A Great and Glorious Romance

P21 Education

P31 how others saw him

P33 a wanderlust — wondering

35 still bumming

64 war + begins College — quits

67 still alone —

69-70 1904 bumming + arrested — best Experience

71 He's selling stereoscopes
    his best friend goes to law school

✓ 72 how he felt about business + Literature

✓ 74 his brother helps him as always

75 — being a fireman + writing

76 His poems published

77 His Difinition of Poetry

78 His fathers concern

89 — 1906 Restlessness

210 Responsible for publishing

A Great and

Harcourt Brace Jovanovich

Helga Sandburg

Glorious Romance

The Story of

Carl Sandburg and

Lilian Steichen

New York and London

See page 319 for Acknowledgments.

Printed in the United States of America

Library of Congress Cataloging in Publication Data

Sandburg, Helga.
   A great and glorious romance.
   1. Sandburg, Carl, 1878–1967–Biography.
2. Sandburg, Helga–Biography–Youth.   3. Authors,
American–20th century–Biography.   I. Title.
PS3537.A618Z865   811'.5'2   [B]   77-84394
ISBN 0-15-136894-5

First edition
B C D E

10,052

*This book is for
my grandchildren*

Sascha Michael

Tristan August

and

Helga Sky

Contents

Illustrations

AUTHOR'S NOTE

I wish to express my appreciation and gratitude to the many friends and associates of Carl Sandburg whose poems, letters and papers were a part of my father's life, and to the libraries and collections that made available their research material, among them the University of Chicago Library for permission to consult their *Poetry: A Magazine of Verse* papers (1912–36).

H.S.

A Great and Glorious Romance

Paula

Woman of a million names and a thousand faces,
I looked for you over the earth and under the sky.
I sought you in passing processions
On old multitudinous highways
Where mask and phantom and life go by.
In roaming and roving, from prairie to sea,
From city to wilderness, fighting and praying,
I looked.

When I saw you, I knew you as you knew me.
We knew we had known far back in the eons
When hills were a dust and the sea a mist.
And toil is a trifle and struggle a glory
With You, and ruin and death but fancies,
Woman of a million names and a thousand faces.

—part of an early poem
by Carl Sandburg

The Search

It takes two cells to begin to make a child. Who has not asked, "How did I manage to get here?" And maybe, "Was I wanted?" The first question is more likely to come up if one is born in America, where the vessels that hold the cells come from such widely disparate religions, languages and bodily differences. I had always planned sometime to look back into my beginnings. What would come to light?

My childhood was serene. Had my parents been looking for a fourth daughter when I came along? I was aware that somewhere along the way was a dead baby sister. I knew that my father had been burned by love of my mother when he first saw her and that he never got over it. I knew that in time he roamed all up and down the country, meeting adoration and adulation, along with some scorn, from the ladies. Did I ever think that he was not true? I wanted to look into it. I wanted to know what drove him and where it began.

The search would take me to the roots of my mother and the source of her power. And into the life of her brother and why and how he happened to be where he was at that time. I had plenty of material. Old letters were stored in the houses we lived in. My grandmothers and my Aunt Mary and Aunt Esther kept correspondence and papers and photographs. My father's friends, Philip Green Wright and Reuben Borough and Alfred Harcourt, among others, saved early letters. So did Carl Björncrantz, my uncle's friend. Grace Mayer of the Museum of Modern Art opened the Steichen Archive there to me. Dr. Rolf Sundblad translated for me the Swedish press accounts of my father's visit there in August of 1959. My daughter-in-law, Elisabeth Steichen, translated my Luxembourg cousins' genealogies and accounts in French and German. Before my father's papers were sent to the University of Illinois at Urbana, my sister Margaret assembled and xeroxed them along with personal correspondence and other records, and made an extra copy for me. Uncle Mart's daughter-in-law, Shirley Sandburg, helped with information on my Galesburg relations, as did a cousin there, Burgetta Young.

Always, I have kept journals and files and photograph albums. They fill shelves, cabinets, drawers and trunks. And there are scribbled records of my mother's recitations during my childhood of the saga of the voyagers, her parents and my uncle, to the new land and what happened before and after. My father wrote of his early days in his autobiographical *Always the Young Strangers.* He wrote further in a recollection, not long enough for a book, that he called *Ever the Winds of Chance* and left behind in manuscript when he stopped writing as he became old.

And there are memories. My sister Janet, as well as Margaret, told me clear ones. And my son, John Carl Steichen, too. My daughter, Paula Steichen, wrote a book about our family, *My Connemara,* that I could leaf through, and she gave me lengthy notes she took down while talking with my mother about family history and stories. One fact comes plain. The shades are drawn on the past and the truth is sometimes hidden as to where and who the people were and when and how the event occurred.

When I began to write twenty years ago and to be published, I used family tales and personalities, hiding them in my stories and poems and novels. I knew what drove the fictional characters. But what drove my uncle? my father? my mother? This is the story of the search, the journey into the past.

January 1974

4

$\mathcal{O}ne$

Am I Dreaming?

Am I dreaming, caught in the web of time? The lake is still and wave-less. The canoe is up a few feet from the shoreline, turned over. The sand is too hot for bare feet and I have rushed over it to the water's edge. It is five in an afternoon in the 1930's. The sun gleams and there is no breeze. I swing the canoe over and drag it into the warm shallows. Climbing in, I paddle slowly out into Lake Michigan, past the first and then the second sandbar. I am nearsighted and the shore is such a vague, distant line that I have a pang of fear. Looking over the green, paint-cracked side of the canoe, I can see the clear sandy bottom, no telling how far below.

We do not dive out of the canoe to test the bottom the way we do on the community raft over there. I cannot see that far, but it will be deserted now, the summer children heading up to the cottages their parents rent each year from our neighbor, Fred Sizer. I am alone out here, my life built on solitude. In our house up on the dune just back of the shore, too far away for my seeing, the wood and linoleum-covered floors are sand-gritted, the grains tracked in by dogs and children. In the kitchen, rolling out a crust and crimping it, Martha Moorman, our household helper, a native of Indiana, is making up a peach cobbler. On a back burner of the stove a spaghetti sauce simmers. Tomatoes of the beefsteak kind gleam on the window sills, got from one of the roadside stands where Martha and my mother stop on their way to the meat market in Three Oaks, a few miles away.

My mother, at her desk at the long, windowed porch, is oblivious of the hour. Tonight we children will go to sleep as usual before nine, and then as she does occasionally for a special event in the sky, she will wake us near midnight to climb to the crow's nest set on the house's roof to see the planets—Jupiter and its four satellites, or Saturn and its ring, or a new comet just discovered by some astronomer in Zurich, visible to the naked eye of some—not to nearsighted me. The telescope my mother recently purchased translates the vague blur of starlight into a place where a celestial body, over a million miles from the sun, will stand clear with its nucleus and its coma extending into a multiple luminous tail.

On a deck built out from his attic rooms, my father is in a chair before a typewriter set on an orange crate. He is stripped of clothes and there is a towel nearby to put across him in the unlikely event of an interruption. His hair is rumpled. He studies the various hand-sawed boards propped before him covered with hand notes, typewritten ones, clippings, and then beats out a sentence on the reconditioned Remington in his two-fingered style. His attention is diverted by a golden-brown wasp that has lit on his arm with a buzz. Its wings are lacy, the antennae wave, the striped body undulates. It clings to his sweated arm hairs and crawls slowly up. He rises absently and taking a sheet of paper with him, goes to the rail of the deck. There he brushes the wasp free with the paper's edge. It scrambles in midair and flies off. He returns to his chair. One of his shorthand notes on the boards goes:

- Scurt eyes: read once
- fresh end day as begin
- ptch 16-ing game
- overdo no: overload no
- acmlt only ncsry
- beware emotndzg pl
- cool that: pln wrk

There is no noise in the house below or in the cloudless sky where the sun burns him to bronze.

From below come three shrill blasts from a whistle. Martha stands at our kitchen door; it is six o'clock and the supper hour is near. I am turning the canoe back toward our beach. In the golden air the only noise now is the sound of the dipping paddle and the water dripping from it. The sun lies molten in the hot blue air over the horizon, beyond which lies Chicago. Sometimes in the sultry nights, if the atmosphere is right, a mirage of the lights of the city will appear sporadically above the lake there.

The canoe slips past the sandbars and into the shallows. I am dragging it up and flipping it over and then trotting toward the flight of green steps that mount the sand dune to the house on top. There are rest-landings with benches where one can gaze down at the silken sheen of the unmoving body of water while hearing the muted bray of the catbird in the bushes nearby and the continued shrilling in the treetops of the cicadas, still called by farmers the "lyremen" or the "dog-day harvest flies," their loud sounds unheard out in the canoe. I take the stairs two at a time; my body, just in its teens, is inexhaustible, its endurance tested continually.

These stairs were set along the dune's face under the direction of my mother. She had hired a carpenter a mile away in Harbert, John Shermak, to build the three-and-a-half-story house; he hauled long timbers across his shoulders and kept his hours in a pocket notebook. The money for it came from my father's two-volume work on the early years of Abraham Lincoln, first called by him *The Pre-Whiskers Lincoln* or *The Well-Razored Abe,* and published as *Abraham Lincoln: The Prairie Years.* He had sent Mother a telegram when the book had been picked up before publication and he'd been notified out in Texas where he'd been lecturing: HARCOURT WIRES BOOK SERIAL RIGHTS SOLD TO PICTORIAL REVIEW FOR TWENTY THOUSAND FIX THE FLIVVER AND BUY A WILD EASTER HAT. The scents of supper—spaghetti sauce and peach cobbler—drift out through the screens of the kitchen. The two police dogs, Jojo and Bosco, drag themselves to their feet to meet me at the brick walk. Flies are buzzing at the house's screens, caught inside. Spiders are weaving webs in high corners, unmolested. Bees and hummingbirds are visiting my mother's flower plantings in the walkways and paths and down the other stairway on the inland side of the dune.

The screen slaps behind me, and Martha, her hands flour-dusted, cutting spaghetti in long strips from the rolled-out dough on the counter, looks up. "Hurry and get out of your suit. It's almost on."

The table is set. There is a white cloth with some flowered decoration which is changed every third or fourth day, washed and ironed by Martha. There is a napkin in a ring to mark each place. Children are expected to wash their hands before coming to the table and to fold their napkin before being excused. There is a platter of sliced tomatoes and celery sticks and a tall pitcher of milk from the refrigerator bottles. Everyone has a glass including my father. Every other morning the milkman, with metal supply racks in either hand, whistles up the stairs from the garage, while the dogs roar and wag their tails and everyone hushes them if the head of the house is at home and not off on a lecture trip.

In the silver bread tray is a white eyelet-embroidered cloth that stays in it between meals. The just-sliced pumpernickel bread is bought at the bakery near Ed Drier's meat market off in Three Oaks.

My mother comes to the table, serene, not tall, with blue-gray eyes, a patrician nose, her hair in a knot at her neck, wisps of it always escaping and curled about her face. "Where's Daddy? Go call him."

Janet dashes for the stairs and rushes up a flight, slim, dark-haired, bright-eyed. She yells into the attic, "Daddy! Supper's ready! We're at the table!" A muffled answering roar is heard and she bounds back down the stairs and takes her chair, satisfied. "He's coming."

The eldest of the three of us, Margaret, urged by Martha, is here by now and unfolds her napkin. Slow-moving and -talking, she is the stubborn one, the first child, not swayed easily or conciliatory as I am. She does not cling the way I do, either, to relatives and animals, and she weighs judgments, wants convincing. She has a sensitive temper and when it rules her there is nothing for it but to let the doors slam after her, shutting out her raised protest. Sometimes my mother will go after her for appeasement but most often Margaret rides the storm out alone, returning before long because the conversation and the doings, the readings, the occasional guests, entertain her. She is the learned one of us girls, self-educated. Her face lights as the voice is heard as he descends the stairs singing a ditty all the family knows:

> Old Man Velerius,
> Looking mighty serious,
> Climbing up the reservoir stairs.
> Took a man's daughter
> And he throwed her in the water,
> Climbing up the reservoir stairs.

"And how are all the shiny faces?" my father asks, not expecting an answer as he settles himself in a wooden armchair at the table's head. His hair is freshly combed. The collar of his blue shirt is turned in and under, making a V at his bronzed neck. He has some papers which he puts beside his plate, a signal to one daughter, at least, that he will most likely be reading something he has written today and will try out on his captive audience.

He quotes a sea captain telling his crew, "All I want from you is silence and damned little of that." He says, "The eleventh commandment is 'Thou shalt not commit nincompoopery.'" And, "When some men get mad, they get drunk. Me—I read the newspapers." And also that writing is only a matter of putting one word down after another and wasn't it Mark Twain who said there's as much difference between the right and the wrong word as between lightning and the lightning bug?

We report on daily doings, the latest fight our Bosco had with one of the dogs of a summer vacationing family, the near tragedy in the basement when a leaking pipe was discovered and repaired in no time by "Mrs. Fixit" as he terms our mother, the letter Martha got from her folks saying that her littlest brother was saving a pair of tame pigeons for me which she'd pick up on her next visit home.

He shouts for Martha, who doesn't eat at the table with us. She appears in the door, clean-aproned, her hands wet from the sink where she's been scouring pots, a smooth-complexioned woman as close to my heart as my sisters and parents. Sometimes when my father reads to us, Martha will come to stand in the doorway and listen. She does this now as he puts his fork down and selects one of the papers. "This is a mock biography of Abraham Lincoln I came on," he says, an edge of derision in his voice. "It's going into one of the later chapters of the War Years. Lincoln was being ridiculed by the opposition during the campaign for his renomination. That would be in the fall of sixty-four. Here it is and intended to wrap him up as entirely ridiculous:

> Mr. Lincoln stands six feet twelve in his socks, which he changes once every ten days. His anatomy is composed mostly of bones, and when walking he resembles the offspring of a happy marriage between a derrick and a windmill. When speaking he reminds one of the old signal-telegraph that used to stand on Staten Island. His head is shaped something like a rutabago, and his complexion is that of a Saratoga trunk. His hands and feet are plenty large enough, and in society he has the air of having too many of them. The glove-makers have not yet had time to construct gloves that will fit him. In his habits he is by no means foppish, though he brushes his hair sometimes, and is said to wash. He swears fluently. A strict temperance man himself, he does not object to another man's being pretty drunk, especially when he is about to make a bargain with him. He is fond of fried liver and onions, and is a member of the church. He can hardly be called handsome, though he is certainly much better looking since he had the small-pox.

Only occasionally does my father's temper, which I know and respect, rise and overflow upon me. Two nights before, I had neglected to polish his shoes, one of my jobs in the busy household, and he had raged loudly. I had fled weeping and furious to my room, cast myself on the metal-steaded bed and stayed there till I fell asleep. In the morning I found an envelope on the study table by the bed with my name on it. Inside the paper said:

Dearest Helgar

Please forget
it - then I won't
need to be for-
given -
with love -
Daddy

And now he is reading more, trying the words out for himself as much as us, Martha still in the door:

"These are my Definitions of Poetry. I've got I don't know how many by now. A hundred? These are first drafts. Poetry is when your bones dream and you take a number and make it dance with other numbers. Poetry is a spot about halfway between where you listen and where you wonder what it was you heard. Poetry is a handkerchief trick with a kite and a balloon—and the neighbors wonder how you got that way."

And then Janet is interrupting, "Roosevelt's on tonight," and Martha is bringing the warm peach cobbler in. She sets it before my mother, who cuts and spoons the slices into bowls. There is a pitcher of cream and Martha goes for a thermos of coffee which she puts by my father's plate. Restless, I am held to my chair, wanting to be off and away, leaping the stairs two at a time, to join the children of the vacationers out by the rented cottages who will be at "Run-sheep-run," their parents not directing them, as do mine, to listen to the president's fireside chat. Indeed many of them are firm Republicans and pained by a reference to F.D.R., whom they look upon as a dangerous fanatic. My mother and father have agreed from the first that he is what the country has needed since the financial crash. They watched delighted when he proclaimed the New Deal and set about using Federal funds for relief and for public works, calling it "pump priming." My father compares Franklin Delano Roosevelt's problems to Abraham Lincoln's, saying that what both men did was "curious, contradictory and preposterous" when viewed with the eye of cold logic.

He looks at my mother. His voice is level and musical. "As the months passed by, Lincoln saw his hazardous proclamation win results. He once referred to it as 'the central act of my administration.' He had proclaimed a status to exist where he had no power to enforce it. And the mere act of proclamation projected an idea that gained momentum from the instant it was spoken."

"No one can put that the way you do, Buddy," she says, firm.

"When some of us look at the bill of rights proclaimed from Washington during the past year, we can see parallels with Lincoln's declaration that a status existed where he had not yet the power to enforce it. The six-hour day, the thirty-five-hour week, a living wage, guarantee of employment or unemployment insurance, the right of collective bargaining to be assured any genuinely organized labor union, these are curious, contradictory, preposterous, to those whose eyes linger on the past and cherish its precedents. And has a hard-working man the right to a little bit of salt down at this end of the table?"

My father eyes me, taking the saltcellar. He turns to fiddle with the radio dial and brings in the familiar, bland voice, with the half-ironic, half-cocky twist to it, the phrases sticking sometimes after one of the fireside talks:

My friends, and all of you are my friends. . . .

The money changers have fled from their high seats in the temple of our civilization. We may now restore that temple to the ancient truths. . . .

There will be an end to speculation with other people's money. . . .

I favor as a practical policy the putting of first things first. . . .

Our greatest primary task is to put people to work. . . .

In every dark hour of our national life a leadership of frankness and vigor has met with that understanding and support of the people themselves which is essential to victory. . . .

It is your problem, my friends, no less than it is mine. . . .

The only thing we have to fear is fear itself. . . .

We do not distrust the future of essential democracy. The people of the United States have not failed. . . .

In the event that the national emergency is still critical . . . I shall ask the Congress for the one remaining instrument to meet the crisis—broad executive power to wage a war against the emergency, as great as the power that would be given to me if we were in fact invaded by a foreign foe. . . .

In the field of world policy I would dedicate this nation to the policy of the good neighbor. . . .

Our Constitution is so simple and practical that it is possible always to meet extraordinary needs by changes in emphasis and arrangement without loss of essential form. . . .

When the voice is done and my father lifts his coffee cup to drink, I have folded my napkin and returned it to its ring, and now grasp my opportunity. "Can I please be excused?"

"She may go," says my father to my mother.

"Thanks." I am out the door and down the hillside and over to the sounds of children. "One two three four five six seven. . . ." Their screams, their battles, their pleadings, their shrill cries, their wild laughter, their secret giggles hang in the green-gold air of twilight.

The sunset sky is fading—all the rainbowed hues are turning into gray. The needles of the pines overhead quiver in the stirring of the evening land breeze. Birds are silent, their evening feeding over. The great body of water below darkens. If I go swimming at night in it, slipping off my clothes and diving under, I stay where I can touch bottom. Where is the land? Nearsighted, I cannot see the dune beyond, the lights of our house where my eldest sister is practicing the piano. The next one is sleeping in her bed, and Martha too. My mother is moving about the house as she has done all the days of my life, wakeful into the small hours, at some chore or studying out a thing at some desk or table, her mind now and then turning to my father at work in the attic.

Before he went up there, after the dishes were cleared, the two had lingered awhile at the table as dusk came on. They might have stepped out for a walk together. The house is a serene one. I know an upstairs drawer which I pull out occasionally when everyone is away, to look over my mother's love letters to my father. Some phrases I know by heart: "Dear Mr. Sandburg, . . . I had to read your poems once before school this morning. . . . The hour had come to say: 'Hail, Poet!' . . . Dear Comrade, . . . You must needs add to the divine madness of poesy the diviner madness of revolutionary agitation . . . My heart so yearning to you! . . . What a Glory that the Soul should be so transfused into the Body! . . . What a Consecration! A realist Pentecost! . . . The thought of you is with me always. . . . I thought of what Service we two together would do for the Cause, somehow, somewhere, sometime. . . . *You to love* . . . Surely I am blest among women."

The letters are a mystery and a talisman to me. From the top window now comes the sound of the Remington typewriter on its upturned orange crate, brought in along with other materials from the sun deck when my father descended for supper. The wisping scent of cigar smoke lingers there too.

Am I back in that time, wet hair stringing, as I come out of that lake of my childhood?

Two

The Gamla Hemlandet

Could I untangle what lay past memory and reality in the *gamla hem-landet,* the old homeland of my father's people? Looking into it, would family stories be shaken and vague photographs become people? Was there glory somewhere? Strength? The tongue was strange to me and mine, the faces familiar in their structure. When I visited Sweden some years ago, traveling for the State Department, I met seven cousins and numerous relations. Some spoke English and I communicated with the others through translators when not kissing, gesticulating, weeping or laughing. Bouquets of flowers were thrust in my hands on arrival and fresh ones continually replaced those faded. I saw the grave of my maternal great-grandfather, Anders Persson, and the font where Grandma Sandburg was baptized, the painting of the old church, long since razed, where she learned the catechism and was confirmed. I visited the rebuilt church. I petted the calves in the stable on the land where she lived. I walked the roads and saw the fields my ancestors knew. I heard their tongue and saw in a news clip:

> Mjölkdropparna på din haka, Helga,
> får inte skymma dina transbärsröda kinder . . .

and it was clearly my father's poem, "Winter Milk":

> The milk-drops on your chin, Helga,
> Must not interfere with the cranberry red of
> your cheeks . . .

The musical language would never be mine to use. My grandparents saw to that. My father has called the Swedish words he learned as a baby before they turned into English "lost" words that he would have no chance to handle again. In the years from 1850 to 1910 more than twenty-five million immigrants poured into America. Between 1870 and 1890 there were 8,058,804, and over a million of these were Scandinavians, most of them young people. Finland was then a grand duchy of Czarist Russia and immigration statistics listed Finns as Russians. Many who came from the northeastern border of Sweden were Finns too, but officially recorded as Swedish Finns or Swedes. As a child, I was told that Grandfather Sandburg was a "black Swede," not blond the way Scandinavians are supposed to be, and that he came from the far north of the country. I always thought he might have been a Finn. It was also related over and again that his parents had died in Sweden, that his name had been Johnson when he emigrated as a young man and that he picked the name Sandburg out of the blue because his paycheck kept getting mixed up with the other Johnsons. Indeed, on the registration certificate of his marriage to my mother in June of 1908, under "Personal and Statistical Particulars" my father lists his mother: Clara Johnson. I had also seen the brief biography of Grandfather Sandburg—he'd died long before I was born—which said that he'd come over from Sweden at the age of twenty-five, and that he'd married Grandma Sandburg when he was thirty.

Most of the story may have been so, although the part that his name was Johnson in Sweden doesn't seem to be. Immigrants, wanting to be a part of the New Land, didn't look back. In one family of cousins of mine that emigrated from Sweden before my grandfather did, three out of their four sons changed their names, and only two took the same new name. When Grandfather Sandburg arrived in America, did he take the name of that family? There were four boys and four girls brought over from the province of Östergotland in Sweden by their widowed mother and their name was Johannsson. Did Grandfather Sandburg Americanize it to Johnson and keep it until the paycheck mixup? His Johannsson cousins had taken the new names of Nyberg and Newberg. Did he pick Sandberg? My father has told how he and Aunt Mary and Uncle Mart decided while in grammar school to change the "e" to "u" and spell their last name Sandburg.

It was when my father, in his seventies, started his autobiography and began asking aging relatives and friends and looking into records in the old country that he began to think that his father's surname wasn't Johnson and more probably was Danielsson. He also believed that his father came over as a young man and worked in a cheese factory in

Herkimer, New York, when he first arrived, and that he came to Galesburg later when another cousin of his, Magnus Holmes, asked him to come on and work with a construction gang of the Chicago Burlington and Quincy railroad.

When my father decided on the Danielsson name, he sent me a photograph and said it was his father and even wrote on the back, "August Danielsson." He sent one of what he said were his grandparents too. "That's Nils Danielsson, father of August Danielsson, & therefore great-great-grandfather of John Carl." The latter is my son and my father had it right, except that a Swede takes his father's first name, not his last, and John Carl's great-great-grandfather could be Daniel Nilsson.

In that photograph, the man who is likely my great-grandfather sits close to his wife, who has a wedding band on her right hand and wears a dark cape fastened with a brooch. There is a voluminous dark apron over her heavy long-sleeved checked dress that falls to the floor and covers her shoes. Her dark hair is drawn back tightly and a white head scarf is tied in back. His dark hair is parted and slicked down. He has a square short mustache. A black neckband is tucked into his brocaded vest, and there is a glimpse of a heavy watch chain and pendant. His pants are baggy and his homemade shoes are worn and splitting at the soles. His overcoat is heavy and long and is open to show the vest. The sight of these two people, with their peasant-heavy hands like mine, sitting for the photographer in that chilly studio, is a treasure to me.

This Daniel Nilsson was a foreman on a Swedish estate at Stralsnas, and had been born in the parish of Åsbo. There is no record on his wife. Southwest of Stockholm is the province of Östergotland, bordered on the west by the lake Vättern. Inland to the east, by the river Svartån, are the towns of Åsbo, Strålsnäs and Ekeby, where the church is and the records are kept. From county archives, from hearsay and from old letters, it is clear that in 1857, in the late summer, the Nilssons were getting ready to come over here. Surely there was trepidation in a family breaking off old ties and leaving tradition. Would a son of theirs change his name to Johnson in time? My father puzzled over it. When he, at eighty-one, visited Sweden a couple of years before my visit there, he met a painter, Severin Fredriksson, whose aunt, Anna Hallgren, seems to have emigrated at the same time as the Nilsson family and would write back news of the Nilssons. Fredriksson's grandfather, Klas Hallgren, could read and write, which the Nilssons could not, and it was he who arranged for the tickets. The Åsbo neighbors helped collect provisions that would last the six or seven weeks of the journey—dried shoulders of mutton, dried pork, hard rye bread and biscuits. The story goes that friends and neighbors followed the family all along the road to Ekeby Church, where a farmer waited with his cart to drive them north to the canal steamer. As they walked they sang to cover up their sadness at their friends' leaving and to cheer the travelers. The Nilssons went as third class passengers—steerage class—and it is said there were a number of children in the family. Who knows? The records differ. Were there seven or just a boy, Alfrid August, eleven at the time of the journey? At all events, they most likely made their way north to Motala on the shore of Vättern. In 1832, twenty-five years before the Nilssons' journey, the Göta Canal had been completed, opening an inland water route from Göteborg to Stockholm. Did they take this way by steamer and board a ship in Göteborg harbor for the New World? When Anna Hallgren would write back to Sweden, it is said that she told of Daniel Nilsson having a job in a railroad workshop. Later she's said to have written of meeting the son, August Danielsson, and of how he had changed his name to August Sandburg. Had the name been Johnson for a while? And did the Nilssons die in the cholera epidemic of 1867? I don't know; some say they did. The truths are shrouded. Perhaps the reality is the story I heard as a child. Perhaps Daniel Nilsson is not my great-grandfather, and there is another man who was anywhere from nineteen to twenty-five when he got here from the Old Land.

I do know that my grandfather, August, worked in a railroad workshop just as Daniel Nilsson did. I know that he was handy with his hands and ambitious. A natural worker, he liked to see the finished product and stash away what he could. He never wrote in any language and signed his name with an X. He learned to read in the English tongue, though he still liked the Swedish paper, *Hemlandet*, best. My father said that sometimes he would set his children down and read to them out of the Swedish Bible. He had brown hair and hazel eyes. He died eight years before I was born and I never spoke much of him with my father. Janet and I whispered that Grandfather Sandburg had fallen out of the great spruce tree in our backyard and that was that. He was a mystery.

And what about Grandma Sandburg, whom my father always spoke of as one with a quick smile and easy ways? She lived a long way from us in my childhood, and we didn't visit there very much. When she came to us, I was under eight, and I think of a frail, kindly, bony lady with bright blue eyes, silver hair parted in the middle and pulled back into a high bun, with knotted veins on her arms, long print dresses down to her ankles and high-button shoes, and a loving way. She never directed me. Did she think me a boisterous one, doll in hand and skinned knees? When she spoke with my father of her marriage in August of 1874, she said she felt her luck. Grandfather Sandburg was twenty-eight or thirty and she was twenty-four, having immigrated the year before. It was her chance. She was working in a hotel in Bushnell, Illinois, as a general maid and kitchen helper. He was in town with the Chicago Burlington and Quincy railroad gang. They met at the hotel, talked, and she got asked to marry. Pretty soon they settled in Galesburg over in the western part of Illinois, where there were many Swedish-Americans.

The Swedish church records on Grandma Sandburg are clear. Her name was Clara Mathilda Andersson (Andersdotter). She had been born on the twentieth of June, 1850, at Lilla Östergården in the village of Appuna about halfway between the port of Motala and Åsbo. Her mother, Eva Charlotta Jönsdotter, was a gooseherder there and had died when Grandma Sandburg was six. Her father, Anders Persson, was a hired farmhand at Lilla Östergården, and Grandma Sandburg was their first child. She never forgot the ways of her mother, and didn't favor the stepmother who moved in a year after her mother died. In the family photograph of the stepmother, Eva Christina Larsdotter, alongside her husband, there is a strong-faced woman. A baby stepsister came along in less than a year, and soon a baby stepbrother. By the time Grandma Sandburg was twenty years old and restless, Anders Persson owned Lilla Östergården and worked it himself, according to the Church books, and one supposes there were many farm chores for my grandmother. At any rate, she seems to have moved a few miles north to Fallsbergs Västergård, perhaps hiring out. The Skänninge Fair was within walking distance. Did she hear talk of America there? The records say that in May of 1873, aged twenty-three, she went to the pastor's office behind the church and got a certificate to emigrate to North America. She said once, long years later, "I left Sweden because my stepmother was so different from my mother." An early picture of Grandma Sandburg shows a girl with high cheekbones and a firm mouth and the beginning of a smile.

My grandparents moved into a three-room frame house on Third Street in Galesburg where, nine months and three weeks after their wedding day, my Aunt Mary was born on a cornhusk mattress. The house was a block from the C.B.&Q. blacksmith shop where Grandfather Sandburg was paid a dollar a day, six days a week. His name was listed on the payroll: August Sandburg. In the photograph of him that my father sent me, Grandfather Sandburg has a little scraggly goatee and wears a wide striped bow tie and a white shirt with a throwaway paper collar (a box of a dozen of the latter cost a quarter). He has slicked back his hair and is a handsome fellow. He was called "Gus" by his worker friends and gradually grew a muscled hump on his right shoulder from swinging the hammer on the anvil. He was no ignoramus and bought and sold a number of houses at a profit, making improvements by himself—brick-laying, painting, carpentry—with maybe a son to hold the kerosene lamp to light some late-hour work. He moved his family into bigger houses so that by the time my father was four, they had a rambling home on Berrien Street, with a roomy upstairs that Grandfather Sandburg could rent out for extra cash. He became a naturalized citizen and a registered voter. Like most of their Swedish-born friends, Grandfather and Grandma Sandburg said "shursh" for "church," "yob" for "job," "dat" for "that," "Sveden" for "Sweden," "velty" for "wealthy," "iss" for "is," and got along all right.

Grandma Sandburg, who could read and write in Swedish, learned both skills after a fashion in English. There is no letter or written record from Grandfather Sandburg, except his X. But Grandma Sandburg was different, and when she was in her seventies she wrote to my mother and used the old-country script. "Dear sweet Lillian . . . How good of you to write me again. Y thank you kindly, it certainly do me a lot of good to think about you all and the later part of the month will meet your faces there in your home. . . . Y am waiting for the pretty spring days to come. . . . Y am not so very well either as Y was sometimes redy to give up but will wait a couple of weeks may be a little warmer weather with sun-shiny days am so glad to look ahead for someting good. Y shall not try to tell any news but hope that all may well go and we will have a good time ones more. untill then Y remain as ever yours. Grandma Sandburg."

And she wrote too, after a visit, "Y am back here again in the old stead . . . and found everything as usuall, the car the train rushed me on so fast Y was home half past tow oclock. Only the memory is left of you and all Y heard and saw a pleasant memory for a longtime. . . . there are so much good in the world for them that look for it. open the hands, heart and take what comes be it storm or sunshine. Y think it all works for our wellfare he who loves God all serves for the best . . . in hope and fait ever yours Grandma."

My father was born in the Third Street house on a cornhusk mattress nearly three years after Aunt Mary came. His diapers, like hers, were of flour sacks. Their tow hair turned brown in time, hers lighter than his. He had hazel eyes as he grew older, and brown flecks danced in them when he was excited. None of blue-eyed Grandma Sandburg's children had her eyes. All of them took after Grandfather Sandburg's side. Mary's eyes were more green than my father's—"cat's eyes" they called them—with the same dark specks. My father was christened Carl August in the Lutheran church and they began to call him Charlie right away, as did his family and Galesburg friends the rest of their days. Growing up in the small house, my father ate bread spread with lard and sprinkled with salt, and liked it.

Other children came along. A year and a half after my father, a boy called Martin Godfrey was born—my Uncle Mart. He and Aunt Mary had a sense of humor that matched my father's, so that my memory of those three is always touched with the sound of their laughter together and a feeling of spontaneous gaiety. In time Grandma Sandburg had four more babies—two boys, Emil Warner and Fred William, and two girls, Esther Mathilda and Martha Clara. Aunt Esther had "cat's eyes" like Aunt Mary, but hers were greener and brilliant. She was taller than Aunt Mary as she grew older and was more serious. She was called in later years by my father "the beautiful girl Esther." My father would say of Aunt Martha that she was the "plain and modest sister." She and Aunt Mary looked more like my father, with the strong nose and wide mouth of Grandfather Sandburg. Barring illness, it was a hardy family, my father, Aunt Mary and Aunt Esther living well into their eighties. Grandma Sandburg's children would span almost twenty years of childbearing. We heard stories of how she would set her children in a row on the kitchen table while she scrubbed the floor on her knees and mopped it properly and then took up the Swedish Bible to read to them while the floor dried.

The New Country was in a time of unease. Strikes, which had become a weapon of labor, were popular during the mid-1800's, although they rarely had any success. In 1877 a nationwide railroad strike had taken place and it was on the sixth of the following January that my father was born. When the Haymarket riot and tragedy occurred on Randolph Street in Chicago after a strike at the McCormick Harvester works, it was 1886 and he was eight years old. Everyone in town kept track through the newspapers of the subsequent trial of those supposedly responsible for the bomb-throwing that killed seven policemen.

Though I've been told that within the household the Swedish tongue was largely spoken, my father has said it was then that he first learned to mouth the new words the adults were using: *anarchist, revolutionist, conspirator, loyalty.* By the time he was ten, four of the so-called anarchists had been hanged, reputed to have said severally just before the trap was sprung, "You may strangle this voice but my silence will be more terrible than speech. . . . Hurrah for anarchy! . . . Hoch die Anarchie! . . . O men of America, let the voice of the people be heard!" The children of Galesburg said, "Well, they hanged 'em." Grandma Sandburg told the family, "Dose anarshists are bad people." Grandfather Sandburg shook his head, "Dey killed and so dey ought to be killed, dose anarshists."

By the time my father reached eleven he had his first job. Every morning before school he swept out the office of a real estate firm, emptied the brass spittoons and rinsed them and occasionally was assigned to polishing them. He got a quarter a week. He took on a newspaper route in the afternoons, six days a week, going to the Galesburg *Republican-Register* with the other newsboys, cross-folding his papers as they came off the press so that they would hold together when thrown, keeping the route for a couple of years, earning a dollar a week. After a while he delivered morning papers from Chicago too, along with the other boys— the *Tribune, Record, Inter-Ocean, Times, Herald, Chronicle*. He also peddled papers from a wagon he pulled, getting a nickel a paper, and he could keep a penny for himself. In the fall of the year that he was fourteen, he hired out to a dairy farmer, George Burton. It was 1892 and hard times. Grandfather Sandburg's work hours had been cut in half and his C.B.&Q. paycheck was down to sixteen dollars a month. My father was expected to help out. My Aunt Mary was in high school by then and her diploma was needed so that she could go into a school-teaching position the following fall which would pay thirty dollars a month. So grammar school was as much formal education as my father was expected to need. The family kept his photograph on his graduation from the Grammar School of the Seventh Ward. He is a little thin, his hair parted and smoothed back; his dark suit and vest are a bit large and Grandma Sandburg has handed him a freshly ironed white shirt that morning. His foot is on a high papier-mâché rock beside him, and an artificial fern in an urn is behind. He carries a round hat in his right hand, which rests on his raised knee. His stance is cocky, it seems.

In the home, in the days to come, he went through Aunt Mary's textbooks and got what he felt like out of them. He walked two miles every morning to the Burton barn. It was October and chill and years later he spoke of frosted toes that winter and no money for proper boots, of stopping in to warm himself sometimes at a stove in a grocery store or in the kitchen of a house, of his uncompromising boss who had a thin face and a long mustache. On arrival at the dairy barn early in the morning, he drove one of the milk wagons loaded with cans and Mr. Burton took the other. They went through town from house to house from early morning to midafternoon, seven days a week, no holidays off. The eight-gallon milk cans stayed on the wagon, and my father carried a smaller can by its bale to the door. There he found the crock or container with its ticket inside—pink for a quart, green for a pint—or else he called out, "Milk!" and the woman of the house came with her pint or quart to be filled. He got twelve dollars a month for the work.

Then pain entered the Sandburg house. The health commissioner nailed a red card on the door: DIPHTHERIA. My father had a sore throat awhile, and so did my Uncle Mart, twelve then. They were put to bed but were soon up. The pretty green-eyed sister, Esther, four and a half, was untouched. Not so the small brother of seven, Emil, and the two-year-old baby brother, Freddie. These lay side by side in the makeshift bed in the kitchen where the family stove was. They were suffocating; the infection was in their larynxes, where a thick white membrane was forming, and because the trachea of each was so small, his breath could barely come through. "All we can do," said the doctor, "is hope."

But the next day Grandfather Sandburg had to go out to buy two small white caskets for his young sons. The funeral over and the flowers left on the double grave, my father went straight back to his job on the Burton milk wagon, peddling from door to door, pouring the fresh milk into the containers the housewives left or held for him.

Death was not so uncommon in that day. Folks had large families and expected to have to let some of them go in childbed and in the early years. Clara Mathilda Andersson Sandburg would live to be seventy-six herself, a decade longer than Grandfather Sandburg. She had had her number of sons cut in half. Mary was away teaching school and perhaps my grandmother consoled herself with little Esther. She was carrying another child who would be her last. Was she hopeful of a boy to replace her lost ones? Surely, though, she was glad of the healthy baby that came in April and was named Martha?

Long, long years later, when Grandma Sandburg was aware that she was nearing her death, which would come on a December morning, she wrote down some thoughts in a blue-lined dime-store tablet, and put it in a drawer where it was found later. The words helped me see glory in this Swedish grandmother, who struggled with the English language and script that never came easily, blessed her life and listed the qualities of four of her children who survived:

> My heart is so full of thoughts and feelings so great so much to be greatfull my heart at times overflow. Therefore help me to be strong and patience now in present struggle for Y am yet on the climing upward path but soon Y shall go down in the silence and the deep peace underground. Most beutifull sacred great and mighty as ocean the gem is called patience. . . . O yes Y am yet strong and filled with desire to live and when Y think of the past the old home and fireside when we were yet all togather. O so many pleasant memories. . . . Martin with his bissness and store and show funny

clowns and marry-making other boys coming and going to it all so full of fun. Carl with his deeper thoughts. Y saw allready in early Childhood was not going to live for money only he wanted to do something more and better with his life his thoughts were allways with his plans in future times to come. How glad wi were to well-come Mary home from her country school all of us were. Later on came Esther with her music so sucssesfull beutifull. . . . is not this enough I say a thousand times enough to make me happy. . . . so help me tho to be patientse take my cross and follow on to the last step lift me up high above those low and simple ugly black waves that only torment chafe upon the spirit and troubled mind. . . . Crushed Y am many times but not yet to death the aprons of silense is with silense is a gift be silent forget it . . .

Three

The Wooden Shoe Ascending

There were the two cells which began myself. I had looked into the Swedish one and found glory at the end. What about the cell that came from my mother? My Luxembourg grandparents lived nearby in my early years and I called them Oma and Opa, in the old-country way. France is to the south, Belgium to the west, Germany to the east, and the Luxembourg language is largely derivative of German, their official language until the end of World War I. I heard the soft tongue over my childhood head, spoken between my mother and Oma to hide a fact from me, and I learned a few German phrases and songs. I knew by heart since I had first listened, the story of their coming by separate steerage, by third class passage, from Le Havre to New York in 1880 in the time when thousands of others migrated from the tiny grand duchy, how Opa came first, Jean Pierre Steichen, with a bit of money and half a dozen trunks of household goods and heavy linen woven sheets and bedding that had been in the family. He was twenty-six. He and Oma, Mary Kemp Steichen, had married four years before, both of them twenty-two then. Opa was a slender handsome man, the darling of his maternal grandmother who raised him. He had vanity and passion and a streak of stubbornness, which my mother was to inherit. She has told me how Oma's family, the Kemps, were not so well off as Opa's, the Steichens, and how it had been considered a good catch for Oma when she got Opa. She was four months older than he. It seems that Opa had been given what inheritance was due him when they married and they had gone headlong into a business. My mother has said that it had something to do with clothing and that she was sure Oma was responsible for the unstable venture, which failed before long. They lost nearly all their money and it was then they decided to emigrate and take their chances on a new life.

Opa was to send for Oma and their eighteen-month-old child, Edouard Jean, as soon as he had a place for them to come to. He landed in New York and was directed to a train for the Midwest and got off in Chicago. There he looked for work among those who understood his tongue and found nothing. Not a strong young man, he became discouraged, then feverish, ill, and soon his cash was spent. His boarding house landlady asked to look in his trunks, and slowly they were being emptied to pay for bed and board.

Back in the village of Bivange, Oma worried over the letters that had come for six months and suddenly stopped. She was frightened for Opa, their child and their life. She had a little money and Opa's letters with his Chicago boarding house address on the back, and she packed her belongings, dressed baby Edouard in long wool stockings and underslip, a heavy homemade dress and high, soft button shoes, and took the boat train for Le Havre. In the steerage of the ship over the days, she hung laundry on a line she strung and compared notes with the other women in their long dresses and shawls and babushkas, holding their younger children like hers. She said years later that then she told baby Edouard all of her hopes and troubles.

When they reached New York, Oma found someone who could understand her tongues—French, German, Luxembourg and the Belgian dialect —and took out Opa's letters. "Chicago. Where is this?" The man pointed to a train. "Take that one. It goes your way." And she did and before long found Opa in his bed in the boarding house. Opa cheered up and began to mend with his strong wife and little boy there. Oma asked questions of Germans in the neighborhood and learned that there was work to be had in the copper mines of Hancock on the upper tip of Michigan. The family story tells of how Oma paid off Opa's landlady and they set out with their depleted trunks and our Uncle Ed.

My mother, like my father, kept a strong sense of her past, her heritage and of the New Country and its hope. In an early letter to my father, she once spoke of "The polished boot descending," and said, " 'The wooden shoe ascending,' that is one of the things I worship! I am proud of my peasant grandfather. My mother I worship for the way she has unfolded from a peasant girl." My mother felt the power of the Old Country that stood behind her, saying she loved "the passion and ardor of the German soul." She had no use for the standard American heroes and the Puritans. And she looked ahead to the "American nationality that is to be—a grand conglomerate of Puritan-Swede-Italian-German-

Russian etc." She remained a patriot all her life.

When I visited Luxembourg for the first time on the same tour for the State Department that had taken me to Sweden, along with the stunning armfuls of flowers, my Luxembourg cousins also gave me genealogies of the Steichens, written in French and going back to the first census taken after "la guerre de trente ans," the Thirty Years' War from 1618 to 1648, and "l'épidémie de peste," the Plague of 1635, when the name appears to have been Steychen. I was invited into the Espresso Bar and Pâtisserie run by one of my cousins and then was driven to Bivange, the small village south of the city of Luxembourg where Oma had waited for news from Opa back there in 1880. I was taken to "rue Edward Steichen" where the house is in which Uncle Ed was born, a tall gabled structure built in 1750, the carved front door having its knob in the center. I was met at the door by two cousins, a sister and brother, Ketty and François Steichen. "The local count gave them the power to live here," I was told. The family story that I'd heard was that Opa was so clever as a young man at keeping the count's dissolute son out of the wine cellar, that the house was given to the Steichen family in perpetuity as reward. This may not be so, for in Bivange they said that this house, called the Steichen house, was first owned in 1879 by a Jean Steichen and his wife Marie Kirch, a couple who had no children and with whom Oma and Opa stayed when Uncle Ed was born.

With my cousins and friends I walked about Bivange, looked at the black-and-white cows, saw the church where Uncle Ed was baptized at three days of age by "le révérend curé Altwies," with Oma's brother, Peter, and his wife, Marie, as godparents. I looked at the rectangular well-swept graveyard laid out between the church and the café. The graves of Steichens were pointed out to me, neatly decorated with rows of bright flowers. We returned to my cousins' house for a *formidable* cake, conceived and executed in my cousin's pâtisserie, and champagne in ancient tall glasses, before driving a few miles further to Monderconge, where Oma's people came from. I learned that her father was Nicolas Kemp and her mother Elisabeth Scholtes, and that she had two brothers, Jean and Peter, and a sister, Grete, who was blind. The family story I'd heard about Grete was that she was married to a "mean man" and that when my energetic uncle had returned to Luxembourg once and met him, he'd knocked him down. As for Jean Kemp, he married Opa's sister Elizabeth, "Lizzie," a red-haired and imperious girl, a year older than Oma, and said to have snubbed Oma a bit. That couple emigrated from Luxembourg to South America—to Buenos Aires, where he prospered as a *menuisier*, a furniture maker. I told family stories on the way from Monderconge back to the city of Luxembourg, which were translated for my cousins. Their stories were relayed to me. When it was time, in a day or two, to take the train to Amsterdam, Dr. Carlo Putz, President of the American Luxembourg Society, handed me an armful of enormous red roses as I boarded. I felt as if I were leaving home.

Both Oma and Opa had had enough education before they came over to write, read and communicate ideas in Luxembourgeois. They worked on the English language, which Opa considered illogical and obtuse. Both learned to read newspapers in it, and they managed to write in English too, in time, using the German script letters, but it never came easy. A later letter of Oma's went, "Dear Helga, How are you getting along in Shool with all the examition, be verry carful, because the end cont, for the most for the passing! . . . Opa is fine and is in the garden working among his flours. . . . Y like to keep you little Girls for a weil yet. That is not only best for me but for you too aldo you won't believe me now but you fint out later that Y was right. Y was toldt the same at your age, but dit not believe et, but et was true all the same. Udels of love and write soon from Opa and Oma."

In my early memories of Opa, he is in the house near ours, as ready in the kitchen as Oma, and usually arguing with her over my head in the Luxembourg tongue. In photographs before my time he wears a white shirt, vest, bow tie, and has a dark mustache. His hero was Napoleon. The father of the grandmother who had raised Opa had marched with Bonaparte to Moscow and back in the winter of 1812. Opa had been told the story again and again through his childhood and related it to us. When I knew him his mustache had turned white and there was an ample beard too; his frame became spare later and he wore galluses and a straw hat with a dark band. It is said that Opa was violent sometimes as a young husband and once hit Oma, though he never tried it again. He did keep a buckled strap hanging on the wall in the kitchen, with which he occasionally beat my impertinent uncle. Oma watched over Opa, convinced all her life that because he'd been a sickly baby, he'd die early. She told my mother, "We've got to take good care of him and we've got to always remember he was once close to death." He would outlive Oma by eleven years, going himself to a few months short of ninety. Didn't Opa in turn always pour the top cream off the pitcher for Oma's coffee? He was a homebody and keen about gardens—flowers and vegetables. In later years he kept track: "So far this year, there have been fifty-three tulips, twenty-seven peonies and seventeen iris blooms. More than last year and that's the truth."

In their early days in Hancock, Michigan, while Opa worked in the copper mines, Oma decided to get into the dressmaking business. She'd never made a dress in her life and so she tore one apart and used it for a pattern. She got an order for a wedding gown for a young Italian girl. The bride thought the resulting billowy concoction was beautiful, but Oma wasn't sure. She was looking around. She was afraid for Opa, because every day there were deaths in the mines. Largely immigrant labor was employed in the copper mines and the life was hazardous.

By then my mother had been born, in 1883 on the first of May, International Labor Day. She was firm and independent and fond of storms. When we were children, living by Lake Michigan, she encouraged us to dash down the dune for a swim during one—the lightning flashing and the sky dark and noisy and the rolling waves cold.

On Oma's urging, Opa finally quit the mines and got work clerking in a general store. The wife of the man who ran the store was a friend of Oma's and pretty soon Oma had backing for a new venture—a millinery shop. Hats were a big proposition in those days. There were frames and elaborate decorations, and some imagination was needed as well as a persuasive personality to keep them moving. The story has been told over and again in the family of Oma and the boxes of roses, how one day she was told by her goods salesman that she could buy a hundred boxes of artificial roses very cheap if she'd take the entire lot. She said she would and Opa threw up his hands when the delivery was made, the boxes stacked on top of each other, filling a storeroom, one layer of roses to each box. He said she'd never sell them. But that week the hatmaker's daughter was sent off to school wearing a hat covered with roses, and on Sunday Oma as well as my mother wore them. My uncle, who was painting by then, set to work and produced posters of fashionable ladies wearing hats covered with roses and put them in the window. Customers drifted through the store, assured by Oma that it was the style in Paris that spring, and before long every artificial rose was gone.

This Luxembourg grandmother was a dedicated Catholic. In time, my sisters and I would be baptized at St. Peter's Evangelical Church in Elmhurst, Illinois. I would already be over nine years old when we lined up and all took her name, Mary Steichen, for our middle ones. It was Oma who recklessly promised her parish priest back there that she'd pay for a statue the church wanted, and somehow in time she did. She was a true believer, and even went back to the Old Country one time after she and Opa had moved to Milwaukee, because the Holy Shirt—the Shirt of Christ—was being exhibited in Antwerp or somewhere and Oma hoped that Grete, her blind sister, might be cured by a miracle. It did no harm to try, so the Kemp sisters cut their hair short, joined the Procession of the Blind and walked with the others as was the custom, taking two steps forward and one step back. Although Grete was not changed, Oma felt better for having gone.

Sometimes these uprooted grandparents in the New Country had trouble making the Reality match the Dream. Searching through letters, journals, and listening, I saw Oma awake past midnight trimming hats and up early doing the washing and scrubbing the kitchen floor to get the housework done before opening her shop. Opa fussed and shouted that she'd be late and slammed the door on her when he left. And then there were the two children to rear somehow, the fulfillment of the Hope. Oma took on the job with ferocity and love. She was an ample woman, larger than my mother, who took after Opa. Oma was always swathed in long dresses and aprons, her hair piled up. And she was vastly energetic. When my father would get to know her, before long he would dub her "The She-wolf." And the family would call her "The Grand Duchess," after the ruler of Luxembourg, because of her powerful way.

Uncle Ed has recounted how, when he and my mother were being punished for some mischief, they'd be sent to the dusky cellar and the door would be locked upon them. They'd whisper and eat the apples and nuts stored on the shelves there, as long as they knew school was on. When the time was right, they'd begin to cry and wail and call about how sorry they were and Oma would let them up, pleased.

He's spoken of how, if Oma thought his misdemeanor was serious, she'd set him down and take a chair and sit before him and explain and reason, her voice going on and on and on. Uncle Ed said he'd promise anything to stop the ever-flowing loving counsel. Once he talked to me about Oma, after she'd been dead for years and he was near his eighties. He said he had come home from school and found the kitchen fragrant with kuchen that Oma was baking for a kaffee klatch of women that afternoon. He was hungry and noisy and demanded some. Oma yelled at him to be quiet and that he'd get his later. He shouted that he wanted some now. She reached for Opa's heavy strap which hung on the wall and hit him with it and sent him to the cellar. As he went down the steps he felt his head, which was wet. He began to scream about blood and how he was dying. Oma ran to take him in her arms, crying, "I'm a bad mother!" Uncle Ed, talking of that time, was nostalgic and tender. Never, if possible, did he miss seeing Oma on his birthday.

When Uncle Ed's book, *A Life in Photography*, was published, and he was in his eighty-fifth year, the dedication was to Oma, "with homage,

29

gratitude, respect, admiration, and love"; and he said, "From my early childhood, she sought to imbue me with her own great strength and fortitude, her deep, warm optimism and human understanding. As far back as I can remember, she was her family's decision maker. . . . In spite of long, tireless hours in her business, she always made time for heart-to-heart conferences with her children. Once, when I was about ten years old, I came home from school, and as I was entering the door of her millinery shop, I turned back and shouted into the street, 'You dirty little kike!' My mother called me over to the counter where she was serving customers and asked me what it was that I had called out. With innocent frankness, I repeated the insulting remark. She requested the customers to excuse her, locked the door of the shop, and took me upstairs to our apartment. There, she talked to me quietly and earnestly for a long, long time, explaining that all people were alike regardless of race, creed, or color. She talked about the evils of bigotry and intolerance. This was possibly the most important single moment in my growth towards manhood."

Hadn't I found glory in my small Swedish Grandma Sandburg? And now strength in powerful Luxembourg Oma, who molded my uncle and my mother to come up to the dream of herself as a young wife who crossed the sea with a son in her arms to look for a lost husband in the New Land.

Four

The Wanderlust

I remember one time in my grade school years in Michigan, seeing my father standing beside our house on the top of a dune and yelling down at some boys below. "Hey, you poet," they were jeering, "write us a poem!" And he with arms akimbo, bellowing back. I was not only disturbed for myself, but for him. Indeed, why a poet? Why not a farmer, lawyer, teacher, like the accepted fathers of my school companions?

I knew he was different. He was off and away from home half the time. And when he was with us, he didn't conform to a normal pattern. The neighbors viewed him with a critical eye, and let me know it at times, aware that he mostly slept his mornings away, while they rose with the sun and were in bed before midnight. They met him once in a while in the neighboring villages of Sawyer or Three Oaks, where he'd ridden in with my mother or Martha to visit the barber shop or drop into the drug store for some cigars. He went out walking after dark had come on, in summers or in a blizzard-time, sometimes nodding and again looking past and through and then striding by a neighbor. He knocked on the doors sometimes of one or another of their window-lighted houses late at night and asked himself in and settled down to talk on and on, on politics, mankind, anecdotes of history.

As long as I was with him on his walks or in our home, I loved and was proud of him. It was when I was away and on my own that it became difficult. I knew that when my father traveled, he was the same way with people as in our neighborhood there in the sand dune country of Michigan. I knew he phoned up friends and acquaintances unexpectedly from a train depot. "I just got in town. Have you got a corner where I could sleep? And maybe I could have a bit of the juice of the java bean?" And they welcomed him, the spokesman of The People.

When had my father's wanderlust begun? Because he was imprinted with the habit. He leapt from job to job as a teen-ager. When he was fifteen, he quit work on the Burton milk wagon route and hired out in a drug store, sweeping, cleaning and doing what he was told. He kept looking around for other work, and when there was an opening for a porter at the Union Hotel barber shop in the half-basement under the Farmers' and Mechanics' Bank, he took it—three dollars a week plus tips and what shoeshine money he could get—anything from a nickel up. There was a little extra when he drew tubs in the adjacent bathrooms; needless to say, no woman or child entered the area. He has spoken of the eight porcelain tubs with partitions between, kept busy on Saturdays especially, for few homes had running water. There were pumps in the yards and folks carried in their water by the bucket for cooking, drinking, and washing dishes and clothes and children. There was a privy in every backyard too, as a rule at some distance from the pump. My father scrubbed the backs of customers for special tips, mopped floors, washed windows and cleaned spittoons.

Then spring came along. He got restless and when a milk wagon pulled up on the street one day and the driver called him over, he accepted the proposition—twelve dollars a month and noon dinner with the farmer, Samuel Kossuth Barlow, and his wife. In those early years my father had odd jobs galore. He was a tinner's assistant for three days, helping take down an old tin roof and put up a new. He washed bottles for two weeks in a pop-bottling works. He hired on in a pottery, until the place burned down. He was water boy for three weeks for a crew of road graders. He worked one season at a boathouse and refreshment stand at nearby Lake George, letting the boats out to customers, and selling ice cream cones, candy and pop. He helped harvest ice on Lake George one January, working from seven at night till six in the morning, acting as "floater" the first week—standing on a raft of ice and coaxing it into the icehouse where it was broken into blocks. The second week he worked in the icehouse, stacking the blocks. He hired out for tips and a fresh pass at the Williams Racetrack, carrying water, sponging the sweated trotting and pacing horses, doing whatever else he was asked to do. It was there that he saw the black trotting mare, Alix, break the world's record, and he never forgot it. Between steadier work, he peddled bills to advertise stage productions at the Auditorium, and he also hired on as a stagehand, helping pull the different curtains, set up props and shift scenes. He saw Eugene O'Neill's father, James, as Edmund Dantes, the Count of Monte Cristo, and said afterwards he went about with the other boys, with arms up to heaven, calling, "The world is mine!" And they would mimic the dying Camille, "He is come! Armand, Armand! You are come, but it is too late!"

My father was eighteen when the wanderlust first bit him. Grandfather Sandburg had gotten a pass for him on the C.B.&Q., and he boarded a train for Chicago, planning to stay as long as his money lasted. He had saved a few dollars and got some advice from a friend, John Sjodin. Once, in their early teens, the two had printed a little sheet called *Not A Cent* that advertised used items for sale, doing the work in a barn loft and passing copies out by hand. John Sjodin had also taught my father a few clog steps, which he never forgot. Sjodin, who would become a radical and an anarchist in time and probably influenced my father's early opinions, had cautioned him on how to make money go far when traveling. And so, in Chicago, he knew to go for breakfast to Pittsburgh Joe's on Van Buren near Clark Street, where he paid a nickel for a cup of coffee and a stack of pancakes with molasses. For lunch and supper the same outfit charged a dime for a bowl of meat stew, all the bread he wanted and more coffee. There were saloons with signs in the windows: WELCOME—FREE LUNCH. He paid five cents for a beer and helped himself to cheese, hard-boiled eggs, rye bread and sausages. He found a walk-up room for a quarter a night at a hotel on South State Street. He said later that he carried no suitcase and in his pockets, along with his cash and his C.B.&Q. pass, he had his pipe and tobacco, his knife, and a handkerchief. For ten cents he bought a top gallery seat at the Variety Show, where vaudeville acts went on. Tickets to the Eden Musee and the Wax Museum cost the same. After three days his money was gone and he rode back to Galesburg.

The experience had been a heady one and it was late in June of 1897, at a little over nineteen years, that my father set out again. The nation had been foundering in Hard Times ever since the Panic of 1893 and a depression still prevailed. Four million workers had been let go from their jobs as factories closed and bankruptcies became common. Groups of men were roaming the country looking for work and gathering in "hobo jungles." My father faced his family in the kitchen, and Grandfather Sandburg frowned and Grandma Sandburg worried. The baby sister, Martha, and the older one, Esther, and Uncle Mart, a bit younger than my father, stood around. Then after the noon dinner he left the house, wearing, as he later recounted, "a black sateen shirt, coat, vest, and pants, a slouch hat, good shoes and socks, no underwear, in my pockets a small bar of soap, a razor, a comb, a pocket mirror, two handkerchiefs, a piece of string, needles and thread, a Waterbury watch, a knife, a pipe and a sack of tobacco, three dollars and twenty-five cents in cash." Again he carried no valise. He walked down to the railroad yards and waited until a freight began to move, ran alongside it and jumped into a boxcar. Through the open side door he watched the land go by. He let the train decide where he was going. He had never been out of Illinois. When the cars started across the bridge over the Mississippi River, my father says he stared because he'd always longed to see that river. His boyhood friends had used to pay a dollar to go along each year on the Grocers and Butchers Annual Excursion, starting by train north from Galesburg to Rock Island, and from there downstream by Mississippi steamboat to Burlington, or even further to Quincy, and then by train back home. My father, without the money to go, had listened to the stories and wanted to see it.

When the cars slowed into Fort Madison, Iowa, he slipped off. A nickel paid for cheese and crackers and he hired on a steamer going down to Keokuk, unloading kegs of nails in trade for passage. The river wound about small towns and farmlands and in a day came to where the Des Moines River flowed into the Mississippi and the Keokuk Canal bypassed the rapids. When the last keg was off the boat, he took a nap on the grass by the canal, washed, combed his hair, filled his pipe and after a while met a professional hobo, the first of many. My father began to understand their lingo and to think of himself as a "bo" in time, so it would be clearly stated years later, in advertisements on the back of his books and in lecture brochures. Hobos called food given from a back door a "handout," being invited into a house to eat with the family was a "sitdown"; "lumps" were handouts that a "bum" could wrap up and stash in a fence corner or under the wood sidewalk while he begged more "lumps" and so got a supply in.

As my father went on his way, he heard the song that the Industrial Workers of the World and the Salvation Army missions would pick up later and which I, in time, learned:

> I went to a house and I knocked on the door,
> The lady says, "Bum, bum, you been here before."
> Hallelujah, I'm a bum, hallelujah, bum again,
> Hallelujah, give us a handout to revive us again.
>
> I went to a house and I asked for some bread,
> The lady says, "Bum, bum, the baker is dead. . . ."
>
> The springtime has come and I'm just out of jail,
> Without any money, without any bail. . . .

And he heard about the bum who asked for a "handout" and how the lady gave him a piece of bread and said, "I'm giving you this not for your sake or for my sake but for Christ's sake." And how the hobo handed it back, "Not for your sake or my sake but for Christ's sake, can you put a little butter on it?"

Telling later of his bumming days, my father said he got jobs along the way. He blacked stoves for a quarter or dinner and supper. He hired out as a waiter in a lunch counter at fifty cents a day and meals. At Bean Lake, Missouri, he worked as a railroad section man in a gang of five, swinging his pick to tamp the gravel or rock firmly under the ties so the roadbed would hold when the freights rolled upon it. And he cut weeds with a scythe, ten hours a day. In Kansas City he answered a DISHWASHER WANTED sign and they took him on, called him "Gus Sandburg" and paid him a dollar and a half a day. He did his sleeping at the end of some hallway, or under stairs where a cot would be placed, or in an unfinished house, waiting until the carpenters had gone, or in a boxcar on the way. When he felt like moving on, he made sandwiches for the trip, left pay in the till to cover the cost and caught a freight out of town.

He learned what "blinds" and "rods" were, and "bumpers." A "blind car" was a baggage car with no front door, hitched in back of the tender that fed coal and water into the steam locomotive ahead. Men in the tender had been known to throw hot water back at the hobos in the blind to discourage them from using it. Under the cars were the "rods," and by holding onto them one could make it from town to town, the gravel and dust and smoke part of the arrangement. It was a bad idea to go to sleep while holding onto the rods. Riding the "bumpers" meant standing on the couplers between two freight cars and holding onto a brake rod. One night my father was planning to leave Salida, Colorado, and head north for Denver. He couldn't find an empty boxcar, so he rode the bumpers, his feet on them and his hands on the brake rod. He kept slipping into sleep, knowing the danger, kicking his legs against each other and shaking his head, fighting the drowsiness and unable to get off the train. Finally he was safe in Denver, and not under the rails.

He slept in flophouses for fifteen cents a night, forty men in a room. There he first met the "graybacks" and "seam squirrels," *Pediculus humanus*, the common louse, coextensive with the human race and apparently inherited by man from his remote primate ancestry, at home in his flophouse blankets. My father climbed on top of a Pullman car going from Denver to McCook, Nebraska, and had the same problem, while holding tight to the roof of the car, of slipping off to sleep despite all his efforts to keep awake. When he got down he was stopped by a brakeman with a star and a club. "You get back on that train." And my father did, wide awake. He reached western Kansas in time for the wheat harvesting, moving with a threshing crew from farm to farm for three weeks. He gazed at the Rocky Mountains, a sight to equal that of the Mississippi River. He saw Pikes Peak. Always he kept company with the men in the "hobo jungles," who washed their shirts and socks and handkerchiefs in nearby creeks, sewed up rips in their clothes, shaved by pocket mirrors, pooled their lumps and cash for shared meals. He stole corn from fields with the rest and boiled or roasted the ears, having coffee on the side and rye bread and cheese. At one house where he'd chopped wood and picked apples for a sitdown, the man gave him an old suit of gray wool, better than any he'd ever worn. He got into a boxcar once on a siding and found others ahead of him, spreading newspapers to sleep on and coats over them against the chill. Finally, shivering, the lot of them left the car, walked down to the local jail and asked to spend the night. They were let in on condition that they'd be out of town first thing in the morning.

Four months and a couple of thousand miles went by, and my father was viewing Galesburg again, this time from the familiar open door of a boxcar. It was the afternoon of the fifteenth of October, 1897. He slipped off, careful, watching out for "bulls" with their dark lanterns and night sticks. He walked down Berrien Street and went up the porch stairs. Did Grandma Sandburg, who probably never understood my father the way she did Uncle Mart, who was always near her, cry to see her elder son safe? She sat him down at the kitchen table, and while he talked on and on into the evening to the family, set coffee and good food before him. My father says he had over fifteen dollars plus the good-looking suit he wore, and that made an impression on Grandfather Sandburg, who asked, "Now what, Sharlie?" My father couldn't answer. He was nineteen and didn't know which way he was going. But he had changed over the past four months, and he would always be a wanderer.

He had to get a job and pretty soon hired himself again to a dairy farmer three miles from Galesburg. Morning and night he was to milk eight of twenty-two cows while the farmer milked the rest. He had a team of horses to curry and hitch to the wagon that he drove into town with the filled milk cans, returning by noon with the empty ones. In town he'd pick up a newspaper, he said later, and read the two-column "Home University" series of lectures by professors of the University of

Chicago on various subjects from politics to literature. Then, as winter came on, he changed jobs again, thinking of learning the painting trade. Mostly he was delegated to scraping and sandpapering, to prepare the wood for his boss. As he worked, he waited for President McKinley to declare war. On the twenty-sixth of April, 1898, two months after the *Maine* had been blown up in Havana harbor, my father was sworn as a private into Company C, Sixth Infantry Regiment of Illinois Volunteers, for two years of service. Though twenty years and three months at the time, he was listed as "twenty-one years of age, five feet ten inches high, ruddy complexion, grey eyes, brown hair and by occupation a painter."

In about three months, Company C sailed from Charleston in the *Rita*, a lumber-hauling freighter captured from the Spanish, which arrived in Guantánamo Bay, Cuba, on the evening of the seventeenth of July. Along the bay were palm trees, live oaks, palmettos and bright flowers, as well as hordes of butterflies which came out to visit the troops and battleships in the bay. The Spanish fleet had just been destroyed in the nearby harbor of Santiago and the ship bands played "A Hot Time in the Old Town" over and again. The song had been written two years before and was used so continually during the war that Spanish soldiers thought it was the national anthem of the United States:

> Please, oh please, do not let me fall,
> For you're all mine and I love you best of all,
> You must be my man or I'll have no man at all,
> There'll be a hot time in the old town tonight!

There was yellow fever ashore and the officers who left the *Rita* returned quickly. It was thought that the cause of the "Yellow Jack" was miasma or poisonous night vapors, and that the disease was infectious. No one heeded the mosquito, *Aëdes aegypti*, which was considered a nuisance and no more. Shore casualties from the fever multiplied swiftly. The glow of houses and hospitals that were ordered burned in the hope of controlling the spread of the fever could be seen from the vessels in the harbor. Certain of the ships were quarantined and yellow-flagged. Years later, my father-in-law, Dr. George Crile, Sr., fourteen years older than my father, and on another transport in the bay, would write that one of the yellow-flagged ships was "the harmless RITA, that carried Colonel Foster's men and had offended only by landing one sick man. . . . A pall fell over those jubilant Illinois men after the yellow flag was raised on her. They were as silent as a funeral. Not even their band played."

Preparations were under way for the invasion of Puerto Rico, and in a few days the *Rita* set sail for the southwest coast of that island, landing at Guánica. My father wrote long letters home to the Galesburg *Daily Mail* as he went along, and they published some. He put down observations in a small notebook, describing Guánica as "a one-street town with palm and coconut trees," and said he "found the coconuts rich and the native cigarettes elegant. The natives take off their hats to us whenever they meet us." The United States Intelligence Department knew little about Puerto Rico. No one in the expedition had ever been there. Nothing was known of the climate or the topography or whether any of the flora or fauna were poisonous. The soldiers, cooped up on the ships for the past days, were unused to exercise. My father, clad in the blue wool uniform of the Civil War of more than thirty years before, marched with his buddies halfway through the island. His journal recorded, "July 26—Had crackers, bacon & coffee at 8:00 o'clock. Relieved near sunset. The co. was marched back to seashore where we struck tents & went for swim before supper. . . . Aug. 6—After dinner got Krag-Jörgensen rifles & knife-bayonets. All of the men highly elated, some of them played with the guns like boys."

My father-in-law wrote of the time, "Our rifles were the old Springfield type, the model used, I think, in the Civil War if not in the Crimean. They had a range of only nine hundred yards and were loaded with black powder. The Spaniards had Mauser rifles of the most modern type, which used smokeless powder and cartridges that were loaded in clips of five as against our one. They could kill at fifteen hundred yards. There was, however, one advantage in our black powder; it acted as a smoke screen, and prevented the enemy from aiming quite so accurately. It made no difference whether or not our men could see, as our bullets did not carry far enough to hit a Spaniard. The detachment of the Sixth Illinois was firing supposedly over our heads at the enemy, but the spent bullets were continually falling among our men, occasionally wounding them."

And there were the mosquitoes, huge and hungry. "One could kill a dog," said the volunteers, "two could kill a man." My father noted, ". . . Slept along the road with the mosq. . . . As one man commented, 'They came in brigades, accompanied by bugle corps.' . . . Started march at 8:00 A.M. A very hot day with uphill walking. Scores of men prostrated by heat. Many serious cases. About ⅓ of C Co. finished. . . .

We stood in a downpour of rain . . . there was almost continual rain till daybreak . . . The hillside presented a strange spectacle with 1000 men standing about with only their ponchos for protection . . . The camp was one grand, slippery mudhole." It was August in the tropics. Besides the rifle, each soldier was carrying a bayonet, blanket roll, pup tent and poncho. He wore a cartridge belt and canvas leggings laced from boot to knee.

When they reached Utuado there was the news that on August twelfth the peace protocol had been signed in Paris and Armistice declared. It was less than four months since my father had signed up. And so Company C marched back down the island roads in the rain, the men sleeping one night in the bins of a scented coffee-drying building. At Ponce they compared weights. My father, who had weighed 152 when he volunteered, had lost more than twenty pounds. They were shipping out for New York. On board there were discussions about the future and searches were in order. Someone would shout, "Time for inspection! Shirts off!"—at which every man would remove his and search the cloth and especially the seams for lice, which had been familiar to the Company C men for the past months. My father, due to his stint as a bum the year before, was more skilled than most in methods of hunt and destruction.

As luck would have it, another of the privates on the ship was George R. Longbrake, whose backyard in Galesburg touched the Sandburgs'. He'd been one of two students from Lombard College who had been inducted into Company C. The other, Private Lewis W. Kay, would die shortly of fever. Aboard ship, Private Longbrake talked with my father, urging him to think about going to their hometown college of Lombard. Longbrake said he'd be returning there in fall and thought they might give free tuition for a year to war veteran Charlie Sandburg. Longbrake would put in a word if my father was interested. He was.

His wandering as a soldier had taken my father just short of five months. On the twenty-first of September, he was given his muster-out pay of $103.73. Again, he was back in Galesburg and going up the porch steps of the Berrien Street house. He was thin and Grandma Sandburg noted again that he could use some feeding up. The little girls, Esther and Martha, in pinafores and black stockings and hair ribbons, welcomed him, as did Uncle Mart, weighing more than my father now. When Grandfather Sandburg arrived, my father handed him half of his pay.

"Well," said Uncle Mart, who worried sometimes about his wandering brother and even in years ahead, it is said, would pawn his watch and chain to send money to my father when he got a hungry letter, "Well, last year you were a hobo and this year a soldier. What's next?"

"Maybe I'll go to college," my father replied. He was not yet twenty-one. Did he pick college because it made more sense than going back to his apprenticed trade as a painter? Would he have picked it if free tuition had not been offered by Lombard College? Who knows? Not I.

Five

Young Edouard Steichen and His Little Sister

I shall leave my father now, drifting and going along with his destiny, and back off into the past—a decade—to 1887. It is the copper-mining town of Hancock in upper Michigan, and Oma's busy with her millinery shop and Opa still clerks in a general store, but is helping out with housework more and more. And he's always got his vegetable garden, which Opa is happiest with. My mother, Lilian, is four, with black curls and blue eyes. Sometimes she is called Lily, but the family pet name for her is Paus'l. No one seems to know where the name came from. "Puss" is a term for kitten and "li" is commonly added to Teutonic names for endearment. Little Kitten perhaps. I called my son John Carl "Butch" when he was tiny, and my daughter "Missy." My father called the latter "Snick" and me "Swipes." That's the way tenderness is. My uncle, Edouard Jean, is eight and his family nickname is Gaesjack. Little Jack maybe. At any rate it stuck through his life. They called him Eddie too, and at this time he has a basket in his hand, filled with beans, carrots, cauliflower, from Opa's garden. He goes from door to door, selling them.

Oma worried about Uncle Ed. The mining town was made up of immigrants, many of them a rough lot, and the children that he ran with used a variety of street obscenities picked up from fathers and older brothers, as well as common slang. She had high hopes for Gaesjack, and the next year when he was nine, she took him down to the town's railway station, tied a tag to his coat lapel with his name and address and sent him off to Pio Nono (Pius the Ninth) College and Catholic

Normal School in a suburb in the south side of Milwaukee—St. Francis. The priests who ran the college were not too different from some in other institutions where the only women around are cooks and house-keepers, and my uncle, observing what went on, had no use later in his life for most priests. Perhaps, as with a Catholic friend of mine, who says he became disenchanted with his faith when he "caught a priest kissing a nun," something similar happened to Uncle Ed. He never told me what he saw or knew, and my mother, talking of it to me, only nodded and said it must have been scandalous, and that was that.

Anyway, at Pio Nono, Uncle Ed's classmates were mostly older boys, headed for the ministry, and he wanted to do well. The family story goes that in drawing class, he was assigned to make a picture of a tulip. He found a large botany book and, placing tracing paper over a picture of the flower, transferred it. He brought his final product to the class, where the priest exclaimed over it, held it up to the class as an example of how to follow instructions and apply oneself, and declared that Eddie Steichen had talent. When Oma heard of it, she was confirmed in her idea that her brilliant son would be an artist, and as for my uncle, rather than expose himself and his unlawful act, he applied himself to learning to draw well.

The next year, in order to be close to the school, Opa and Oma took the lake boat and moved their household to Milwaukee, where she set up her millinery shop. My mother was sent, along with the other Catholic girls, to a Catholic school. In 1892 my uncle began seeing the reports in the newspapers about the coming World Columbian Exposition to open in Chicago on the next May Day. Machines fascinated him and he de-cided to go. He was thirteen years old and he went to the Milwaukee Western Union office and proposed delivering telegrams by bicycle, a new idea. They took him up on it and paid him fifteen dollars a week instead of the usual ten. He saved the money, one eye on the papers, which reported on the "hootchy-kootchy" girls and a cafe where one could "Smoke the Chibouk" in the "Egyptian Village," and a new amuse-ment designed by George Washington Gale Ferris to upstage the Eiffel Tower of Paris—a wheel 250 feet high and carrying thirty-six cars up into Lake Michigan's high winds and down again.

Later my uncle said that during the week he went to the 1893 Ex-position he lived mostly on chocolate, saving what money he had to buy a motor. He stood with the crowd and watched the dynamo, the first ever on exhibit, converting mechanical energy into electric. Then, back at home, he made a miniature railroad engine that pulled cars over a track. He had already taken his bicycle apart and put it together, and my mother related later how he took his Waterbury watch to pieces and successfully reassembled it, with an unneeded part left over.

The next year Uncle Ed was fifteen and his formal schooling was considered to be over. He was apprenticed to a Milwaukee lithographing company, the terms being that he would work for a dollar a week the first year, two dollars a week the second, three the third and four the fourth. He was assigned to the typesetting section until one day the firm's owner came through and observed him painting a watercolor for Oma's fortieth birthday—three bluebirds on Queen Anne's lace and buttercups. He transferred Uncle Ed to the art section.

My uncle was sixteen when he bought his first camera. "You press the button," said the Eastman Kodak Company advertisement, "we do the rest." He had gotten the money for it from Oma, one more machine that interested him. It was called a "detective camera" because it was small and exposures could be made secretly—some models were even disguised as parcels, books or suitcases, or were made to be hidden in a hat. The roll of film contained fifty exposures and Uncle Ed went about photographing everything that appealed to him. Then he took the camera back to the dealer, who was to remove the roll himself and develop it. Only one picture from that first roll was worth printing—of my mother playing at the family upright piano, aged twelve, in a full-sleeved, long print dress, her dark hair pulled back with a ribbon. There is a picture of Napoleon Bonaparte along with the other photographs clustered about on the fringed shawl that covers the piano top. The print was tiny, about 1½ x 2 inches, and my uncle took it to the manager of the lithographic firm and suggested that photographs might be made of products, so that posters and advertisements they devised would have an up-to-date accuracy that would please the customers of the firm—meat packers, brewers, patent medicine vendors, and the like.

He returned his camera to the dealer, got a more professional one, which used a single plate at a time, and set up a darkroom in Oma's jam cellar. She said later that she moved out all of the canned foods so that his chemicals and poisons wouldn't taint them. Opa pronounced that his son had gone crazy and he also didn't like the way he was wasting water.

It wasn't many months before my uncle began to think of himself as a photographer as well as painter and poster craftsman. He roamed about the countryside outside Milwaukee during his free time, taking the tram to the end of the line and walking back into the woods in the evenings to try to capture the mood there in twilight scenes of trees and pools. The prints he made look very much like the watercolors he was painting at that time, monochromatic and the opposite of the clear photographs of ears of corn or wheatfields or pigs that he made for the commercial advertisements. When he was eighteen, Uncle Ed got a prize for an envelope he designed for the local committee of the National Education Association, and one of his posters—of a lady sleeping on a C which was elongated into a slipper moon, on which were the words "They work while you sleep"—was widely printed in papers and magazines as well as spread out upon tall billboards. The message was: PLEASE TRY CASCARETS CANDY CATHARTIC. He drew posters for Oma's store windows too, and he photographed groups at social outings and did portraits in the conventional fashion. It was not long before he was getting together with other young men interested in photography or painting. They named themselves the Milwaukee Art Students' League and Uncle Ed was their first president.

He was using new techniques that he liked—letting rain fall on the lens or spitting on it or setting the camera out of focus or jiggling the tripod a bit. When he was twenty, he submitted two prints to the Second Philadelphia Photographic Salon and had them accepted. One was a composition study of himself, and the other was called "Lady in the Doorway," done when he was eighteen. Was the girl one he loved, perhaps called Rosa? She stands slim and dark and sunlit and vague in a bough-decorated doorway. Who is she? The print was made at one of the Art Students' League outings at Gordon Place on the Milwaukee River, the estate of the mother of one of the students. My uncle says he deliberately made the photograph out of focus. Of it one critic said ". . . original, if not artistic or serious."

Uncle Ed got his first one-man show in Milwaukee in 1900. Paderewski had given a piano recital and my uncle had attended and then done a lithograph, which was placed in a window of Gimbel's store. A neighbor, Mrs. Arthur Robinson, saw it there and bought it. Uncle Ed went to her house to ask her why she liked his lithograph. She said it was very good and even if he was unknown now he would not be for long. She asked to see more of his work and Uncle Ed brought over a portfolio. Fifty or more photographs and sketches and paintings, matted and a few framed, were set up in her parlor—among the potted palms and ferns, on the piano top and the sofa and tables and chairs, and some strung along a wall. Mrs. Robinson asked her friends to come by and they bought one or two, but mostly they just looked. Some of the photographs were later noted by art critics. They were of misty woodland settings in summer and snow and then many portraits, one called "La Rose," of a dark-haired, full-lipped beauty, eyes half closed, that later would be a success in Europe.

And how was my mother faring? Were her ambitions, lofty as they were, being fulfilled? It seemed that Oma's idea of her future, and Opa's too, differed from hers. For the seventh and eighth grade she'd transferred from the Catholic school to a public one, and she graduated at the age of fifteen, receiving, as she later said, "a big bunch of lilies" along with a green velvet box. In the lid of the box, in which in later years she would keep her love letters to my father, was pasted a water color of a pool and trees and violets, and the message "Congratulations and Loving Wishes to Lily, From her big Brother Eddie." Mother had brought a medal home from the eighth grade class—it was for the highest grades, 103%. Opa declared that she was to learn a trade suited to her sex and he'd stand for no nonsense about the education of women. And so Mother was apprenticed in Oma's hat shop. There were eight preparers and two trimmer girls, and they said it was a great opportunity for Lily. It was Oma's secret hope that she would in time take over the business. As a child, I was familiar with a photograph my uncle made of my mother then—round-faced and serious-eyed in a wide-collared white shirtwaist and a broad-brimmed straw hat from the store, laden with artificial roses.

Mother worked in Oma's shop for a year, arguing with Opa, stubborn as she, until she learned of a convent boarding school, the Ursuline Academy, over in Chatham, Ontario, across Lake St. Clair from Detroit, where the mother of a friend of hers had gone. Feeling the safety and protection of the nuns, Opa at last gave in, and my mother would be allowed to attend for one year. She spoke later of how the Luxembourg language was spoken in her childhood home, so English became an acquired tongue. Always a bookworm, she said that her speech and written word came to be somewhat scholastic, backed up by Latinisms.

At that time Mother was writing poetry, having what she later called "literary aspirations," saying she had "written my apostrophizings (however crude) to the Stars etc. I have even labored lovingly setting together little word-melodies with nothing to them but the sensuous music of the words. . . . In my teens I used to dream of being a poet." Uncle Ed believed in her genius and her future literary career, and she told later of how close the two were and how they "made pilgrimages together on moonlit nights to birch woods, listening in the silence for the heavy fall of a dew drop." She was sixteen and he twenty.

When Uncle Ed had completed his four-year apprenticeship at the lithographing company, they had hired him on right away, at twenty-five dollars a week the first year, and the following year at fifty. It was a fine salary, so when my uncle announced that he was about to quit work and be off to Europe to look around and to study, Opa got upset, convinced that Uncle Ed had once more lost his mind. But not Oma. She emptied the money drawer and gave it all to him, and she would do the same when he wrote home from abroad that he needed help. "The Lord will send us a customer who wants to order a hat," she told Opa.

Oma promptly bought an enormous scrapbook, which she planned to fill with news accounts of the successes of Gaesjack, in whom her faith never wavered. One of the first news clips she pasted in had to do with a show held in Chicago that April and cosponsored by the Art Institute there. Of one of the entries, the report said:

> "The Frost-covered Pool" was the product of Edward J. Steicher [sic], Milwaukee, Wis. The picture, if picture you can call it, consisted of a mass of light gray ground, with four or five vertical streaks of darker gray upon it. Even those who claimed to admire this production admitted that the "frost-covered pool" could not be discerned by the very closest scrutiny, and that it was a mooted question whether or not the vertical streaks represented trees . . .

So off my uncle went, stopping in New York to meet Alfred Stieglitz at the Camera Club of New York and to show him his portfolio of sketches, lithographs, paintings, and photographs. Stieglitz offered him five dollars each for three of the latter and Uncle Ed accepted, delighted. He also had stopped off at the Ursuline Academy in Ontario to see my mother. There the two had reaffirmed their belief in Art, Work and each other. In a photograph he took of them together during that visit, each wears a high white collar—hers soft and lacy, his stiff and with a dark tie; each wears a hat; their eyes are steady and sure and their mouths are set in a stubborn way. He is twenty-one and she seventeen.

It seemed that Opa's concern for my mother proved to be not unfounded. When she returned from that convent she had not only lost her religion but had been a star student, and she was heady with her new knowledge. At the Academy she had taken fifteen subjects, from logic and Christian doctrine to botany and astronomy. She had arrived at the school with a fiery faith and had earned the respect and concern of the nuns by kneeling on the stone floor below the altar all night long, as she had seen them do. And she read the *Confessions of St. Augustine* to try to untangle the theology. Then, in the *Atlantic Monthly* or perhaps it was in *Scribner's Magazine,* for the story varies as the years go on, she read an account by Mark Twain on "White Slavery" and forthwith began to deny the existence of a God who would allow that trade to go on. When she returned home, she told Oma and Opa of her new conviction. Opa, in his expansive Luxembourgeois, shouted about the deceit of schooling and what it had done to my mother. Oma retorted as loudly, weeping as well, and turning to Mother, explained how she feared for her soul. Oma took her to see a Jesuit priest, Father Langner, who reassured Oma, "As long as the child believes that what she does is right, she is still one of us. She has lost faith but it will come back." Ever after, my mother has had a soft heart for the Jesuits.

As for my mother's further education, ignoring protests, she set about studying during the summer and early fall so that she might take college entrance examinations to cover four years of high school. On the first of December, 1900, she was notified by the University of Illinois that she had passed. She left Milwaukee for Chicago, this time hatless and independent. She changed on the Illinois Central for Urbana, where the university was, down in mid-Illinois, prepared to absorb whatever education could bring her to prepare herself to Better the World and Mankind.

Uncle Ed, meantime, had sailed in the spring of that year, 1900, at just twenty-one years of age. He took the French Line steamer *Champlain,* along with a close friend, Carl Björncrantz, a member of the Milwaukee Art Students' League. They booked passage by steerage, storing their bicycles in the hold. Uncle Ed later said that the bunks were "tiers of three shelves one above the other, with straw and a blanket for bedding. Food was ladled out from buckets into tin plates that the passengers had to wash in cold water. Having been warned that the food was poor, we took a number of loaves of bread, a ham, and some cheese with us." The two young men bicycled from Le Havre along the Seine to Paris, on the way setting up makeshift easels, getting out their palettes, and painting and sketching as well as photographing. Confident of their genius, they went striding through the Grand Palais. They were stopped by the guards when they tried to ride their bicycles into the marble halls. They were undoubtedly Americans, my uncle wearing knickers, a sports coat and soft checkered cap, stumbling in the French tongue. They headed for the exhibition of Auguste Rodin, held just outside the entrance of the Paris World's Fair of 1900, where the statue of Balzac was. They had seen photographs of the statue in the Milwaukee papers, and my uncle had said that "it looked like a mountain come to life."

47

Then they continued their tour, taking their bicycles through France and Belgium and Luxembourg. When they parted company, Carl Björncrantz went off to Sweden, where his ancestors had lived, and Uncle Ed to Austria. In May he was back in Paris, where he spent time at the Louvre and got himself a studio in the Latin Quarter—83 boulevard du Montparnasse. "I wish he were a little less wild," my mother said of him later, "a little more practical. . . . An artistic temperament has its drawbacks!" And, "On second thought I believe I did my brother an injustice in referring his shortcomings to his supposed artist's temperament. I'll take that back—say his shortcomings are due to plain 'cussedness.' . . . For Edward hasn't any nonsense about him."

Uncle Ed would spend two years and four months abroad on that first trip, later saying it was perhaps the most exciting time of his life. It stamped his character thereafter. He looked upon himself as a painter as well as a photographer, and enrolled at the Académie Julian to study sketching and painting. After a month he declared that he had no use for schools, that "Julian's has killed more artists than one can number," and that "the kind of work that was admired there was cold, lifeless, slick, smoothly finished academic drawing."

My uncle refused to recognize the sharp line between the photograph and the painting, and began using a technique involving gelatins, colloids, gum and other materials so the negative was soft enough to be worked over and the results could be controlled in a variety of ways. The resulting prints satisfied his desire to see "whether such and such a painting could also be done by photography." It had been his custom since he had roamed the woods outside Milwaukee, filming stands of trees and mud puddles near them, to sign many of his photographs and particularly those resembling water colors or oil paintings, with his name: STEICHEN, and below the date in Roman numerals: MDCCCCI.

He submitted his work continually. In September, the London Photographic Salon hung some in a huge exhibit. Then the Royal Photographic Society showed twenty-one prints, and he went on to London for the show. Papers in the States and abroad reported:

VIEW PICTURES BY AMATEURS

Women Visitors Pass Criticism Upon The 900 Photographs Shown.

. . . Edward J. Steichen's picture "Keats" puzzles them also. This "Keats" was a beautiful woman, with very big eyes. She was clasping a book with a "soul's-awakening" clasp. "Is it a wallet or a datebook?" asked one of these critics. "It's her Keats; that's where the name comes in," explained the Milwaukee originator of the idea.

48

Mr. Steichen, as becomes a leader of the new movement, has a portrait of himself, which he terms "Self Portrait: Composition Study," whatever that may mean. Mr. Steichen represents himself as partially dressed, trousers, shirt, and braces being in position. The print is so trimmed that one side of Mr. Steichen is cut away, and had the knife slipped a little there would have been a print without Mr. Steichen. Such work is interesting to those who study the philosophy of clothes, for all the elements which go to compose the young man who follows the new American School are clearly placed before us. This photographic eccentricity was, we presume, perpetrated at early morning, as was also doubtless "Nocturne No. 12 Miss G."—also shown at the New Gallery—which depicts a young lady in a pair of corsets seated at a piano. This is a very low tone effect, the top of the lady's head being lost in the background. Apparently Mr. Steichen objects to including the whole of a head in the picture.

The Proper Old Lady and Martha have now laboriously reached "Self-Portrait," by E. J. Steichen.
The P.O.L. Why have they put the figure up in the corner like that? The camera can't have been pointing straight.
M. It's evidently a piece cut out of a big picture. Perhaps they had this bit over and thought it was a pity to waste it.

. . . Again, take "Self-Portrait," by E. J. Steichen, of Milwaukie [sic], U.S.A. We should call this "Wanted, a Pair of Braces," for his trousers are tied up with string.

Back in America the same photographs were shown in the Third Philadelphia Salon at the same time. The report there went:

Mr. Steichen sends a "Self-Portrait"! We do earnestly hope that the phrase will not become current over here. Imagine a young man clothed only in shirt and trousers, standing before a light wall, quite bare, save for a black picture frame that he could easily swallow at a gulp, and you have a self-portrait. It is probable that his missing half is at the next door neighbour's, for we notice that his address is 342½, Seventh Street, Milwaukee.

And then another kind of item appeared about my uncle, who enjoyed the ways of Paris and would eventually live in its environs. It was carried by the Paris edition of the New York *Herald* among others, two days after Christmas that year of 1900:

"BANQUET D'ATELIER."

Mr. Edouard J. Steichen, who is studying painting in Paris, gave a Christmas dinner in his studio at 83, Boulevard du Montparnasse, in honour of the arrival in that city of Mr. Holland Day. No one would expect this brilliant young member of the New American School of Photography to give a dinner in quite the ordinary way, and he didn't; the whole of the elegant little function being worthy of Mr. Steichen and the Latin Quarter. Covers were laid for six, Mr. Frank Eugene, of New York; Mrs. William E. Russell and Miss Mary Devins, of Cambridge; and Mrs. Elise Pumpelly Cabot, of Boston; with Mr. Steichen and Mr. Day. The studio was lighted with the red glow of silk lanterns, which Mr. Steichen was fortunate enough to obtain from a Japanese Government official at the Exhibition, and was decked with holly and mistletoe.

Toasts were drunk in honour of the newly-elected American members of the "Linked Ring" [an avant-garde London photographic society], Mrs. Gertrude Kasebier and Mr. Clarence White. Before breaking up the banquet, a curiously improvised medley of the "Marseillaise," "God Save the Queen" and "America" was sung, and toasts were drunk to Her Majesty and the French and American Presidents.

Some of the items of the menu were ingeniously described. Particularly happy, for instance, is "salade *Hollandaise*, sauce *developpement à la glycerine*," "marrons glacés *au gum bichromate*," "choux de Bruxelles au *carottes des Ecoles Nouveaux*," "vin de Xeres en l'honneur *des nouveaux lincks Américains*."

It was January then; my uncle had not yet been in Paris a year. His friend Carl Björncrantz was returning to the States and Uncle Ed wrote him, "Bon Voyage—old man good luck to you. Through the smoke of my cigarette I see you now—on board ah—you will be there soon in that blessed land—U.S.A. and then in Milwaukee.—Don't forget my parents— see them often. My mother likes you and I'm sure will be good to you. If they are lonely cheer them up. Tell them I'll be back *some* time and bring back the reward. To those who profess to be my 'friends'—just tell them that you saw me. . . . If people pick because I don't write tell them I'm *busy*. . . . bless your heart and accept the love of your friend, E."

Uncle Ed continued to exult to Björncrantz upon his successes, while hesitant before Oma and Opa. On his birthday he wrote from 83 boulevard du Montparnasse: "Mon cher Carl—I have not written for some time I know—I am bad—but busy the last few weeks have indeed been hustle.

—Salon.—Today the result.—I have had a picture *accepted*.—Naturally I am feeling good. It is a birthday present—and a beauty. There are no official statistics, but I am told that over 3000 pictures were submitted and only *200* accepted. Of course this is only the one salon. You know there are two—the Champs de Mars (the new)—and the Champs Eleysees [sic] (old)—that is the one stands for modern art the other for the old academical.—I am naturally 'new school.' The old salon will certainly be accepting more things. Just think Carl—of having one of my things hung in the *Grand Palais* where we went strutting through together but a few months ago. The two Salons exhibit in the same building at the same time of course. I got in a portrait—which is particularly good because the portraits admitted this year have been *very* few and the majority submitted consists of portraits. It is a portrait of F. Holland Day who you know has been visiting with me, and it was done in *one* sitting of about 2 hours. If I get it fotographed later when hung I shall send you a print. I painted a rather large thing also but as I expected it did *not* get in. This cost me lots of work & money but I learned very much by doing it—and shall do it *all over* again now.

"There is going to be a great retrospective exhibition of childrens portraits at the Petite Palais during the same time as the Salon. This shall consist of great loan collections from all over the world of the old masters and the great modern works. There is also to be a small collection of modern fotographs of children. I have been *invited* to contribute 6 things of this—so I will be represented with my painting at the Grand Palais and with my fotographs at the Petite Palais—and that at the two greatest events of the year in the art world.—Don't think Carl that I have a swell head because I tell you all this and because I rejoice—but I know you are interested and understand.—

"Last night I wrote a rather blue letter to my parents.—discouraged and with very little hope ahead about the salon.—What I am writing to you is different.—Now I can't write more now.—but you will hear from me again soon. Tell me about yourself. Yours, Ed."

Then he sent the same news home, but on a postcard. My grandmother promptly called up the Milwaukee *Sentinel* and pretty soon she had another clipping for her scrapbook. It was Sunday morning, a year after Uncle Ed had left her arms, and her triumph was there for all to see:

THE SENTINEL, SUNDAY MORNING, APRIL 14, 1901. AN HONOR TO MIL-WAUKEE. Striking Success Won Abroad by Edward J. Steichen, a Young Local Artist. NOTABLE BIRTHDAY GIFT. Though but Twenty-two Years of Age One of His Pictures Is Accepted by the Salon.

Some celebrate their birthdays in one way and some in another, but few are so lucky as Edward J. Steichen, the Milwaukee boy who went to Paris to study art less than two years ago and who on March 27, the day that he was 22 years old, was officially notified that the Salon had accepted his portrait of F. Holland Day, of Boston. The news reached his parents in this city on a postal card phrased in the laconic fashion of youth and it marks another upward step in a career that is attracting wide attention even in the French capital, where artists are as thick as blackberries in July. . . .

The clipping went on at length about Uncle Ed's beginnings in Milwaukee and his triumphs in London and Paris. And, "At any rate, it is quite certain that the Milwaukee young man has succeeded in getting himself and his art talked about, which is something that a good many older artists have striven for and failed of doing." And Oma saw to it that my mother was in the article too:

Mr. Steichen expects to return to Milwaukee some time next winter, but it is doubtful if he will remain here, as his parents are planning to remove to Chicago to be near their daughter, who enters Chicago university in the autumn. This daughter, who is named Lilian, and who is only eighteen, is as clever in her way as the son, for she entered the State university of Illinois after only a year of study at Ursuline convent in Canada, following the completion of an ordinary course at the Sixth district school in this city. She is making a special study of languages and expects to be graduated from the University of Chicago in two years, the professors at Champaign having assured her that that is possible. Some of her brother's cleverest photographs have been studies of his sister, one which shows the two in animated conversation having been one of those that struck the popular fancy at the recent London exhibition.

It was like Oma to contemplate moving her business and transplanting Opa and the household to be near their vigorous daughter. I'm sure Mother discouraged the idea, for they never made the break from Milwaukee. It's true too that my mother was as brilliant as Oma claimed, receiving her Bachelor of Philosophy degree after two and a half years at the University of Chicago. When the Award of Honors would be made to her graduating class, out of the seven students who excelled, my mother, listed as "Lilian Anna Maria Elizabeth Steichen," would be the only one mentioned four times, and she and one other student would be elected to "membership in the Beta of Illinois Chapter of Phi Beta Kappa" and be given the key.

Like Oma, my mother always believed in her romantic, tall, slender, handsome brother, with the striking birthmark on his left temple. Somehow, possibly because there was only one sibling on my mother's side—Uncle Ed—our family was always very close to him. I loved my father's siblings but in a different, quiet way. I was especially close to Aunt Mary and Uncle Mart because they would visit us. But when Uncle Ed came, hearts beat fast and there was general commotion.

In 1901, my uncle exhibited a "Portrait of Miss C.E.S. by Eduard J. Steichen"; she was an American, Clara Smith, whom he would marry two years later. I would hear stories from my mother all through my childhood of my uncle's way with women. One of them told of a young and wealthy heroine who fell in love with my penniless, talented hero uncle who would not marry her because of her money. Was her name Rosa? When she was seventeen, she followed Uncle Ed to Europe to study music with a master in Germany. She tried to coax my uncle into jealousy by becoming engaged to her music master. She went to my uncle and said that she would buy a painting from him for her new home. He was enraged and said none were for sale. My mother's story told of how the heroine returned to her apartment and, holding some token of his in her hand—a print, a painting, a memento—shot herself. My mother said that the tragedy struck the heart of her hero brother and that the girl was buried in a famous cemetery near Paris. There were other stories of how Uncle Ed brought Mother a magenta dress from Paris on one of his trips, and how when he visited Oma and Opa he wore a black cape and swaggered, elegant.

There is no doubt that my uncle, called by one critic at least, an "ultra impressionist," knew what he was about at the age of twenty-two when he calculated on how to get paintings or photographs into exhibitions. Ebullient, energetic, quick-moving, he staged his way through his life. When he would have a second wife after he broke up with Clara, it was told by my mother, to my young satisfaction, that theirs was a common-law marriage. She would be elegant and auburn-haired and creamy-skinned, an actress, and I would adore her, feeling that by no miracle under heaven could I ever attain a romance to approach theirs.

Back then, he was writing to Björncrantz again, "My dear Carl.—Well —h--l what's up, old man, why don't you spit it out. —Let me feel with you, as I can but feel now I would. This world is a great storehouse of pain for us all. None escape—some of us receive it physically and they are to be pitied indeed—but those who suffer the pain that is of the mind and the soul live in a realm so beautiful that the pain comes as a great gift from God. It is suffering and sorrow that makes us *men*—that exalts us.—It is suffering and sorrow that gives birth to *great art*.—and therefore we are blessed when it is ours. —What is it, Carl.—I am in a mood to appreciate it all the time for you can realize my feelings, when I tell you that I have not heard a word from Rosa since she left me here at the Gare St. Lazarre.—I don't know where she is or anything.—Believe me Carl ever your friend.—Ed."

Some critics sensed this feeling, which was evident in his work, one saying, "To a casual observer it must be quite apparent that Mr. Steichen, who is said to be as deft with the pencil and brush as with the camera, is imbued with an unveiled mysticism, that he revels in melodramatic sentiment, and gloats over imaginative chaos. He is nothing if not an impressionist—an extremist of the extremists."

Uncle Ed had a plan in his assault upon the art world, saying, aged twenty-three, "It is my ambition to produce a photograph gallery of great people, present the series of enlargements to a big museum and publish the same in book form. It will be my life work." A Norwegian painter, Fritz Thaulow, introduced him to Auguste Rodin, whose notorious Balzac statue he had admired. Together they bicycled outside of Paris for ten miles to the hamlet of Val-Fleury near Meudon, on the Seine. Above the village on a hill covered with an orchard was the home of Rodin. My uncle and Thaulow stayed on for dinner cooked by Rose Beuret, called Madame Rose, the common-law wife of Rodin, shy and sometimes spoken of as "a primitive woman, a peasant." They drank the wines brought up from the cellar by their host. Then my uncle called Rodin *cher maître* and said, "The ambition of my life, master, is to make a great photograph of you."

Rodin liked him and in time would call him *mon fils*. When Uncle Ed's first child would be born, it would be a girl. He would hope the second would be a "little brother," whom they would call Auguste after the master. When the second baby would arrive though, as my mother said, it "turned out to be a little sister! (Will she be called Augusta?) . . . no one in the family seemed to think it could turn out to be a *girl*." They would puzzle about for a name for a while, Uncle Ed writing home that ". . . . she has a number of names—Charlotte & Kate and I generally call her Mike—I don't know which will last but I guess we will call her Kate." And they did and gave her a middle name too: Rodina.

When Uncle Ed had been granted permission to make a photograph of Rodin, he wanted to study him beforehand. And so, at the sculptor's invitation, he spent his Saturdays for a year visiting the home and studio in Meudon and watching Rodin among his works. It is told of the sculptor that his method of work was to employ several nude models, who were told to walk about or rest as they pleased. *Le Maître* observed, became familiar with the play of muscles in movement, and according to one biographer, Paul Gsell, Rodin "follows his models with his earnest gaze, he silently savors the beauty of the life which plays through them, he admires the suppleness of this young woman who bends to pick up a chisel, the delicate grace of this other who raises her arms to gather her golden hair above her head, the nervous vigor of a man who walks across the room; and when this one or that makes a movement that pleases him, he instantly asks that the pose be kept. Quick, he seizes the clay, and a little figure is under way; then with equal haste he passes to another, which he fashions in the same manner."

When my uncle finally was ready to make his study of Rodin, he decided to combine two negatives. The photograph, which would become famous, was called "Le Penseur" and showed Rodin with his marble "Victor Hugo" sculpture in the background and in the foreground the bronze "The Thinker." Uncle Ed said later, "When I showed Rodin the combined print, he was elated. . . . It is probably more of a picture *to* Rodin than it is *of* Rodin, because after all, it associates the genius of the man with that expressed by his work."

By now the name Eduard Steichen was established, whether his viewers agreed with his style or not. One critic called him the *Enfant Terrible* of the New American School, while another said, "One should not say he recalls Rembrandt, but rather at this rate Rembrandt will, in time, remind us of Steichen!" One critic complained of studies Uncle Ed made in Italy, saying the Etruscan "skies seem slightly obscured with London fogs." And of "Le Penseur" and other studies at an exhibit:

> It would pass very well for a dream of Rodin lost in contemplation of one of his rough-hewn masterpieces. We think the light behind the head is a little inartistically forced. As to the "Pool—Evening," we can only say that when evenings are as dark as this they are called night. "The Black Vase" is one of those queer things that are nothing and mean nothing. . . . why it should be called "The Black Vase," rather than, more obviously, the white window or the stretched neck, does not appear. . . . Mt. Steichen overreaches himself in his artistic strivings. He is a contortionist. Who would fancy Velasquez perpetrating these follies, and asking from five to ten guineas for them? But, of course, it is easy enough to put a price on any work, and quite another thing to obtain it.

Despite the complaints of the critics, it seemed that the Belgian government was about to purchase "The Black Vase" for the Bruxelles Museum of Fine Arts. It seemed too that it would be the first time a government would buy a photograph to hang among its old masters. This pleased my arrogant uncle. An interviewer for *The Paris World*, Katherine Knode, spoke of calling "on Mr. Steichen in his secluded and picturesque studio at the back of an old garden in the rue Boissonade. I had come expecting to find a man well on in life—perhaps in the fifties —with a somber face and massive physique. I had only known the artist by his work and its invariable strength, its sane and reposeful sentiment, its absence of that quality designated 'chic'—in a word, its dignity and maturity—had all induced me to the belief that here was a man advanced in years. When, therefore, to my summons at the knocker there responded the antithesis of all my imaginings, and he told me in reply to my question that he was Mr. Steichen, there must have been plenty in my face to inspire the merry smile with which he greeted me."

On the thirtieth of March, 1902, the New York *Herald* ran the headline: "PHOTOGRAPHS IN THE SALON. Innovation To Be Introduced for First Time in Paris Art Exhibition." And press cables that followed said "The photographs were submitted by Mr. Eduard J. Steichen, a young New Yorker, and are regarded as a great triumph. The decision to admit photographs almost caused a split in the jury. The pictures were, therefore, entered under the title of engravings, although really they are nothing but remarkable photographs."

Oma at once informed the local press again and they ran a headline:

MILWAUKEE BOY HONORED

Edward J. Steichen, the young Milwaukeean, whose artistic photography has created such a furore in Europe, where he has been studying and working the past two years, is coming home in July to spend the summer with his parents. In the autumn he will go to New York to execute several commissions there, and later will return to Paris, where he intends to keep his permanent studio. Just at present he is resting in Rome. . . . "I suppose," he writes in a recent letter to a friend here, "I have had more success photographically than with painting, but you must bear in mind that I have only been painting in a serious vein for the two years I have been here, while I have been puttering with the camera for about eight years."

And an English paper reported too that "Admirers of the pictures by Mr. Eduard Steichen will regret to hear that, owing to continued ill-health, caused we believed by overwork, he has left Paris for his home in America." There was no question that Uncle Ed was exhausted, besides being broke. He'd been abroad more than two years and needed to see Oma and Opa again. And my mother would be home too on her summer vacation from the University of Chicago. The clipping of August of 1902 that Oma pasted in her giant scrapbook told of many changes in her son:

. . . the gray linen shirt with loose "kimono" sleeves, soft turnover collar and black ribbon scarf at the throat, to say nothing of hair of a significant length and degree of unkemptness, would have proclaimed Edward J. Steichen, the artist, even if he had not been caught this morning in the act of placing a large photographic plateholder in a favorable position in the sunlight before his mother's home, 423 Fifteenth Street. Mr. Steichen reached Milwaukee about a week ago after two years spent in Paris and after a fortnight longer here he will go to New York where he has taken a studio and is ready to resume his work. Mr. Steichen should surely be considered among the foremost of Milwaukee boys to reach high place in the world without, for by art critics everywhere he is regarded as a master innovator in photography and all the French, German and English art journals have devoted much space to discussions and examples of his work. During the two years abroad, the young Milwaukee artist has made the acquaintance of and photographed nearly all the personages known to Paris. . . . Mr. Steichen is a most delightful person to interview, and his simple, frank talk of his work, quite free from any self-consciousness is a pleasure equalled only by a glimpse of the few examples of his work he has with him. His boxes have not yet arrived from London, and he had planned to have them sent to his New York studio, but his Milwaukee friends are anxious to see his recent work, and it is probable he will consent to a private exhibition some time next week.

Mr. Steichen said, "I am going to open a studio in New York, but I mean to keep in touch with the art work of Europe, because I believe that art is cosmopolitan, and that one should touch it at all points. I hate specialism. That is the ruin of art. I don't believe in art schools. I believe in working in every branch of art. That's what Michael Angelo did. He was painter, sculptor and architect and supreme in all. No man will ever be great who specializes."

Mr. Steichen is a boyish looking chap, and in his negligee attire, his speech punctuated with expressive gestures made with a brush, he could fittingly pose for the accepted type of the artist.

And Oma, gazing out the window at the *Sentinel* reporter talking with Gaesjack in flowing gray shirt and black silk scarf—was she surprised at his success? Was Opa? The news item clearly stated that Mr. Steichen put his developer "in the sunlight before his mother's home." Did Oma think back on the smelly third class steerage of the steamer that brought her over the Atlantic with the eighteen-month-old child, in search of Opa? I know she thought ahead, confident of the future triumphs of her Boy Wonder, now twenty-three, and of her Girl Wonder too, now nineteen.

$\mathcal{S}ix$

The Shifting Stars of Destiny

Until the Swedish and the Luxembourg sides of my family get together, there is no way but to follow their separate beginnings. What had been happening over in Galesburg, Illinois? Perhaps Grandma Sandburg was beginning to feel hopeful about my father, now that he'd been enrolled as a student in a college. Since the photograph had been taken of "Charlie" on his graduation from grammar school, he'd not had any formal education. He was self-read though and spent a lot of time with the newspapers. The shelves in the house held Bibles in Swedish and English, Mary's and Mart's schoolbooks, some stereographs, newspapers and not much else. My father was a "special" student, taken at the age of twenty on a recommendation, even though he lacked a high school diploma.

He said years later that Grandma Sandburg told him then, "You do the best you can, Sharlie, and maybe you make a name for yourself. It don't do any hurt to try." She made griddle cakes and coffee for him at dawn when his bicycle arrived at the porch steps. He had a job as a "call man" at the Prairie Street Fire Department, eight blocks from home and down the street from Lombard College, and was paid ten dollars a month. At night he slept on the second floor of the station house, wearing an undershirt, drawers and a blue uniform shirt. Later, telling of it, he said there were seventeen iron frame cots and beside each was a pair of rubber boots with pants attached. When the alarm bell rang, every man slipped into his pants, buttoned them on the way to the brass pole, slid down, leaped on the horse-drawn chemical wagon or hose cart and was off. My father bought a bicycle so that when the fire whistle sounded during the day while he was in class, he could leave and pedal to the burning building. His hours were ten at night till six in the morning. On the way to breakfast at home, he'd pick up a penny newspaper.

Grandfather Sandburg had moved his family into a roomier house just across Berrien Street from the old one. My father had his meals with the family and a room to study at the end of a hall, its windows overlooking the front yard where a tulip tree stood. Below was a wide porch with curlicued columns running along two of its sides. There was a well and a pump in the yard and a privy in back, clotheslines, a barn for storage, a big garden for potatoes and cabbages. There was a furnace, with registers in most of the rooms, and a bathroom upstairs. In the big downstairs front room was a piano bought by my Aunt Mary, then at her schoolteaching position. My father's room was heated with a little kerosene stove, and he has told of how he smoked his pipe and studied in the evenings there by a lamp that he kept wick-trimmed and filled. He had elected to take Latin, English, philosophy, history, as well as drama, public speaking and elocution. It seems that he shone as a basketball player, leading the team in that new game. There was no coach in those days, and no more than twelve men in the school played basketball. The total college enrollment was about a hundred—eighty or so in the Liberal Arts Department and less than twenty in the Divinity School; a third of the students were female. In the team photograph that I have, my father's dark hair is parted in the middle. He wears a sleeveless jersey with an L sewn on it, knickers and a wide belt and ribbed socks. As captain, he holds the ball. He played back position and right guard and in later years the young man who was center, Athol Ray Brown, described the "battle cry of the Terrible Swede: Lima-lama, jima-jama, 18-16-24, Willy, Willy Willy! That meant simply to get the ball to Cully. . . . Sandburg would raise his arms high over his head and heave the ball crashing against the backboard." The college paper reported on a Saturday evening game in March, "Up until the last few seconds it was a tie with the score 10 to 10, when Captain Sandburg threw a difficult goal from under the basket and saved the day for his team."

It seemed that my father liked that year of education his stint of soldiering had got him into. And when, in the following May, some of the officers of Company C, Sixth Illinois Volunteers, offered to put him up for appointment by the local congressman, George W. Prince, as a candidate from the Tenth Congressional District of Illinois to the U. S. Military Academy at West Point, he accepted and headed for his room. He had three weeks to cram what he could from old school books. Then he took the train to Chicago, changing there for West Point. He passed the physical and then took the written preliminary exam. By the thirteenth of June, the adjutant was mailing a form to the Sandburg house: "Mr. August Sandburg . . . the Superintendent of the Military Academy directs me to inform you that your son Charles A. Sandburg conditionally appointed a Cadet in the service of the United States, has been pronounced by the Academic Board as not qualified in Arithmetic and Grammar. . . . Very Respectfully. . . ."

In the afternoon of the same day, my father sent a wire to Uncle Mart, in care of Schultze's Cigar Store in Galesburg: FAILED EXPLAIN SHORT PREPARATION TO PRINCE FOR REAPPOINTMENT IF POSSIBLE. CHARLIE. My father boarded the train back to Chicago and settled down in one of the smoking car's wicker seats, gripsack at his feet and pipe in hand. He enjoyed the fall scenery and got off in Albany to walk about and browse in the bookstores. Then he was back in a wicker seat again in a smoking car until he reached Niagara Falls, where he descended again just to have a look.

Home in Galesburg, he made what explanations he could to a cool Grandfather Sandburg and a steadfast Grandma Sandburg, and returned to his firehouse job for the rest of the summer, supplementing it with extra work as a handyman at the Union Hotel, which flew its own flag from the front roof above the entrance. A trolley ran along one side, and buggies and carriages and horseback riders moved by in the street outside. At four-thirty every morning my father slid down the brass firehouse pole and walked to the hotel to stoke the furnace, clean out the clinkers, mop the floors, fix the fires for the chef and the pastry cook, do whatever he was told and get to have any of the breakfasts on the menu for the day for free.

In fall he left that job, though he stayed with the firehouse work, and returned to school. In exchange for tuition he arranged to perform janitor's jobs under the direction of the regular janitor, along with his basketball teammate Athol Brown. After a while, with Brown and another student, Howard Lauer, my father got together to form the Poor Writers Club, led by Professor Philip Green Wright, teacher, poet, and learned man, one who exercised a direct influence on my father's literary development. Wright, Boston-born, had an accent, was in his forties and had a way of stirring up students. He took his astronomy class out at night to study the stars and tramped with some of the young men into the country on Sundays, reciting poetry and discussing ideals. On Sunday afternoons the Poor Writers Club met in his study to read and criticize their own work "in prose and verse, and any other sports of the spirit which we happened to run across during the week," Wright reported later. And, "We were poor, we were, or wished to be, writers, hence the title. . . . Very delightful, innocent, and refreshing were these meetings, when our minds wandered the free fields of fancy and imagination." On Sunday evenings around seven-thirty, a dozen or so students would gather in the large front room of the Wright house on East Knox Street to read from current or ancient authors and discuss the works under the guidance of Professor Wright. At nine o'clock Mrs. Elizabeth Wright served Nabisco wafers and cups of hot chocolate and at ten the evening ended.

My father had enrolled in the elocution class and practiced hard before the members of the Poor Writers Club and the evening groups in the Wrights' front room. He entered the Swan Oratorical Contest, held once a year in the College gymnasium. Halfway through he went blank, stuttered and stopped. His story is that Maud Miner, his teacher, who was in the wings, supplied a sentence and he plowed through to the end, the fifteen-dollar first prize going elsewhere. By the next year he was ready to try again. He was a member as well as the secretary of the Erosophian (love of wisdom) Literary Society, its objects "the improvement of the members in oratory, debate, literature and parliamentary law." As business manager of the college monthly periodical, *The Lombard Review,* and then editor in chief, he had had an opportunity to express himself in writing as well as elocution. He felt prepared, having memorized every word from start to finish, and so in February of 1901, at twenty-three years of age, listing himself as Charles August Sandburg, his hair parted and slicked back, in high starched white collar and black bow tie, in the same gymnasium, he delivered his oration for the Swan Oratorical Contest. He captured first prize. The talk was devoted to the work of John Ruskin, its title "A Man With Ideals," and it called for higher progress for mankind. "Let us have more happy homes," he declaimed, "and less traffic and war; less hate, less pelf, more hope, more love!"

It was not an uncommon theme for my father. He used the pseudonym "Karl August" in *The Lombard Review.* "The most faithful advocate of socialism is the man whose occupation is the creation of things; the dreamer who writes, paints, carves and works. . . . His mind is generally so enwrapped in his work that he has no thought for propagating and his belief in socialism is brought to mind only when he must needs leave his intellectual heights and go down and rub against the earth for the purpose of, say, eating, i.e., buying bread. Buying! Pitting his dreaming, aspiring soul against that of some grocer whose highest ideal is written in dollars and cents." As editor in chief he had an audience when he railed in print against his society: "More and more do we hear of the man who says: I love action, but I hate hurry; I adore beauty, but I detest display; I marvel at Venus de Milo, but believe corsets a curse! I like electric displays, but prefer stars; I would rather have the ripple and sparkle of reality than any play-show of power hemmed in by footmen, card-trays, cheese-straws, debutantes, automobiles and Bourbon-like riots of spangles." In my father's review of Robert Hunter's first book, *Poverty*, there was the same drift: "It is not a cheerful subject that this book handles. There is little pleasure to be derived from observing 'poor people,' the hungry, the dirty, the ragged. The vicious are not pretty to look at, and most persons, when they read a book prefer to have it deal with 'high society.' The Smart Set may be more adulterous, covetous and lazy, comparatively speaking, than the masses, but the pomp and circumstance of their surroundings, the footmen, the card-trays, the cheese straws, the gowns and tailorings of the 'rich people,' these things are much more pretty to look at than a mob of dusty workingmen carrying dinner-pails."

As an orator, he defined his goal in *The Lombard Review*, signing himself "The Knight of the Grip": "An orator's purpose, like that of every man, should be to have men say when he is gone, 'He was gentle, and the elements so mixed in him that nature might stand up and say to all the world, "This was a man."' . . . if I were to name a few who are really chosen out of the many who are called, the list would have men like . . . Elbert Hubbard . . . Eugene Debs. . . ."

In January of 1902, he wrote of the class-day orator at Harvard for the next June: ". . . when the nearly one thousand seniors have their time-honored class-day exercises, a full-blooded negro, the son of a slave, will stand before an audience of the most fashionable and cultured whites. . . ." The man was Roscoe Conkling Bruce; his father, after the war set him free, had graduated from Oberlin College, and he attained, among other positions, that of U. S. Senator from Mississippi. Young Bruce had graduated from Phillips Exeter Academy and entered Harvard in 1898; he had won a number of prizes and medals, and my father reported, "he is a remarkable orator and popular for his personal qualities."

In the last issue of *The Lombard Review* for which my father was editor, he spoke of those who had "gleaned from it something of sense of duty, perhaps some good cheer, perhaps some courage, and to each and every one of its friends it says, 'Oh, old heart! The world is not bad, and every day, as there is a God, it is growing better. Live life to the full. Suffer. Be glad. Work hard, be cheerful, be gracious. And God will rest ye!'"

Then my father, after four years counting the one as a "special" student, abruptly left Lombard College without waiting to graduate. With him went a fellow student, Frederick Dickinson, who had taken the fifteen-dollar first prize talking on "Robert Burns," the year my father had gone blank, stuttered and stopped on his first bid for the Swan Oratorical Contest award. Dickinson and my father had gone off together two summers earlier during vacation, bicycling about the countryside, selling stereographs and viewers for the Underwood and Underwood Company. They had worked together on editing the "Jubilee Year Book," *The Cannibal*, which celebrated the college's fiftieth anniversary, listing themselves as "Editing Manager" and "Managing Editor." Both had belonged to the Erosophian Literary Society, as well as to the Glee Club, the latter recording them as "Charles Ole Bull Sandburg" and "Frederick Clementine Dickinson."

It was the spring of 1902 and my father was twenty-four. He packed the front wire basket of his bicycle with his valise and a shoe-box-size black leatherette canvassing case, lined with blue plush and containing two dozen stereograph cards, a viewer and order blanks. He put on his soft cap and wheeled out of Galesburg. The young men liked the occupation. My father had said before returning to Lombard that other summer, "I am becoming such an enthusiast over stereographs that I may keep all I have over at the end of the season." He had put a notice in *The Lombard Review* about their vacation work, explaining, "Stereographs as seen through a good glass are the best possible substitute for travel. They bring a scene before the eyes with startling reality and impart much of the inspiration that the original scene would. These, when studied in the same spirit of investigation and love of beauty that one should have in the study of art, history, geography and books of travel, are of inestimable value. To neglect them is to forgo a genuine pleasure and a real addition to your stock of knowledge. They are . . . the connecting link between illustration and reality."

I suppose many of the immigrant farmers and country people, like Grandfather Sandburg, didn't read books, and the stereograph filled a need. In my own childhood, the sets were lined up on shelves in boxes the size of a thick book or in double-volume size too, each containing from fifty to a hundred of the cards. On these were mounted two slightly different photographs of the same subject, taken with a double-lens camera. The card fitted into a sliding bar of the viewer—the stereoscope—which one held while looking through the double magnifying eyepieces. There was a three-dimensional as well as enlarged effect. As a child, I was instructed to keep them in numbered order within their boxes, and not to leave fingerprints. The scenes varied from the "Winged Victory" statue in the Louvre to "Peasants Before the Walls of the Alhambra" in southern Spain to the "Throne Room of the Royal Palace in Berlin" or "Rhinoceros Captured by Natives," portraying the animal with hind leg chained and roaring. On the backs of some were elaborate descriptions of the sight and sometimes on the front too: "Sunset at the Grand Canyon: 'Over all broods a solemn silence.'" Or: "Earth proudly wears the Parthenon as the best gem upon her zone!" Or even: "When you grow up and have a gun, shall you go to the woods to hunt for a rhinoceros? . . . Perhaps you will be lucky and find a rhinoceros and shoot him."

My father wore a cap and a long light-colored jacket and knotted his dark tie and went from door to door. He described the process in a letter to my Aunt Mary, "Here I am yet all the while . . . zigzagging toward the ideal, and every now and then sending my smile crashing thru some sourface and splintering the gloom behind it. You see, when canvassing, I so often run against an icy exterior that I have to challenge, defy, slap, coddle, calm, enjoin, exhort, thaw out and warm up, that I believe I am evolving a small-size *aura* . . . I am begetting a self-respect that borders on conceit. . . . So long for this time, sister. I love you. Charlie." He said, "We have been working in the country and enjoy it keenly . . . couldn't keep awake to write half-decent during above. In the evening we went on a moonlight picnic and it was 3 A.M. before we got back. You could not have ordered a more beautiful night."

In the Sandburg family, and especially in Aunt Mary, there was doubt about how my father was handling his future. He wrote Mary, "You perhaps know of other periods in my life when I was undergoing experiences that I considered developmental to a high degree—and which time proved to be such—but which at the time, I did not think would interest you and of which, I therefore did not write. You haven't a great faith in stereographs and their future in education, nor do you see clearly that I am passing thru a sort of apprenticeship in salesmanship and dealing with people. I could go into some world-old work at or near home that would reflect more honor on the name Sandburg than that in which I am engaged now. But it takes time for big results—And I hope this is an explanation that explains that sometimes, 'I am doing a work and cannot come down,' in which I hope I am not a 2nd Jonah . . . —I am a fool, but I know which way I am going. . . . I will not let correspondence, or anything else that is not eternally vital, rob me of the sleep or recreation that I must have if I am to have health, do my work, and carry on my studies . . . believe me always truly yours with deep brotherly love."

As the year's end neared, he wrote her again, "I thot I would make my Xmas remembrance in 'views.' Sent a box with a Rome Set, and book, for you, and a Yosemite, Niagara, Is Marriage a Failure? and a few miscellanies, as a combination Yule-tide thought for Mama and Papa, Mart, Esther and Martha. If I remember right, there is a scope at home." And he added, "I feel something of a brute. I wrote to Mother yesterday, and was going to write to you and tell you why I'm not coming home this Xmas. I don't lack the carfare, but I wouldn't have a kopeck for the old gentleman—it seems almost unnatural sometimes to say 'Father.' I haven't any resentment toward him, but neither can I make any affection blossom. And there is that in me, be it right or wrong that will not permit me to face him again till I can have some of that Stuff to hand him . . . I expect to be home in proper condition to please papa's and other's expectations,—well certainly before summer."

My father was drifting about. It was the wanderlust. When he had been over a year at selling stereographs, he wrote back to Professor Philip Green Wright that he enjoyed it: "Canvassing is like being a Swede —you can squeeze pride or shame from it. . . . Frankly, if I had been a canvasser all the time, I would have a thousand banked now. But I have been a canvasser only about ¼ the time, a scholar, a poet-taster, an athlete and a social lion (or cub) the rest of the time."

He told Wright, "I am pegging away at old plans hoping I am as boyish and enthusiastic as ever." And on the Fourth of July of 1904, "On this glorious day wherein we celebrate political independence and industrial servitude . . . I spent the day with men and maids in the woods; did a stump speech; recited Shakespeare; impersonated a nigger preacher; . . . I have a splendid idea in my head tonight, which if I worked out would be a great literary hit. But if I started to develop it, it would mean 1:00 or 2:00 A.M., and when I woke up tomorrow, I would feel more like a man of thought than of action and business. I often deny myself and the world this way . . . Yours for the Better Day, Charles Sandburg."

It was a time of new interest in a sound body. Everyone experimented with special diets and exercises, as the machine age took over. My father and Dickinson tried out the Kellogg fad that had been started by the Battle Creek Sanitarium, originally the Western Health Reform Institute. They didn't go to boarding houses anymore, but had their breakfasts and lunches in their rooms—cereals, nuts, fruits and sometimes cheese and cold ham.

My father wrote home that he had taken an eight-mile walk with friends over the hills on a Sunday, telling his sisters, "Walk in the country very much . . . very very much. Understand? Or I will scold. . . .

Take long walks outdoors and breathe deep as you can letting the air out slowly, and you'll feel that you have 'go' in you, and everybody likes women and men with 'go.'" He told the younger one, my Aunt Esther, "Whatever we want real strongly—and try hard to get—we will get—or something just as good. . . . Give my love to mamma and papa, and kiss Martha for me." He wrote Aunt Mary, ". . . 'follow the gleam' as you have been and you will realize the truth that 'the soul grows by leaps and bounds, by throes and throbs. A flash! and a glory stands revealed for which you had been groping blindly thru the years.' . . . Charlie."

He was thinking of going to England with Dickinson and perhaps also Professor Wright during that summer. He wrote the latter, "I am set on a European tour before making any place my permanent home." They thought of taking passage in a cattle boat perhaps, and planned to sail the first week in July. Over in West Derry, Rockingham County, New Hampshire, was Robert Frost on his thirty acres, milking the family cow at noon and midnight so that he would not have to rise at the crack of dawn and might sit by a kerosene lamp to read or to write out poems— to be published in London later in *A Boy's Will*. Frost was four years older and would be going to England before long. My father's trip was called off, but suppose it had not been? Would he and Frost have inevitably met over there? Would my father's course of life have changed? Restless, he was roaming east with his canvassing valise—Pennsylvania, New York. From New Jersey, four states south of Frost's country, he wrote Aunt Mary, "I was in Walt Whitman's old home last Sunday and on Memorial Day threw a rose in his tomb at Camden. . . . The chances are that by falltime, I will have a book published in deluxe style. Prepare yourself for those who will extol and laud—and those who hoot and smile and deride." And he added, "Some way I feel as tho I am not doing as much as you had expected me to—that I have fallen short of the standard of achievement you had your eye on for me."

And he told Aunt Esther, "I have your picture on a mantel in my room and am sometimes asked if that is my sweetheart. And I say, 'Yes, but that picture don't give any idea of her—she has such a quiet, witty way about her.' . . . Always keep your hope high—and smile, smile no matter what comes, as mamma does . . . give my love to the whole household. . . . Your loving brother, Charlie."

He felt his aloneness. "If I could only meet the Ideal Woman, I believe I could pull myself together and set the world by the ears. As it is I shall continue to prepare my cocoa myself, sew on the trouser-buttons, and be an itinerant salesman, a vagabond philosopher-poet, and most unworthy descendant of Leif Erickson."

The book he had spoken of to Mary would be his first and one of the results of The Poor Writers Club and his close tie with Professor Philip Green Wright. The latter had a press in his basement, on which he already had printed some of his own work. Wright was preparing the Foreword to my father's book, to be called *In Reckless Ecstasy*. In exchange, my father would write an introduction to Wright's collection of poems, to be reissued by him: *The Dial of the Heart*. My father would dedicate *In Reckless Ecstasy* to Grandma Sandburg: "I dedicate them to one who has kept a serene soul in a life of stress, wrested beauty from the commonplace, and scattered her gladness without stint or measure: MY MOTHER."

There were sixteen poems, free verse and rhyme, and five prose pieces. In the introduction, my father explained that he got the title from Marie Corelli, a romantic novelist of the day, who had said that ideas that couldn't be put into direct words might be brought home by "reckless ecstasies of language." He said, "The Bible contains one incomparable specimen of the reckless ecstasy. 'Vanity of vanities, all is vanity.' . . . But it is Christ who surpassed them all in the pathos of that infinitely tender wail: 'The light that is in them is darkness, therefore how great is that darkness!' This paradox poetizes the awful fact as does no equal amount of words in all scripture, sacred or profane. . . . I try to express myself sensibly, but if that fails, I will use the reckless ecstasy."

It is clear that the work which made up my father's manuscript was outright derivative of his college years and his delight in oratory. Half the verses were in a rhyme pattern and half free. He said later of this early time, that he "wrote sonnets and triolets, long and short rhymed verses, ballads and ballades, rondeaus, pantoums, all kinds of formal verse." One of his rhymed poems in the book, called "The Quick and the Dead," went:

Was the wind only jesting last night when it said,
"The days are not long from the quick to the dead."
For the house-windows shook and the tree-branches tossed;
The rain-bells rang for the souls that are lost.

I asked of the wind where the lost ones sequester,
In days that are now or days that are yester?
While the muffled rain beat, moaned the night-wind low,
"To the hell upon earth do the lost ones go.

"In the bed that they make must the lost ones lie,
On the roads that they choose must they run and die;

The quick are the lost and the dead are the found—
There are no souls in the dust underground!"

And then a prose piece before the ending "Invocation" went in part:

I am the one man in all the world most important to myself. I am
as good as any man that walks on God's green earth. I am also as
bad as any creature that ever transgressed a law of life. . . . Above
all other privileges vouchsafed us earthly pilgrims, I place the
privilege of work. . . . The brightest, most lasting happiness I know
is that which comes from yearning, striving, struggling, fashioning,
this way and that, till a thing is done. . . . I am not a thing that
hurries and worries. . . . I am careless, graceful, easy. . . . I never
slam a door, and I would rise above all the petty, inevitable vexations
of each day. . . . I will lose myself, lash, taunt, and shame that man
who by his superior gifts or situations knowingly darkens the lives
of others. . . . I pray for a heart unspoiled. . . . Captains, toilers,
kings, queens, drudges, vagrants, fools, would know me all. I would
pass thru the world one of the masterpieces of God, a man. And
having tried to live thus, I cannot think but that I would be of use
in some way, even down among the dead men.

While my father was looking ahead with some nervousness that mid-
July of 1904, to his first proper literary output, his present situation was
that he was down to his last ten dollars and needed to quit meandering
about the East and head back to the Midwest. Dickinson had invited
him to come to his home in Freeport, Illinois, for the rest of the summer,
where he would have free board and could work the surrounding countryside. My father sent his stereographs and valise ahead by express and
one moonlit night swung up on the bumpers of a moving westbound
freight car. Later he wrote Professor Wright about the way west, "I
wandered across Pennsylvania along the beautiful Susquehanna, past the
coal mines and along mountainsides whence I could look down on
smelter-works in lurid light." He walked out to gaze at the Monongahela
River and then took a trolley out to the Pittsburgh freight yards, where
he climbed into a coal car. There, with five others, he was "captured by
railroad police." They were handcuffed and marched to a justice of the
peace, who stated that each must pay a ten-dollar fine or put in ten days
in the Allegheny County Jail. Needless to say, no one came up with the
ten dollars. My father's cell was four tiers up. His companions were a
gray-haired Civil War veteran out of a job and a teen-aged husky

Bohemian steel mill worker who had gotten drunk and decided to fight a policeman. The boy knew a hundred words of English and as the days passed, my father learned a dozen Bohemian words and how to count in that tongue. The sheriff got fifty cents a day to feed each prisoner and my father said they got five cents' worth of food. If the warden wanted he could "shake the plum tree and fill his own pockets. . . . For breakfast, we had a half loaf of bread, and a cup of hot brown water masquerading as coffee; for luncheon a half loaf of stale bread again,—soup on Wednesday & Saturday; for dinner—but there was no dinner. How can we sleep on a big, heavy dinner?" The prisoners were allowed to buy tobacco and to send out for the daily paper.

My father valued the experience, though. "It was a lark on the whole, and I think gave me new light on the evolution of a criminal." Later he would regale my sisters and me when we came along, naming the event his "forcible detention." He continued his journey west by freight car bumpers and soon joined Dickinson, setting out on the selling trail again, walking "on an average twelve miles a day." He said, "We are getting hard as hickory." There were instructions on how to sell the stereographs, the Underwood and Underwood brochure stating, "We must insist that the First Selling Talk be thoroughly committed to memory, word for word and we strongly advise committing the Second Selling Talk. . . . This does not deprive you of using your own native gifts nor of throwing your own personality into your work." The salesman was to say of the equipment:

> This is satin-finished aluminum (pointing), that is imported mahogany (pointing). The combination of aluminum and mahogany presents a rich appearance. This beautiful hand-engraved aluminum is very strong and very light, and won't tarnish under ordinary circumstances. The hood (pointing) is arranged to exclude all surrounding local objects, thus closing one in with the scene itself. You feel that you are in Jerusalem, in the cotton fields, in Norway or whatever the scene is laid. The lenses are the purest made, perfectly ground and are put in to stay. This 'scope is guaranteed to last a lifetime.

And of a sample stereograph, that it was of an

> enormous 11-inch shell from Japanese siege gun, beginning its deadly flight into Port Arthur . . . this is war in reality. Directly in front of us is the enormous cannon. That man to the right (pointing) has

just discharged it. All these men stuffed cotton in their ears to save the ear-drums from bursting. . . . You see the dense clouds of smoke rising; the shell actually caught in the air, on its way over those hills to Port Arthur three miles away, where it will explode and do its havoc. Our war-tours are the best possible record for all future time to show accurately and in detail the different phases of modern warfare. Well, I will put you down for an instrument and some of these, may I, please?

My father defended his occupation and said he felt that his work was more than "a means to a living." He had "sold to Negroes who can neither read nor write, and I sold to the state governor . . . and practically the same class of subjects to both." He said that a Columbia University psychologist as well as Oliver Wendell Holmes believed that although they had never been to Rome they could, through the stereoscopic tour of that city, in combination with a map detailing each place represented by a stereograph, have an experience the same as being on the spot. He wrote to Wright, "I only wanted you to know what fascination and pleasure and intellectual profit and recreation I am afforded by the line of goods I am handling."

He also told Wright, as fall came on, of his solitary life, "I am like Keats at least in this, that the roaring of the wind is my wife, and the stars thru the windowpane are my children." Keats, in October of 1818, had written his brother and his wife in America, George and Georgiana Keats, after describing a walk and a visit with a lady, "I hope I shall never marry. Though the most beautiful Creature were waiting for me at the end of a Journey or a Walk; though the Carpet were of Silk, the Curtains of the morning Clouds; the chairs and Sofa stuffed with Cygnet's down; the food Manna, the Wine beyond Claret, the Window opening on Winander mere, I should not feel—or rather my Happiness would not be so fine, as my Solitude is sublime. Then instead of what I have described, there is a sublimity to welcome me home—The roaring of the wind is my wife and Stars through the window pane are my Children." My father liked that passage and would use parts of it again.

Then he was moving on, lonely and independent, as Dickinson went back in fall to law classes. He took a room in Aurora, just west of Chicago. It was furnished and unheated and he spent a good deal of his free time at the comfortable public library. He told later of how he broke ice in his water pitcher in the mornings and managed a sponge bath; he boiled two eggs on his Sterno lamp and made cocoa in the same water and got along. At this time my father was thinking about writing proper biographies of old-time Swedes: Gustavus Vasa, the sixteenth-century Swedish patriot who had disguised himself as a peasant and gone about to raise an army to drive the Danes out of his land, and who was made king; or of his grandson, Gustavus Adolphus, called The Lion of the North and The Snow King, who died a mysterious death in a famous battle. Or of Charles XII, king in the late 1600's, noted for his bravery and charisma. My father had written of him in one of the free-verse poems in *In Reckless Ecstasy*. It ended:

> Immortal Swede! Across the years
> There comes to us a glint
> Of how a man should laugh at luck;
> And whether it was sleet that beat athwart thy brow,
> Or sunshine bathing thy proud locks,
> Steady and straightforward, smiling,
> Did you face the shifting stars of Destiny.

My father had asked Aunt Esther to send him the *Life of Charles XII* by Voltaire. "I have decided that Charles XII was my namesake and I want to post up on him. Have you read The Book of Esther in the Bible —about your namesake? Here are kisses for my three loves—Mama, Esther, Martha. . . . Charlie." He said of Voltaire's work, ". . . he does not leave with a reader an adequate conception of the noble self-denial, and the sublime self-confidence of the man." My father wanted to do it right himself, to render these men with a "living touch," with their "blonde, curly hair," mocking blue eyes, and terrible fervor. "Now, this scheme —that of giving a more correct and vivid portraiture of these men and their times—is getting such a strong hold of me that I've either got to carry it out completely, dropping all business completely, or I've got to postpone it . . . and get down to business and acquire such a fund as will last me through."

He felt he had reached a parting of the ways. "There was a time I could equalize my attentions to business and to literature, but of late the latter has been drawing me away from business. And the time I have given to books and reflection has given me a conviction that if I had the leisure I could produce several essays and studies that would be welcomed in the literary world. . . . It seems to me . . . that if I could . . . instruct and entertain the public, gets its ear, show it that I am a self-contained individual, still 'in love with enraptured life,' that what I would subsequently say about the need for a social and industrial revolution, would be more quickly and attentively heeded. So I am thinking about formulating a vow, and on New Years Eve to stand on a stack of bibles, lift my right hand toward the vault of heaven and let the gods know by wireless that they may strike me with epilepsy, then paralyse me and disembowel me if I during the coming years entertain for a moment a dream of writing anything but letters, and orders for goods."

But it didn't work, for in December *In Reckless Ecstasy* was in my father's hands. Professor Wright, with the occasional help of his wife, Elizabeth, and his sons, printed a hundred copies, to be sold at a dollar each, on the small Truddle Gordon press, setting the book up in Caslon Old Face type. Wright wrote to my father, "My dear Sandburg. . . . It is a perennial wonder to me the improvement you are making in the ease of expressions and facility of your verse."

Aunt Mary wrote too in compliment and my father responded, "Never forget that . . . I look on you as one of the blessings and inspirations that has entered into my life. . . . Your good little letter of appreciation . . . is a little treasure-note to me. . . . wait till the professor prints about a dozen other efforts of mine. . . . Yours lovingly, Charlie."

My father told Wright, "I am delighted that you should choose to put a literary effort of mine into such a charming and delectable environment of paper and type. . . . I do wish my mother might see a copy of this. . . . And now, 'may all the gods go with you and smooth success be strewn before your feet.'" He said, "The finished book lies before me—'a bubble blown from our dream-skulls' . . . my regard for you is one of the admirations that adds immeasurably to the brightness of my comings and goings. . . . Of course, I see all sorts of flaws in my work now, and I am grateful that they have been brought home to me. I enclose a late sonnet. . . . Fraternally yours, Charles Sandburg."

Spring came around and in March my father was writing Aunt Mary, "I am at a queer place in my life and feel all sorts of things buzzing merrily or snarling viciously about me." A publisher in Boston, Richard G. Badger, who had brought out Wright's first book, had noted some of my father's poems and had written that he would give "immediate and careful attention" to any material he wanted to submit. "It's new to me," my father said, "to have publishers write that way. So I expect to put in about a week or two at home in April revising and typewriting about thirty-five poems of greater or less merit and length. I have been writing when I felt the mood and business has gone to the dogs."

And then from Galesburg to Aunt Mary, after he'd gone to his old Berrien Street room again, taking meals with the family for a few days, "I have been firing off a lot of stuff the past week here—just fixed a bunch of sixty poems now . . . make them go through them anyway, and put them through the exertion required for a turndown. . . . With love, Charlie."

When he got back to Aurora, he gave a try at making some money in a vaudeville theater, going on for a couple of nights in a Swede getup of red stocking cap and lumber jacket, reciting a dialect version of "Dawvid an Goliat" and telling jokes. A man asked his grocer, "Haw much ban potatoes?" And the answer, "Five cents pound." "Bat Yimmy Yonson down street salls for three cents pound." "Go buy from heem dan." "He don't got no more." "Ven I don't got no more, I sall for three cents pound too." My father decided after the second night to give up show business.

Then who was it that got my father out of his difficult time but my Uncle Mart? This uncle was gay, resourceful and loving. He was twenty-four then and married, with steady employment at the Adams Express Company. My father was unmarried, restless, and already twenty-six. Uncle Mart rode a railroad car regularly back and forth between Chicago and Galesburg and sometimes stopped off at Aurora to see how my father was getting on. Now and then the two took the car back home and the family visited. Aunt Mary in Albany heard from my father, "I was home last Saturday night and Sunday—they were quite a happy household. . . . I enclose clippings of some stuff I have had in the G. *Mail*, and will ask you to take care of them and return when you are through. . . . yours lovingly." The Galesburg *Evening Mail* occasionally printed prose pieces my father sent to the city editor, who was his old basketball teammate, Athol Brown. The pieces were called "Inklings and Idlings," and the two hoped the work might be spotted by some big-time paper looking for fresh thinkers. One was signed "Crimson" and was about the problems of the laboring man:

> . . . The garment workers, in 1904, had agreements with the employing tailoring concerns in which wages and conditions were specified. But the employers began to send part of their work out to sweatshop concerns to be finished. The coat of a suit would be made entirely by union labor and the inside pocket would bear the label of the International Garment Workers. But the vest and trousers of the suit would be finished or "trimmed" in homes where generally the entire family, from the father and mother down to the smallest child, ply needle and thread from daybreak till late at night. This is the method by which these greedy plunderers produce a "union-made" suit. . . .

74

Uncle Mart seemed to see what Grandfather Sandburg never could—that "Charlie" was different. Uncle Mart told my father, "What you want is plenty of time to read and write and you can do that in a fire station and you won't have to fuss around and worry about that damn view business. All you have to do is take care of two horses, less than two hours a day, and the rest of the time you're free—unless there's a fire." Uncle Mart talked to people he knew in Galesburg and found a position for my father if he wanted it in the Brooks Street Fire Department. It paid seventy-five dollars a month and the station house was three blocks from the Sandburg home. My father took the job, grooming the horses, oiling harness, polishing the combination hose cart with ladders and cleaning up around. Later Uncle Mart said that his brother would get so deep in his writing or reading that he'd not hear the alarm sounding about him and would miss the horses clattering and the wagon clanging as they left. Then it would dawn on him and he'd rush to a phone to find out where the fire was. He'd leap on his bicycle and be off. By the time he reached the fire, it was sure to be out.

The chief at the Brooks Street station was Jim O'Brien, who had known my father before at the Prairie Street Fire Department. He gave him leave to use a corner in the upper floor where there was a table and chair. My father went out and bought a second-hand Blickensderfer typewriter for fifteen dollars. The machine had been invented twelve years before and was a formidable affair. When one letter was struck, it brought down a cylinder covered with all the alphabet. My father sent out editorials on it that were published unsigned in the local *Labor News*. And made copies of poems:

> It's me
> To the perpetual poem
> Of the free fresh air,
> And insolent blasts
> Of winter,
> And the soft low zephyrs
> That come lulling
> In mid-summer,
> They tap me in the face,
> These things, and then they flit,
> And call out,
> "Gee! Ain't I glad I'm here!"

The books piled up on his table. He read Charles Darwin, "The desire to ascend is there before the wings." And Robert Louis Stevenson, copying it into the notebook he kept, "Shelley was a young fool; so are these cock-sparrow revolutionaries. But it is better to be a fool than to be dead." And Tolstoi and the essays of Charles Lamb; and he went through Herbert Spencer; Karl Marx's *Das Kapital*; Upton Sinclair's *The Jungle*, just out; and Jack London, of whom he said, "*The Call of the Wild* and *The Sea-Wolf* are his masterpieces. . . . If he were not a Common Man I would call him a Great Man." And all of the poets of the 1800's, liking Emily Dickinson and Stephen Crane, and then always Walt Whitman, copying into his notebook long sections and committing passages to memory. And Thomas Gray, memorizing the thirty-two stanzas of "Elegy Written in a Country Churchyard."

My father was finding an outlet for a few poems now in a new monthly magazine called *To-Morrow*, published and managed by Parker H. Sercombe in Chicago. The magazine was odd in appearance—nine inches high and five across, with the message on the masthead: *A Monthly Magazine of the Changing Order*. It was one of many sporadic organs of opinion of the day. Sercombe had a reputation for eccentricity and liberality. He lived in an old mansion house, where he held a weekly salon or open house and friends and students could gather for talk and refreshments. An associate editor of *To-Morrow* was Oscar Lovell Triggs, professor of English literature at the University of Chicago and a writer and a liberal too. He liked some of the poems he saw of my father's, and put one in the February issue of *To-Morrow*. My father told Professor Wright he had jotted it down on a trolley car and sent it off at once, adding, ". . . what dreams surpassing all I had dreamed or welded hitherto may come I wonder." Three more poems appeared in the March issue of *To-Morrow*, one, "The Pagan and The Sunrise," starting:

> Swarthy, dusky, dappled, alive,
> Off in the East, reds and purples plash,
> And beams of silver suspire and glow,
> And a disc! huge, white, and glistering.

Triggs told his readers, "Charles A. Sandburg is a young man unknown to fame, but if one may judge by the few poems he has written, he will not remain long in obscurity when once his quality is appreciated." My father took the express car with Uncle Mart to Chicago and visited the *To-Morrow* offices at 1926 Indiana Avenue. They also ran a lecture bureau, Sercombe acting as secretary. In the April issue of the magazine was the announcement of a Thursday evening talk by Sercombe on "The

Soul of Whitman's Poetry." There was also another poem by Charles A. Sandburg, "A Fling At the Riddle," which began:

> I think to filch a Story from the Sphinx,
> Outface that old Egyptian questioner,
> And cry, "Behold! I know! I know!
> I know I do not know!"
> Poignantly sad, and beautiful unspeakably,
> That we must pass, that all must pass,
> And change and pass away again . . .

Then my father was getting before an audience again, a pursuit which he seemed to be born for. Sercombe also ran the Spencer-Whitman Center, for which *To-Morrow* was the official organ. When my father gave a talk, they praised him: "Charles A. Sandburg in his lecture on 'The Uses of Poetry' pointed out some of the beauties of the commonplace and brought out a very lively discussion of the 'utility of beauty.' " The Center defined its purpose and the inspiration for its development as stemming from the "Synthetic Philosophy of Herbert Spencer and the Cosmic insight of Walt Whitman, the Poet-Seer." Free lectures and discussions were conducted at the Center on Monday and Thursday evenings. They also had established cabinet-making and book-binding shops in the rear of their Center.

To-Morrow would review Philip Green Wright's new book, *The Dreamer*, and so would William Marion Reedy, who published *The Mirror* in St. Louis, one of the magazines to which my hopeful father was submitting his poems. Reedy termed Wright "A Socialist Poet" and said that for all of its faults his work was still poetry. "There are crudities, absurdities, a monstrosity now and then in the scansion of the blank verse, but in its totality it is the authentic voice of the singer of a full, not an empty day, of life with ache and vision and upward urge in it. The foreword by Mr. Charles A. Sandburg, and the brief apology by Mr. Wright, are two excellent specimens of nervous, well-knit, savory prose."

In the Foreword to *The Dreamer* my father had said, "Poetry is one of those flowing, spontaneous results of nature like the air and the sea and the rain. . . . The interplay of forces by which poetry is produced, the process whereby experience after experience so impels a man that he seeks to give lyrical expression to the more vivid phases of his life, is not to be gathered into a formula."

I have wondered if Grandfather Sandburg, skilled and clever, about sixty years old here and with no time at his age and in his life for non-sense, ever untangled his son's meanings or wishes? Did Grandma Sandburg? Their fireman son would up and leave now and then, riding up to Chicago for a week, where *To-Morrow*'s column would report, " . . . the To-Morrow family was made glad by his presence at their home during his stay in the city. Our readers will remember Mr. Sandburg's poems in our March and April numbers, poems which it will pay them to hunt up and read again." Long years later, my father said that when he decided, after eight months at the Brooks Street Fire Station, to quit and told his family that he was going up to Chicago to try his luck, Grandfather Sandburg took him aside, "Iss dere any money in diss poetry business, Sharlie?" He said he answered, "I guess, Papa, though I haven't got anything but hope."

He hitched a ride to Chicago with Uncle Mart on the Adams Express Company car. He went down to the *To-Morrow* offices to visit, and then over to Sercombe's mansion house for an interview. He got offered a job. There was no pay except room and board, and the work was helping edit and proof manuscripts that went through the *To-Morrow* offices. My father wrote home on the new stationery, ". . . for a time am going to act as associate editor of *To-Morrow*. Will write you a letter when I am not so rushed. . . . Until I let you know otherwise, my address is as above. . . . Love to all . . . Charlie."

Later that spring he sent sheafs of poems out on the same stationery. And in the same office, he looked over his rejections, "We are returning to you herewith the following poems. . . . We find in all of them . . . a good deal of real poetry. Our objection is chiefly that, while we have no battle against poetry like that of Walt Whitman, these poems of yours seem to follow his style too minutely; and, while we do not regard rhyme as necessary in poetry, we feel that there should be a little more rhythm than we find here. We should be very glad indeed to examine more of your work. Yours very truly, Watson's Magazine." He had sent them eleven poems. He had seen the advertisements for the magazine in *To-Morrow*, stating that they were "The leading exponent of Jeffersonian Democracy, Edited by Hon. Thos. E. Watson, of Georgia, the father of Rural Free Delivery. . . . He is today heading a middle-class reform movement . . . Watson's Magazine is not a Socialist publication." He tried them again later and they responded. "Dear Sir:—We are returning to you herewith the following poems. . . . The rhythm in these is perhaps a little smoother, but they do not on the whole seem in content to equal the ones you sent formerly. We are, however, much interested in your work."

He was turned down too at the St. Louis magazine, *The Mirror*, their editor saying, "My dear Mr. Sandburg, . . . The fact of the matter is that all the verses suffer from vagueness. . . . I know that you say that you are modeled more upon Henley than Whitman, and yet, to be quite frank with you, I do not think that you conform to Henley's idea of rhythm. . . . As you are perfectly aware, there is no disputing about tastes. According to my taste there is a tremendous lot of flub-dub and tommy-rot in the work of Whitman. I have no doubt, from what I have observed of these poems of yours that you could write poetry but I think you will have to do it by getting away from the Whitman obsession. . . . It may be, of course, that I am blind in my observations. . . . Cordially yours . . ." And he had said, "I suppose, however, that your profession is that you are more of a radical than a poet. It surely is not impossible that one should be both. . . . Faithfully yours, William Marion Reedy."

What next? By now my father could no more stop himself from writing than from eating. He would be twenty-eight before long. Where was the elusive thread on which to string his life?

Seven

On with the Fight

During the long days of the late summer of 1902 in Milwaukee the Steichen family had a reunion. Mother was on vacation from the University of Chicago. Uncle Ed was back from two years and four months in Europe, where he'd traveled about, rubbed shoulders with famous people and felt his power. He'd returned to the applause of his hometown and the outright adoration of Oma and my mother. Opa was reserved and I expect his view, like Grandfather Sandburg's view of my father, was that he never quite understood the occupation of his artist son. Opa was happiest in his garden and he would have liked to get out of Milwaukee onto a piece of land. He sat in his chair in the kitchen, his hands on his knees, listening, ready for argument if one seemed called for, prepared to go to his weeding in the backyard garden or to checking the kegs in the cellar where the dandelion wine was settling, just as soon as the dishes were washed up and the house was still again.

Oma, an ample apron tied about her long-skirted dark dress, her sleeves pushed up, cooked everything she could think of, from crusty apple pies to stuffed glazed chickens, while she endlessly questioned her two Products of the New Land. The family spoke together in Luxembourgeois much of the time. My uncle told Oma that my mother was an artist and a genius. In a letter once to Mother he had advised her to keep her independence and freedom, "When you marry, you as a woman will be gradually forced to give these up. You will be a mother and those instincts will get the better of you. I do not discourage you in marriage . . . but you will be a greater factor in humankind if you can be a mother intellectually and be mother to modern humankind. I see in you things great and glorious—in any way you go if you will always be but true to your best self. Be it as a Joan of Arc or as a wife and mother."

And she said in later years that it had been when she first heard Uncle Ed say that he would go to Paris and would photograph the great of Europe that she had felt his destiny and her own, and had begun to gear herself for a life of work and became interested in the cause of socialism and turned to books and an atmosphere of learning. My mother had some radical notions at that time. She became a vegetarian, and refused to kill even houseflies. At the university she would go to eat at the Seventh-Day Adventist dining room, where the fare suited her. When she had first stated at home that she would not eat meat, Oma had pleaded, sure that my mother would die without proper nourishment. Opa had raged and ordered that she should not get any food at all if she would not eat the meat set before her. So she said she would not eat then and he let the order go. Later, in a letter to my father, my mother would make her points clear, "No artificialities for me, no corsets, no French heels, no patent medicines! No formal receptions! No mad chase after the very latest styles in dress! . . . I stay at home, walk, read, work, do as I please. . . . Put me down as 'peculiar' but don't molest me! . . . I don't go to church Sundays. I talk socialism, and radicalism generally, whenever I get the chance. I am regarded as harmless—they do not see that my non-conformity is part and parcel of a large, really formidable movement—a movement that threatens to overturn their institutions. If they scented the danger, they would cease to be tolerant."

At the university, she stayed out of the social life, going her own path. Her political ideas suited Oma, who was readily converted to socialism. Among Oma's good friends in Milwaukee were the Charles Whitnalls, he the state treasurer of the Wisconsin Social-Democratic Party. Opa may have voted the socialist ticket, but I'm not sure. I know that he argued about it with Oma. And I know, too, that he remained at home content when Oma and Mother went out to attend a meeting of Social-Democrats in some hall. My mother went over to visit the Social-Democratic headquarters when on vacation from the university or during the summers, handing out leaflets, helping translate English texts or editorials into German, or the other way around, and contributing money to the paper that was the party organ—*The Social-Democratic Herald*. She planned to be a writer—essays or articles or poetry. As for my uncle, he told the family that he thought he would get into commercial photography, where the money seemed to be, while keeping up his career as painter and getting his oils and water colors and lithographs into exhibitions along with his photographs.

Fall came on and my mother returned to the university, where she shortly joined a new radical socialist club. Uncle Ed took the train for New York, ready to plunge into his plan to make money by his craft. He hunted for a studio and finally found a small top-story room that suited him in a block of old brownstone residences between Thirtieth and Thirty-first streets on Fifth Avenue that had been turned into offices and shops. He set up a small showcase on the street level and put up a sign to say that "Eduard Steichen" was available for portrait photography at 291 Fifth Avenue. According to a family story, my uncle continued to use a system he'd worked out in Europe whenever he got money, of cashing it into small change which he threw about his rooms. When short, he could always manage to scrape up a little from under the bed or the carpet, or in some corner. The days passed and he wrote to my mother from his new studio, "Dear Sweet sister, . . . Don't worry. Cheer up. Everything lies before us. We'll *do it sure*. Lovingly, Gaesjack."

In October of 1903, Uncle Ed married the American girl he'd known in Paris, Clara E. Smith, the subject of his "Portrait of Miss C.E.S." I never knew Clara, but my mother has told me that she was a strong woman, vivacious and energetic, and that she wrote very good poetry. My cousin Mary was born on the first of the next July and I have seen Clara in early photographs Uncle Ed made—beautiful and light-footed in a filmy long white gown, her dark hair looped, holding the baby in ruffled white cap and dress up to some sun-lighted, white-flowering tree. The tales were related to me of the stone-walled place they lived in later outside Paris, called Villa l'Oiseau Bleu, The Villa of the Bluebird, in Voulangis, which I never saw except in albums, and of how he painted and photographed there and how famous people came to visit, among them Isadora Duncan, the dancer, who may have wanted to have a child by my uncle, who said no because children always complicated an artist's life. The story went on about other beautiful women loving Uncle Ed, and how when it finally came to divorce and alienation suits and newspaper accounts, Isadora herself was said by some to have danced nude in the garden among the lilies for my uncle, and rotogravure sections carried sketches of Isadora's dance, too. And then the "other woman" was there in a courtroom. And Clara, a child at her side, pointing, "That is she!" Mother told me who the "other woman" was and I wrote it in my journal, but I said I'd never tell, for Mother was fond of her and hoped Uncle Ed might marry her. There was a pretty little boy that might be my uncle's child too. I was involved in my mother's reminiscences, and too young to sense the tragedy that must have stalked through some of them. I only admired my uncle as the most fulfilling romantic imaginable and provided my mother with a rapt audience at kitchen table or bedroom or her desk.

When Mother graduated in spring from the University of Chicago, she stayed on, working at various jobs. She translated two books from German for the Social-Democratic Party. And she translated quotations from Latin and German into English for a proposed new book of quotations to, as she said later, "rival Bartlett's." When the project was abandoned, she returned to Oma and Opa, who had just got a little farm. They had put their savings—and Uncle Ed had helped out as his work in New York flourished—into a four-acre piece of land three miles from Menomonee Falls, fifteen miles northwest of Milwaukee. Opa, a natural man of the land, was happy there, but Oma became lonelier than she had thought she'd be. There was no trolley line to their place, and when Mother went home she would take the train from Milwaukee to the Falls and be met by Opa and horse and buggy. The country was open farmland and their home had a bit of woods and plenty of space for corn and potatoes, apple trees, a grape arbor and a small house. There was a coal bin in the cellar, kerosene lamps and candles, and they called it The Simple Life. During the summers Mother and Oma would set up a tent in the orchard and sleep outdoors. But Opa stood firmly against "new-fangled notions" and slept round the year in his own upstairs room.

My mother said it was she and Opa who had managed the move from Milwaukee to the farm. She grew fond of the small white farmhouse and busied herself at house and garden work while sending out letters inquiring about a teaching position. She said, "When residing among retired farmers, one must live in books and letters," and so she continued to write poems—her "word-melodies." She sent two of them to Uncle Ed at "291," since he had said he'd help try to place any of her writings.

My uncle was not just being well paid as a commercial photographer, but was being sought out for his portraits. He has said that perhaps his "most concentrated and exciting experience in portraiture" came when he was twenty-four and photographed both Eleonora Duse, the Italian actress, who was in her mid-forties and would be quitting the stage in a few years, and John Pierpont Morgan, the banker and financier, within less than an hour's time.

The photograph of Morgan had been commissioned by a German portrait painter, a friend of Alfred Stieglitz, Fedor Encke, who was painting the financier's official portrait. Finding his subject restive, Encke asked Uncle Ed if he would photograph him, saying that he could make an extra photograph for himself and would certainly have orders from

Morgan or the family for it. Morgan, tall, in top hat, cigar in mouth and carrying his gold-headed cane, arrived with Encke and took the pose that Encke was using for the portrait. After the first exposure, Morgan became restless and moved about, and when he took his position again, possibly irritated, the new pose pleased Uncle Ed. "I saw that a dynamic self-assertion had taken place, whatever its cause, and I quickly made the second exposure. . . . Then he clapped his large hat on his massive head, took up his big cigar, and stormed out of the room. Total time, three minutes." At the elevator, Morgan had taken out a roll of bills, peeled off five hundred-dollar notes and handed them to Encke. "Give this to that young man. I like him."

My uncle packed up his equipment, took a cab and half an hour later was at the Savoy Hotel with the "immortal Duse." The actress was noted for using no makeup on or off the stage. She ignored the camera and moved continually, so that of the six exposures made, only one was not completely blurred and would do. Uncle Ed said later, "Never before nor since have I photographed any person so completely unconscious of the camera." He had told her to hold some roses and stay still. She put her head down to smell them and then looked up, and that was the print he saved—she is filmy and tragic-eyed.

The Morgan portrait has become well known, his eyes fierce, glaring, his mustache and eyebrows bristling, his gold watch chain and pendant gleaming, his bulbous nose, deformed by a skin disease since his early years, only slightly retouched, his left hand clenched upon the chair arm, the light caught upon it giving the illusion that he holds an open knife. When Uncle Ed brought the two photographs of Morgan to him, the financier was pleased with the one made for Encke, which had been retouched, particularly about the nose, and he ordered a dozen prints at a good price. He disliked the one that was not touched up and called it terrible and tore it up. The act so infuriated my uncle that when in time Morgan heard that a print of it was on exhibition and much admired and offered five thousand dollars for it, Uncle Ed let him wait three years before he made copies for him. As for the chair arm resembling a blade, my uncle always refused to take any notice of comments on it. "It is not only photographers who read meanings into their photographs!"

And then Uncle Ed was writing Mother back on the little farm, "My dear Paus'l . . . Well dear girl I am just in a mood and in a leisure moment to write . . . it's a hard row to hoe devilishly hard—one must be agressive—agressive—agressive—I have little hopes to place either of the poems you have sent me—they are too lovely too subtle. . . . however I have not given up. Send on essays—nature articles . . . anything—but on with the fight. You have the art and the ability, it is merely a fight for the recognition of it. It will be that always and the greater and better we do the harder the battle . . . contact and conflict always—ce la vie. [sic] . . . I myself can hardly make both ends meet—but the outlook is brighter every day. I live on that physically.—The other thing we live does not fluctuate with Wall Street but within ourselves—be it the belching and bellowing roar of Pittsburgh with its wealth and its slavery, with its genius of labor and ignorance or be it the calm and silence of the snow and moonlight.—it lies within *us* the beauty of all these.—and it is for us to create and give—and it is art.—lovingly—Eduard."

By now Mother had landed a position at the State Normal School in Valley City, North Dakota, west of Fargo on the Cheyenne River. She went out there in September of 1904. She was to train high school graduates to teach and would be in charge of the plays given throughout her two years there. My uncle approved of her job. "I am glad you are going to teach, Paus'l—it is better for us all just for a while to hack—hack hack.— It will help us plan and achieve a bigger goal in the end.—Paus'l—you said it to me—and I've always listened—*'aim high'*—I felt you had missed aim when you spoke of the position in a publishing house.—you could do lots of little bits of good that way—but they are drops in a bucket.— big game is your hunting and you can do this best when independent.— Your life—your time—your where—your when—must always be yours. . . . Lovingly, Gaesjack."

Uncle Ed was on the move in New York. Twenty-nine of his paintings had been on exhibition at the Galleries of Eugene Glaenzer and Company and the show was a success. He could afford to pay a little more rent and when a room with a big studio skylight became available next door to the 291 Fifth Avenue brownstone residence where he had the top-floor room, he switched his lease and took it also. The buildings stood side by side off Thirtieth Street and a common central hallway and elevator existed, so the adjustment was a simple one. The old room adjoined two vacant ones and the situation seemed ideal for exhibition galleries. He tried to interest his friend, Alfred Stieglitz, in the idea. Stieglitz was fifteen years older than Uncle Ed, with an international reputation, the leader of American photographers in their battle for recognition in the arts. Since photographs had not yet been hung in any art gallery in the United States along with paintings, my uncle wanted to invite painters to come to an exhibition gallery that had just that in mind. 291 Fifth Avenue was the address and the gallery would be called "291" and be sponsored by the Photo-Secessionists. Their aims were to push photography everywhere, to arrange exhibitions and to bring photographers together. Stieglitz was against the idea of a Little Gallery, saying that there would never even be enough photographs in the world good enough to keep a continual exhibit going at "291." However, at length he was persuaded, said he would stand the cost, and Uncle Ed set to work to design the rooms and plan the exhibits.

And wasn't it about at this time in the lives of my family that my father was seated at his books and papers in the large upper floor of the Brooks Street Fire Department, about to quit and go to Chicago to see if he could get a job on the *To-Morrow* magazine? Where was my uncle at the time, elegant and assured? Why, in an upstairs private room of Mouquin's, a French restaurant in New York. The glassware and silver glinted, the room was decorated with green vine leaves, the cuisine was excellent. Alfred Stieglitz and others of the Photo-Secession society were there. The first exhibit of their members had just been installed at the "291" gallery and they were toasting the occasion, and later would go over to look at the reality. The exhibit would last two weeks and in time the three rooms of "291" would see controversial drawings by Rodin, watercolors by Cézanne, sculptures by Matisse, abstractions by Picasso, Brancusi and Braque. It would be said that you could gauge a man's attitude toward the arts—radical or conservative—by whether he was for or against "291."

Ever since he'd taken his first photograph—of my mother at the family piano—in 1895 at the age of sixteen Uncle Ed had been making portraits —some with oil and brush, some with camera. He said at this time, "As a matter of fact, I began to be troubled when I heard that being photographed by Steichen was considered quite the thing to do." He waited until he had made his selection for a Photo-Secession exhibition at the Pennsylvania Academy of the Fine Arts in Philadelphia, and then he took a liner with Clara and Cousin Mary, almost two now, for France. "I made up my mind to get away from the lucrative but stultifying professional portrait business." He wanted to talk with Rodin about "291" and see whether le Maître would allow an exhibition of his drawings. It was May of 1906. My uncle felt the looming future.

And where was my mother? She had gone on in 1906 from the State Normal School in Valley City, North Dakota, where they had given her letters of recommendation that had helped get her a new position: "Miss Lilian Steichen is a young woman of superior ability and pleasing personality . . . she is considered an excellent teacher and one that this normal would like to keep. . . . It is to be regretted that lack of funds compel the board to make her present salary a maximum one. Respectfully. . . " Her new job was at a high school in Princeton, Illinois. Mother has told me of her days there, how she roamed the woods and streets hatless and indeed often with a muddy skirt, for she liked long walks in the rain. She was a cynic, she said, about old-fashioned art, and approved of Uncle Ed's modern work. She declared that art was "by and for the privileged minority . . . a thing of Snobbery—a diversion of the leisure class. . . . Give me something that is for the Masses."

She put Shelley on the shelf along with what she called the "poet's poets," and read Robert Hunter and Thorstein Veblen and violent novels such as Upton Sinclair's *The Jungle.* She gave up the idea of being a poet herself as she neared her mid-twenties, and looked for a Life of Action. She said, "If I had the choice between on the one hand accelerating (tho by ever so little) the progress of the Socialist movement, and on the other writing another 'Prometheus Unbound'—I should choose the former. The time for writing lyric dramas is past." She called her times an Epoch of Struggle and looked for comrades about Princeton, and aside from another teacher, Elsie Caskey, found none. She liked teaching and said that "the whole existing educational system is based on discipline which involves threats. But I don't believe in discipline. Would substitute interest." She said none of her pupils stood in awe of her and that was the way she wanted it.

She would not go to church either. By then all her theology was gone —"not a shred remains—not so much as the word 'God.'" She had "a horror of being mistaken for a militant atheist or some such monstrosity . . . I recognize a universal religion of humanism and joy-in-life—a religion common to all—to those who accept theologies and to those who have no theology."

And as for sex and love? In that day, plays and novels by Ibsen and Shaw and Chekhov and Strindberg were laying bare psychological situations between parents and children and between lovers in and out of marriage. My mother read them all. What of herself? All she would ever say, when pressed for details on her love life, was that she had been as much as engaged to a writer who was prominent at the Milwaukee Social-Democratic Party headquarters, brilliant and elderly. Do I know who he was? Did she ever say her comrade-lover's name? Or only, retrospectively, "He was a good man, but one day I looked into his eyes and saw that they were old." After that, she said, the affair was off. And there was another vague tale of romance told in an early story to me and retracted by her when my mother was in her seventies. It was all about an Important Personality in the party, also along in years, who wanted not just to make love to Mother, but for her to have his baby, which would perpetuate his acknowledged genius. It seemed she turned him down too.

I know I despaired in my young teens, listening to my mother talk, of ever equaling her ways. I swore to learn Latin and Greek and unriddle politics. Listening to her, I wanted nothing more than nobility and purpose. And what happened? None of my lofty dreams came to pass. I became a storyteller, a plotter of fiction, a poet, thoroughly versed in English alone. And love? Secure in my mother's encompassing affection, I was able always to give love and to love.

Eight

Orator and Organizer

My mother has told me of my father's early days before an audience, how he would come to a stop, and while the people stirred and turned to each other and waited, he would sometimes go long moments before resuming. Was he collecting his thoughts? Was he looking for the right phrase or word? Was he disturbed by those he wanted to convince? My mother said she did not know.

In the summer of 1906, the restlessness had moved in my father again. Since his triumph at the Swan Oratorical Contest back in Lombard College, he liked to stand before an audience and try to hold them. These two sides of my father's character formed a way of life that always delighted him—going continually from place to place, and then holding an audience, large or small. While he was with *To-Morrow*, he would get himself scheduled to speak at the Monday and Thursday regular lectures given free at the Spencer-Whitman Center. He was determined, and fought his way through the stuttering and stammering, working out his system of memorizing an entire talk which he could rattle off. He attended Chautauquas at Plainfield, Elgin and Aurora, putting in less and less time at his *To-Morrow* desk. He would be in Chicago for a week and then back to the room in Aurora. He wrote Aunt Esther in Galesburg, asking her to send him a library book, *Wit and Humor of the Bible*, and said that he had practiced his Whitman lecture on a group of friends and been asked to give three talks in Racine, south of Milwaukee, in the early winter. "I have other lectures arranged for, but these three are the first I am to be paid for. It is a low rate for lecturing but not bad for a beginner, $25 for the three. . . . About pay you won't say anything in G.—They will pay me $25 for a single night before next year passes. . . .

89

Give all my loves at home a thought from me, and mother, the best love, a kiss. Charlie."

He wrote to Professor Wright, "I have just returned from a five-day stay in Chicago—feeling for and hammering away at this and that—I have arranged dates in Chicago, Blue Island, Racine, Detroit, and while at present see barely expenses, a future looms up big with mighty fates and hopes. My future is not behind but careering like blazes ahead of me. . . . No man can say what the morrow bringeth forth." In the notebook that he kept was a sentence, "Sometimes when fate kicks us and we finally land and look around, we find we have been kicked upstairs!"

My father was about to leave his post at *To-Morrow*, where critics of the magazine said it was not radical so much as eccentric. He wrote another *To-Morrow* contributor, a reporter in Fort Wayne, Indiana, Reuben W. Borough, to see whether he could get him a lecture in that town. "My dear Borough:— . . . the terms on which I will come are these: I furnish circulars, window cards and pay for newspaper advertising. I receive 50% of the receipts after my hotel & railroad expenses are paid. If receipts do not cover expenses, I foot them myself, thus involving no one else in risk. . . . I want to have a long talk with you. . . . I want to meet another youth who throws his poetry into loose, disarrayed rhythms, and lets rhyme go hang. . . . Faithfully yours." Borough and my father became close friends. When Borough went to Chicago as a reporter for the *Daily Socialist*, my father and he called each other Rube and Sandy. The one smoked a pipe and the other what Borough called "Sandy's cheroots, long twisted stogies which he bought packaged by the dozen." The two roamed the town, fellow socialists, both lonely, both unmarried, although Borough was engaged to a girl reporter for a Long Beach paper out in California, Laura Bradley.

Then my father got himself a new job. He'd gone over to the Steinway Building in Chicago to see the man who put out *The Lyceumite*, Edwin L. Barker, publisher, editor and critic, who called himself "The Lyceumiteman." Barker had offered my father a position at twenty-five dollars a week and my father had taken it, telling Wright, ". . . meseems I will cut out vagabonding a year or so."

Among the performers who came through *The Lyceumite* offices was a Viennese magician advertised as "Joseffy the Great," a prestidigitator, ventriloquist and master of the art of illusion. My father called him "Joseffy, the necromancer," for the magician claimed he could foretell the future by communicating with the dead. Joseffy played the violin and spoke six languages; he was tall and thin with wild hair, a bushy mustache and piercing eyes. He and my father became good friends. Rube Borough had no use for Joseffy and when he heard that my father was writing a piece on him, said that it "was too bad Sandy had to make a living that way." Borough stated further, "This fellow, said Sandburg, had technique, imagination, and artistry with his rabbits popping from his coat sleeves and his many-colored flags pirouetting over the stage. He took me to see the chap, an uninspiring semi-illiterate with an irrepressible flow of crude puns."

By then my father, feeling his future, was ready for his next book and wrote to Wright about it, "I have a number of things I am going to have printed in some sort of folio this summer. About six essays of 1000 words, eight of 500, and paragraphic dissertations, about enough for a 32 page book—they are to be the choice selections of a box of stuff. . . . It is to be on thin paper, not necessarily rough. The cover is to be the coarsest, thickest, heaviest, most durable, gray or red, you can crease without cracking. . . . I shall have about 2 or 3 thousand run off, and put on newsstands —$.25. . . . This is all between you and me. Let me have a dummy, and some idea of prices, and then I can make a proposition as to whether I can pay for the paper alone, or paper, ink, labor, and all." He was thinking of the title, *Careless Essays*, and he wanted the cover design to be "something bold, black, careless."

At this time my father was giving advice to Aunt Esther, ten years younger than he and talented on the piano and organ, who was thinking of perhaps performing on the Chautauqua route, "If I should try to say something short and to the point that tells what seems to me is necessary to make a success as an artist of any kind, a musician as well as anybody, it would be this: Work and love, love and work. Live as your soul tells you you ought to live. . . . Thank God if you're not satisfied with your work. And don't worry. Go after big things. . . . Think yourself a piece of God's finest stuff and you will think better and do more for all others. All this is much like preaching, but the reason I have written it down for you is because I think you show promise of being an artist, a pianist of more than ordinary talent. And I know that if you work in the right way and get the right ability, I'll be able to put you in the way of good things before the public. . . . You needn't show this around. Just put it under your hat and work and love. . . . Last of all, don't let your work wear your health down. Of all things, get out into the sun and pure air every day, and walk in the mist when it's cloudy. Vitality, bounding, exuberant health, is a characteristic of every artist worth hearing. All of it, Esther, with love, Charlie."

My father's advice to Aunt Esther stood him in good stead for himself when, after four months with *The Lyceumite*, Edwin Barker sold the magazine to a lecture bureau combine which ran the competitive magazine *Talent*, with which *The Lyceumite* would be merged. Barker moved on to the International Harvester Company and my father was, as he said, "tossed out of the deck like a dirty deuce." And he said too, "If I did not enjoy a scrap I would be crestfallen, undone, down and out." He signed up with the Midland Lyceum Bureau, and was to go out into the field to contract for lecture courses for them in Indiana. My father was anxious about having his new book published and wrote to Wright, "The printing of the Careless Essays will depend on my success in Indiana. I will write you from the gas belt how things go, whether the oil wells run well, etc." Wright assured him that he wanted to do the book. "I feel that a great moral wrong would be done if any of the works of Charles Sandburg should be printed elsewhere than at the Asgard Press."

But the job in Indiana did not pan out either, the area assigned to my father being already covered by other bureaus. Did he feel this to be a blow? Already Rube Borough was about to leave Chicago, the weekly salary he received at the *Daily Socialist* not enough, Borough said, to pay debts he owed, much less to marry his fiancée, Laura. By the next summer, he would have returned to his hometown of Marshall, Michigan, where he would work as a salesman in his family's buggy factory. And my father? He planned to go back into one trade he knew well—selling stereographic views. He would combine the work with lecturing, though the latter brought him little or no income. He told Professor Wright, "I shall get a map tomorrow and decide where I go. At present only God knows, but tomorrow both God and I will know. Yours fraternally, Sandburg."

He wrote to Borough too, from Hinckley, Illinois, "Tonight both God and I know where I am—yesterday only God knew I was to go here. Green-crested hills surround the town and white roads lead off into grey, mysterious distances. I will be in dire peril of tossing off a poem or two. . . . Yours in comradeship, Sandy."

My father seemed happy to be out of the city and roaming the landscape again, and with a book approaching publication. It was a pattern he would follow the rest of his life. He sent off another letter to Borough. "Dear Rube: Some hatless runt of an individual got away with that proud, natty Stetson of mine—I was in the reception room . . . and when we came out lo! the skypiece was neither here nor there. Again lo! Also, hell, and Dam. Please send me that boxed up black Fedora. . . . Otherwise, I will have to push on wearing a golf cap and you know I don't play golf. . . . Sandy."

My father was twenty-nine. He wrote to Wright, "There is a place for me somewhere, where I can write and speak much as I can think, and make it pay for my living and some besides. Just where this place is I have small idea now, but I am going to find it. . . . If you see fit to go ahead and print a 32-page folio of Careless Essays, I will be able to pay something on it this summer, but it would probably only pay for the paper. . . . I cannot see why I should not dispose of several hundred of these after my lectures next season. The socialist orators all sell a good lot of books." He had had offers for jobs—one from an advertising agency in Milwaukee at twenty-five dollars a week—but he told Wright, "I have thought I will keep up this fight a year or more yet, before even partially abandoning it. I am planning to work independently with my lectures next season, going on percentages under auspices of Womens' Clubs, Socialist branches, single tax clubs, &c." And, "I wish you would write me what you think are some of the pieces that need editing, that I might later wish were not in cool, irreparable type."

One man who had given my father a quote he could use in his circulars to persuade an audience to attend was Elbert Hubbard, a businessman who had been able to retire in his thirties and establish a small press in upstate New York where he could put out magazines and small books that he edited. It was called the Roycroft Press and was patterned after the Kelmscott Press, founded in England by the socialist and poet, William Morris. Hubbard ran the Roycroft Inn also, where large meetings could be held, and the Roycroft School for Boys. "We teach boys to work. . . . Half a day at the books, and half a day at useful work—that's the plan." And there was the Roycroft Shop, where home industries were taught and practiced and the produce sold. It was Hubbard who had written the essay which became so famous that forty million copies of it were sold—"A Message to Garcia," that told of Lieutenant Andrew S. Rowan's journey to meet the leader of the Cuban insurgents in 1899. At his Roycroft Press, Hubbard published a booklet called *The Philistine*: A Periodical of Protest, stating on the cover that it was "Printed Every Little While." It contained what Hubbard described as "a fund of useful information, keen comment, and real humor." As a child I saw copies of *The Philistine* on shelves of the household and wondered how it related to the Bible. On the cover of one was, "Blessed are the belliakers, for they shall receive absent treatment," and inside, "If you do not understand *The Philistine* you should get a copy of The Essay on Silence, and commit it to memory." Of this essay, my father told Professor Wright, "It has never appeared in the Philistine or Little Journeys. A very strong thing—very suggestive. Purple ooze—calf cover, and 32 pages of vellum and not a word of print on them—only the hand-tooled title outside

'Essay on Silence'!" Hubbard also printed tiny booklets called *Little Journeys*, which brought the reader to a hundred and seventy homes of famous men, one at a time.

My father and Professor Wright mailed Hubbard their recently published small books, *The Dial of the Heart* and *In Reckless Ecstasy*, saying, "Dear Fra Elbertus: . . . we are sending you a contribution to the Roycroft Library—the printing was done by a college professor and his wife and boys. . . . We have been assured . . . that these cannot qualify in the Burn Book collection." My father openly admired Hubbard's philosophies and his way of life, so that when William Marion Reedy over in St. Louis had written to my father in his small room in Aurora, Illinois, he'd said, "My dear Mr. Sandburg:—Why not change your address to *West* Aurora?" Elbert Hubbard's establishment was East Aurora, New York. And that summer my father, who had as he said "very little cash," was given "transportation and 'keep' at East Aurora" at the Roycroft setup. He had told Wright once that he ranked Hubbard the highest as an essayist among contemporary writers. When he wrote to Wright about the advertising circular that was being set up by the Asgard Press, he said, "I hope the Hubbard endorsement can get onto it, even if it means sacrificing some. . . . Possibly the Hubbard testimonial may go on the first page." It stated that "Charles Sandburg is a most interesting personality—earnest, enthusiastic, wise. . . . His religion is the religion of service, and that he has a distinct message for the people and knows how to give it, I am firmly convinced."

East Aurora was south of Buffalo, New York, and northeast of Lake Chautauqua, where large assemblies would gather on the shores at the towns of Lakewood and Chautauqua. A convention was being held at the Roycroft Inn at the beginning of July, 1907, and my father was to give some talks. Hubbard had offered, besides expenses, to put him in the way of a few dates, hopefully for the coming fall and winter. My father sent handbills to his friends, printed by the Roycroft Press and announcing that a "Saturday Evening Socialistic Symposium" would be held at the Roycroft Chapel and that one of the speakers of the evening was Charles Sandburg. Hubbard had said, "Sandburg knows his Whitman as very few men do." The inn was overcrowded; many of those who came, including my father, were put up in tents.

The oration was a success. "They are sort of crazy here about the lecture I gave yesterday," my father wrote to Wright. "They drew out of me my best. Mr. & Mrs. Hubbard say I have 'a world-beater.' The crowd caught things right on the wing all the way through & when I was done & had seated myself & was talking nothings with somebody Hubbard grabs me by the arm & pulls me to the front again—they were clapping & yelling for an encore. For the tribute as far as approbation is concerned I don't care any particular dam, but that I now am sure I have trained my powers, so that they can be of *service* to men, pleases me. . . . I have changed it from a strong literary lecture into an oration. . . . You won't pass around this effusive message. . . . While I was writing, Hubbard tells me that an insistent demand for more of my stuff dictates that I go on for at least a half-hour talk tonight. . . . Yours faithfully, Sandburg."

Then my father left East Aurora to do once more what apparently pleased him most, taking up his black satchel of Underwood sample stereographs and heading into the countryside to inveigle farmers and small townsmen into the excitement of adding to the sets they had or buying a "view" and beginning fresh. He would be a walker all of his life, roaming city blocks in areas where many hesitated to go, and down dark alleys and sidestreets. He has told me how he would keep his hand in his pocket sometimes in more risky places, so that someone desperate might think he had a weapon. He never carried anything more dangerous than the slim small pocketknives he fancied to cut his cigars in half or to slit out newspaper items. He was mostly a night walker and carried a flashlight, using it sparingly, only in rutted roads now and then, seldom by the lake, and then simply to find the twisted way that led there. He liked mostly to let his feet find the way in the dusk or moonlight.

All the time of course, he was writing poems. Back then, in the fall of 1907, he called one "May":

> I wonder as of old things
> Once again made fresh and fair,
> Hangs over pasture, pathway and road.
> Lush and renewing, the lowland grasses rise
> And upland beckons to upland.
> The great strong hills are humbled
> As if in some deep throb of joy.

And another, "Under the Trees":

> After the day's work,
> In twilight and slow gloaming
> We love the friendliness,
> The deep and quiet friendliness
> Of Trees.

After supper,
The dusty roads of day
And bitter and weary things
Put by, remembered not,
Under the calm, green trees . . .

And "Solitude":

I can have this cool loneliness
And you can take along what you want
Here of this cool loneliness.
It is not like prairie land
Nor a single crag
Nor a level ocean.
Little hills around it
Keep off winter,
The big rough player.
A disc of cool loneliness,
I always ask it:
What are you waiting for?
It seems so sure somebody is coming.

Rube Borough arranged some lectures for my father, one in Marshall, Michigan, Borough's hometown. He reported in the Marshall *News*, "Walt Whitman loomed large and persuasive as the spokesman of a great democracy in Charles Sandburg's lecture, 'An American Vagabond' given last night at the Universalist church. . . . An unadvertised feature of the lecture was the appearance on the platform of two gray and white cats, one of which rubbed itself affectionately against the leg of the orator as he was getting well into his subject." And my father said, "There were only 30 at my Marshall lecture, but they were the cream of the town. . . . They have hired me at $10 to repeat the stunt, with variations, two weeks from now, and are going to throw it open and free to the town. They want to know why I haven't a book out."

Abruptly, my father was offered a position. "It is twenty per week and I can do my work any time I please just so I get it in. I am in the office part of the time, tho no regular hours." It was on a new magazine published monthly in Chicago, *The Opera House Guide*, and my father was also to write their weekly letter, *The Billboard*, giving current Chicago stage listings. On its masthead was stated that it united "The Lecturer, The Lyceum, The Platform & Chautauquas." And my father worried about the book Wright was bringing out. He changed the title from *Careless Essays* and began thinking of it as a smaller and less expensive booklet. "When I am better 'heeled' than now, I shall say my say more emphatically, and paint with a bigger brush. I think of calling the folio: Incidentals. . . . About the 'swag' in this momentous deal, suppose we arrange it that after a sufficient amount has come in to pay for printing, we take half and half. If there is any kind of a Chautauqua season next year, I am satisfied we will sell enough copies to pay for printing."

There was another book in the offing that my father wanted Wright to print also. It was *The Plaint of a Rose* and he thought of changing its title too. "What do you think of the title Among the Roses in preference to The Plaint, etc.? . . . It may be I am pushing the thing too far, plunging unwisely, and not catching the tide at the crest as I think. If I lose it is I alone who loses and I am willing. But with you it is different and if you are taking any chances in backing Sandburg, don't do it. For I will get it done some way without involving others in any serious risk. You know the situation.—It is a case of the way through the hill being the way out. Where I talked in ones last year I talk in tens this year and next year will talk in hundreds. I have given good years to art alone and for a while I am not going to think of art that doesn't have an 'economic conquest' attachment. . . . Fraternally yours, Sandburg." Wright wrote back to say that he would be "more than glad to print the Plaint of the Rose (and in the name of all the gods I protest against the change of title). We will consider the details of this little booklet later."

My father described the short tale as ". . . poetization in prose of the theory of economic determinism. God knows the latter needs poetizing." The story was of two roses—one "the most haughty, the most loved, and the one most in love with life," and the other living in its shadow, protesting its fate, unheard by the other. " 'When I was a bud, one day a tiny, delicate tracery of crimson appeared on my petals, but as I have told you. . . . no water! . . . no sunlight! . . . so I faded. . . . Sister. . . .' No answer came from the upper rose to the rose below."

Again, out of the blue, my father was jobless. "Once more Fate has kicked me," he declared, "and I am waiting to see how far upstairs the impetus will send me." He wrote Wright, "It was a very sudden move. . . . the expense of a special editor for the lyceum is inadvisable and I have two week's notice. . . . I have several good prospects in view, and think I have a good many assets left besides my honor!" And he said that he had finished his sketch of Joseffy and that the *The Opera House Guide* was going to print it. The magician liked it too. My father said that it was "one of the best things I have ever done, whatever that is saying. He is going to have it printed in a booklet for publicity purposes. I shall try to get the printing of it for The Asgard."

The piece was called *Joseffy, Necromancer* and told of the magician's beginnings in Europe, of the devices he had created and sold to other illusionists, of his skill with the violin, and how "he always mingles the gay, fantastical and whimsical in a way to capture his audience and hold it attentive." One of Joseffy's props was Balsamo, the Living Skull, made of copper and inset with real human teeth which clicked as it answered the showman's questions. I clearly recall Joseffy coming to the house of my childhood carrying Balsamo, who was kept in a velvet-lined dark box with a hinged door. I knew the skull was alive and my recollection is shrouded with terror. I was also afraid of the magician himself, strange and wild and foreign. He claimed that some centuries past he had visited a certain Joseph Balsamo, Count de Cagliostro, who was incarcerated in the dungeons of the Inquisition; a few weeks before he was put to death, the count had promised Joseffy his skull. There it was.

When Wright would print a piece by my father on the magician three years later, it would match *Incidentals* in size and style and be called *Joseffy*, subtitled *An Appreciation*. A picture of the magician, signed "Mysteriously yours," as Joseffy was said to sign all his correspondence, would precede the text. The same illuminated block with a rampant lion would be used by Wright to start each of the small books, which began with the word "It." *Joseffy* started, "It was in Vienna," and *Incidentals*, "It may be I will some day look back on these incidentals."

My father was stirred at this time by the nearing publication of *Incidentals*, "Dear Professor:—The proofs and specimen you sent are here. I like the make-up of Incidentals. It ought to have an artistic dishevelledness. . . . I had thought a cover which had 'give' to it, which would bend with a pocket would be more suited for a pocket then one of the stiffness which would crack, while a stiffness that wouldn't crack would be too expensive throughout. If you had thought the colors of the inside paper and the cover paper did not harmonize, your doubt would have tallied with mine, for I wasn't certain on the point, but in the weight I thought I had hit on the right thing. Here I am pleading like a man about to be hung. I believe I have more convictions on printing matters than I have on politics."

In the Apologia prefacing the small book, my father had said, "It may be I will some day look back on these incidentals as youthful impertinences. I have not yet rounded into thirty and many years remain in which the bacilli of repentance may get at work. But this consolatory fact I have: The moving finger has written, I have said what I wanted to say of what I thought was the highest and happiest in me. . . . Life is more vast and strange than anything written about it—words are only incidentals." One of the pieces in the book went:

Never were the masses so alive and intelligent as they are today. The common people want better houses, better food, better clothes. They want pictures, music, books, leisure. Man does not live by bread alone. He has a soul. This soul imperiously asks to be fed. It wants art, beauty, harmony. For sweet sounds and forms of beauty and things that caress the eye and thrill the touch, it asks and demands.

And then copies of the book arrived. "You went beyond what I expected," my father wrote Professor Wright. "It's a premier piece of printing. . . . By all means, fire an Incidentals at each of the local papers. I want them to know I'm growing. They will get my tone one of these days." And he added, "I have only one suggestion to make for The Plaint and that is the point I spoke to you about last summer—the ribbon or cord binding has an amateurish flavor, a novitiate air, that Asgard is above." He was anxious: "The design for The Plaint cover doesn't appeal to me strongly. . . . The border is too ornate. If the triangular design consisted of two roses, I know how hard such a drawing would be to work out. . . . here goes another demurrer—one against using gold on the front of The Plaint. I have seen hardly any work in gold on book covers but had a tinsel suggestion, a look as of striving at the durable and striking the ephemeral."

Before the end of the year, *The Plaint Of a Rose* would be published, the cover done by Mrs. Wright. Professor Wright said, "I am sending cover design to the engravers today. It is Betty's work and I hope you will like it. We have really spent a lot of time thinking about it." My father did. "The work and thought you have given The Plaint is in evidence. It is simple and direct. . . . This cover design outclasses all the others you showed me. Mrs. Wright may be proud of it. . . . I enclose a dollar for as many copies of The Plaint as come to me for that amount."

Since *Incidentals* and *The Plaint Of a Rose* were published at about the same time, both booklets carried advertisements of the other. In a back page of *Incidentals* was a line, "He gives us brutal materialism interwoven with lofty and glowing idealism . . .—the best Sandburg has done and that is saying much. RUBE BOROUGH." My father used Borough's name in one of his lecture brochures also—*Sandburg on the Platform*. ". . . tall, lean, proud, strange. . . . He speaks slowly in the beginning and gestures little. . . . Suddenly he pauses and swings into one of his wonderful climaxes. . . . Epithet, denunciation, and eulogy leap and pour from him. . . . There are times when Sandburg means what he says, absolutely." The praise was credited to "Rube Borough in the Marshall (Mich.) News." It was made up, and my father wrote, "Dear old Boy: . . . I hope you won't mind the liberties taken with your name in my new circular. Yours is the only one that is entirely a fabrication. I am a ready liar in a good cause and will bicker until the cows come home on the question of whether there is any absolute truth expressible. . . . Let me know what parts of the country you're in. Our ways may cross. With love, Sandy."

And then he was writing Borough, "I have not seen the trees change this fall—that is, not a real woodland that looks like it was on fire. And it's a month since I've seen a real sunset. I go up to Manitowoc, Wis., next week and am going to get out where there are hills and woods and air—before I come back here to Chicago, 'where God ain't.'"

My father was restless now. Did he have a girlfriend? Almost thirty, had he made love? Was there someone who had turned him down? Had he been wanted by some woman he didn't want? Questions I never asked my father, perhaps because I preferred to listen. At this time he told Borough, "Since I saw you I have fallen in love and fallen out again, —the moth just dancing through the flame—with a crack violinist, a reader, an amateur palmist, an actress, a chorus girl, a newspaper woman, and at present don't know what I'll do about a live pundit and poetess.— If I had no work 'twould be dangerous. . . . Here's my hand. Yours, Sandy." The next to the last piece in *Incidentals* was called "To You." Was it for an imagined or a true lover?

I love you for what you are but I love you yet more for what you are going to be. I love you not so much for your realities as for your ideals. I pray for your desires that they may be great, rather than your satisfactions which may be so hazardously little. A satisfied flower is one whose petals are about to fall. The most beautiful rose is hardly more than a bud wherein the pangs and ecstacies of desire are working for larger growth. Not always shall you be what you are now. You are going forward toward something great. I am on the way with you.

Up in Manitowoc, my father set down a moody memo:

> It was in Manitowoc, Wisconsin. The
> world-sorrow was gnawing at my heart.
> I walked down by the lake shore
> and communed with trees, shadows,
> stars, old gray houses, dead ghosts
> of sometime homes, black piers
> that shoot arrow-like out into
> the waters, and over it all a steely
> sheen of sky and thru it all a
> wavering, hovering stuff of the moon.
> I began to feel different. I saw
> that I had thought myself too
> Important a unit in The Great Scheme.
>
> Sometimes my hopes are great and
> I plan. Then I tumble the hopes
> and the plans into nothingness.
> For I have seen plans crumble and
> dreams fade and ships of hope go
> out on the tides of time and never
> come back.
>
> The clock of destiny we hear tick.
> But what time it is, nobody knows.
> A week, like an aeon, is an abyss
> toward which we plunge not know-
> ing what is ahead.

He wrote to Borough later that he "had a great time up in Manitowoc and learned many things. . . . They have a splendid constructive move-ment in Milwaukee, from which socialists all over the country are taking lessons. I shall probably do some organizing thru the northeastern part of the state this winter, possibly making my permanent residence in Manitowoc or Oshkosh." And he added, "I consider now that I am trying out the lyceum, not that it is trying me out. If it is not big enough for my stuff, I will not change my stuff. I will climb out of the lyceum and make it sue me for my time."

My father's lecture in Manitowoc had been "under auspices & for benefit of Daily Tribune there, a workingman's paper. It's a socialist town, you know,—the mayor and alderman—& I expect to learn things there." The Manitowoc *Daily Tribune* reported enthusiastically that, speaking to the largest audience ever gathered for any purpose by any newspaper in this city, Charles Sandburg, Chicago, held a capacity house enraptured for an hour and a half at the Opera House on Saturday night. Taking his hearers thru the tortuous declines and apexes of the career of that great poet, Walt Whitman, drawing from each phase a lesson, finding in each event something of good, drawing an inspiration from the entire life seldom equalled on the lecture platform in this city, Sandburg proved himself a man of deep thinking ability and great oratorical power. The boldness of the idea of the entire argument was well voiced when Mr. Sandburg exclaimed, "The men who have seen visions have been the great men of the world. The men who have propounded great doctrines have been the men who have seen those great ideas in visions, long before that great book 'Capital' was written." . . . Thru the hour and half of the lecture there was the most marked attention, the most feeling response, the greatest tribute to any speaker.

My father was working on a pamphlet at that time which would be published shortly and which he hoped was pretty inflammatory. One statement in it went:

Socialism holds that your hat, your house, your books, your piano, your carpets, your toothbrush, shall be your own as your private property. But the great tools of production that are necessary to the life and well-being of all, these should be owned by all. This is collectivism. Today, men are lucky if they have a chance "to earn a living." What the Socialist wants for every man is the chance to live a life.

It was December of 1907 and he was starting a new aspect of his life. He had offered to be an organizer for the socialist party in Wisconsin. E. H. Thomas wrote to him about the position. She was Miss Elizabeth Thomas and not only secretary of the Social-Democratic Party of Wisconsin, but a good friend of the Steichens out in Menomonee Falls. She had been out to the Steichen farm for a week's vacation the previous summer and had been asked to come again the next year. Sometimes my mother and Miss Thomas went to musicals or plays in Milwaukee when my mother was home on vacation. Miss Thomas had written my father that she had sent three telegrams about trying to locate him. "Dear Comrade:—We have had the greatest difficulty in reaching you. . . . The State Executive Board decided that if you were willing to try the district

organizership for three months, they would appoint you as district organizer in the Lake Shore and Fox River Valley district. . . . I am most
sincerely sorry that there was so much delay. . . . When you go to your
new field of labor, we should like to have you stop over a little in Milwaukee, so that we may have some talk with you before you begin your
work."

My father accepted at once and wrote to friends that he was "prepared
to batten on the epithet of 'agitator.' " He told Borough that he had "been
rounding up dilatory locals, trying to put new spirit in them. . . . One
word for straight socialism now counts for more than ten maneuvering
opportunist words. It's the only program that will rouse the stupor of the
masses." And he added, for Borough had sent him the address of Ethel
Dolsen out on the west coast, a friend of Laura Bradley's, "I looked and
looked for the letter you wrote me, having that Los Angeles girl's name
and address. . . . Let me have it again. I want to see what sort of a
letter a socialist woman can write. . . . As ever yours in brotherhood,
Sandy."

After Christmas of 1907, my father took the Chicago and Northwestern
train to Milwaukee, stopping off in Sheboygan on the way, as he said, "to
talk with comrades there if nothing more." Miss Thomas had written my
father that although there were difficulties she believed that the "comrades have the right spirit, but need just such organizing work as you
are in Manitowoc to do. Their dues need to be collected, they need to be
urged to attend meetings, new members ought to be brought in, and
subscriptions to the Social papers, including not only the dailies, but also
the Social-Democratic Herald, the Vanguard, and the Wahrheit ought
to be very persistently and systematically collected. Get the people to
reading, and the organization will follow naturally. But Socialists who
do not read have very little conception of the movement, and can with
difficulty be held together in an organization. Hoping that you will be
able to handle the work . . . Fraternally yours, E. H. Thomas, State
Secretary."

He got into Milwaukee on the twenty-ninth of December, a Sunday,
and went over to party headquarters at 344 Sixth Street. He hoped to
visit with Winfield Gaylord again, and he wanted to meet Victor Berger,
a national committeeman and a power in the movement. Berger, eighteen
years older than my father, had been born in Austria-Hungary and had
come over with his family in the year my father was born—1878. Berger
had mended boilers and polished metal for a living, until he got a job
teaching German in the public schools. After twelve years as a teacher,
he became editor of the *Zeitung*, a German language newspaper. Later

he helped bring the *Social-Democratic Herald* from Chicago to Milwaukee. Berger, like my father later, was a close friend of Eugene Debs. The latter has said that it was when he was jailed after the Pullman strike in 1895 and was beginning to read and think about the cause of the workingman and "when the first glimmerings of Socialism were beginning to penetrate, that Victor L. Berger—and I have loved him ever since—came to Woodstock, as if a providential instrument, and delivered the first impassioned message of Socialism I had ever heard—the very first to set 'the wires humming in my system.' As a souvenir of that visit there is in my library a volume of *Capital* by Karl Marx, inscribed with the compliments of Victor L. Berger, which I cherish as a token of priceless value." Both Debs and Berger influenced my father's early views on socialism. Berger, unlike the tall, gentle, clean-shaven Debs, was a heavy-set mustached, dark-haired man, freely voicing strong opinions. Later my parents would call him "The Bear."

It was at this time that my mother and father were about to meet. My mother would be twenty-five on the first of the coming May. She had the classic Steichen features—blue-gray eyes, dark brows—and stood about five foot five. She had been teaching at the high school in Princeton, Illinois, since the fall of 1906, and had just spent her Christmas holiday with Oma and Opa at the farm. Opa refused to stir from the place except to harness the horse and go down to the station. But Oma welcomed change and when Mother was home, the two would go into the city to shop and attend Social-Democratic meetings or musicals or the theater or a concert, go to a restaurant or have dinner with friends of the Steichens in their homes and stay over—sometimes with the Charles Whitnalls, active socialists, or with Louis Mayer, the artist, and his wife, May, socialist "sympathizers," as my mother called them, or with others. Oma and Mother took the train in on Saturday and that night after dinner, went to a meeting hall of the Social-Democratic Party.

Family stories differ on whether they went to hear a party man speak that night or another, but in my journal it is so. And there is a letter of my mother's, written a few months later to my father, that gives her feelings and a picture of an evening like the one on that Saturday in December of 1907. Oma, May and Louis Mayer and Mother had gone to hear Emil Seidel, their friend on the state executive board of the Social-Democratic Party of Wisconsin. Benches had been set up for the audience and as they came in a Polish immigrant named Anielewski was addressing the crowd. "I don't understand a word of Polish but I followed his speech fairly well—the general drift of it, from his gestures, his voice, and the proper names used. . . . The audience was thinking—

it was still in the hall." When the man left to make more speeches that night at other halls, Seidel began his talk, in English. My mother's letter went on, "No wonder the Milwaukee movement is so solid. This was straight socialist education work, not academic, no 'holy words'. . . . He didn't talk about class-consciousness, but his speech was interspersed with the spirit of it—and it was a geniune class-consciousness . . . that gave fire—real fire—to his speech. . . . I was moved—so were we all—each in his own way. There were some 120 men in the hall." Mrs. Mayer, Oma and my mother were the only women present. ". . . there were young boys, fourteen years old, mere kids, in the audience, so they'd talk and make a little noise at times. Seidel didn't seem to notice it, no one seemed to. And there were great hushes whenever he was especially impressive—showing that they were listening. And a few times men in the audience put in a few words—backing Seidel up. Some earnest soul that exploded—couldn't hold in! Oh it was great! And this was in the Polish quarter—the priest-ridden Polish Catholic quarter! After the meeting a young fellow begrimed of face—stunted of growth—but with fiery Isaiah-eyes—distributed literature. One of the silent heroes. He was a worker. Showed us his button—said he had been a worker in the party for eight years, and his eyes gleamed! Isaiah without the prophet's tongue! Distributing literature! He was quiet, repressed, but the eyes! The eyes! . . . A worker losing himself in the cause! God bless him! . . . How a meeting like this stirs me! Such exaltation! Such hope—such faith in man! I *see* the dynamics of the movement! I *see* the yeast that will leaven the bread! And there is plenty of yeast! Plenty. . . . It was great . . . to see those Poles, some stolid, just a gleam of thought, a momentary rapt attention now and then—some passionately alive to every word, the majority somewhere between these extremes, but all at least *there*—listening or trying to listen—thinking, thinking, thinking. . . . Oh it's a great great time that we are living in, when workingmen sit in little halls on benches and stand around the walls thinking, thinking—the thoughts of social-democracy! When I left the hall . . . my head was striking the stars! Such exaltation."

My mother was on fire with the cause. She did what they asked her to at headquarters when she went in—passing out leaflets or translating Victor Berger's editorials for the German party paper, the *Wahrheit*. The people in the office were her friends—Miss Thomas and then Carl Thompson, an organizer as well as a national committeeman for the party, as was Berger. Sometimes Oma and Mother had dinner at the Berger home or met the Bergers at a restaurant before a meeting. "The Bear" had strong ideas on love and marriage. During one dinner discussion, he declared to Oma, Miss Thomas and Mother that he considered himself a "varietist" and believed in continual changes of mates as one went through life. He even advocated late marriage in the hope that by so doing one might manage to remain with one spouse. Berger himself had married about ten years before, at thirty-seven, and had two daughters, both brilliant and both to become doctors in time. Mother and Oma considered Berger a genius and the Steichen family, along with other socialists of Milwaukee, followed his editorials in the *Social-Democratic Herald.*

It was Sunday, the twenty-ninth of December, 1907. My mother and Oma said good-bye and Mother went to look in on party headquarters before taking the train to Princeton. Miss Thomas introduced her to the new organizer for the Lake Shore and Fox River Valley district, who had just come in to visit and discuss his work and was in Berger's office. Miss Thomas said that while Carl Thompson had faith in my father as a coming agitator and called him a "hustler," she herself was afraid that sometimes Charles Sandburg was "talking over the heads of the working-man."

Here again, the family story, in the way of folklore and song, holds the central thread though the action may differ. Some say my mother planned to have dinner with friends and go to a concert afterwards, and so she turned my father down when he offered to take her to dinner. But I heard that she was returning to Princeton that day and that she paid little attention to the young comrade. She mainly felt pity. He was gawky and intense and not much to look at. His thirtieth birthday was just coming up. He had hazel eyes with brown flecks in them, cropped dark hair, and was thin and tall. He wore a bow tie, a white shirt with a celluloid collar and a dark suit. She was fancy-free and self-supporting, and had been photographed since the age of twelve, when she wore her black hair long, by one of the coming artists of the day who adored her—Eduard Steichen.

Did my mother say, as I remember, that she had a train to catch and was in a hurry? My father walked her out to the trolley. He told her that he wanted to send her some of his propaganda leaflets and some of his other writings too. Would she comment on them? She gave him her address in Princeton. And then, as my mother lifted her skirts and boarded the trolley, was my father quickened with hope? I think so.

Nine

The Little Green Velvet Box

When I was a child I knew the drawers in the houses we lived in. Some contained jewelry, keys, ribbons, tins of buttons. When the house was quiet and the people were away, I would wander to the drawers and pull them open and rummage through the treasures carefully. It was an introspective occupation and made the house and the family mine. In one of the drawers there was the green velvet box presented to my mother by Uncle Ed when she graduated from eighth grade, in its convex lid the tiny watercolor done by him. In the box were those of my mother's love letters to my father that he had saved, and I became familiar with them. The first was dated 17 January 1908: "Dear Mr. Sandburg, I have your leaflets 'Labor and Politics' and 'A Little Sermon.' Do tell me how you contrive to be a moral philosopher and a political agitator at one and the same time—and especially how you contrive to write such Poets' English one minute and the plain vernacular the next. The combination is baffling! Artist, poet-prophet, on the one hand; man of action on the other. You must explain yourself else I shall 'have such misery' trying to crack the hard nut myself. Thank you for the leaflets. And good-luck to you in all your work. Yours cordially, Lilian Steichen."

There it was. He was gone, my father, after that, caught in the web of love, entangled, so that as he went about his work, going from place to place, changing his collarless shirts and fixing the paper or celluloid collar in position, or wearing the fresh-starched collared ones that the wives of comrades washed after he left their houses and kept ready for his return on his next swing that way to collect the membership dues from the locals and give them more party literature to distribute; as he presented his addresses to four o'clock afternoon "People's Meetings" in churches for free, or for small sums in lecture halls; as he wrote by himself in the single rooms he took in boarding houses, the fire began to burn that was his feeling for my mother—mingling admiration and desire.

Along with *Incidentals* and his propaganda papers and pamphlets, he sent her a poem of his that *The Lyceumite* had once featured as a frontispiece, "A Dream Girl." And he asked when her next vacation was and when she would be in Milwaukee again. "My dear Mr. Sandburg, . . . This is an *age of action*—not of dreaming or contemplation or gratulation . . . it's only once or twice a year that I *read* pure poetry like Shelley, Lanier, Keats. Not that I no longer appreciate the lyric loveliness of Shelley's *'Life of life thy lips enkindle'* or of Lanier's *Marshes of Glynn* —but that I am called away from such aesthetic enjoyment by a Voice from the World of Action—a Voice unmusical, strident even, but *Compelling* for it is the *Cry of Life*. There you have it. . . . It's good to have loved the poet's Poets and to have soared a little on the wings of poesy oneself! But it's good too, and better . . . to move on to greater things, the every-day life of Action—the politics of constructive socialism! . . . Your *Dream-Girl* . . . is indeed a dream girl—not of our world today but of the Millennial Epoch of Rest. In our Epoch of Struggle girls must be made of sterner stuff. Too bad, but it's so. My hope is that socialism will gradually create an environment favorable to the development of such a Millennial *Dream Girl*. But meanwhile under capitalism your Dream Girl must be a leisure class product. . . . As for *Incidentals*—it is all right. . . . But—of course you've guessed it— I like *Labor and Politics* best. It belongs to the sphere of Politics, of Action. . . . You ask when I shall be in Milwaukee again. Our spring vacation lasts from March 27 to April 6. I shall spend it partly in Milwaukee and partly at my home. I told you—didn't I?—that my home is in the country—a little farm. . . . If you should be in Mil. at any time during my vacation I should be so glad to see you there or to have you come to see us at the farm. I am sending you the February Century containing an article about my brother. . . . you'll come across a reference to myself. I must tell you that the credit I am given is not deserved. Everything else in the article is true—but this is pure fiction. I was at school while my brother was studying in Europe—both of us supported by our mother. All the credit belongs to her and brother himself. The article does not tell the half of our mother's wonderful goodness. . . . Forgive this long letter. . . . Sincerely yours, Lilian Steichen."

The *Century* magazine had carried a piece, "Progress in Photography—

with Special Reference to the Work of Edward Steichen," along with six of Uncle Ed's photographs, for which he'd been paid fifty dollars apiece. The previous November, *Century* had run an article, "The New Color Photography," and used two of my uncle's Autochrome Process color transparencies, and paid him three hundred for the lot. The Lumière Company had developed a technique of making direct color photographs in the form of Autochrome plates and as Uncle Ed said, "The results were extraordinary. . . . I took some color plates with me to London, where I photographed George Bernard Shaw. Shaw's rosy complexion and luminous blond-red hair and beard made him a natural target for color photography. . . . He was easy as a big dog to photograph." Alfred Stieglitz met my uncle in Europe and was excited by the photographs and asked to reproduce them in *Camera Work*. Uncle Ed gave Stieglitz a batch of Autochrome plates to try out himself and brought his own prints over to America for a Photo-Secession members' show at "291." Uncle Ed also brought back the drawings of Auguste Rodin, as he'd planned, and they were exhibited in the Photo-Secession Galleries under Stieglitz' direction, the first showing of modern art in the states. Before long my uncle would introduce the work of Henri Matisse there. Uncle Ed lived most of the time at Voulangis outside Paris now. He had brought together some of the bolder young painters and they formed the Society of Younger American Painters in Paris. He would draw from them for gallery exhibits at "291" in the next few years —Max Weber and Paul Cézanne among others. And now and then weren't paintings and photographs shown together in the same exhibit? My uncle was feeling his power in his art. *Everybody's Magazine* was preparing an article to be called "What the Matter Is In America and What to Do About It," by Lincoln Steffens, on the coming Republican convention, and for a thousand dollars my uncle gave them reproduction rights to two photographs—one of President Theodore Roosevelt and the other of the former secretary of war, William Howard Taft.

Uncle Ed was a success and the delight of Oma's life. And my mother wanted everyone to know that he was her brother and recognized. My father's situation was different in most ways, and particularly financially. He wrote to Philip Green Wright, "Dear Professor . . . At present there is practically only expenses in this job of organizer, but by spring I ought to have the district in shape to pay me from $50 to $75 a month and expenses. . . . Yours as ever, Sandburg." And to his new correspondent, from his room at the Athearn Hotel in Oshkosh, "Dear Miss Steichen:—It is a very good letter you send me—softens the intensity of this guerilla warfare I am carrying on up here. . . . The Dream

Girl is Millenial [sic]—formed in the mist of an impressionist's reverie. . . . But, my good girl, she is not of the leisure-class, as we know the l-c. She is a disreputable gipsy, and can walk, shoot, ride, row, hoe in the garden, wash dishes, grimace, haggle, live on half-rations, and laugh at Luck." Wasn't my father writing almost directly from the poet he admired, Walt Whitman? In the first volume of *Leaves of Grass* in the section called "Children of Adam" in the poem "A Woman Waits for Me," Whitman says:

> They are not one jot less than I am,
> They are tann'd in the face by shining suns and
>   blowing winds,
> Their flesh has the old divine suppleness and strength,
> They know how to swim, row, ride, wrestle, shoot, run,
>   strike, retreat, advance, resist, defend themselves,
> They are ultimate in their own right—they are calm,
>   clear, well-possess'd of themselves.
>
> I draw you close to me, you women,
> I cannot let you go. . . .

Then my father sent my mother a sheaf of his poems and wrote, "Am going to send you The Plaint of a Rose. It was written as and marks the half-way point on the Journey 'from Poetry to Economics.' A protest and justification of the universe! . . . I shall plan to be in Milwaukee the last days in March and one or two in April, and will hope to see you then. . . . Charles Sandburg."

Three days later he heard from Princeton: "Dear Mr. Sandburg, The poems—the poems are wonderful! They are different from the poems in the books that stand dusty on my book-shelf—how different! Yes, from the best of them too—from Shelley, from Whitman, from Carpenter! Oh, if I had a volume of your poems, dear Poet-of-Our-World-Today, it would not stand on the shelf dusty but would be read and wrestled with for the life-strength it could give! . . . I may keep them a little while— may I not? Could I keep them one week? I shall want to read them often. The *Cry of Life* will not call me from your poems—it is *in* your poems—poignant, intense!" And she said, "Have you really turned from poetry for good? Shaw is our dramatist—why shouldn't you be our Poet? The American movement doesn't seem to be in pressing need of a poet, at the present moment—*perhaps. Perhaps!* But surely the time isn't far off when it will need its Poet. . . . And yet—it's *great* work what you are doing now—as S.D.P. organizer! You seem to have a genius for that work too (I received the Manitowoc newspaper with your article—an article that ought to take hold sure). Would it be possible to be both organizer and poet? Or is it a case of having to forego one service in order to do the other? And if you have decided to forego being a poet, why? Why? More anon—And great thanks for the wonderful wonderful poems. Sincerely, Lilian Steichen."

In the mail to her were more poems from my father, some done back in the firehouse days, others by the lake shore recently, one of a group of three called "An Autumn Handful" going:

PERSPECTIVES

(Inscribed to Saugatuck)

Always in what I love
Is something yet beyond.
I see the lake expand,
The broad blue vista
Lures the gloaming and the dark.
The somber woodland rises
On the farther shore
And cool-deep open places
Ask the wanderer to enter.
Transitions on the slopes occur,
And ever half-caught phantoms
Gesture from a hilltop.

But ever farther yet
Is meaning after meaning,
Shadowed in the onset
Of the dusk—over there
Where day-things vanish
Into silhouettes that also disappear.

My mother replied, "Dear Mr. Sandburg. . . . I had to read your poems once before school this morning, at noon and again this evening— each time to reassure myself that it was really so—that it wasn't some passing glamor that made the poems seem so wonderful—that they really were the wonderful poems I thought them. And every time the reassurance was complete. The hour had come to say: 'Hail, Poet!' The three poems in 'An Autumn Handful,' the poems 'The Pagan and Sunrise,' 'The Rebel's Funeral,' 'A Fling at the Riddle,' 'The Road and the End'— all great, great, great! 'Hail, Poet!'"

Perhaps Mother was already thinking of bringing this poet she had found together with Uncle Ed. "I'm glad you are interested in photography as an art—a distinctively modern art. And that you appreciate my brother's work. . . . I have some faint hope that my brother will come over to America this spring. . . . If he does come he will plan to be home at the farm during my vacation. I should so much like to have him meet you—he would appreciate your poems and love you as an S.D.P. organizer! . . . You say you will want to hear some of my word-melodies in vacation. I'm beginning to feel uncomfortable over the prospect. . . . I used to dream of being a poet—I suppose because I loved poetry. And dear-Brother-Mine shared these dreams. He was sure I was a genius. It has been the hardest job disillusioning him. . . . For my part I am content to be, instead of a genius, an average human being. There's wonder and joy enough in being a mere human being—a Woman! Anyway there is something tragic to me in the combination—Woman-Genius. The constant struggle between two kinds of work she has to do: as mother of children, as master-workman. Of course the true Woman-Genius takes up her double life-work, accepts it, rejoices in it, just as the true Mere-Woman her one work! . . . It must be glorious to be such a woman-genius these days—doing her woman's work of bearing strong children to carry forward the Movement in the next generation; and doing besides the man's work of carrying on the Movement now. . . . I see I'm rambling on and on and on. And it's past bed-time again! Goodbye. Sincerely, Lilian Steichen."

As a child, I only knew my mother's love letters to my father, kept in that green velvet box. His were stored away somewhere and it is only in these late years that I have seen them—the ones she saved. After interfiling their letters, the pattern of this time before their marriage comes clear. An orderly man and falling in love, he seems to have kept most of hers, while she was careless of his early ones and many are lost. Continually he pressed his poems upon her. "Dear Comrade," she wrote him, "I am happy to hear you say that my letters have given you something. . . . What joy for me to read and know by reading that there are more and still more such wonderful poems as those in the first bunch that so completely upset my notions about modern poetry! . . . 'coming, coming, coming' out of the great source within you—*if* your strenuous life as agitator leaves you energy for it. And a formidable IF I know this is! As if it were not enough to be possessed with one sort of divine madness! You must needs add to the divine madness of poesy the diviner madness of revolutionary agitation—Bless you! . . . I like to get the thought of all this great great poetry in my mind—and then think of you knocking about in the 'Lake Country' not as a wandering minstrel, but as a plain practical S.D.P. organizer giving talks to hard-headed working-men and organizing them for political action. Wonderful! How Shelley would have envied you! He tried so hard, poor boy, to do what you are doing now—to be a man of action helping to carry forward the political movement of his day. But it wasn't given him to do such work—he wasn't hardheaded himself—lacked genius for practical action. You see the gods have been very good to you! . . . I confess your genius. . . . L.S."

Three days later she took her pen again, "My dear comrade, Just a word of cheer to you in the midst of your arduous labors in the faraway North! . . . Bravo! The world could not move on without you! without your help! . . . Glad thanks! Lilian Steichen." It seemed that in one of my father's lost letters, he criticized her choice of words here, for she wrote back, "Yes, it's a go. I'll try always to say 'hard work' instead of 'arduous labors' hereafter. 'I'll try,' I say. But doubtless I'll blunder into scholasticisms now and then. That's what schooling did for me. . . . I got my English from books, largely academic books at that. I've tried to get free from Latinisms—and talk idiomatic English. It's been up-hill work. But I'm at it still—will try harder than ever, I promise you. And you trip me up, please—when you see me going in the wrong direction. And don't give up hope for me if I sin often—backslide often—you know why I'm liable to now. . . . L.S."

"My dear comrade," she wrote, ". . . your letter tells me that I'm helping you. I like to hear that. So I shall be able to help the world on a little, through you. Directly I don't touch the world these days. Princeton is outside the bounds of the world. . . . Thanks for the 'Sun-shine-Slanting-Across-Shadows' and 'the crimson turban in a Corot land-scape'—I accept both! With a glad heart! My Religion is *Joy-in-Life* you know." The days were going by so that it was March now and her vacation at the end of the month was approaching. She was determined to bring Uncle Ed and my father together. "I have had the best news from my brother—he is on his way to America! Now I am waiting to hear definitely whether business in New York will not interfere with his being home during my vacation. It is just barely possible—or my fears make it seem so—that he may have to hold his exhibition that week. So I'm waiting anxiously. The short spring vacation promises so much this year! You *must manage* to spend a day at the farm. It's not very accessible—no trolley-line and a poor schedule on the railroad. . . . I suppose you'll look at the schedule for trains back to Milwaukee. If so, don't imagine that we'll let you leave on the *afternoon* train from Menomonee Falls. . . . You'll either have to stay overnight with us or leave from another station on an *evening* train. The *better* plan would be to stay overnight—*if we can lodge you comfortably enough.* The farm-house is small—it's a dear little, old little, white farmhouse. . . . Papa sleeps in one of the upstairs bedrooms and you could have the other. But Papa doesn't mind the cold—and maybe you do. (The up-stairs isn't heated.) So whether we can lodge you comfortably enough will depend on how cold the weather is—and how much cold you can stand. There are plenty blankets and quilts—by the way—if you can get any comfort out of that thought! Perhaps you can put up with such 'simple life'—can you? . . . How long do you expect to remain in Milwaukee? Do you know? . . . Spring is here too—and Gladness! From glad heart to glad heart —Greetings! L.S."

And then, ". . . the other evening I came in to supper after a splendid walk—in an exuberance of joy! It had been raining hard all day till late in the afternoon. The streets were muddy and pools of water were every-where. The air was sweet and fresh after the rain. At sunset the sky had cleared in the west along the horizon—the rest of the sky was still overcast with great heavy clouds—slate-blue. I was walking toward the sun-set. The street was bordered with elm trees. Thru this vista of arching elms, I saw the sky a-glow! And the ruts in the road caught the glow—two ribbons of burning gold. And my heart caught the glow—burning intense. So there I stood and looked and looked. 'Let it be said I have lived'!"

There are fewer letters of my father's from this time so the story is hers now rather than his. "I feel glad for the life that is given me to live —I think of how I shall soon see my brother. I think of the splendid letter—the last one—from you, my good comrade. And I think of how I shall see you soon. I feel exuberantly glad for it all. . . . If the weather is anything like this when you come out to the farm we won't have any difficulty making you comfortable for the night. By leaving the door from the living-room to the stairs open, we can arrange to have the up-stairs bed-room reasonably warm and fairly well ventilated too. With a hot fire in the living-room and windows open—you'll get fresh and warmed air upstairs all right. And I wish you would plan to stay several days instead of one! Provided you would enjoy it—of course! L.S."

The spring vacation was three weeks away, starting on March twenty-seventh. My father was traveling about as always. He wrote to Aunt

Esther, "I am writing this on a sleigh stage crossing Green Bay from Mariette to Sturgeon Bay." He wanted Aunt Esther to forward copies of *The Fra,* the new magazine that Elbert Hubbard was just putting out from his Roycroft Press, which had some of my father's poems in it. One was called "Backyard Vagaries," and was part of the "An Autumn Handful" set of poems that he had sent on to my mother:

> Hollyhocks uprise erect and bold
> And look wide-eyed to other lands
> As though to pass by merely seeing.
>
> Poppies flaunt their discs . . .
> Mock-mournful brown-eyed Susans
> Hush the queries of a bumble-bee;
> Sunflowers tanned and hardy,
> Gaze across the fence at Pansies
> Pampered in a tended, level bed.

My father had had a new leaflet printed, which he passed out on his travels and he enclosed it in a letter to my mother too:

> What do you think about these things? To get into the game of life, take chances, make decisions, and keep moving. . . . To acquire friends with whom you can babble of stars, roses, coffee, and the weather. . . . To use every possible tool and situation for the advance of The Great Cause; to distinguish between intelligent discussion and futile rag-chewing. . . . To pity the respectable and satisfied and see in the heart of the jailbird your own impulses; to be patient with the stupid and incompetent and chat reverently with the town fool about his religion . . . to realize that the grafter, the scarlet woman, Rockefeller, Thaw and the one-legged man on the corner selling lead pencils, are each the result of conditions for which all of us are in part responsible. . . . To spell Art with a capital A and enjoy paintings, poems, stories . . . to hoe in the garden, split wood, carry out ashes, get dirty and be actually useful every once in a while if not twice. . . . To live in a bungalow, with bathrooms, music, flowers, a beautiful woman and children healthy as little savages. . . . how about these things, Brother? Are they worth while?

This leaflet was reprinted later in various forms. It may be compared again to lines in Walt Whitman's Preface to *Leaves of Grass,* published over fifty years before, with which my father was familiar, "This is what you shall do: Love the earth and sun and the animals, despise riches, give alms to every one that asks, stand up for the stupid and crazy, devote your income and labor to others, hate tyrants, argue not concerning God, have patience and indulgence toward the people, take off your hat to nothing known or unknown or to any man or number of men, go freely with powerful uneducated persons and with the young and with the mothers of families, read. . . . in the open air every season of every year of your life, re-examine all you have been told at school or church or in any book, dismiss whatever insults your soul."

My father mailed another poem to my mother, "Lines on a Paradox," beginning:

> All the beautiful thoughts you send,
> In a sheaf I gather and give back to you.
> > Yet I keep them, too,
> For that is the way with beautiful thoughts;
> Into and out of their trackless routes
> They pass and repass and no man loses . . .

And she replied, "Dear poet and comrade, . . . The 'lines on a Paradox' are well worth while! You are a Joyous Heart—a Sweet Boy—to have thought the thoughts in them! And a rare Poet to have found the sweet simple words that tell the thoughts! Again Glad thanks!" She said of the leaflet, ". . . the prose enclosure is splendid. Strong, simple, direct, and full of joy and wisdom—it shows the noble strength and stature of your soul. . . . No more today. Good-night, L.S."

She told him, "Today I got a short note from my brother saying that his photographic exhibition opened last week (I inclose announcement) and that it will continue till April 2. I hope the exhibition won't prevent his coming home March 27 as he first planned. His note didn't mention this possibility. It was very typical of Edward's notes—short, brisk, full of the rush of work—'hastily but lovingly, Gaesjack.' When you've read the note you've gotten a vivid impression of the rush, rush, rush—of getting up an exhibition in very short time—But you haven't any facts—practical points like dates—He's a wild boy—Gaesjack! . . . I wish he . . . would write definitely whether he'll have to stay in New York till the exhibition closes." She said, "Now *you* haven't Edward's sort of 'cussedness.' Your letters are always satisfying—they come to the point. However I take for granted that you have a peculiar brand of 'cussedness' all your own. It's only a question of finding out wherein lies *your* 'cussedness.' It's not human nor comradely to be angelic, and until the contrary is proved beyond a possibility of doubt I'll consider you innocent of any such uncomradely deficiency in plain human 'cussedness.' That's all for today. Here's Good Luck to you and your work! L.S."

It was the sixteenth of March and two and a half months since my father had escorted my mother to the trolley and got her address. Then she had thought him not much to look at and felt pity for him—intense and lean and somewhat worn. Now it was eleven days before they planned to meet for the second time, and it seemed that the written word—the flood of poetry and propaganda—had brought her near to passion. "Dear Charles Sandburg, your two beautiful letters which came together today have left me full of Wonder and Hope! To think that one day can hold so much happiness! and it's You, my Poet, so free with the warm human gifts of your dear words and rhythms, that have filled the day brimful with Joy for me! 'So glad am I that on the great wide way we have met, touched hands and spoken.' This thought 'I give back to you—yet I keep it too'—And I have really some part in the making of your warm human poems! Really? This thought is what fills me with such sweet wonder and hope. I have been conscious in rare poignant moments in my life of something very beautiful deep deep within me, but the Voice from those depths has always been so small, so still—more a *hush* than a *voice*—that I never dreamed that anyone but myself would hear it. But so finely attuned was that heart of yours, you caught the fine vibrant note from the depths—and . . . gave it strength and quality. In your poems somehow (I dare *hope—believe* it!) the sweet still hush of my heart has become blended with the clear strong proud Music of yours and so is heard! It is heard—and the farthest star and the last son of man will vibrate to it. But for you, the sweet small hush yearning upward toward light and utterance would have subsided back to the dark depths—subsided and subsided—till it lost what small strength for upward yearning it had—and so died forever! So glad thanks to you—for Voice! for Life! This is the Wonder and the Hope! . . . L.S."

My father gathered up more to send her—Asgard Press circulars, more poems, a copy of *In Reckless Ecstasy*. Did it seem to her that the gates of love were opening and she was set upon finding the words? "Wunderkind! I've got to call you that even if you don't know what it means. The name has been on my lips before when I read some account of what you were doing—or when I read some splendid poem of yours. . . .

Now that I've read 'In Reckless Ecstasy' and the rest you sent today—why nothing short of *Wunderkind* will do! If there's an English equivalent I don't know it—my English vocabulary is small. . . . You call a *Wunderkind* a boy that makes you lift up your heart to him and sing: 'Hail, thou young god!' Such worship and rapture and wonderment are embodied in *Wunderkind*. 'Wonder-child' would be the literal translation—but English has not crystallized a thought, a name in any such word combination. The German soul had greater need for the word—and so it made for itself the word! The German soul—you get it in a Wagner opera—knows how to feel the passion, the tumult, the rapture of Worship. And there is nothing under the sun that has so good a right to inspire such Worship as a proud, free, tender, strong, brave Boy! This Boy the Germans call *Wunderkind*! the Germans who know how to worship, the Germans who have given us the Wagner opera *too*! (And you are Norse! Splendid! That is the superlative of German! It was not enough, it seems, for you to be a young god—you add to this that your race is the Young God among the nations!—You glorious young Norse God) I want to say so *much* more—but I must stop. I've read and read in 'In Reckless Ecstasy' (O, you Wunderkind!) and read the circulars—and have thought and thought looking at you in your different aspects together—Lyceum speaker, Poet, S.D.P. organizer, Boy—and it's to you—this complete many-sided *you*—that I say in glad worship recognizing in you a glorious achievement and a still more glorious Hope:—'Wunderkind! Wunderkind!' . . . L. S."

It seems my mother was caught now too. Had she ever dreamed of her good fortune in coming by chance on a *Wunderkind*? Did she ever think back on the reality of the tall, not very romantic stranger she'd met in Berger's office and try to remember what he'd been like in the flesh? She described him to her family in what my uncle later said were "glowing phrases." And Uncle Ed said too that "all the family knew about him was that he was a poet and a socialist and that was it."

In the Foreword to *In Reckless Ecstasy,* my mother read what Professor Wright had said, "The boys called him the terrible Swede: not such a bad characterization, after all; for it is a quality of this old viking blood that it enables its possessor to land on his feet in any and every environment. . . . The Poor Writers Club is now disintigrated [sic] . . . , but Sandburg, true to his Norse instincts, disdains harness. In these days of frock-coat degeneracy he could hardly build a dragon ship and scour the seas like his viking forebears, but he is making the nearest approach to this which modern manners permit; he is traveling, selling stereoscopic views for Underwood and Underwood. And he is doing it quite in the old viking spirit."

"Dear Comrade," my mother wrote, "I've been reading *In Reckless Ecstasy* again today. How this Voice of your past self helps me to understand you as you are today. I feel surer of you. You aristocrat, You! This monument out of the past shows that your blue blood is not of yesterday. Wright testified that your blue blood showed itself to him when he first met you in '98—ten years ago! So I'm sure that your present self is built on sure solid foundations. You, Charles Sandburg, as I have known you these few weeks . . . have a past self that contained the embryo of your present self. It was a natural growth and gives sure promise of further beautiful growth. . . . In but a little more than a week we shall see each other face to face! This time I shall really see you. The first glimpse I had of you was not *seeing*. That we will be good comrades I know. For the rest, we know not. . . . I shall probably arrive in Milwaukee at 4:45 P.M. Friday, the 27th. I *may* have to go straight thru to Brookfield . . . where father could call for me with horse & buggy. It will depend on whether brother will be at home then. (the 27th is his Birthday—a great event in the family! so if he were home I'd have to hurry home as fast as possible to celebrate with mother and him). If brother isn't home—as seems likely now—I'd like to wait over in Milwaukee till a later train to Brookfield, either the 6 or 7 o'clock train. That would give us time to see each other. . . . I hope you'll like it at the farm well enough to stay there most of the time till you return to Oshkosh."

She told him about Oma. "You will like my mother I believe. She has such a Heart! And such strength and dauntlessness! And such Hope! Mother comes from plain unlettered peasant stock in mediaeval priest-ridden Catholic Luxembourg, with its religious processions and pilgrimages and the rest! Yet mother understands me, an 'infidel'—and is half an infidel herself, tho she won't quite admit it! And she's a party member and a private agitator! . . . I notice you dedicated *In Reckless Ecstasy* to your mother. What a mother she must be—to have such a Wunderkind as You! What a Mother! . . . How proud she must be of having born You! I suppose you'll be in Manitowoc, when this reaches you, hard at work again! To think of your making a speech—2 hours & 10 min. long— as you did at Green Bay. . . . Good-luck! L.S."

My father was indeed in Manitowoc and was asking Professor Wright to send Miss Lilian Steichen *The Dreamer,* which contained my father's Foreword. He added, "I shall eventually get more of a material compensation for my work. Never had such luck as the past winter, along that line. Have lots of hope and a number of chances yet left for ringing the bull's eye of fate. . . . Am head over heels in work up here. It's merely a choice of what handles to take hold of! All luck to you, old heart. Fraternally yours, Sandburg."

My mother sent my father a photograph Uncle Ed had taken of her sitting on the farmhouse steps; her thick black hair is pushed back; she is wearing a long unironed skirt and a loose white collarless blouse, the long sleeves rolled up. She wrote him that her family always called her "Paus'l." He signed a letter with his nickname "Cully." My mother was finding ways to make my father's coming visit longer than had been originally suggested. "How do you like this plan? We visit in Milwaukee together till 6 o'clock. . . . Then take train *together* and reach the farm that evening *together*. . . . Father or someone would call for us at Brookfield—and we'd have the ride home together. Wouldn't that be better than the old plan of having you come out to the farm the next morning? . . . I enclose a letter home from my brother. So you can see what his plans are. He writes that his nose is 'to the grindstone'—the letter shows it. It's surely work-work-work with him these days. . . . Must stop now or I won't make the mail. . . . L.S."

He answered, still in Manitowoc, "Dear girl:—I will look for you on the 4:45 P.M. . . . on Friday the 27th . . . I expect to have everything cleared up and be ready for anything that can happen, gallows or throne, sky or sea-bottom! . . . You will announce the events and the gladiators will gladiate like blazes! The joy-bells on high will clang like joy. Motley will have vent and psalms will be sung and three or four peans will go up to the stars out of pure gladiosity.—I believe you asked about my cussedness. This is some of it. I am cussedest when I am glad, and so are those around me. Admonish me gently to behave and I may or I may not. . . . I promise tho, that while we are on the cars and respectable people who pride themselves on demeanor are about, I will not, 'Rah! rah rah!' nor sing 'The mother was chasing her boy round the room' with all forty four verses. . . . Just glad, L.S., just glad, that's all! . . . So interesting a brother you have! The letter gives me a glimpse of him. 'My tricks and carelessness' how naturally that drops from him—with those he loves confessing a little waywardness, knowing they love him for it. Will you bring along and wear once that Graeco-Gothic white thing you have on in that picture? Just frinstance! . . . C.S."

She wrote him and analyzed both of them in what he called an "obsession of nationality." Was it because the Luxembourg household my mother came from was somewhat intellectual and worldly, what with Uncle Ed going and coming between London, Paris, New York, wearing perhaps a cravat and a grand black elegant cape, whereas in Grandfather Sandburg's house, they had dropped their Scandinavian ties and felt totally American? Mother proposed her point. "Dear Charles August Sandburg! What a glorious name it is!—Strong and proud and free—just the right name for you whom I call in loving worship, 'Wunderkind!' . . . I know why I'm glad that you are of the race of the Far-North Teutons. It's because Scandinavia has given us Ibsen, Björnson in drama —and in music so many names of the newest Pioneers—I don't remember the names of these 20th century Scandinavian composers. I do remember getting the impression . . . that the most daring moderns, who *carry* forward the Wagnerian idea, are Scandinavian. What you remarked about individuals is true of nations too—'the polished boot descending, the wooden shoe ascending.' Germany is in its *prime* now—Scandinavia fresh and vigorous in its magnificent *youth*. Hence the *daring*, the pioneer-spirit of Scandinavian art! And you are an incarnation of that spirit— you Wunderkind! As for an 'obsession of nationality'—of *course not*! You know how every true patriot among the Germans hates Heine for the way he has satirized German nationality—more particularly the *phlegmatic middle class* of Germany. And I—I love Heine! But mention Heine to a typical German and he will cry 'Renegade!—traitor!' Yet Heine and I both *so* love Germany! *So* love the passion and ardor of the German soul! The very reason why we would mercilessly lash her phlegmatic flesh! . . . But Americanism! What does American nationality stand for? Anyway!—Is it 'our Puritan fore-fathers?' . . . I prefer Ibsen-Hauptman-Sudermann—That is, I prefer 'Joy-in Life.' I prefer Life to Death; service to self-sacrifice, etc. So for me German-Scandinavian! instead of Anglo-Saxon. Yes, I'm glad I am German and you Swede! Of course there is something to be said for our Puritan brothers! As a human being, I take pride in their achievement too—I'm broad enough for that, thank God. It is possible to love one's own people and take pride in other peoples too—Fourth-of-July patriots to-the-contrary-notwithstanding! . . . Must change the subject abruptly. I have your glad glad glad letter—all alive with *a very cussedness of gladness!* . . . I like your kind of cussedness! It's fine, dear-boy, magnificent! You *are* a Gay-Heart! . . . Goodnight! L.S."

My father sent her a last letter before they met, from Sheboygan Falls, ". . . Slept last night looking out on a sky of stars and a winding river. Saw the sun come up the other side of a ridge of hills. So I knew whatever was mine would come to me, 'reply somewhere on the tide of the years, today or tomorrow.' And it turned out to be today! Anybody that can put it down in black and white 'I—I love Heine!' has mounted far toward the summits of freedom. Dear, beautiful girl-heart—proud, mystery-woven girl-heart—Lilian Steichen. We see great days of big things—so shall we be like what we see."

Ten

The Great Ride Together

How can I reconstruct the past, wanting to know how it was, so that the photographs in my albums and on my walls could come alive? Family stories help, but like folklore, they change continually this way and that as time goes on, so that history may be distorted. I hoped for the original truth and luckily I had my parents' love letters. There is the fact of what happened, Mother writing to my father when that week of vacation was over, "You're such a Beaute when you're not looking worn-out, dead-tired! It's a fact. . . . I can't forget how old and tired you looked March 27! I couldn't help feeling a kind of pity for you then. . . . And then after two or three days of rest, what a change! . . . You were ten years younger *at least*. . . . What hours you must have kept working and working to have brought yourself to that worn-out state by March 27th?"

It seemed that my mother had gone to the little farm before the twenty-seventh to help Oma with preparations for Uncle Ed's birthday and to be there to welcome my uncle. Perhaps she wanted time too with her family so she could hear Uncle Ed's news and give him her "glowing" account of her young man. Oma worried over Gaesjack and, as always, urged him to stay on for a long visit. Were the family in suspense when my mother declared she'd go off in the horse and buggy herself in the approaching storm to fetch her poet at the Brookfield station? It did no good for Opa to say he'd go instead. She only wanted him to hitch the horse to the carriage for her. My mother had been falling in love through letters and it had been three months since she'd seen my father. She was noted in the family for her headstrong ideas and ways. She wanted time alone with him as she left Oma and Uncle

123

Ed in the kitchen and slapped the reins on the horse and set out while thunder muttered overhead, the sky darkened and Opa shook his head and went back into the house.

There are letters from my parents to each other about their ride to the farm from the station. He said, "Such a night as it was, slashing rain & a wind that almost took the carriage off its braces—our hands talking louder than the howling gale." And she spoke of that "Great Ride To-gether—from Brookfield to the farm in storm and wind and lightning and black night! Such a ride! 'We have lived.' How the elements love us. . . . We didn't beg the wind and the lightning and the thunder and the rain—we didn't *beg* them to give us their company! It wasn't a ceremonial 'call'—we hadn't given out that we would be 'at home.' Out of sheer love for us, they *intruded* their presences upon us—shouted to us—slapped us in the face with love's abandon. . . . And didn't we shout back tho! And didn't we give these rough old intruders to understand that we love their sort . . . for their lusty mad gayety and their free common ways!"

They would call it The Great Week later on. "Ah, those days at 'the farm,' such days, such days . . . I see you going up the narrow stairs candle in hand—saying good-night and good-night—your eyes full of love —you, Cully. . . . You must speak those poems to me again that you spoke: 'Among the Hills'—'When I was a Tad-pole and you were a fish' etc. That voice of yours, Cully, with its richness and resonance . . . I want to hear it!" They began to give each other new names and to learn ones that the other already had. Once she had called him "Comrade" in letters and signed herself "L.S." That formality was gone. At the farm she had told him how Cousin Mary couldn't say "Paus'l" and called her "Paula." My father liked that name and accepted it for my mother's ever after. When they ran in the woods, they named themselves "Mickey" and "Kitty Malone." When they were serious Social-Democrats, they called themselves "Sandy" and "Liz." If she would call him "Wunderkind," he would call her "thaumaturgist," from the Greek: thauma = wonder, + ergos = working; a wonder worker. She declared she would call him "Carl" thereafter and not "Charles," and she liked the sound of "Cully" too.

Uncle Ed viewed the newcomer somewhat coolly, I think—a poet and a socialist organizer without a penny in sight. My uncle took time to make some camera studies of my father. There he is, his black, cropped hair combed, his elbow on the table beside him, his hands just clasped, his eyes intense, in dark suit, white shirt and bow tie. Later Mother wrote to my father about the result, ". . . the proofs came of the pictures

Ed took of you, and he's got the eyes! Bless Ed—he's got the eyes! . . .
Ed got . . . the Wunderkind and the Sweet Boy. I love these pictures
of you—the eyes are yours sure. . . . Of course the proofs are mere
sketches to be changed, filled in, etc. They are pictures in embryo."
My father answered, "That proof is a wonder. I don't know why. What
will the artist say when he knows I look on it as great stuff for publicity
use! . . . Eduard Steichen is an artist. We all know our best selves, the
selves we love. And he caught a self I pray to be all the time! By what
wizardry of sight & penetration, he came to get that phase of me in so
little a time, I don't know. It took more than eyes—it took heart & soul
back of the eyes."

My uncle took walks with my father too, knowing how anxious my
mother was for them to get along. Were the lovers less tense when
Uncle Ed had to leave, busy with another exhibition to come off, this
one at the Pratt Institute in Philadelphia in mid-April? Oma mourned
his leaving as always. My mother said, "This short visit from Ed upset
her, and she is worried about his health and happiness."

My father never mentioned romance when he wrote to Professor
Wright from the Steichen farmhouse during that week. "After strenuous
weeks northward, have been spending a few days, living the Muldoon
life, on the Steichen farm, with the folks of Edward Steichen, the painter
and art photographer. The March Century has its leading article about
him but does not mention the fact that he is a warm socialist. Into the
harness again next Saturday, going down to Manitowoc, where we have
big mass-meetings. . . . Yours faithfully, Sandburg."

My mother spoke of the "soft blue shirt" he wore that week, and how
she'd been busy about the kitchen from "churning butter to washing
dishes." She showed him around the farm—the apple trees, the arbor, the
horse's stable, Opa's gardens where he put out corn, potatoes, flowers,
vegetables. They roamed the woods. My father wrote later, "Do you
remember the House in the Woods, Paula?—how the reprimanding winds
and the sullen clouds tried to scare us—how we were too warm to be
frozen out. . . . How you had the impertinence to call me 'Fool' and
I resented it with wild circling motions!" She wrote, "Sweet Fool! Playing
in the woods—playing house! 'We braggarts' paid spot cash for all our
furniture (including hat-rack) no installment plans for us! . . . I had
not played with anyone since I was twelve . . . till you, Cully, infected
me with your Gladness."

He declared that "I learned in The Great Week that you're absolutely
fearless to obey your heart-promptings, that you're hardy. The Soul of
You, all that Sea of Singing Thought & Tinted Dream that is in you, all

the sky of love and earth of beauty in you, I knew from your letters. . . .
In The Great Week, I learned all the rest, found you The Daughter of
the Regiment, fresh as all youth, gay as all holidays. . . . that it happened! that you came!"

She wrote of the week's ending, ". . . think of that last glorious night
on the farm—we-two so happy under the eternal silent skies." And then
they were packing their bags and stepping up into the buggy on an
April morning. Oma waved good-bye and Opa drove them to the station
to catch the coach car for Milwaukee. My mother's train for Princeton
was not due till early afternoon and they parted. But my father saw to
it that he was there when her train came through, so that later she said,
". . . that sudden Joy of coming upon you—1:30—Saturday—at the depot.
My heart so yearning to you! . . . What a Glory that the Soul should
be so transfused into the Body! The Body no more a Hulk—no more a
Thing of Wood—but etherealized—a Speaking Flame! What a Consecration! A realist Pentecost! . . . 'the kelson of creation is love'—Isn't it?"
They both had read and re-read Walt Whitman, my father knowing long
passages by heart, so she was sure he knew her reference to the passionate verse in "Song of Myself":

> I mind how once we lay such a transparent summer morning,
> How you settled your head athwart my hips and gently
>   turn'd over upon me,
> And parted the shirt from my bosom-bone, and plunged your
>   tongue to my bare-stript heart,
> And reach'd till you felt my beard, and reach'd till you
>   held my feet.
> Swiftly arose and spread around me the peace and knowledge
>   that pass all the arguments of the earth,
> And I know that the hand of God is the promise of my own,
> And that all the men ever born are also my brothers, and
>   the women my sisters and lovers,
> And that a kelson of the creation is love, . . .

He wrote also of that brief meeting before her train left, "You're a
Great Soul—a Wonder Girl. How we rushed together! What a flaming
mad glad glory of a folly it has been & is & will be! . . . We stand with
a choice of forty roads. We pick one, saying, 'This is the way and the
only.' It is a winding road into an untravelled country. It is a road we
can learn only by touching the dust of it . . . Carl."

He said, "I have felt strange and unusual of late—neglected the more practical things—moved in sort of reckless and ecstatic moods—but mostly in a calm—bathed in contemplations and conjectures. . . . with you I am proud of all romance in my blood—you embody all the heroines of history to me. You are all the actresses and all the prima donnas—yet you are also Paula, Lilian, this figure caught on your brother's prints, an individual—the glad laughing girl and playmate with whom I built a House in the Woods, whom I carried over the bogs of marsh on high-windy days, going with me on every intellectual ascent, every play for foolery. . . . I might use all the superlatives of language and every caress that short Saxon words will carry to you. You are the most beautiful, graceful woman in the world, the most splendidly equipped of heart, intellect and feeling, in all the world. Yet through and over all this is better and more beautiful and inspiring—some spirit of You, quiet, homely, brooding, steady, unfaltering—always, always mantling me day and night. . . . I am committed to this thing, lost and abandoned with You—the Ideal—The Woman who has lived and knows—the Woman who understands—You."

Perhaps they had spoken of marriage. Who knows? They were lost in love. He sent her a note the day after they parted: "So here, kid, is a poem. Such a day as today during the past week would have been too much and killed us dead, for sure." And he quoted from *Romeo and Juliet* a line out of one of the notebooks he kept filled, "Well-apparelled April follows on the heels of limping Winter. The lake was so blue, such balms floated on the breezes, the sunset fell in such ruddy beauty, today. And over all of it, as a capsheaf of glory, is The Great Fact—we have met—YOU ARE!!! Cully."

She wrote, ". . . the thought of you is with me always . . . I thought of what Service we two together would do for the Cause, somehow, somewhere, sometime. We will do it! We may have to change our plans as to the *how* and the *time* and the *where*. But the Service we will render! We will! So we may walk the earth, we two, our 'sublime heads striking the stars.'" And, "Cully, are you taking care of your health? You must! . . . When you look fresh and strong, you can inspire hope and splendid discontent! But a worn-out face can't radiate hope! (All it can do is to preach self-sacrifice! And that isn't a final thing—an end!) As Cully, the one-time baseball player, you can bring such hope into the movement! . . . You know what dear old Walt says:

'Is reform needed? is it thru you?
The greater the reform needed, the greater the Personality
    you need to accomplish it.

You! do you not see how it would serve to have eyes,
    blood, complexion, clean and sweet?
Do you not see how it would serve to have such a body and
    soul that when you enter the crowd an atmosphere of
    desire and command enters with you, and everyone is
    impressed with your Personality?
O the magnet! the flesh over and over!'

. . . Thus old Walt 'To A Pupil!' And he's right . . . your body—such
a fine athletic body it is. I'm afraid you don't fully appreciate it. Take
Walt's words to heart."

It was a symbol of the eventual union of Sandburg and Steichen when
he called them the S-S. "The S-S stands for two Souls. The hyphen
means they have met and are. S-S stands for *poise*. It means intensity
and vibration and radiation but over and beyond these it places harmony
and equilibrium. Don't ever write when you're played out or needing
sleep. . . . There will be nights when I get to my room and will not
dare take a pen and talk to you—thinking, dreaming, loving, planning—
because it will mean out too late in the morning for work! On what roads
we have not yet gone in our lives we must go hand in hand guiding
each other. . . . All your pictures go up on shelves and tables the
minute I locate in a room. You are with me always as a redeeming,
transcending Presence. The intangible You floats about the room. I con-
jure scents of your hair (that copper gleam in the black!) (You posed
for Titian—I was marauding on a Viking ship but I missed you then—
That was why I kept on marauding!). Always you are with me, giving
me your smile for my failures and mistakes, accepting everything, having
seen in me as I have seen in you—a something last and final of sacred
resolve and consecrated desire—the something that gave us each a Tint
of silver in our youths—by which each interprets all that the other does,
always seeing *intentions* if not accomplishments. . . . No poem, nor
biographies will ever analyse or depict the S-S! Paraphrasing the exas-
peration of the critics who fumble in futility attempting to epitomize
the meaning of Shakespere, it will be said, 'The S-S? It *was!*' And today:
IT IS!"

He told her, "I will strike my old pace in a few days, keep up with all
district correspondence, write circular letters, and socialist stuff for newspapers, work on my three economic lectures for next winter, read to keep
in touch with the world-currents, hold noon and evening meetings, look
up professional & business men & trade-unionists who lean our way and
put the thing up to them and at least sell them a copy of Thompson's

pamphlet, solicit pledges, urge the secretaries to keep dues collected, drag delinquents back into membership, get a line on the records of congressmen & legislators for use in the fall campaign, and to keep from going crazy sit by a riverside under trees and starlight and think about this wonder and glory of You-Me—the S-S. This will all mean short notes to you, we knowing that back of the great love must be great action. . . . Carl."

Her letters were equally intense—pages and pages covered in her clear handwriting, one letter fifty pages long: "Page 50—isn't it awful!! I'll never do it again! I want to write now about the poem I got from you today—and the sweet letter to your 'delectable Liz'—but I'll leave that for another time. I *do* need sleep!"

Did she have time ever to say it all? "Such letters, Heart, such letters! What a Man you are! You are the Miracle that I have looked and looked for these years! The Miracle has come to pass . . . lo—the Ideal become Real! *You to love.* . . . Surely I am blest among women. . . . And what forces made you what you are! All those years of struggle when you were 'a heart where hope fought hard for life.' . . . When you told of the struggle of your young days, I understood! That boy-heart of yours undaunted. . . . That in spite of all and thru all you developed the genius in you, is wonderful! That you developed the heart you have . . . that is more wonderful still! . . . Soon we'll settle down again to Work and Rest and Exercise. . . . You'll work as you've never worked before—and you'll rest too and take care of your health as never before! So will I. The Commune will not be found wanting in world-service. And these days in the Clouds are needed—'it's some sort of gathering of forces'—The greatest things are doing—hidden even from us—in the dark womb of Nature. What things we know not!

"After a while will come a beautiful calm acceptance of the S-S, something really grander than this present exclamatory ecstasy! . . . You are all the separate intensities of Shelley, Bebel, Kautsky, Walt Whitman, Marx, Wagner, the Vikings, Christ, Buddha, Lincoln, Heine, Browning— you are all these separate and different intensities! But *harmonized!* Brought into equilibrium! You are *Poise!* The S-S is Poise above all things. . . . We shall do the best we can to make 'two blades of grass grow where now there is but one.' We shall do our best *to do something* —to leave some *thing* that we have produced here on earth as a bequest! But we'll remember that *the life we live* is more important than *the works we leave.* Yes. Sometime this earth and all the works upon it will be Dust—Dust—Dust! But the S-S cannot be reduced to cosmic dust! It is a Real Fact that defies dissolution! Suns and systems may perish but We-Two *Are*. This isn't mysticism. It is the very realist Truth—as true as that fundamental fact 'I am'—which is its own proof."

Would she ever finish telling him of the miracle of meeting? "The World has created us and has brought us together: it has produced the atoms and has given them to chance to unite in the S-S molecule! Our first duty is to appreciate this gift of Nature's. It has cost eons of agony and toil and blunders to fashion and shape our two atoms. And for eons Nature has sought to bring these two atoms together—but always we just missed each other and Nature was baffled for the time! Now she has achieved her purpose: *the S-S molecule is*! . . . We will give the S-S the best chance! . . . And then to do what service we can for Society! How we do not know! Whether we shall make much of a splash we don't know nor care! . . . We have 'sacred resolve and consecrated desire' in our hearts—and courage—and hope—and physical strength. 'We will do' good. Somehow. In this field or in that. Organizing, or private agitation—Editing a paper—or contributing to many papers— Poetry or the lyceum—Who knows which of these fields we will do our best work in. . . . Paula."

And my father? "Such a girl you are. . . . Poet you are too—you blow blossom-odors on your letter-pages—sweet-breathed girl. . . . Had a Bohemian dinner this noon—really Bohemian—the comrade's name is *Kratochvil*. . . . Doughballs, roast pork with carroway seed & black gravy, sour cabbage, a bottle of beer, coffee-cake and black coffee—a symposium right from Prague itself—the stuff they build *Kubeliks* of—you vegetarian!—Then I walked two hours in the sun & wind. . . . Carl."

She said, "Have played all day—went to the woods at nine this morning with a flock of children—little girls, preps and freshmen, about a dozen. Stayed till five in the evening. We picked flowers—mostly hepaticas (I inclose a few—pressed) . . . such a variety of hues in them— some deep purple, some white with a spirit of a purple tint just suggested—some pale pink—some lavender—some blue and more blue—some purest white. . . . And such fragrance—not heavy and voluptuous—but hardy and bitter-sweet with all the vigor of March winds and the strong tang of a succulent green thing that has sprouted in forest mold! No pampered hot-house flower—this child of March winds and April sunshine! . . . If we had had a woods like this at the farm—and such weather as this—my God!—it would have been something all but 'beyond human power.' Bryants Woods is a winding ravine, a stream meandering thru the bottom, with side-ravines and tributary brooks branching off— the banks of the ravines very high and finely wooded with beautiful old trees and young ones scattered between and lots of underbrush, the banks sloping gradually sometimes, but mostly sheer and steep, or terraced. Imagine these winding ravines flooded with sunshine—swept by strong yet sun-warmed winds—fragrant with spring-odors of earth and flowers. Hear now the poignant call of a bird from the shadows of some side-ravine—or now the tinkle of the brook clear and sweet below. . . . Sometime we must pitch our tent in some sweet sunny spot like this! . . . We had each an orange and as many egg-sandwiches as we wanted! And it was a good dinner. We enjoyed each mouthful—masticating thoroughly in true Fletcher style! . . . No more tonight. I must make up sleep. I'm recovering my equilibrium again in the matter of taking care of my health. . . . I think we-two are the sort who will do our best work between forty and sixty—if we don't spend our strength recklessly. We-two have good constitutions and fairly good physical-culture habits as a basis for a long life. I said long *life*—not merely long *existence*. We have kept our childhood long—we should keep our prime long. . . . Goodnight! My Poet! Lilian."

Did my mother, in the way often of women, make the decision that she wanted to be with my father and not off teaching another year at Princeton? She would be twenty-five on the first of May. She said that the "*how* and the *time* and the *where*" ought to be soon. So they picked a date—the end of her school term. He wrote, "You're such a devil, regular she-devil, of a socialist; & then such an individual, artist (Miss L.S.), wild girl (Fanchon), merry girl (Kitty), sweet woman (Flavia), whatever there may be of privation in material living (knocking around barnstorming as Minnie Maddern, Bernhardt, Maude Adams & all the stars did), won't equal the deprivation, the want of avenues for expression, in your life should you teach another year.—And I, I know I'll NEVER be any better prepared to live the Life-With-You than *now*. I burn up vitality & live intensely—so the longer we wait, the poorer prepared I am . . . VII!—one finger less each week! Then the leap! Then the scramble up the bank of the other side of the Rubicon, marching in the dust and sun, loafing in blue twilights and sleeping under the trees & stars. . . . You're the Soul of All Great Romance or you wouldn't dare! . . . Carl."

At the farm my father had spoken to my mother of his few close friends—Professor Wright, Joseffy, Rube Borough. She talked about the house they'd have: "And then for a roof—four walls of a room—three chairs (one for you and one for me and one for company—Joseffy or Rube or some other of our Comerados)—also a hat-rack!—and a breadbox!—and an ash-tray!—and some bowl or glass for wild flowers! Oh—and of course—a coffee-pot!! . . . Very likely I could get pupils in

Oshkosh too—to eke out what income we get from the movement. But the ideal thing would be if I could help swell the income from the work in the movement, so I wouldn't have to do any or not much tutoring—for tutoring is mere money-getting, like stereoptician-selling—not work, service. . . . I'd rather be *most* poor so we gave the S-S the best chance, than live comfortably but at the risk of the highest development of the S-S in love and service."

My father seems not to have said a word to his family or friends back in Galesburg. "My folks I shall calmly inform when it is all over. Merely more of the unexpected which they regularly expect! Charlie has been so queer in his tastes—they will look so and so at you when we go to Galesburg one day! Gee! that will be fun—and downtown and at the college they will look and they will find you baffling and only sense something of power and beauty & wisdom & love—something as far-off and cross-textured as my poetry and warm and open as myself. They won't understand you anymore than me—but they will love you—yes, you will be good for them! A few, a precious few, homely and yearning —O so yearning—will understand. My mother out of her big, yearning, hungry heart will hug you before you leave and with a crystal of tears will find the soul of you. Mary & Esther and Martha will all like you deep—but they have not starved so hard nor prayed so vainly—they will get only sides of you. We should have a whole day with Wright (The Dreamer) of Asgard—he will do us a poem!"

As for my mother, she told everybody, including their mutual friends at the Social-Democratic headquarters in Milwaukee. She wrote my father that Miss Thomas had "changed her mind about your talking over the heads of the workingman. . . . I inclose letter received today from Miss Thomas. You see she 'gives us both her blessin'.'" And of Victor Berger, "He said you weren't good enough for me! But when I put it up to him straight—he had to say, 'Honest—I don't know him.' . . . My hope is that B will like you—that you'll work together well. B likes me—so if he's just he must like you." And then she wrote of hearing from Oma, who had had dinner with the Victor Bergers in Milwaukee: "In mother's letter that I got today she mentions something that B said . . . to the effect that we ought to wait a number of years, not only that then our growth would be finished and so we could perhaps choose mates that would be endurable for life, but also that you might work up to a securer position by that time. And mother adds: 'But I don't agree with him. . . . It doesn't matter much about "securer positions"—if Carl is "good to you" that's what counts.' . . . I understand dear comrade-mother! Thru thick and thin she's backed us up.—

And now she understands me—understands that we are happy and that We-Two are One. And she knows that that's the best thing in life. . . . I told father. He grumbles and acquiesces. . . . Of course he thinks we ought to wait and wait and wait—until the coal-cellar is filled with fuel, and the larder with food, and the money-bag with shekels!—But I put it to Pa kindly but firmly that *that* was our business. . . . And personally he really likes you! You have tact, man! And that's the way—Pa has his points and I want him to be as happy over my forth-going as can be! . . . I received a gratulatory note from dear Edward today. . . . How I wish Ed could have seen more and more of you—the Cully in you! The time was too short. We are going to have great times together yet!—So much and so much before us! . . . Now I've written Ed just today that we have decided to have the marriage this summer. And I've asked him 'how about finances?' Now we'll wait and sip our coffee the while! . . . If Ed can't help out the finances—my little hoard of $400 more or less will be devoted to that end. To make it dead sure—secure mother against the chance of this hoard being lost in a busting bank—I could put it in postal money orders in the box mother and I have in a Safety Deposit Vault in Milwaukee! We could marry with clear conscience—with mother provided for for this year and next. . . . Pshaw! It's so dead easy!—But I didn't realize before that you had enough resources to be able to cope with the baby-possibility within the year. But you can. It's all right, old pal! My I'm happy! For I *don't want to wait*! LIZ."

And my uncle, how did he take the news from my energetic mother who never wrote letters not spangled with exclamation marks? He was bound for France and had planned to have Oma and Mother come over to Voulangis during the coming summer holiday. His little daughter, Cousin Mary, was nearly four, and Clara was expecting another child in late May—the one they wanted to be a boy to name Auguste. My mother would never get there. Uncle Ed wrote from on board the Dampfer *Kaiser Wilhelm II,* a ship of Bremen, "Dear Paus'l, Just a hasty line before the pilot leaves the steamer. I simply have not had a chance to write. You are evidently in a bad way as far as being in love is concerned. Prosit. Do just as your heart dictates if your good sense will permit you, and then it is sure to be all right. At any rate you have only yourself to be responsible for. Of course I will always be on hand when I possibly can to fill in the cash account on the farm. Your reducing the whole thing to an even 300 is a demonstration of your impracticalness. Have they ever done it for a year on anything like that. —The exhibition was more of a success than I had hoped and I can see my way clear for another year and of course that means that I can also take care of Ma & Pa.—I am sending Ma a check for $200.00 now. As for all the rest that will be taken care of. I had planned to have you and Ma come over to Paris for the vacation weeks but your wedding changes that. And I am sure you will all have a full summer with that. I am glad for you, Paus'l and *hope* it will turn out right, hope oh so hard— and love you. Ed."

In her same mail was a letter from my father in his hotel room in Two Rivers, Wisconsin. Was it in the least concerned with money or practicalities? "Just had a five-mile hike—over sandy hills wild & wind-beaten—and into pine woods along the lake shore. Grand somber glooms under wide branches, thickets & pools, & all the weird orchestration of frogs, crickets, night-birds, & what-nots with tongues & throats & voices. A bog kept me from reaching the shore. I could hear the surge. . . . So I took a seat (nobody asked me, Kitty, I wanted it & just took it—that's the way with S-S!) Yes I took a seat on a mossy, big log and lit a cigar. I read out loud to the tintinabulation of the frogs some lyrics to you. Some were original and some not so original but they were all lyrics! I spoke them to You—the 'rhythmic time of the metronome of want' was in them—the want of *You* to be there—warm hand & wild hair and good face. The shadows had come a-creepin', slow and quiet but sure as shadows. The dusk had fallen all around when I was getting the last puffs on the cigar. I looked up at the sky and startlingly near, thru the green-black boughs of a massive pine was a burning, glowing star, a glittering, melting, concentrated flame seen thru this one hole in the roof of the forest. I called out to the Booger-Man, 'You know the name o' that star?' 'No.' said the Booger-Man. 'Well,' I said, 'You Ignorance! You, if anybody asks you, the name o' that star is *Paula!*' And the Booger-Man mumbled something and took hisself back where he come from. Wouldn't talk no more! Whatdye think o' that? . . . Good-night, Paula, my great-heart—it's a night of grandeurs—and you are its star . . . the last glory of this night of glories. Carl."

What was my mother's mind on? Not fanciful notions like my father's, but rather a romantic wedding. "Do you think the knot had better be tied in Milwaukee? . . . Here's my picture of the 'nuptial rites solemnized' at the farm. Gaylord and Thompson arrive about 11 P.M. . . . received with glad gay shouts—rah-rahing etc!—trumpets—yawps!—'any noise good or bad.' Then maybe we'd all take a look at Pa's corn and potatoes—see how they're doing—discuss whether it's a good potato year or not!!—too wet or too dry!! etc! etc!!! Then dinner. . . . Then a walk thru Zimmer's orchard—Thompson would be moved to talk about the farmer question—agrarianism. . . . And when Thompson & Gaylord felt

they had enough of tramping—were ready for work—back we'd hike . . .
and under our own apple trees maybe—or in the arbor—with as much
despatch as pleased the 'holy man' who officiates, the knot should be
tied! You in your blue shirt, sleeves rolled up—Kitty dressed ready for a
romp over the hills. . . . I confess it would be a lark too to just go to
Milwaukee off-hand and do the thing up still more simply—if possible.
. . . Paula."

My father was still out there, walking the lonely Wisconsin lake
countryside. In his room, he wrote her, penciling sheet after sheet of
notepaper, unable to stop himself, "Back from a long hike again—sand
and shore, night and stars and this restless inland sea. . . . On the left
a ridge of jaggedly outlined pines, their zigzag jutting up into a steel-
grey sky—under me and ahead a long brown swath of sand—to the right
the ever-repelled but incessantly charging white horses and beyond an
expanse of dark—but over all, sweeping platoons of unguessable stars!
Stars everywhere! Blinking, shy-hiding gleams—blazing effulgent beacons
—an infinite, travelling caravanserie—going somewhere! 'Hail!' I called,
'Hail! do you know? do you know? You veering cotillions of worlds beyond this world—you marching, imperturbable splendors—you serene,
everlasting spectators—where are we going? do you know?' And the
answer came back, 'No, we don't know and what's more, we don't care!'
And I called, 'You answer well. For you are time and space—you are
tomb and cradle. Forever you renew your own origin, shatter to-day
and reshape to-morrow, in a perpetual poem of transformations, knowing
no goal, expecting no climax, looking forward to no end, indulging in
no conception of a finale, content to move in the eternal drama on which
no curtain will be rung. You answer well. I salute you to-night. I will
see you again and when I do again I will salute you for you are sincere.
I believe you O stars! and I know you! We have met before and met
many times.'—All this time I was striding along at a fast pace, to the
music of the merry-men. The merry-men, I forgot to explain, ride the
white horses and it is the merry-men who give voice to the ecstasy and
anger and varying humor of the sea. The tumultuous rhythms of the
merry-men and a steady, ozone-laden wind had me to walk fast and
when I turned from the sea, there burst upon my vision, the garish
arc-lamps of the municipality of Two Rivers. So I turned to the sky and
said, 'Good-by, sweet stars! I have had good companionship with you
to-night but now I must leave starland, and enter the corporation limits
of Two Rivers town. Remember me O stars! and remember Paula down
in Princeton, Illinois! and if any agitators appear in starland, let them
agitate—it will be good for them and for all the little stars.' And as I

plodded down a narrow street past the hovels of fishermen and the tenements of factory workers, I quoted from the barefooted, immortal Athenian, 'The gods are on high Olympus—let them stay there.' Yes, let the gods who are on high Olympus stay where they belong. And let us turn to the business of rearing on earth a race of gods. There—it's out of me, Pal. It was a glorious hike. I shall sleep and sleep to-night. And you are near to-night . . . My Lilian—Carl."

Had he finished there in the dark of night in the small room, having filled twelve pages? Could he leave the table where he wrote and go to sleep? Wasn't there more to say to cover eight more pages with his pencil? "P.S.: P.S.S.!—No, I will never get The Letter written & finished. It will always need postscripts. I end one and six minutes after have to send more. All my life I must write at this Letter—this Letter of Love to the Great Woman Who Came and Knew and Loved. All my life this must go on! The Idea and the Emotion are so vast it will be years and years in issuing. Ten thousand love-birds, sweet throated and red-plumed, were in my soul, in the garden of my under-life. There on ten thousand branches they slept as in night-time. You came and they awoke. For a moment they fluttered distractedly in joy at stars and odors and breezes. And a dawn burst on them—a long night was ended. God! how they sang. God! The music of those throats—such dulcets and diapasons of song as they sang! I hear them & I know them. These birds want freedom. These imprisoned songsters are all to be loosed. But I can let out only one at a time. Each letter, then, is some joy till now jailed—but now sent flying—and flying and flying!—at the touch of release, called out by The Woman Who Came. So Paula, you have letters and letters to come—and we will send birds, love-birds with love-songs, flying out over the world. We cannot live the Sheltered Life, with any bars up. It is us for The Open Road—loosing the birds—loosing the birds! Jesus wept, Voltaire smiled, William Morris worked, the S-S flung the world twenty-thousand beautiful, vibrating, fleeting, indomitable, happy love-birds singing love-songs swelling the world's joy."

She wrote with her mind on a picture of what the future would clearly be: "As for household goods—I say: *as little as possible*! I like the way the Japs have!—I have such supreme contempt for even the better class of furniture produced by our Occidental Civilization, that it will be no deprivation for me if we never *never* own a piece of it!! When the time comes that we feel we *have* to own a few things why 'all right' —'What must be, must' you know! But neither of us has a hankering *after the stuff*! I have a way of comparing frescoed ceilings with the sky set with stars—Orion & the rest—that always nips in the bud any possible infringement on my part on the 10th commandment 'thou shalt not covet thy neighbor's goods!' The sky is the big arched ceiling—the only one in the world big enough for us anyway—(we who strike the very stars with our sublime heads!!)—the sky is the really beautiful ceiling that's ours for the looking, since we have eyes that see. With such eyes as we have our only difficulty will be not being able to enter into possession of all the things that *are* really ours—ours for the mere looking. We won't have time enough to walk over all the land we really *own* (because we have power to appreciate it!) we won't have time to walk to the ends of our domain—says the Duchess to her lord, the Duke of Buckingham-and-eggs! . . . Paula."

And then Mother began bordering on making an issue with my father about her role in their marriage. I have always known her as totally female, her power over my father continuous and subtle. There never were loud arguments back and forth in our house. My father raged and roared, and often. But it was one way. She coaxed him out of it. When he was very old, I saw them standing in the kitchen together. He had pulled at a door handle which stuck. He rattled it and shouted. A small woman, she looked up at him and patted his chest, "What a fine strong voice!" Disarmed, he stood there in love. It was a thread established early and woven through their life.

Back then, she said, "I might try writing on 'Art and Life'!" And again, "I made a start on 'Woman and Socialism' this evening. Just sketched it out. Had to stop because my brain got tired . . . when I'm rested I'll attack 'Socialism & Woman' again. . . . Together we ought to make something really worth while. . . . And for the district, if only I can make good, Cully! As a speaker, I mean! That would be great—great— GREAT." About the play she coached for her Sophomores, she said, "The Play was a brilliant success!—Also I made an after-dinner speech . . . which was applauded and applauded and applauded . . . who knows? —maybe I *can* do things that amount to something in the ten minute speech line. . . . Hum, Carl? . . . I haven't been able to work on that 'Woman and Socialism' paper yet! It always seems just ahead—the time for it! . . . It can wait a little—can't it? . . . love and love."

She wrote on and on, setting straight the position she wanted for herself. "Do you know, Carl, I've never once told 'a good story?' Never once! —Not even in conversation, I mean. Now, *are* you disillusioned? What hopes are there on the platform for one who can't tell a good story!! . . . it's not my fault that you will persist in thinking I have real abilities. Didn't I protest at the very start that I was no woman-genius, but a mere-woman! . . . I've met second-rate geniuses of the Petticoat sex, enough and to spare. (I don't think they count for much—they are simply second-rate or fourth-rate *men* in petticoats.) . . . Women are physiologically, I believe, constituted to excel in power to *love*—while man is physiologically constituted to excel in power to *work* . . . women will never equal men in any field of *work*. That's not saying that the sex is inferior. . . . I say all this talk about inequality of man & woman is due to muddled brains—lack of clear thinking. . . . We're equal, Pal! Do you hear? Equal even tho I can't write poems! Some day I'll give you a demonstration of heart-power—there will be times to test my woman's soul. . . . I am your equal mate, because I can follow you to your heighths & depths, as your comrade-mate because I can appreciate *all you do,* tho I cannot do as well myself. . . . I want you to accept me as I am—not to imagine that I am more—perhaps a genius. I know I'm not a genius. The poems of the S-S will be *written* by the Sandburg-S tho the Steichen-S will help with inspiration and love. . . . And the Steichen-S will do some good general organization work—planning—correspondence—circular letters—etc. etc. . . . Paula has spoken! . . . *You* must understand, even if the rest don't. About the rest I care very little— whether they understand or not. . . . You mustn't have any illusions about me. See? Else you would be loving some Paula-phantasm, not the real Paula—not *me.* I shall never write for print. I feel as sure of this *now* as of anything that refers to the future. Absolutely positive. As far as I am concerned it is settled. I'm glad that it's settled. Tho it's a disappointment—for from childhood I had 'literary aspirations.' . . . The problem of life is to find your sphere—find what you *are* qualified to do and then do it. When you're working at what you *are* qualified to do, work is a joy though it be only sewing on buttons. But trying to do what is beyond you, is sheer agony.

"Do you understand, Carl? This means somewhat. It's a serious matter. You must get readjusted to this decision of mine. . . . I write no leaflet. I write no review of Hunter's Socialists at Work. I write *nothing* for print—not *now* nor hereafter. . . . I can lead a discussion! And I can help with the correspondence. Also I'll be able to sell literature—tho *what degree* of success I'll have in this we can't tell till I actually try it this summer. But I've sold hats—so I ought to be able to sell literature about which I know so much more! . . . Now do write me that you understand."

And my father? He said it was fine with him. "Getting ready for the meeting to-night kept me from writing. What the hell do I care whether you go in for literary work or not? Don't we each give the other free loose for anything & everything? We go we know not whither? All I know is you are a great woman, a splendid girl. In some way you will express yourself. <u>you</u> *decide on the way*. . . . What would I be to insist that I know the road of expression You should move along? Great you are—great, beautiful, inclusive, daring, quick, original. You are big enough to do as you dam please. I would rather be a poem like you than write poems. I would rather embody the big things as you do than carve or paint or write them. You inspire art—& that's living! You may cut out writing, but Paula—please don't say you'll never pull my hair nor improve my MSS nor a hundred different things I'm too sleepy to name! Love, Paula. Carl."

It was true that she had chosen her way. It has been said by some that my mother's talents were turned aside by the power of my father's genius. I never thought it was so, but in these segments from her letters of this time, it seems clear that she made her own decision. Because my mother took an ancient female way, insisting on his dominant role in their life, she may have been wise. I know it made their home a tranquil one.

Eleven

The Rubicon

How can there be suspense in looking into the past? The story has already been told. Did I want to be assured of what I thought to be the truth? It was near mid-May in 1908 when my mother wrote my father, "The way to learn how is to jump in and swim. In the end we'll make it, all right. If no other way then along the Starvation Road! Other great souls have won out that way! Browning recommends it. . . . It was the road Marx took! (. . . maybe you think Marx was a celibate! Maybe you think Marx had a comfortable bank account!!! Study the life of your Prophet! and cease doubting!!)."

My father, who'd not had a bank account as yet in his thirty years and who would always leave the family finances to my mother, wrote, "Paula . . . I'm sending a five with this—it leaves me broke—but I can't raise money when I *have* money—and I'm going to try to have $50 or more for starting. We'll make a compact that all money from literature sales will go into the Baby-Fund—it should range around $15 or $20 a month & increase at that. I'll turn over some dust to you every once in a while if not twice, all that there is to spare over our material needs— if we ever save anything, ever have a good bank-account or not—that's up to you, after the stuff is once in—and the stuff will come in, eventually. We are about where Gaesjack(?) was the day before he sauntered into Stieglitz office the first time—so."

She said, "I'm getting a few more clothes made in view of the fact that we must live in a couple of dress-suit cases for the summer . . . a trunk is *out of the question*. . . . And if you're broke, you know I hold the S-S funds in trust. We have $28.00 (I don't believe I told you that I got the Five you sent from Appleton all right) . . . don't work too hard to make our funds $50.00 to start on. We can start on less—and why shouldn't I have the fun of adding a little to the Starter-Fund. Why?"

They spoke of a child, my father telling her, "*Plant* that fund of yours where it's absolutely safe—and it's not to be thought of except for last & unforseen contingencies—call it the Desperation-Fund. The Baby-Fund will grow—and such a Baby! such a Baby as it will be—such a reckless cub—never to hear a 'Don't'—learning fire by getting burnt—getting religion & ethics & love-powers from our kiss-microbes—never knowing *he's* (or *she's*) being educated—just living & unfolding—such a cub! . . . Carl."

The story unravels in their words that went back and forth daily, from my mother teaching in Princeton and my father going from town to town. She wrote, "It's up to you now. From my angle of vision I see no IF. . . . And you, Carl, haven't hinted that you saw any IF from your own angle of vision. . . . We ask for so little of the things that cost money. We have your room now. I have clothes to last awhile. And I can live and *thrive* on a diet of bread and peanuts and walks and fresh air!— Surely I'll be able to do enough for the district to compensate it for at least enough bread & peanuts and water and fresh air to sustain life in me!"

Her next letter went, "And this morning came your letter saying 'There's nothing left to consider' . . . I haven't told mother yet that we are planning to be married so early this summer. I had a letter from her to-day in which she speaks of some sewing that she and I could do toward the trousseau!!—I see I'll have to do some explanationing! What do *we-two* want with a *trousseau*! Ain't it? . . . I don't believe I need anything at all in the way of new dresses—unless there's something you particularly want me to have—something you have a particular fancy for. If so, let me know *now*—and I'll have it made here."

And then telling him, "The Rubicon *is* crossed. Paula has done with every last shadow of a But or an If. . . . Paula is willing to starve—to take in washing, if need be! But Paula is *not* willing to live the lie of separation. . . . Privation and toil—*anything*—she's equal to, only she must be *along*!"

"Just a wee note, dear sailor girl," he said, "I'm plugging away at several things now, that I want to get out of the way before the bigger togetherness begins. . . . Yes, buy *good* clothes—they can be hocked in emergencies. People enjoy a certain carelessness in dress about a man, the which is unforgiveable in a woman. . . . Difficulty we will know— But defeat—never—never! Free and large and lavish, we shall insolently and triumphantly sail and sail."

She wrote, "Together, we-two! Yes, and ready for any luck! . . . Such a glad mad sweet world! And whatever crag-born agony may come to us, the world will still look good—we will see the meaning and understand and love the more for it."

My father asked Carl Thompson from the Social-Democratic Party headquarters to marry them. Thompson was a minister as well as a party officer and national committeeman. And my father wrote that he'd told "Win" Gaylord of their plans and Gaylord said "Good! You won't be sorry." They wanted him at the ceremony too. "You're a wonder! my thaumaturgist!" my father wrote, "I like your picture of the wedding doings at the farm—it would please your mother better probably than any other plan—I had thought of our taking a car out to Thompson or Gaylord—get the knot tied much as we might wash our hands at a wayside hotel—a few minutes chat—a stop and chat at T., or G., whichever lost the toss (!), attend to business and greetings at headquarters and then ho! northward! . . . If Joseffy has no Chautauqua dates then, I will have him on hand, with the skull of Balsamo, and the violin."

He liked his work. In the men my father met and talked with, and in the outdoors he continually walked through, he found his themes for his poetry and prose. "The district has so much of natural beauty, Lilian. That was one of the things attracted me up here. All nationalities are represented in it. You will find wilderness unspoiled in Ocanto. You will find civilization at its best and worst along the Fox River—black, choking industrialism, and libraries, concerts, women's clubs and art from Schumann-Heink to 5¢ vaudeville. All big, pulsing, turbulent, panoramic! I have for it all the passion & enthusiasm Walt had for

'Proud, mad city! my city!
O Manahatta! My Manahatta!'

And all our efforts, dear, will be cumulative—the more we do the more we can do along any line. Our income will always be on the increase. Continued agitation and organization will familiarize us intimately with the various situations making us increasingly competent to advise, guide & direct the comrades. Loyal, whole-hearted friends, like bitter, implacable enemies, will constantly multiply. Such a trip as it will be."

And she said, "The Dutch-Ess will work up a little 10-minute German talk to warm the hearts of the clamorous Dutchmen who want a German organizer! Ya! Ya! We're the 'Internationale' allright! When you get your Swede talk ready—and I my German talk—we can give them a sort of club-sandwich—the Swede & German talks sandwiched in between

142

your English Oratory and Mine!" She spoke of Oma saying that "she feels she is losing her little girl etc. etc. etc!" So that he replied, "To her girl, the Golden Girl, the dear mother is beginning to cry 'So Long!'? Wonderful Mother—and Wonderful Daughter. It's a rare thing—so deep and close a chumminess—with such a foundation in the things that are everlasting. She was one of the factors in That Week at 'the dear little, white little house'—as unique in her way as you. I said to you, 'She's Whitmanic.' And she is. Nothing but the Limit, the farthest and highest, for her boy and girl. Nothing but the Limit for herself, working in the scope of her chances. A rapt enthusiast, giving all, risking all, and no surety of returns."

My father always held Oma in a kind of awe. She was "The She-wolf." He spoke of her to Mother: "If there's anything in the story that a Recording Angel puts down all the 'good' and the 'bad' we do, how easily and calmly she could look that R.A. in the eyes! . . . I think her mother-heart sensed it that I'm the kind of a boy the girl she reared ought to have. I know her. I had that wave of feeling toward her and I believe she's toward me as I am toward her. So that she knows the S-S is wise, that else is impossible. And this in the long run may be true too: That she not only not loses her Golden Girl but is gainer by an attachment, a companion piece which goes with the Golden Girl! She not only keeps Lily, the choicest book in her library of life, but she gets a Volume Two!—Not a whole Volume maybe, but a kind of glossary, something that will show her new meanings in Lily, the G.G.! All this in the long run, by the big way, the far look! She will understand if the love for her girl is as big as the wide, fine life she has lived. Even so."

My mother was restless off there at school. "I study and study the calendar these days hoping that I can find some way of figuring it so that the time of waiting won't seem so long. But no matter how I count the time, it's sure to come out too long. . . . I hope you'll find time to run out to the farm for a day. Telephone mother from Mil. or from Menomonee Falls or from Hartford, or write her—R.R. 17, Menomonee Falls."

My father did find time. Oma was noted for her argumentative spirit and she looked ahead to the visits of the radical poet organizer soon to be her son-in-law. She liked the cooking and serving of food too. My father wrote from the farm, "What with yesterday afternoon & last night (it was 11:30 for the mother and me) & walking in to M. Falls this morning . . . the air is all flying ribbons and clashing melodies, warbling birds, brass bands—Ess-esses!—wild circles! . . . A beautiful day here at 'the farm.' We were going to sing 'The Vacant Chair' but nobody remembered the air. Out on the parade-ground (between the studio & the garden, you remember) a bright half-moon shines down, a big silver star burns and flares as for joy—all is balm & quiet. . . . Paula, I can't write seriously here. I'm careless—careless! It's the woods and the You-You! that's lingering around here. Always, Carl."

He told her that there would be a Social-Democratic convention in Chicago on the sixteenth of May and he'd been elected a fourth alternate delegate. "On the go, on the go all the time. But Paula, Paula, I wish I could have been with you— . . . I had just so much time to see so many people that had to be seen to-day, or you would have gotten a regular cyclopedia of inquiry & murmurings. . . . A *Mr.* Stewart here, who is 'a literary man' & has stuff regularly in the Atlantic and Century (Lord help him!) says I present a fine life-philosophy in splendid English (I was so pleased he should approve of my English—him a-writin' for the Atlantic) and sublime force, but that I don't interpret W., who was such a egotist; that what I say of W. might all cling about an old cook-stove! so—Mister Stewart is unique." My father asked my mother to come along to the Chicago convention if she would. "Whatever Paula's heart tells her. . . . love and love . . . Breath of my Breath—Heart of my Heart! . . . Carl."

My mother said she would come to Chicago, wild to see him. "Just Thursday to live thru—then Friday and I'm off to Chi.! Will you be at the Union depot at 9:30? Or are there night sessions too at Brand's Hall? And if I'm to pilot myself to Brand's Hall—tell me about where it is— street & cross-street. Hope this reaches you Thursday morning or noon. Would like to get a reply so as to know whether to expect to be met by you at the depot in Chi. . . . Lilian."

An unhurried man, my father always arrived at train stations and airports at the last moment. He looked forward to the leisurely trip over to Chicago from Milwaukee by boat, telling my mother, "This is the 5th time I have made this trip—each time marking varied epochs. And never was life bigger, both with clash & conflict, but with the fine lure of beauty & far stars. . . . It was 'worth the money' to hear your mother call me 'Carl.' You have been doing some sort of educating sure! . . . At present looking, some of the Wis. delegates will not be at the convention all the time, which will mean, I sit & vote & see & absorb & refrain from expostulation, muttering Paul Jones, 'I have not yet begun to fight.' "

He wrote her, "(Lights of red & white along the river flash into the dusk. The water repeats each of them instantly, as tho, 'Hello, hello Night!' The materialities may not have a language but they seem almost to talk to each other.) . . . Miss Thomas is *so* good with me—as tho you had helped her see things—trifles of solicitude she never evinced before. —Is thinking about us. Murmurs a fear that the district finances will not

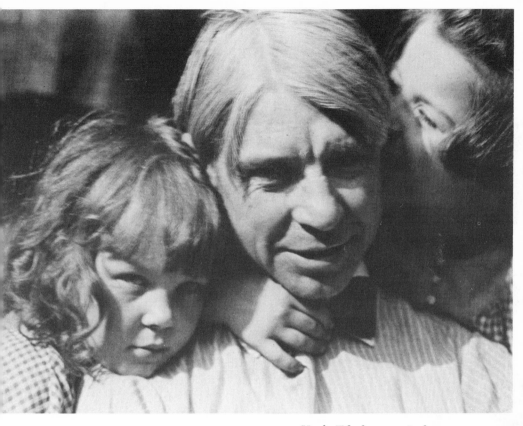

Uncle Ed photographed me on
my father's shoulder, and
Janet whispering in his ear.

My Swedish grandfather and grandmother,
August and Clara Sandburg.

My Luxembourg grandfather, Opa,
with the family cow.

Eugene Debs is holding the rose
I have given him, 1924.

Grandma Sandburg and me,
posing for a picture in
the Elmhurst garden.

Uncle Ed and my mother in 1886—he is about seven and she about three.

My father on his graduation from grammar school in 1891.

My father's friend, Frederick Dickinson, standing beside him, Lombard College, 1901.

My father at Lombard College, listed then as Charles August Sandburg, 1900.

My uncle photographed my father when
he met him for the first time at the
farmhouse in Menomonee Falls, 1908.

My father is about thirty years old here.

Mother in a school play, about 1898.

A photograph by Uncle Ed of himself and my mother in 1900 before he left for Europe and fame.

When Uncle Ed left for Europe in 1900, he sent a postcard home of himself
with his friend, Carl Björncrantz, on the French steamer, Champlain.

A self-portrait
by my uncle,
Edward Steichen,
in the 1920s.

Mother's chicken project got a
write-up in the Milwaukee *Journal*
in September, 1910.

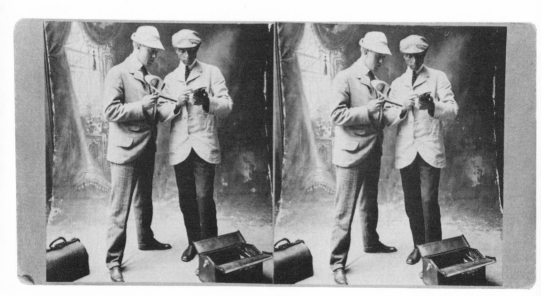

Frederick Dickinson and my father
sold stereographs for the Underwood
and Underwood Company, 1902.

My uncle sketching on his
bicycle trip from the port
of Le Havre to Paris, 1900.

My mother, Miss Lilian Steichen,
photographed by my uncle on
the farmhouse steps, about 1906.

Opa with Mother who is holding
Margaret, at the farm, 1911.

My sister Janet in the
Elmhurst garden, about 1920.

My mother, about
thirty-three years
of age, holding
my sister, Janet.

Margaret, Janet and me at
Williams Bay in the 1920s.

During World War I,
Uncle Ed came home
to visit my Luxembourg
grandmother, Oma.

My sister Margaret,
eight years old, with
me at eighteen months.

Mayor Emil Seidel
appointed my father
his secretary in 1910.

My father as City Hall
reporter in Milwaukee.

Edward Steichen at thirty years
of age—*l'Enfant Terrible* of
the photographic world.

My father in his forties—
the People's Poet.

My mother with Margaret
and her monkey, about 1915.

My father, Grandma Sandburg,
me and my doll, Betsy.

With my father on the swing
in the Elmhurst yard.

With my father in the garden at Elmhurst.

Uncle Ed took a picture of us at our
Lake Michigan sand dune home: me,
Janet, my father, my mother, Margaret.

be large enough (she didn't say for what!) & intimates that I deserve more speaking dates outside the district. We will do the best we can with what we have to work with. We will surprise them in increase of income. But always the literature sales go to the Emergency Fund—and if the rest is not enough, from elsewhere more will have to come. . . . It's almost dark. After the boat starts, at 8:30, I shall walk & breathe for an hour & then turn in. I've got plans & details of plans for several things. We will talk about 'em."

And there was my mother. "Yesterday evening I wrote you definitely about my train. I gave the letter to someone to mail it for me. They *may* have forgotten to do it. So here are duplicate 'instructions'! I arrive on Burlington train at Union depot, Chi., 9:30 Friday. If you're not there, I'll wait for you—unless I get different 'instructions' from the Dook meantime . . . Lilian."

But, as was usual with "the Dook," my father, he arrived at the depot just as she came from the train, bag in hand. She told me of that time long years later, how she'd thought of separate hotel rooms, but how he'd said they'd share one and save money, as "Mr. and Mrs. Charles Sandburg." The schedule at the convention was a busy one and she stayed with him all of the time, due back in Princeton on the late Sunday night train.

They slept together in a double bed during the two nights. They called the room their "home," and while they were in love, my mother said they didn't have intercourse. When I asked her why, she said they wanted to wait until their wedding, which was to happen so soon. They lay in each other's arms and it seemed enough, she said. They were totally content. My parents naturally made a couple. When troubles came up in their lives, my father said later to me, "I'd tell your mother to come lie down. 'Put your head on my shoulder and we'll talk it out.'" That's the way it was.

Back in Princeton on Monday, she wrote him in the evening, "I am so sleepy I can't write—can't keep my eyes open—understand your condition Saturday morning when you were *so* sleepy—You—My Boy. Good-night! It's no use trying to write—This is just to tell you that I'm sleepy, sleepy, sleepy. My Boy, my Boy—I love you and kiss you—Goodnight!" And then, "It's the Presence, Carl . . . You with me! . . . you left some visible tokens—mementos—of wolf-tooth love! You! And Kitty is glad for it! Glad for the unsightly blemishes! the black and blue marks! You—you're going to be arraigned in court for cruelty to animals! Micky Malone! Says Kitty."

A day later, ". . . those two honey-sweet days in Chicago. You with me! . . . These two mad feverish days together—such days to look back to and live over again! But what will the real life together be. . . . No feverish haste then—but time for the whole gamut of love to be sung! . . . Carl at Chicago was dearer than Carl at the farm. The more we know the more we love. The acme is always ahead. We'll never reach the mountain peak! (There'll never be the other side—the down-grade!) Always you shall be dearer and still dearer at each further revelation! . . . Cully, that $4.00 makes it $34.00. But you let me put 6 to it and call it 40.00. It won't be 'me' that's putting the 6 to it—*you saved me that much in Chicago*—so the 6 are *really* from you. So it's 40.00."

He sent her a poem called "You."

> You are slanting sun across the dark,
> You are dew and calm and fragrance,
> You are fire and gold and sunset peace,
>   You lure and you lead
> And the look of your eye is light
> On the path of the dream we dream.
>
> The touch of your hand is hope
> And the sheen of your hair is glory.
> You are the sea with its mystic song,
> You are the stars and dawn and morning.
> You are a woman, you are a comrade
> We will do, we will hope, we will live,
> We will rest in the hearts of remembering men
> Who saw us as we passed.

My father seems to have had a curious shyness about my mother. He didn't tell Grandfather or Grandma Sandburg of their wedding plans. When he'd visited the Steichen farm during the Great Week, he never mentioned a word about her when he wrote Professor Wright of the "Muldoon life," implying rather that he was there as a friend of Uncle Ed's. When Rube Borough wrote of those days, he said the marriage of my parents was "without a previous word of warning to me."

There was to be a Social-Democratic state convention in Milwaukee on the thirteenth and fourteenth of June, and my father wrote Aunt Esther, who'd been finding fault with him for not communicating with the family, "You wouldn't reproach me with not writing you if you knew how lean I am and how I am plugging away day & night for socialism & the socialist party up here. You will come to see some day, my dear girl, why almost all the great artists, painters, musicians & dramatists, are socialists or in sympathy with us. Socialism, if you will look into it, you will find means greater art—more of music for more people. . . . I do wish you could arrange to come to Milwaukee for the S.D.P. State convention, the 13th and 14th. If you haven't had the lake ride from Chicago to Milwaukee, by all means take this chance to have it. You could take the boat from Chi. the morning of the 13th, getting to Milwaukee in time for the convention opening in the evening. Leaving Sunday night for 'the lake by starlight' you could be in Chi. again Monday. This round trip would be $1.50 or $2.00 and $10.00 extra for berth."

With never a mention of the "wild socialist girl" he was planning to marry on the fifteenth of June, my father went on, "We ought to have some pleasant hours together, tho I will have some speaking & committee work to do at the convention. And you will meet some great people—people with fine hearts and big souls.—The most of the summer I will be in the farther northern part of the state, about Marinette & Sturgeon Bay, and as this is campaign year it means extra effort all along the line. Next winter I am going to put in lecture courses in a number of towns up this way, at least five, maybe fifteen."

As always with Aunt Esther, he spoke of her possible career as a pianist. It was a thing between them. "If you can really raise hell on the keyboard, in a way *to wake up and give enjoyment to an audience strange to you,* this is your chance to break into public concert work! Honestly, as brother talking to sister, I doubt whether you are reckless and proud and bold enough for public work. But maybe you have changed from a good, quiet, behaved girl into a genius! If you have I will be able to get you some dates next winter up here, tho there would probably be hardly anything more than expenses the first season! Yes—meet me in Milwaukee the 13th of June. Charlie."

There it was. Why was he so careful? My mother couldn't wait. "That Galesburg trip is something to look forward to—I suppose we'll see some eyes as big as saucers, will we?! . . . And they won't understand Charlie's other self any more than the original Charlie! Rather the puzzle will now be a genuine prodigy! Charlie was baffling enough, but lo now a duplicate-Charlie, a woman to watch Charlie! ye gods, a Prodigy! a Prodigy! So much for the town. But the Mother—that will be different. I love her, flesh of your flesh, Cully—heart of your heart! The mother who bore the Wunderkind! I will find *You* in the Mother, Carl—*You* not yet unfolded—yet still *You!* all the possibilities of *You* in the embryo!—I love and love the Mother—and I know she will love me."

My mother went on in an almost literary sense, romantic. She had read Robert Browning backwards and forwards, and knew my father had too and would understand her reference to Browning's poem "Memorabilia," in which the first stanza goes:

> Ah, did you once see Shelley plain,
>   And did he stop and speak to you
> And did you speak to him again?
>   How strange it seems and new!

She wrote, "The girls I don't see so distinctly yet—but I'll love them and Mart too—there will be *something* of Cully or Carl or Sandy or Micky in each of them, surely! Or if not, at least they are wrapped in the glory of having lived years and years with you 'seeing Shelley plain' all the while! 'How strange it seems and new'! . . . Galesburg! Galesburg! Old Town, I love you—because Cully played in your streets—and suffered—and hungered with the heart's hunger—and struggled—and won out achieving *Himself*—so that now *Cully is!* My heart will go out to everything and everybody in Galesburg that meant or means anything to *You! Cully!*" Did she understand something of his shyness, his reticence, when she added, "Maybe we'll make that Galesburg trip a year from this summer! No matter *when*, tho."

June was going by and she said. "June! June! of roses and the WEDDING! . . . What will June do to Two-Hearts that were mad in chilly March!?!" And she thought again of Grandma Sandburg perhaps coming by for the celebration: "Wouldn't we both like an S-S festival (not a registration-of-the-body festival)—and Rube and Joseffy and your Mother should be there—and my Mother and Ed . . . yes, and Wagner and Robert & Elizabeth Browning and Edward Carpenter and Ibsen and Shaw and poor old Walt—all these should be there as well! . . . What say you?" And, "There's one thing about inviting people that struck me just this minute. That is presents! . . . You know weddings are commonly regarded as a sort of hold-up game! What do you say to this awful possibility! . . . maybe we could write the invitations in such a way they'd all know we weren't 'holding them up' for wedding gifts . . . it might be necessary to write plainly in the lower left-hand corner: 'No presents accepted'!" She explained to him about another custom that she felt firmly about too, for in all the days that I knew Mother I never saw her wearing a ring. "I've written mother urging 'no rings' on the plea that I gave up wearing rings about 10 years ago because they seemed to me relics of barbarism on a level with earrings and nose-rings!"

My father said, "I go to Appleton to-night & give my 'The Poet of Democracy' to a literary society out on the edge of Appleton—about 30 people, of all sorts—mostly indecisive types, 'sober & industrious,'—the kind the local newspaper says of, when they die, 'He was respected in the community and loved by all who knew him. He was kind to his mother.' A sort of deviltry possesses me at times among these—to talk their slangiest slang, speak their homely, beautiful home-speech about all the common things—suddenly run a knife into their snobbery—then swing out into a crag-land of granite & azure where they can't follow but sit motionless following my flight with their eyes."

She told him, "May the S-S be many many years together. It's a solemn thought—the thought of death. It never used to worry me. While I was alone, a single separate person, I laughed at death—so genuinely careless that I couldn't even *understand* the common human cry, the yearning for immortality. I was impatient with people for not laughing up at death as I did myself, careless, almost challenging! Now it's different. I haven't thought it out to the end yet from the new viewpoint of hyphened Double Ess! Someday I'll feel a need for thinking it out to the end, maybe—and then I will—and I suppose it will spell PEACE—Peace, when it is thought out to the very end. But now I see only that it is a *solemn thought*—that I cling to Life with a new tenacity, because *you* are *of life*."

He responded, "Nor have I worked it out—thought my way thru this thing of death. There's something running thru life now I never knew before. I'm not afraid of it, but I don't understand it, and its some new filament of power, a new Chance, I've never seen at work. The coincidence of our ideas and plans and whims is something I would not have believed till—the Wonder-Woman came!"

She wrote, "My walk this afternoon was under a sky of storm clouds. I was out on a country road where I could see the full sweep of sky—get all the changing cloud effects. . . . Now the sun would be hid behind massive lowering clouds—now it would shine thru a rift in the sky flooding orchard and pasture and roadway in a fresh golden light. The odor of apple blossoms freshened with light spring showers was in the air. Toward sunset when the sun again broke thru the clouds suffusing everything in a mellow glow, I threw myself in a bank of lush grass by the roadside and watched the lengthening shadows of tree and of the cattle —or I looked up into the arching boughs of great shade trees overhead— and watched the great clouds sailing and sailing past. All the while little gray and brown birds in the hedges were shaking the sweetest warbles from their little throats—and the fragrance of apple-blossoms was wafted to me from the orchard, all pink-and-white, across the road."

By now my Aunt Esther had decided to take the lake boat to Milwaukee for the state convention on June thirteenth. Aunt Esther was twenty that year of 1908, young and fresh, a ways from marriage, her ambitions centered in music as a talented pianist and organist. Aunt Mary was going to come also—thirty-three by now. It would be nine more years before my Aunt Mary would find the one she wanted to marry—a handsome man fifteen years younger than herself, Allie Johnson. Had my father told his sisters then that he was about to take a wife? I don't know. I never asked. But my father wrote to my mother that the girls were coming and she was delighted, ". . . the news that I'm going to meet Mary & Esther has come. Good! And Saturday is only 4 days off now! IV, Carl, IV! And we meet! . . . And when I see them I'll want to say: and you were near Cully all the years when he was a boy—you ate with him—played with him—shared the common life with him for days and days and weeks and months and years! 'How strange it seems'—and new. I hope they'll talk about the days when you were kiddos together. I must know all about it and live it all over with you. . . . Love and love to the Wunderkind. Paula."

He wrote, "Oho! Kitty Malone—3 days—3 days!—Oho! You'll be put to it—hard put to it again—no good to run nor dodge. You will find yourself surrounded so you can't get away. . . . Micky."

And she, "I was hearing my classes for the last time. . . . No absentees this last day. We had flowers and flowers! Peonies Red—Pink and White! And Roses. And Roses. And Roses. A deluge of them. No desk visible— or books or anything. Just a mass of flowers! Very sweet of the youngsters really. I read them Russel's article about S. Carolina slavery—Contract Labor of Convicts. Some of the girls wept! Some of the boys wanted to stay after 12 o'clock thru the dinner hour to hear the rest! What with the flowers and the interest in Russel's article, it was a day! . . . Now I must start to pack. I leave here at 6 A.M. tomorrow. . . . Paula."

Oma was meeting Mother in Milwaukee the next day, a Wednesday. They spent their time shopping and stayed over, going out to Opa and the farm on Thursday. On Saturday the convention opened, Victor Berger as state chairman calling it to order. My mother and father sat side by side at last. There were my aunts. Mary was a handsome woman; her brown hair, which had grayed prematurely, was waved and pinned back. And Esther, her light brown hair hanging straight and naturally, sat beside her, taller and slimmer. Did the green eyes of the two of them light up when my father spoke? Were they delighted with his delivery and command? Were they surprised? Did either of them ask after Uncle Ed? Clara's baby had come on the second of June—little Kate Rodina Steichen. My uncle had sent a cablegram: MOTHER AND CHILD ARE DOING WELL.

On Sunday, there was a morning meeting at ten o'clock and noon dinner was served in the hall at thirty-five cents a plate. The afternoon was taken up with reports on the locals given by delegates led by Miss Thomas. An orchestra of two violins, one cornet and a piano played between events. Berger gave a speech on the approaching presidential campaign and asked for comment. At four, Carl Thompson and "District Organizer Charles Sandburg" talked on the organization of locals and methods of propaganda. At six, it was announced that there would be a "Banquet for delegates and party members, served in the hall at 35¢ per plate. Toastmaster, W.R. Gaylord." In the hall "Charles Sandburg of Oshkosh" gave the first talk.

Were my aunts impressed? Was my mother proud? Did my aunts have the news by now that my parents were to be married the next day? My mother had had to go off by train to get the license herself, not at the Milwaukee county courthouse, where she learned that she must go to the city hall of her own county twenty miles away in Waukesha.

And then, where and how was the wedding carried off? Who came? There was no skull of Balsamo, no Joseffy's violin, no Victor Berger or Miss Thomas, no Rube Borough, no Uncle Ed, no Grandma Sandburg, not even Opa and Oma at the ceremony. There was no ring. Carl Thompson said the words to them in his own home, leaving the word "obey" out as he'd promised. My parents had agreed on that and it was a family story that we all knew well. They said they would, and as perfectly as they were able did, love and honor. But in their household no commands were given. My aunts were on hand—Mary and Esther. And Winfield Gaylord was there with his wife, Olive. The latter, along with Thompson's wife, Kate, served as witnesses. The marriage certificate listed Lilian Steichen as "teacher" and Charles A. Sandburg as "party organizer."

Reminiscing in a long talk once, my mother told me that their marriage night was spent in a Milwaukee hotel. There was no honeymoon, though my father planned to join her at Oma and Opa's farm whenever he was able, while they worked out how and when they would start what she called "housekeeping" on their own. It seems my father had had to be off first thing in the morning. Something had come up. A friend, the editor of the Manitowoc *Daily Tribune*, Chester Wright, was involved in a libel suit and had asked my father to come and watch the trial and write it up for the paper. My father told my mother he couldn't help her with her bags as he had to report to Milwaukee party headquarters first. Then at the railway station, heading for the farm, Mother ran into Miss Thomas, who said that my father hadn't gone to headquarters after all, but straight to the depot, and seemed to have left right away. Telling the story to me, my mother spoke in her usual contented way, countering

151

my protest that my father had no manners or chivalry, with her tale of the young married lady who lived on the floor above them in a rooming house sometime later, whose husband brought her candy and flowers regularly, but who was consistently unfaithful. Mother added that that pair had eventually divorced too. Never to my knowledge did my father bring my mother flowers, candy, diamonds or rings. From the beginning he placed his earnings in her care, and if in their later life he kept a small separate bank account, she spoke of it to me with some interest, but not to him. "He ought to have what he wants," she said. Back then, he wrote to her, ". . . be careful how you give me money. I am 'a son of fantastical fortune' and a spender. We will buy what we need. The rest goes into your hands. Now, having sent you all my money but fifty cents, I have incentive to hustle. . . . Cully."

My father did write up the trial in the Manitowoc *Daily Tribune*. It was featured as the top headline: BATTLE FOR FREE PRESS IS NOW ON IN CIRCUIT COURT.

> It doesn't look dramatic. There are no noises, no loud cries, no torchlights, hurrahs and fireworks. But in the court house of Manitowoc county where the circuit court is in session, a battle is being fought. And it is a battle that concerns every man, woman and child in the county. It is one of those rare, unusual law cases where principles are concerned. It is a quiet battle but is one that touches vital issues. On one side in this battle is District Attorney Kelly and William Rahr, the boss MALSTER. If they can win their case, newspaper editors will find it harder than before to expose political graft or business corruption. On the other side in the case is the defendant Chester M. Wright and his attorneys, I. Craite and Daniel Hoan. If they win their case, it will mean a fair and decent freedom for newspaper editors in discussing and criticising public affairs—it will mean that any business man or group of business men who have rigged up a game to plunder the public will be more likely to be discovered and brought to light.

Three weeks later my parents were together again at the farm. On the sixth of July the *Daily Socialist* carried a headline: GIVE SOCIALIST A "CHARIVARI." WHEN THE WEDDING DIN SUBSIDES, ORGANIZER TAKES COLLECTION. The account stated that

> . . . the young men of the neighborhood, all farmers and "hired men," gathered at night with all the cowbells, horns, tin cans and the like they could get hold of and made night hideous with discord. They

wanted the bridegroom to hand out money for beer and cigars. . . .
Shortly after the din started two of the huskiest young farmers went
to the door and demanded that Sandburg come out and "set 'em up"
to the crowd. A motley chorus greeted him when he appeared. Tin
horns and cowbells were used with the utmost efficiency. There was
a hush of expectation when Sandburg put his hands in his pockets
and stood facing the crowd. "Boys," he began. "That's the stuff! Be
generous, Charlie!" shouted several of the "boys." Sandburg continued, "The Socialists are fighting your fight." "Hurrah!" came a cry
from the crowd. "We'll have a drink on that!" "You work hard all
your lives," resumed Sandburg. "That's why we're dry," shouted a
voice from the crowd. "You harden your bodies and twist them out
of shape," said the impromptu host. "How about those cigars,
Charlie?" cried a friend. "You are victims," Sandburg persisted, "of
a system which cheats you out of the time that should be yours to
use for play and development and all the better and higher things
of life." Cries of "Three cheers for Sandburg! Hurrah for the Social
Democracy!" "We Socialists are fighting for a better system. If I had
a million dollars—" Cries of "We wish you had!" "I would not give a
cent for beer and cigars. A Socialist gives his money to the cause he
is fighting for. The Social Democratic Party of Wisconsin has no
traction companies nor 'criminals of great wealth' to support it. A
little from each man will help. We depend on the workingman for
support." Then he passed the hat. Some paid and others walked
away. They gave one last grand chorus of noise—a sort of infernal
finale—and then a cheer for the Social Democracy.

And word came to the farm from Voulangis, where Uncle Ed was
content with his Clara and Mary and baby Kate: "My dear Ma & Pa.
. . . We are all settled comfortably at last. . . . The country all around
is very beautiful and I shall have a chance to work. So much for us. I am
glad the wedding turned out such a simple affair without any monkey
shines. And from now on it is up to the Sanborns to make good. I certainly
did not think when I met him out at the farm that he would so soon
become a member of the family. It certainly turned out to make a fine
combination—and I have that peculiar feeling that I sometimes get about
such things, sort of a premonition that it will be great. And now how is
our garden at the falls. Love & lots of it to you all from the villa l'oiseau
bleu. Gaesjack."

Twelve

Down Whatever Road

Marriage—would it settle my father down? Would he find a stable job near their home where my mother would be "housekeeping"? It seems not really. A wanderer always, he would find reasons for remaining one. I have thought they may have been closer because of his absences, when she wanted him there in the bed and by the stove. For a while after their marriage, she stayed on at the little farm with Oma and Opa, seeing him only occasionally. But his letters came: "Paula—I don't know what you're doing. To-morrow it will be a week since I had a letter from you. I don't know what your fingers are working at nor what problems your brain is feeling its way about. But all last night your heart beat close to mine. I heard its pulsings & I knew thoughts of yours—all the great real dangers & all the great real splendors that you and I have touched and dared these days we touched & dared again. I saw you back across the years facing all the dark questions of life & always giving them answer, always unafraid—often sad & often with high-keyed joy, but always answering, always facing them unafraid. I remembered your low-voiced talks to me as we lay close to each other, between kisses,—the rarest, highest thing I ever touched in life or work or books—your talk of what life is & what life may be—Deep you are & fine you are & with mystic strands of power running all thru you. Down whatever road your soft eyes look & your little feet go to-day, they go with beauty and sweetness & poise. And always and always & always I am with you and I love you and I love you. Foolish and rough & often thoughtless I have been & may be again but what there is of me—loves and loves. Two children turning pages in a big book under a high tree. May all the gods of luck watch & speak wisely with them. Love and love. Carl."

My father had a notable temper, which the family respected but didn't fear. He never laid a hand on a child. A piece of advice that checkered my childhood was, "Helga, learn to control your temper!" My parents didn't squabble the way Oma and Opa did, continually and casually. There would be an occasional word battle, roars on one side and soft remonstrations on the other. I would slip out of my room to listen at the stair-top till it died away. My father's anger at his family would rise when, working in his attic rooms, the noise below got too loud. He would thump on the floor, shouting, "Pipe down all that yammering!" And we would. "Hush!" My mother says that in those first days of marriage when cash was scarce, if my father became infuriated in some way, he would pick up a chair and smash it to bits or tear off his shirt and rip it up. She said it as if it pleased her in the telling of it later on. "And we didn't have the wherewithal to buy a new shirt or chair in those days either!"

Perhaps she had looked for a child right away. She was restless on the farm as September came on. They were not sure of their future in any way. She sent news to my father, "Steichen S. *not* on the way! Learned this today—just 8 weeks from July 2nd! The news came as something of a surprise—." And later, "Again the old news renewed: Steichen-Sandburg *is not on the way*. All's well!"

When my father came to the farm, there was some friction, it seems. Oma was always around, talking constantly and worrying. Some dispute would be going on between Opa and Oma that my mother ignored easily, but that bothered my father, not used to it. And he would be in and then out again, sometimes arriving when not expected, upsetting Oma's routines. My father admired her, but Oma had as strong a will, had always run her household, and the two grated on each other's sensitivities at the farm.

Mother took the train to Milwaukee occasionally to shop and visit party headquarters and once in a while to hear my father give a speech. After one of them, they parted and went their separate paths, and she wrote to him from headquarters right away, wanting to care for him at the farm, "Now you obey orders—*don't wear yourself out!!* Save your strength. Don't draw on the future. You've done that far too much already. . . . Gaylord is the only one here who looks at all worn. He has a nervous temperament like you—but he isn't as worn as you. As for coming to the farm— . . . You know how things will affect you! I think I could plan things so you'd get more rest perhaps! Early to bed—between 8 & 9—out of bed 8 in the morning—breakfast—that would satisfy mother. Then you off to the orchard all by yourself with a few novels—and Paula.

Dinner 12. Right after dinner off to orchard again—alone with novels or a hike together. Supper, very light, at 6—short walk, and to bed at 8! You see we would have to make the concession of regular mealtimes. . . . What do you say? Shall we give the farm one more trial. It really seems to me that it is a better resting-place for you than with any comrades. . . . If we conform to meal hours, mother will be satisfied—and there won't be that grouchyness and criticalness in the air that your nature (and mine) is so sensitive to—spoiling the rest—ruffling one all up! And the food will be good and wholesome and we'll have a fair amount of time to ourselves. What do you say? Now be good! Save yourself. That's my last word . . . Paula."

Back at the farm, she wrote another letter and added that Oma understood the need of rest for him. "When I told mother about your exhaustion in Milwaukee she suggested that you drop everything and take a week's vacation at the farm—for mother's idea too is health first and the movement afterward. Mother added that she would not talk much so you could rest better. What do you say, Carl?"

There were books for my mother to read at the farmhouse, and newspapers and magazines. There were chores that she helped with—picking the vegetables and fruits to put up, sweeping the rooms. My father came to visit and she had letters to write when he was away. But I think her thoughts, day and night, were always on him. She needed to get involved in some way with the cause, as he was. She had friends in Milwaukee and there were amusements in the city too—concerts and the theater. She thought about getting a room there. She visited the Social-Democratic headquarters and reported to my father, ". . . everyone was cordial of course. Thompson said if I cared to do some office work, there would be some I could do later on. Pay—one dollar a day. Deduct $2.00 room-rent and $2.00 for food—net gain $2.00 per week—minus carfare, laundry etc. However I told Thompson, 'Yep.' I'd be glad to. . . . What do you think of the proposition anyway? Its just general office-work—writing addresses, folding letters, etc. We can talk it over when you come. It will depend too on how soon we start housekeeping. . . . I've put up 15 qts. of apple butter! Now I quit. 15 qts. ought to be plenty. It costs us so little—just the sugar—that I thought best to run the risk of putting up too much—rather than too little. Apple butter ought to save us the expense of buying much dried fruit and dairy butter. . . . Those 15 qts. cost us about 75 cts—for sugar & parafine!"

I think my father wanted my mother away from Oma and Opa and the farm too—on his own ground. He spoke with a Social-Democratic friend, a mailman, George Fox, about letting my mother use the Foxes' back room while she looked for a place. "Comrade Fox" and Hope, his wife, called Hopie by her friends, lived in Appleton, Wisconsin, on the Fox River, thirty miles south of Green Bay on the railroad line from Milwaukee that passed through Menomonee Falls, Fond du Lac, and Oshkosh before reaching Appleton. The town was on my father's organizing route, and he stayed with the Foxes when he came through. When they told my father certainly, Mother packed and said good-bye to Oma and Opa.

While Mother and Hopie visited, on the way to becoming fast friends, Comrades Fox and Sandburg talked about the party and how for the first time it looked as if the socialists might have a chance for power in Milwaukee. My father had written in the Manitowoc *Daily Tribune*, "It is not an absolute surety that socialism, if put into practice, would make a nation of happy people, but if we can bank on any certainty in modern affairs, that certainty is this: the socialist makes people think. . . . Socialism is educating the people into new modes, habits and attitudes of thought." Fox agreed, although much of the nation did not—"red vermin," "crackpots" and "wild-eyed Marxists" were a few terms used for the party.

Before long my mother found a place in Appleton that she liked— three upstairs rooms that suited them both. Her letters had the flavor, the texture, of their new life in their own home: "I got all the letters you dictated, off on Sunday. It just occurred to me you might be wondering about it! . . . Also I've wrapped (most beautifully & securely & safely—) 50 good circulars to Sprague, 50 good circulars to Marshall. And I've written a note to each telling them that I am sending them the circulars under separate cover. . . . Then to-morrow after the mail is off—it's me to the job of cleaning up the house."

She had determined to master his old Blickensderfer typewriter, and said, "Blick is all right. I copied 'Lost' and 'Men Out of Jobs' on Little Blickie—and sent the two poems to the American Mag. My copies were works of art! You'll have to admire my work when you get home! I'm practising for speed too—repeating common words. I try to find the keys by touch. . . . My copies are b-e-a-u-t-i-f-u-l! like our midnight tomato soup! b-e-a-u-t-i-f-u-l!! Will you arrive Wednesday morning? We don't want to dance to the tune of 'The Mother was chasing her Boy round the room'—nor to the revised version of this old song 'Paula was chasing her Boy down the Road!' as we did last time! Probably there'll be a morning train that isn't too early. . . . I'll not go beyond where the road forks—

so we won't miss each other. And dearest, you're planning to stay at least 5 days, aren't you? You need a real rest—and you can't get that, if it's only a couple of days, and you are thinking of going away very soon."

Did it sometimes seem to my mother that she saw less of my father than had been planned and promised? Did she remember his words about "marching in the dust and sun, loafing in blue twilights and sleeping under the trees and stars"? She wrote him, "How does it feel, Carl, to be 'plugging away' at lists?—Hah? Hm? How many will have fallen before the onslaught of your spear, my valiant knight, when you return home from 'the list'! . . . every incident will interest me, whether it's comic or tragic or both or neither. You get something from meeting people—you know how to learn things. . . . If you work on poems and lyceum stuff when you should be resting—you will be tired for the campaign work, and it will be no go campaigning. Be sensible, Carl. Be good. Quit the poems and lyceum staff till after election. . . . Now's the time for political work." And she added, "I'm glad you are in the midst of it—rather than here in the Wilderness. . . . I'm with you, my love, wherever you are—You, My Agitator—Mob-orator."

The "political work" she spoke of had to do with the national presidential campaign. Teddy Roosevelt, still shouting about the money changers, was going out and the Republicans were doing their best to put in William Howard Taft. The socialists were running the same man on their presidential ticket whom they'd run in 1900 and 1904 and would run again in 1912 and 1920—Eugene Debs. Debs was born in 1855, twenty-three years before my father. His parents had immigrated from the Alsace in France. He'd worked in a railroad shop, become a locomotive fireman, clerked in a grocery firm and then begun his life work when he organized his hometown Terre Haute Lodge of the Brotherhood of Locomotive Firemen. My father first heard Debs's name in 1894 when a strike called "Debs Rebellion" or the "Red Revolution" took place. It started in Pullman, Illinois, on the outskirts of Chicago, a "model town" where even the public works were the property of the Pullman Company. As a child I learned songs from my father about men who never saw regular money and went to a company window and drew brass tokens against their accounts, which could be spent at the company stores:

> We live in company houses, the company runs the schools,
> We're working for the company according to the company's
>   rules,
> We all drink company water, we all burn company lights,
> And the company preachers teach us what the company
>   thinks is right.

At the head of the Pullman strikers and the newly organized American Railway Union had been Debs, thirty-nine years old then, and he managed to tie up most of the nation's railroads. At his direction all the men had laid down their tools and not a Pullman car moved. When, within a few weeks, rail transportation became paralyzed, the federal authorities had stepped in with an injunction against all strike activities. Troops had been ordered to Chicago by President Cleveland, despite the protest of Governor Altgeld of Illinois that states' rights were being violated. The strike had been broken and Debs, who refused to obey the order or even to acknowledge it, was jailed. The labor unions barely survived, but the socialists had their leader.

The 1908 socialist campaign was being run on a platform of public ownership of railroads and communications, municipal ownership of public utilities, progressive income and inheritance taxes, universal suffrage and free school books. My father was involved. He wrote my mother, "Have cancelled the date for Mishicot and will meet the *Red Special* tomorrow at Green Bay. Wish you could be along. . . . Turning pages we are, leaf on leaf together—Together!"

The Red Special was Debs's campaign tool—a locomotive pulled a coach, a sleeper and a baggage car. On board, the campaign party ate, slept, and planned whistle-stop speeches as they crossed the country. My mother said, "There'll be so much to talk over, Carl! Got your Red Special letter from Green Bay—so glad you were along! I want to hear all about the Train—and the meetings—and Debs. . . . I've been reading the Daily Socialist and understand what the Red Special means. I'm so glad you are going to be on it two days—you'll get in touch with the national movement. I believe the Red Special *is* good propaganda. I should think that right after the Red Special passes thru a district would be the psychological moment for agitation—or at least advertising later meetings or distributing literature."

When the Red Special screeched to a halt at a town or crossing and the people gathered around the rear of the car, one of the campaigners, maybe my father, would introduce Debs, who would step out, lean and lanky. When Debs's friend, James Whitcomb Riley, spoke of him, he said, "God was feeling mighty good when he made 'Gene Debs, and he didn't have anything else to do all day."

Debs harangued his gatherings, "Why should any man, woman, or child suffer for food, clothing or shelter? Why? The question cannot be answered. Don't tell me that some men are too lazy to work. Suppose they are too lazy to work, what do you think of a social system that produces men too lazy to work? If a man is too lazy to work, don't treat him with contempt. Don't look down upon him with scorn as if you were a superior being. If there is a man who is too lazy to work, there is something the matter with him. He wasn't born right or he was perverted in this system. You could not, if you tried, keep a normal man inactive, and if you did he would go stark mad. Go to any penitentiary and you will find the men there begging for the privilege of doing work. I am not a prophet. I can no more penetrate the future than you can. I do study the forces that underlie society and the trend of evolution. I can tell by what we have passed through about what we will have in the future; and I know that capitalism can be abolished and the people put in possession. Now, when we have taken possession and we jointly own the means of production, we will no longer have to fight each other to live; our interests, instead of being competitive, will be cooperative. We will work side by side. Your interest will be mine and mine will be yours. That is the economic condition from which will spring the human social relation of the future. When we are in partnership and have stopped clutching each other's throats, when we have stopped enslaving each other, we will stand together, hands clasped, and be friends. We will be comrades, we will be brothers, and we will begin the march to the grandest civilization the human race has ever known."

My father wrote, "Aboard Red Special—9/24—Green Bay. Paula: All tumbled and hurried and dusty, here we are. The success of the Train has been understated, if anything. Debs is superb. Crowded house, all kinds of enthusiasm. Fine bunch aboard the Train. Lapworth, the Englishman, is very interesting. He's Hunter's secretary, you know—has done much of Hunter's writing—so. Remembered Ed very well, and regreeted me and congratulated, on learning of the June proceedings of You and Me. More later along this line! Will sleep on the Train to-night—not very restful, but hell, the revolution tingles and whirls around here. . . . Am in Manitowoc the 25th, Kaukana the 25th, Oshkosh the 26th and 27th; Campbellsport the 28th, West Bend the 29th. Then for The Wonder-Girl!"

Debs wrote later from his home in Terre Haute, "Mr. Chas. Sandburg, Appleton, Wis., My dear Comrade:—. . . I remember and shall always remember the service you so freely rendered on the 'Red Special' and your fine spirit and wholesome presence. May you find many to engage your service and give you the chance—all you ask or need—to deliver your message and do your work. Count me always Your loving comrade, Eugene V. Debs."

My father had been working on long prose pieces for some time, using the form of letters to a mythical "Bill," and signing them "Sandy." It was the same technique used by the Englishman Robert Blatchford in his book on socialism, *Merrie England.* Now my father had an interested publisher for one of them, Charles H. Kerr, who put out a Pocket Library of Socialism in Chicago. Kerr also monthly published *The International Socialist Review,* and six days a week, the Chicago *Daily Socialist.* Two other writers for Kerr's Pocket Library of Socialism, out of the series of about sixty, were Jack London and Eugene Debs. Kerr, back in 1901, had published *Socialist Songs with Music,* translating "The Marseillaise" as well as "The International Party" for it:

> Arise, ye pris'ners of starvation!
> Arise, ye wretched of the earth,
> For justice thunders condemnation,
> A better world's in birth . . .

And so my father asked my mother, "Paula—Will you go over that Dear Bill & get it in MSS shape for Kerr? So we can work on it together when I arrive on the 25th or 26th? I miss you—but it's just sort of abstractedly—You are so near! Always! Always! For you, I find myself muttering gratitude and prayer of a kind—so utterly superb you are. Carl."

When Kerr would publish a "Dear Bill" letter as a booklet, it would be called *You and Your Job.* The piece would also be printed as a pamphlet by the Social-Democratic Publishing Company in Milwaukee to help the present campaign for Debs. It would be used in the coming elections in Milwaukee. It would circulate widely—one time published in the Western Federation of Miners Journal in Denver. *LaFollette's Weekly Magazine* would feature a series of "Letters to Bill" in 1909, one beginning, "Dear Bill: I wish I could get straight on this thing. Maybe you can help me out some but I doubt whether you can solve the puzzle. Some big brains are bucking this proposition and most of them are up a blind alley on it. It isn't exactly a puzzle. To be real correct, it's a problem—with a capital P. Have you heard anything about The Problem of the Unemployed? Well, that is the one big, immediate problem. That is the one staring, heavy Problem that stands across the road of Progress barring the way like a big rock, just as though it could talk, saying, 'You've got to clear me out of the road before you can go any farther.'"

The long letter ended, "The time is coming when we will see that it is a matter of common sense and common weal to pay some attention and give a little real thought to the Unemployed. The man out of a job has his choice of three things: he can beg or steal or starve. . . . So long as a man lives and eats, somebody pays for his living and eating. What a man eats and wears, he has either himself produced or somebody else has produced it for him. So if a man who has no savings, is not at work earning a living, then society, all of us, support him either as a criminal or a beggar. When the next wind blows the driven snow around the roof you sleep under next winter, old boy, remember that somewhere between two million and four million men are unemployed over the country, without any chance to earn a living by honest work. And some of them are out of the coin to pay rent and they don't know where that coin is coming from. Yours always, Sandy."

My mother wrote my father about the manuscript and about her editing. "I have just finished making *beautiful copies* of 2 Dear Bill letters. . . . And do you know, Wunderkind, the letters grow on me. These two, anyway, are splendid! I did not make many alterations. One you may object to is substituting 'dragging' for 'sluffing' boot-soles along sidewalks. You remember I particularly liked the word 'sluffing!' But it isn't a word at all—not in that sense. Sloughing means 'casting off, as an old skin by a snake'! There is no other meaning. Maybe you were thinking of 'shuffling' but that isn't used transitively. I made a number of other minor changes. But you have the final chance at the Ms. to change it back—or any way you like." And a day later, "They're all done—the Dear Bill letters are all copied—and the copies corrected—all done! You ought to be here, Cully, to celebrate with me—swing me round the room and all. The copies are done! The copies are done! . . . As soon as you know when you'll be home, write me. . . . (if I should set bread one evening, expecting to bake the next morning). . . . Knock many short loud knocks. I'll hear all right. . . . Be sure you leave your address with the editor to whom you submit the Dear Bill letters. We want the copies back, if they are rejected! (Such beautiful copies! and—They are done! They are done!)"

He wrote her back and sometimes he seemed to have the blues: "The melancholy of autumn is cast over the country. Trees and grass and air hover with wild, somber expectancies. Something of ours, something that you and I hold high and beautiful is interfused and kin with it. One tree on a wooded slope is a blaze of scarlet and brown and I murmur, 'Paula.' A tall slim birch lays its sheer white out across dusky, contrasting green and again I murmur, 'Paula.' Across the dark last night at Cuiejla's the lake-song swept on the wind, a restless, indefatigable song, with the plash of surf and the voices of waves—and Paula was with me, listening,—and we said, 'It is our song. What we hear is the vivid and reckless sea. It is the chant of our hearts, the anthem of our strivings, the oratorio that is an accompaniment of our faring-forward toward the Ideal.' . . . I have been sort of fumbling at times lately—groping—it is Monday evening—and I have not had a word from you since last Friday. I've thought you may be under the weather—or you sent mail to Kewaunee. God reigns & the government at Washington lives—but I want—words, eyes, little feet—Paula! . . . It has been fight & fight lately —inside the organization. Debs is superb. His face & voice are with me yet. A lover of humanity. Such a light as shines from him—such fire as burns in him—he is of poet breed, hardened for war. . . . I can't talk about myself or anything tonight. Think very cheaply about everything. I am going out into the mist and wind. A throwback from over-reaching, being too serious, too deeply wistful—'wanting and wanting and always wanting'—."

She had the blues as well: "We must have our home soon—feeling bad. No use writing. Paula. This note is just to let you know that I'm not forgetting to write—simply can't write." And the next day, "Feeling all right again to-day—was blue and blue yesterday and the day before— so lonely and homesick for you, Heart. . . ." And again, "I feel lonesome for your eyes and hands and your beautiful head of hair—and the low resonant Voice! Still—in some ways, as you've often said, it is better that we are apart now and again for a little while."

He wrote her, "Now the thunder is growling, rain is beginning to patter. And it comes to me clear that Home is more of a Home when the open is stormy.—I want you for the sun and the flowers, Paula, but I want you for the rain & the dark too."

And from "The Rooms," she mourned after he came and left, "I've put everything to order—came upon pipes here and there—and I laid THEM away, alongside of The Flickers, to rest and rest—and the spittoon —that too is put away to rest and rest. . . . Dear Heart—it's lonely and lonely. I think I'll get the pipes down again tomorrow and pretend that you are around to use them. I did not know I could be so lonesome. The tears are coming again. So . . . maybe when the sunlight streams in in the morning, and the sparrows come to feed, and I am strong and refreshed with rest—maybe then I'll have a gladder heart to show you. . . . I don't understand these tears and tears. Missing you, is natural. But that I should miss you *so*, with such aching pain, and tears and tears— that cannot be good. Rest and work and broader interests—reading and all—must save me from *that*. . . . I send you love and love. I kiss your good, true eyes—."

When her letter came he answered, "I can't say what my heart feels

—things clattering around me—but Carl knows—he knows this you fling around him. The tears of separation on Monday, & the bigger & fresher outlook Tuesday—they were mine too, tho with such life & pictures and hustling around me, it was harder for Paula. About VII fingers now— and then Home Again—Lilian and The Man Who Smokes Around the Rooms. . . . Remember—you are unafraid—absolutely unafraid, of anything that walks, creeps, crawls, swims or flies—So. I'm sure the Thoroughbred has not had enough fresh air the last month. Two hours in the open every day—two hours—make that an average, Dear. Chicago almost gagged me; my hill-bred lungs revolted in the air. . . . Walk all over & around Appleton. Enclosed is the 5 I meant to send earlier. Wine —and love—and all—to Paula. Carl. P.S. How I love you—worship you— with the finest as well as with the commonest everydayness of me. *You* satisfy *all of me*—the K.M. [Kitty Malone] cooking apple butter—the red-hot girl-socialist worshipping the street-corner agitator, the mob orator—the dreaming woman with eyes for the Beautiful, praying under the stars, to you! to you! . . . When you write, don't wear the white sweater & put your chin in your hands that way—I won't be able to read for the want of lookin' at you."

And then my mother got an idea. She had inherited Opa's love for the land and his feeling for plants and animals. She wanted to get out of "The Rooms" where she was lonely and cooped-up. She had read a book called *Three Acres & Liberty* and she told my father, "I spent yesterday evening 7–9 at the library reading this book—all about hoeing, and ploughing, and weeding, and guano, and plaster etc. etc.! WONDERFUL! . . . I am in favor of planning things somehow—someway—(you know the 'how' and the 'way')—so we'll get some simoleons— . . . We mustn't look to the Views to pay too much—else—where will the cash for '3 A' etc. come from! The more I read, the more I realize the advantage of a little capital for current expenses—fertilizers, tools, trees & bush-fruit to set out, strawberry plants etc. etc.—But, Carl, you know how you feel—and when you need rest—and where you can live best today, to-morrow & the day after! And I want my boy all right! I do! So I'm hoping you won't be long—on the way home! Tho—if you think it best to be long on the way home—why Paula is something of a soldier-girl—and can wait—for the sake of Three Acres & Liberty! Sure!"

Sometimes, when in the neighborhood of Menomonee Falls, my father got off at the depot to visit with Oma and Opa. Their horse had gone lame and been sold, so my father walked the few miles to the farm. Mother advised him, "If you can get any pointers from Pa how (not) to manage our chicken farm—so as to have our eggs cost us 5 cents a piece (nit)—why get the Pointers! Go ahead! Paula's gone daffy—what with this glorious air and sunshine—and the house all clean and mopped up! —and Three-Acres-and-Liberty Ahead! . . . I've a lot of literature on Poultry, which the Fox's gave me . . . and they make exciting reading! The poultry game is great, Carl! They are selling their 200 egg incubators at $10.00—they paid $16.00 for them. That would be the right size for us. . . . We can also have their chicken-wire, just as good as new, but at reduced price because second-hand. . . . We would need $200.00 to start on. That would build us a coop (counitng $60.00 for that and posts for the run etc.)—buy good fertile eggs, 600 eggs at $4.00 a hundred. . . . supply the chicks with food till they reached the broiler stage, about May, when we would sell 200 chicks . . . etc etc . . . And chicks started in middle of Jan—beginning of March—ought to weigh 2 lbs in May. The broilers would bring $100.00 in May. That would raise the other 200 chicks. . . . etc. etc. The garden might bring in something— but we didn't figure on that—except for supplying our own table . . . and won't we be Pals tho—together—on our farm! Three Acres and Liberty! Do what you think best. But let us get a few simoleons to- gether, if possible! . . . Let's try to scrape together a few simoleons!"

Although my father was never a family yard man—we children raked and hosed out the garage—we weeded, hoed, milked, cleaned the chicken houses and barns—still he preferred the country atmosphere, the air and the food, to anywhere else. He had chopped wood since a child and did it expertly. In those days my parents had kerosene lamps and a wood stove and she spoke of ". . . enjoying the wood-shed and pilgrimages to it daily! enjoying fire-making in the morning with 'kindling to burn' left by the kindling-boy!"

And so he began to think of "Three Acres and Liberty" also. "Oma got on at Granville and poured out a torrent of speech the way to Milwaukee. Is now a bit more adjusted to the '3 acres and liberty' idea. Is inclined to get an incubator & test the scheme herself before fully endorsing us. . . . I hope to leave Chi. sometime Monday. May stop at Kenosha, Racine, &c. inquiring about land—LAND! In that case I won't get to THE ROOMS until Tuesday or Wednesday."

Then she wrote, "The folks have a horse now—so in case you decide to 'run out' to the farm, you won't have to walk. (!!) They would be glad to see you—but I suppose you haven't the time to spare. . . . if the roads are good enough, Pa will bring eggs & butter there (provided you pass thru before it gets dark) . . . you should telephone in good time from Milwaukee. . . . Pa's eyes are poor—he can't drive after dark."

My mother joined my father for a farm visit, and she praised him for controlling his temper with Opa's speedy new driving mare, Fanny, that Opa liked to give a free rein to. Fanny was an ex-racehorse and Opa encouraged her to pass any vehicle in sight. My mother said, "And the way you were so calm and reasonable with Fanny! From seeing you rip up shirts and swear at inanimate things, I half expected you'd swear at a horse that had got into trouble! (I had some fears for our chickens —they are so foolish you know, and try one's temper.) But there you were, talking so gently and reassuringly to Fanny—doing *just the reasonable thing*—not a hint of temper—Good-Sense—sheer good-sense! You're all right, Boy:

> 'There's a time for swearing
> And a time to refrain from swearing'

as the preacher saith in Ecclesiastes. . . . It does no harm to swear at shirts. So we swear—once more—all together d—— d—— d—— ad infinitum! But now I know you won't swear at the chickens, nor at the dog,—nor at anything that oughtn't to be sweared at! You—blessed reasonable cussed Boy!"

He sent her a poem about them on the roadway to the Menomonee Falls depot:

> In a wagon, on a roadway
>   From Menomonee to Home,
> With the mist upon your hair
> And the wind upon your brow
> And the wonder and the welcome
>   Of the calling wanderlust,
> You keep a-looking forward
> On the winding wayworn road,
> By house and hill and random boy
>   That drives the cattle home.
>
> O tousled girl! dishevelled head!
> What musses your hair and makes you look
>   A thing for picture, poem, story?
> For your face is set with glory
> And your eyes are dusky mirrors,
> Sky and wild and birds cawing are there,
>
> In a wagon, on a roadway
>   From Menomonee to Home.

When my father needed more room to carry his clippings and papers and pamphlets, Mother cut into the linings of his jackets and coats to enlarge the pockets. That was how the French students did in the 1800's, she said later. He had a system for pressing his pants when traveling by smoothing them flat under his mattress, the way sailors did. He also spread newspapers on the floor for a clean covering in his work area and when they got messy, laid fresh ones on top. In "The Rooms," she used their trunks and packing boxes for furniture. Her letters of the time hold the disheveled picture: "I hope the FIVE was not lost in the mail, for there was none inclosed in the letter. I suppose you forgot to inclose it—my forgetful Genius, you! . . . No matter. I am not lacking for simoleons. The Foxes handed me FIVE on pledges . . . I immediately blew myself for some cheese cloth for curtains for pantry & dresser, and burlap for covering. . . . Also I've stocked up on whole-wheat flour and un-milled wheat. . . . I am getting lots of fresh air. This morning I piled wood in the wood-shed—the door wide open. . . . House begins to wear a look of settled housekeeping—the kitchen no longer looks like a warehouse. Boxes are all covered—dressing table—typewriter stand—and all. You shall see! It is all *Magnificent*! Love from The Carpenter of Appleton, Liz. P.S. And WINE!!!"

She said "wine" because it was a symbol between them. He toasted her in many letters, one ending, "Here is Wine—for the wine we did not have with the fried ham tonight. Here is Wine!—the dear, beautiful S-S vintage of 1908—You. Cully."

Opa and Oma had known the wine-making craft from Luxembourg. Years later my mother would make it in the days of Prohibition. There would be kegs of it in our cellar rooms always. When my father cautioned Mother in one of those early letters on a remedy for the blues, she said she was about to go on a spending spree: "And now I'm going to blow myself! first a cord or two of wood! And then maybe will follow some less discreet 'blowing' myself! I shall heed your injunction not to refrain longer from drink!—drink!!"

"How do you feel—" she asked him, "with 75 cents in your trusty trouser pocket—and maybe Whitman & 20 dollars ahead of you! . . . Have been sewing—finished 2 pajamas for you and 2 nighties for me— all warm outing flannels. The pajamas are beautiful—and I know you'll look *magnificent* in them! . . . There is wheat (chicken-feed wheat) in the Miracle box cooking toward breakfast tomorrow. But you'll not be in on it! Too bad! And dried peas are soaking in cold water overnight— to go into the Miracle-box pease puree and bean puree and chicken feed (oats & wheat) and vegetable soup and—and—and—when Cully comes home."

Besides the butter and eggs that came from the farm, my mother bought a pint of milk a day from her landlady who kept a Jersey cow. Her letter told of how one day they almost lost the source of it all: "We 'purtnigh' lost our milk-machine here! 'Tim,' on the drunk, sold the cow for $25.00 to a man who came up here, got her out of the barn and was half way down the block before Mrs. Wms was aware. Lewis called the man back, and when Mrs. Wms joined Lewis in calling for the return of the cow—the man came back with her, protesting all the time he'd paid· for the cow and he was going to keep her. No man could buy her back from him, not for fifty dollars! Mrs. Wms gave him some talk and he led the cow back to the barn! So we have our milk machine again! There will be real milk in the morrow! as before. And say, Cully, Mrs. Wms is all right. And 'Tim' is a bad boy—if he is good-hearted when he is sober. So. Here's love, dearest! And don't you go on a drunk!! And, maybe, sell my dream-chickens for a song!"

He wrote back, "I wish I could have seen the comedy entitled, 'Mrs. Wms. Cow.' If we didn't know them as we do I would pass the story on to some of the papers—so tragically funny!"

All the while, the Blickensderfer typewriter was at hand. "I have started on the poems. But it doesn't go. No use trying with the 'T' off. I am going to try to get a T here in Appleton. If I can't get one, I'll let you know—and on your way home you may be able to get one at a Blick shop in Chicago. . . . I'd like to get at the poems. Meanwhile I'm getting them all together. . . . The Poems are great, Carl. It would be 'all wrong' to give them up. We must give the Poet every chance! If we can only assure ourselves enuff leisure for this—you will arrive! You've got it in you. The only question is—can we get enuff time to get IT out of you! You are great and great and great! Greater poems than some of yours have absolutely *never* been written! It's only a question of time till we come to our own—via the Incubator-Brooder-Chick-Machine plus the Potato-Tomato-Bean-Cabbage-Factory! It's all coming, dear—coming sure!"

She took the trolley to hear him give a talk and wrote him when she got back to "The Rooms." "You were a 'Terrible Kid' at Greenville. How you warmed up to the work—how you felt it all—and analysed—and showed it up—and got impassioned! Wonder-Boy! . . . And you have such a way with people—such beautiful fellowship. What you said to the men on foot whom we overtook—it couldn't have been better! You gave them poems—living throbbing poems. No-one could have said a 'righter' word. For that too, I am proud of you! You have such a way with people! Fellowship! And the power will grow too—with more strength, more health—and so more to give—and lavish—and spend—on Men. . . . When you do finally arrive (it will take you longer—there are so many of you to look after!)—but when you do arrive, what a company of geniuses you will be—Poet—Essayist—Agitator—Orator—Organizer—Lover of Humanity—and Lover of the Wonder-Girl! Such a bunch of you there will be. . . . We can wait—and work—and pray—all in our own S-S way—and all the while we will be arriving—arriving!"

Without their letters, I would never have understood their style of living then. He was away so much of the time and her life, as before their marriage, was concentrated on his work as much as their love. "I do the best I know how to do, for the S-S. God bless what comes of it! Where are we going Carl? Where and where? And what will we do when we get there? Questions and questions—Carl—and how will the answers look —when written out in the life of the S-S—all the days we live under the sun!"

She advised him of train schedules and how to drop in at the farm. I am sure that she missed Oma and Opa. She was living a different way, uprooted. "Give Oma and Opa my love. . . . If the roads are good enough (which I doubt—you know we have no sleigh, only a buggy), Pa could drive you." She invited Oma to come for the New Year holiday. And Oma approved of all. "Ma is here—thinks the rooms GREAT!! . . . Also Ma is proud to see YOUR name in print! . . . There are three photos from Ed—more Xmas presents! . . . And there's a stuffed chicken and butter and fresh eggs and cottage cheese! Cully! You can be home New Year's Eve, can't you? There'll be something to drink too maybe? hum? . . . Come!" My parents had made a promise that each would let the other go his way and she didn't forget. Their wedding had been a little over six months past and she was polite, "When you can! Unless the work calls too loudly the other way. But we both *hope* & *hope* it'll be 'us together' tomorrow evening . . . Ma and I will sit up till twelve or after to see the New Year in."

I hope my father made it. The letters don't tell. But then his birthday was near, the sixth of January, and knowing how Oma felt about Uncle Ed's birthday, my mother told my father, "I'm going to write to Mother Sandburg so she gets my letter to-morrow. A Birthday is really more a mother's day than a child's day. Anyway, Cully, I am grateful to the mother and to all the forces that made & shaped You!" A birthday package came. My mother didn't yet know that Grandfather Sandburg couldn't sign his name, and she wrote, "The Galesburg postal looks as tho it was written by the Governor! Signed 'A. *Sandburg*'! So! Is it? The box came this morning! And there's plum sauce—a big 2 quart can—for the boy! It must be the kind of plum sauce you told me you used to like so much—the kind you used to eat so much of! It's a beautiful golden yellow—pure sun-shine! When you come home, we'll open the can and celebrate! and there's jam & jelly & raspberry sauce—and a fruit cake, and half of an orange layer cake (I tasted both! Both delicious!)—and home-made candy—and oranges and apples. Altogether a delicious box of good-good things! Such a birth-day supper we'll have when you come home!! The plum-sauce especially! I bet the Mother remembered it was your favorite. . . . We are saving contents of the Birthday Box till you return. I have cakes in crocks so they will keep moist. The candy is delicious—home-made—and beats the S-S brand!! . . . And I bought a 5-cent candle-stick and candles—so we can sit over our supper in the half-light of a candle! . . . Here's Love—Carl—and Love—on your Birth-day! . . . Who could have guessed from your first lusty cry when you entered the World—what a Wonder-Boy you were to become! Who could have guessed the Poems and the Dear Bill stuff and the Voice—from that first lusty cry of a tiny bit of a baby! Wunderkind!"

He said that it was "fun to have fellows ask, 'What kind of a girl is she?' And it's me to the Expatiation— . . . Less than a week sure—& we will again drink coffee & babble of cabbages & kings. *And* Paula will climb onto a chair & curl up & look out of her deep child-eyes & talk wisdom and love—and look like a consumate last satisfying glory—You. Carl."

Then spring was there and summer was near. Uncle Ed, who had given up on my mother visiting him in Voulangis, urged Oma to come over. She wrote Aunt Mary, "Dear Miss Sandburg: . . . I have half way my mine made up to go to Paris this sommer to see the Babys and all of them, and my Brother in Luxemburg. this are my plans, but I am stil considering et all." Oma was lonesome for my uncle though, and feeling her age. She decided to make the voyage. My mother moved out of "The Rooms" in Appleton then to be nearer to Opa. She packed their things and went down to Beaver Dam, fifty miles from Milwaukee and not far from Menomonee Falls—the address 122 4th Street. She wrote Aunt Esther of her visit home, "Dear Sister Esther: . . . Monday & Tuesday of this week I was at the farm to say 'Good-bye' to mother. She is not in the best of health, but we are hoping the week crossing the ocean will do her good—the salt air, the change of scene and everything. . . . Two women friends from Milwaukee will make the trip from here to New York and across the ocean, with mother. And of course, on the other side, brother will be. . . . By the way, I know Mother would greatly enjoy a little letter from you on ship-board just before leaving. . . . The boat sails Tues A. M. . . . Here is the address: North German Lloyd, 'Kaiser Wilhelm der Grosse,' Hobocken, N. Y. Mail is distributed on shipboard just after leaving land. . . . Charlie & I are looking forward to Mart's visit. . . . Once more love to you all . . . Lilian."

And sure enough didn't word come back soon from Villa l'Oiseau Bleu, Voulangis, where Cousin Mary had just had her fifth birthday and Cousin Kate was a little over a year, Oma writing Aunt Mary, "Dear Miss Sandburg: . . . there is so much to see here and the Babys want most all of my spear time. . . . I enclose you a Card were you can see (Grandmother) Oma in all her Glorie. You see what a nice little girl Mary is, and Baby Kate is so sweedt and big and strong and the Baby Donkee arrived just a few days after me so Mary is under the impression that I had something to do with his arrival. The mama Donkee is a fine animal, she can run as fast as a horse with all of us on the Basquet Cart. All people here who got little Cildern keep Donkees ensteadt of horses because the ar not afraid of everething as horses, and so is more save for the Children. Paris is Beautiful Wunderfull . . . I can't tell et in a lettre, only wish Lillian and Carl could see all, hope the can sometimes, but after all, I like et the best here were the Babys are, and et is such lovely place, . . . a 6 foot wall all around, and so manny fruit trees of all kind, and flowers roses all colors, in fact everebody here has so manny roses France is a big rose garden. I love et, but after all I am like a Cat, you know, the allways go home again. Somme times I get lonely for Mr. Steichen and my two tramps, but I am verry happy that the are in Milwaukee, so I can see them often, and the can have so manny good things from our little farm to eat. So I hope the will make there home there, and then you must all comme to see them, and us old people at the dear little farm as Lillian allways named et. I wish I hear how you all are, and just love to get a Photo of Ester in her Cap and Gown. I told Ed and Clara so much about here, that the would like to see her Photo. I am here until about the 6 or 8 of August, after that I am going to my dear old home and my adress will by, C/O Vivin Wagener, Monderconge, Conto E/A Grande Duche de Luxembourg, Europe."

My father, meantime, was job hunting, true to their "Three Acres & Liberty" plan, "Paula:—Nothing doing at Sentinel, Free Press or Eve. Wis. . . . Had an hour and a half talk with Hoyt, pub. of the News. He will put me on within 2 or 3 wks, he thinks, first at court reporting, then editorial writing—was struck with the Bill stuff. Wanted my antecedents.

I confessed everything in my dark past except tt I had been an organizer. Didn't say what my politics are. Am wondering what kind of a liar I am. . . . An editor is wanted on a Sheboygan daily. I may go up there & look it over tomorrow." My father had had a lead on a job as advertising manager at Kroeger Brothers, a department store in Milwaukee. "They will probably not be able to interest me, so from present looking the plan is to be home Monday night with the Wonder Girl till God calls us elsewhere or we are moved by The Spirit of the Job to take our baggage into another biding-place.—Love and love—."

But then he sent off a series of letters to my mother as the job—the first of its kind for him—gradually became a fact. "Monday—3 P.M. Have just come back from Kroeger's. Will start in as ad-man Wednesday morning, at $20 per wk.—Don't pay rent for the next week till you hear from me. . . . It is a try-out at Krgrs. I don't know whether they will let their old man go this week or not. . . . They didn't like it tt I had no references or previous experience in store advertising. Took me on my bluff!—It will be a better job than reporting." And then, "Monday night. . . . I wish I could say how long I will last with Kroegers as I could then tell you positively whthr you ought to come on or not. I don't see where my fall-down can happen. The K. brothers rather like me personally & look for me to be a kind of a bright light around the place. They like my general build & style or they wouldn't have taken a man minus store experience . . . it seems to me I can swing the thing all right & raise hell to the total satisfaction of my German-Jew chiefs. (Ach! a Swede married to a Luxemburger working for German-Jews in an English-speaking commonwealth where not even the streets are common wealth inasmuch as they belong to the automobiles.) And, "Tuesday—2 P.M. I've rented a room at $1.50 per week. . . . Yesterday afternoon & today I have been rambling over & back & thru all the dept. stores in the city, & buying armfuls of papers & studying ads & reading signs. Some of the job will be very pleasant, as I will be very much A Boss, as to when & how I do most of the work. . . . The apart-days aren't for long now, that's sure." Then, "Tuesday—Bulletin No. 2—6:30 P.M. They will fire the other man in the morning & begin taking their chances with me. When you land here . . . we can both use the room I have now till we get another—there is a plenty thereabouts. Delicatessens, dairy lunches, moving pictures, all kinds of things to keep Paula's eyes open. . . . I have walked six or more miles to-day. Had lots of good sun. . . . Maybe we are on our way to a little land and a living. Already we have much love and a little living—the little land we want will come—."

On Wednesday night my father reported to her on the stationery of his employers with the motto: *The Store that tries to Please.* "Back from the first day with the store tt tries to please you. The dept. heads send me in the news from their fields. I edit this store news for a Bargain Circular issued twice a week. Four other days of the week there is copy to prepare for 3 dailies—also 3 weeklies. . . . I write what is to go on the window show-cards. I keep records of what advertising goes to the papers & how many inches each dept. gets in total. I am quite a cog in the machine if I make good. W.J.K. says when I have demonstrated this there will be from $1000 to $2000 a year in it. That is to say, they will either raise my pay or fire me within a few weeks. . . . It beats newspaper work of most kinds. The only fault is it may be a little hard on my eyes. But with Paula here & right living, I think not. So I am going to say: If you don't hear from me on the Thursday night mail at B.D. [Beaver Dam] then *come on* here! *Come on, Paula!* . . . pack & skiddoo —flit from B.D. & get here as quick as you can. . . . I am rooming at 338 Hanover St. Don't bring any baggage (more than a case or two) here—you may want to look up another place for the Two-of-us."

It was June, a year since their wedding, and she came on. My father, while keeping the regular hours, the routines and the stability of the department store, still managed his newspaper work. Into the nights and in spare moments he wrote feature stories for the Milwaukee *Journal*, sometimes using a pen name, Armstrong:

THE CIVILIZED SAVAGE. What is this brute instinct to kill that lurks in human nature? What is this impulse set on a trigger and ready to shoot even when there is no danger? What is this peculiar, hungering desire to take life? . . . The man who "carries a gun" knows well if he looks into his heart that down deep is a hidden, furtive desire to kill. He does not say so openly either to himself or his friends, but in his fingers is the itch to pull a trigger and blow out the light of a human life.

A MINUTE OR TWO OF COMMON SENSE by Armstrong. THE CHANCE OF A CRIPPLE. You were told last week in The Journal the story of William Prust, the 20-year-old boy out on Forty-first-st. A year ago both his feet were crushed so that the doctor had to take off both of them. All of a sudden, in one short day, his two good feet that had always made him an EQUAL of his playmates, are taken away. In the race of life he is now HANDICAPPED. . . . If we did our thinking with our feet, then Willie would be bad off. But we do our thinking with our BRAINS. That is why Willie has a good chance yet in the life struggle ahead of him. Handicaps don't always count. Senator Gore in the United States senate is BLIND. But in the many bills and resolutions that come up for action he can SEE a good deal farther than most of the other senators.

Armstrong. THE VALUE OF A CHILD. How much is a child worth? That is an interesting question. Last week in New York a man and his wife offered their baby for sale at $500. John Graham Brooks says that the average cost of bringing up a child from the time it is a little bald, red thing in a cradle until it is old enough to vote is $25,000. But these figures give no idea of how much a child is worth. The little baby boy, Abraham Lincoln, was certainly worth more than $500. If it cost $25,000 to bring up Thomas Edison, he was a big value for a low price. . . . It is a good sign that the world is waking up to the truth that the more healthy, happy, sensible grown-up people there are, the more healthy, happy, sensible children there will be.

He didn't last long at Kroegers. But the *Journal* liked his Armstrong pieces and when they offered him a job doing features, he accepted and left the other business for good. After a short stint at the *Journal*, he moved over to the Milwaukee *Daily News,* taking the desk of one of their editors who was on a two-week vacation. When the editor returned, my father went to the Milwaukee *Sentinel* for a while and then back to the Milwaukee *Journal,* where he was assigned the post of City Hall reporter, which seemed to satisfy him. The 1910 elections were coming up in Milwaukee, the *Journal* was a forceful paper and my father wrote "Among the Workers" and "Labor" columns, all about hazards to working-men and what building would be best suited for labor headquarters and about street cars and the tobacco trust. He compiled little pieces printed as "ZIG-ZAGS," out of the material he collected in the long stuffed pockets of his coat:

Every man ought to read a good book once in a while. There are some men who read too much. They read so much that they know more about books than they know about life.

We all see the odd streaks in other people. We can't see our own with a looking glass.

America has many business men but no poets. The reason for this is that we are a nation of hustlers and no poet can be a hustler. All poets from Homer to Swinburne have been vagabonds, spectators of life. They sat by the wayside and watched the procession go by.

The man who knows a good cup of coffee and kicks if he doesn't get it is generally a man of good judgment in the world's affairs. Only a quitter will take bad coffee without making a murmur.

The hardest calamities are financial. When a man shoots himself, he is either a banker gone broke or a workingman out of a job.

The only thing we are afraid of is the future. The past is gone and can't touch us.

In late 1909 he was asked to tour Wisconsin for a few weeks, visiting forty-five cities as a special representative with the "Flying Squadron" of the Wisconsin Anti-Tuberculosis Association. My father liked to speak and he showed lantern slides too. "Illustrated Free Lecture. WAR against Tuberculosis, by Charles Sandburg," ran the posters. The routing called for him to talk in public schools, churches and auditoriums on mornings, afternoons and evenings, for seven days a week during the tour. The papers reported on his style: "Charles Sandburg is an intensely earnest speaker who makes all his points as clear as daylight so that everybody can understand. He has a set of stereopticon pictures that are not only instructive but entertaining and enjoyable."

The tour over, he threw himself into the coming Social-Democratic campaign. It was 1910 and the party candidates in Milwaukee were running on the issues of honest and efficient government and the overthrow of the vice and corruption and graft that flourished at City Hall. The papers reported on my father, who was doing his part in the campaign:

SOCIALISM IS COUNTRY'S SALVATION. So declares Charles Sandburg in lecture at Empire Theatre Monday Evening. "No other way than that proposed by the Socialists will save modern civilization from the crash of disaster," declared Chas. Sandburg of Milwaukee, last evening in an address delivered before an audience that filled the Empire theatre almost to its capacity. "Already the concentration of wealth has proceeded to the point where one-half of the citizens of the republic are homeless tenants and where, according to Senator Pratt, editor of the Wall Street Journal, more than one-half of the wealth of the United States is represented at a meeting of the directors of the United States Steel company, when all are present."

Sandburg began his lecture by telling his audience what Socialism is not. He noted that it was "diametrically opposite to anarchism," and that it was not irreligious. It proposed no piling of the nation's wealth, he said, in one big pile and then its equal division among the nation's population. . . . Sandburg will be remembered as the man who lectured in this city two years ago on "Walt Whitman." He speaks as one intensely interested, but he is no fire eater. In a deep, musical voice he tells of the wrongs of the working class and the people listen and think.

The campaign was waged enthusiastically—open air rallies took place on street corners or from trucks stationed outside the Allis-Chalmers or International Harvester factory gates where workers massed to listen. "Bundle brigades" were organized to distribute literature printed in twelve languages, including German, Polish, Scandinavian, and mid-European. The campaign was successful and the nation was startled when the Social-Democratic Party swept into power in Milwaukee that spring of 1910. It was the first time in history that socialists had taken control of a city government.

The new mayor was Emil Seidel, who rolled up his sleeves and kept long hours. Seidel, fourteen years older than my father, was a friend of his as well as a long-time acquaintance of the Steichen family. My father, in his position as City Hall reporter for the Milwaukee *Journal,* had got to know him well. Seidel's parents were immigrants from Germany. During his term, Milwaukeans would call him "Unser [Our] Emil." Like my father and uncle, Seidel had never got past public grammar school. At thirteen, he'd become a wood carver and had gone to Germany to perfect the trade. There he became a socialist. Seidel would be Debs's running mate in 1912 as the Socialist candidate for vice president.

Did my father think then of getting into politics in time? How did he see his future? Was he giving up his literary aspirations, at least as far as pay was concerned? In the Social-Democratic party sweep, Carl Thompson, who'd married my parents, became city clerk; C.B. Whitnall, the old friend of the Steichens, with whom Oma and Mother used sometimes to stay overnight when in town for shopping and a rally, became city treasurer; Victor Berger would be elected to Congress in the fall campaign, becoming the first socialist ever to serve in the House of Representatives. That spring twenty-one of the twenty-five aldermen on the common council were socialists. Emil Seidel held the reins.

Who did he make his secretary? "The first appointment of the new mayor was announced April 12," ran a news item, "his first appointment almost upon his arrival. Charles Sandburg, who has been connected with *The News* and *The Sentinel* and for ten days has been city hall reporter for the *Journal* was named private secretary, at a salary of $1,200 a year." At this point my father decided to officially change his name. When he was home in Galesburg, he would continue to be "Charlie," and he was still being booked as "Charles Sandburg, Lecturer." His propaganda pamphlets and his publications to date were signed "Charles." My mother, calling him "Carl" in letters, addressed the envelopes to "Charles." Grandma Sandburg had named him "Carl August" at birth, and now a news item stated firmly that "Mayor Seidel's secretary who once was Charles Augustus is now plain 'Carl.'" And they said, "His viewpoint is almost six feet above the pavement and under a shag of hair that tousles around recklessly. When he talks to you, he'll lean over close and use his hands much to express his points. That's Carl Sandburg, Mayor Seidel's secretary. . . . an earnest sort of a chap. He can work hard and loaf just as hard when the mood hits. He loves nature, his politics and his wife."

My father wrote to Rube Borough, "Please remember the 'Welcome' sign is out for you on the City Hall tower and remember that you ought to use your Wisconsin home, which is my house, just as I have used my Michigan home, which is your house. I will show you City Hall. The Wonder Girl will show you 200 fluffy chicks she has chaperoned out of eggdom. Yours faithfully, Sandy." Borough wanted to do a magazine story for *Technical World* on the socialist victory in Milwaukee. He wrote later of visiting City Hall and meeting Seidel, "a rather small man with a genial smile, and I liked him although he did not strike me as a commanding figure." Borough also noted my father's "new tailor-made suit (at least it looked like one to me)" and that the "Sandburg home was a plain, almost shabby little house in the Milwaukee outskirts. The rooms were carpetless, with little furniture in them. On the covered rear porch was a large tray of sprouting wheat, an item of diet which Sandy said he liked. Sandy's black bread was excellent and so was his beer, particularly the bock. I found Lilian gracious and charming. . . . Sunday Sandy and I had a swim at the YMCA, and that night the three of us went to hear Friedrich von Flotow's 'Martha.' . . . at home in Marshall I worked hard on my article. . . . It came back with a formal rejection slip."

Now my mother, in her position as wife of the mayor's private secretary, was working for the party too. The Milwaukee *Journal* carried the headline: "SUFFRAGETTES HAPPY OVER THE CHANCE TO VOTE ON BONDS. WOMEN ARE GLAD. Mrs. Carl Sandburg Sees It as Step in Struggle for

Ballot. In speaking of the right to vote on school bonds, Mrs. Sandburg said: 'This privilege means that the suffrage wedge has been driven just a little farther in the right direction.' " My mother marched in the parade of suffragettes too, and even carried a banner. She made speeches for the party. When before the Eighteenth District Mothers' and Teachers' Club on a Monday afternoon, she told them, "If Honest Abe Lincoln, the awkward, horny-handed rail splitter, were alive today, he would be lined up with the Social-Democrats in this campaign. He would feel out of place anywhere except with the labor movement struggling for better food, better clothing and better housing."

Meantime, Oma had returned from Luxembourg, Uncle Ed had come over for exhibitions of paintings and photographs and visited at the farm for his birthday, and Grandfather Sandburg had died on the twenty-second of March. I wonder if Mother ever met my father's father. Not that I knew of. Oma wrote Grandma Sandburg a letter of sympathy, "Dear Mrs. Sandburg . . . wee all love you and wee all wish, we could be of more comfort to you. I am verry sorry that he could not get to know Lillian as Carl of said. he knows his Papa would enjoy her and I often toldt them to go and wisit you all. My son will Sail tomorrow again. I feel sad to, but at the same time, am happy to think he will be with his dear ones soon. . . . I am so sorrow I did not see your son when he was in Milwaukee if thy telephoned to me I would have gone to see him sure. but thy ferget, the dear ones, they were so glad to have him and Lillian thought he was just wright, bless her heart. Once more dear Mrs. Sandburg cheer up as good as you can."

Uncle Ed sent a letter to Mother as he left America bound for France: "A Bord de la Provence. Dear Paus'l—I don't know what to congratulate you on first the chickens or the election—. . . . The world is a great place after all—the old ball does get a big gait on once in a while. . . . Can't you send me a batch of Carl's manuscripts some time—I'd like to read them.—Of course I'm not fooling myself that I know anything about literature—but like the regular philistine and the monkey in the park— I know what I think I like—and have their curiosity. . . . love to both of you from brudder."

Mother's chicken project, which she'd thrown herself into, even got a write-up in the Milwaukee *Journal*:

> Back to nature is the ideal of Mrs. Charles Sandburg. Always interested in farm life, last April she thought she would try and see what success she would have in raising chickens, so she and her

husband, Charles Sandburg, secretary to Mayor Seidel, moved to their present home near the Hawley-rd, where she could try the experiment. "I think it is fine," she said. "It is something that every woman ought to do. It gets me out into the open air, and I never felt better or happier than I have this summer." Mrs. Sandburg started out by buying an incubator and 200 eggs. Becoming more interested as time went on she bought two more lots of 200 eggs each. Although it was her first experience in chicken raising, she succeeded in bringing 300 to broiler size. Most of these have been sold, so that all expenses have been met. . . .

"Do you think one could gain a livelihood from chicken raising, providing one had but little or no experience?" Mrs. Sandburg was asked. "Yes," she replied, "but it wouldn't be play. There would be some hard work ahead." Not the least of Mrs. Sandburg's summer worries were street car fatalities. Fifteen of her chickens were sacrificed on the steel rails in front of the house. When the eggs were in the incubator there were many nights when sleep was almost unknown and there were many sorry days when little fuzzy chicks dropped dead, but after all Mrs. Sandburg isn't sorry for her work and her experience. "I have had a lot of worry and work," she said, "but a lot of keen enjoyment at the same time—and just think of the fresh air I've had."

Their first child was conceived that autumn. I think my mother was content at the Hawley Road house near John's Wood on the outskirts of the city where she'd made her start towards "Three Acres & Liberty." As always, my father continually wrote love poems to her. And all of them had the same title:

PAULA

Star-eyed girl of the heart that knows,
Where did you come by your eyes that see?
Where did you get your heart that knows?
    What passing ghost of silver breath
    Blew on your hair that breath of white?

You tell me of dreams, sea-tinted, sky-fashioned,
You pour out sweet thoughts like baskets of flowers,
You scatter me whimsies, wide-handedly tossing.
Tree-top anthems, smell of the rain, and shy wood-blooms,

The wind that goes winding the sunset trail,
The mud and the bugs, the red spring wonders,
You know them all and you pass them along!

Where did you come from?
Where are you going?
And what are you going to do when you get there?

PAULA

When I looked in your eyes today
And saw the play of lights there,
Your face shining arcs and triangles
Of sunshafts between summer showers,
With mysteries of rainbow color flickering
On a great curve of sky, such as the breath
Of a farm in the hills of the lake country
Of Minnesota—when I looked today
This was the singing there. It is a cry
Losing itself in the hill pines,
Finding itself in the rolling horizons.
You and I must go far.
There is no other way, you and I
Together. It is the law.

PAULA

The mists of night go trailing all the hills,
They feel their slow gray-ghosted way
And hunt for outlet down the sloughs—
Then fade away for other worlds and other forms.

In the running dusk of an upland rise,
High and far on the end of a slope,
At the rim of the world stands Paula,
Looks to the pit and the dome of worlds
Where dawn leaps out flame-fingered and tressed of gold.

At her hill-born neck and hill-loved shoulders
The sunrise flashes its banner and dream
Vibrant and flinging with wonder and daring.

The gods of beauty know her all,
The gods of service give her passwords,

Low love-shadows, deep love-lights
Gather and flit to her hands and face.

Woman of a million names and a thousand faces,
I looked for you over the earth and under the sky.
I sought you in passing processions
On old multitudinous highways
Where mask and phantom and life go by.
In roaming and roving, from prairie to sea,
From city to wilderness, fighting and praying,
I looked.

Dusty and wayward, I was the soldier,
Lone-sentinelled pacing the night,
Who heard your voice in the breeze nocturnal,
Who saw in pine-shadows your hair,
Who touched in the flicker of vibrant stars
        Your soul!
Woman of a million names and a thousand faces.

In the hammering shops I stood,
In the noise of the mad turmoiling,
In the clanging steel and grime and smoke
And dreariness numb of hand and brain.
To a heart where hope fought hard for life
You called from out of the years ahead,
Woman of a million names and a thousand faces.

When I saw you, I knew you as you knew me.
We knew we had known far back in the eons
When hills were a dust and the sea a mist.
And toil is a trifle and struggle a glory
With You, and ruin and death but fancies,
Woman of a million names and a thousand faces.

You are the names of all women who are and have been,
        Your face is the sum of all faces.
Tumble your hair and give us that look
And the wrongs and shames and shattered dreams
Are explained and gone like the yesterdays.

For you are the light of the world's dim dawn
And eternity speaks in the hum of your voice.
Out of days bygone rise your gesturing arms
Resplendent of poems and systems to-morrow.
You are statue and eaglet and priestess,
You are folly and beauty and laughter and wisdom,
You are the woman who understands!
Woman of a million names and a thousand faces.

Music came into their home then, my father writing a friend, "We 'plunged' on a Victrola and got a dandy. You will be in for a fine concert when you make Milwaukee again." Those first 78 rpm records broke easily, fragile as glass. The needles came in tins and were fastened into the head of the Victrola arm with a built-in screw; they dulled after being played a few times and it was necessary to put in a new needle frequently. A removable handle fitted into the side of the Victrola, and when the spring ran down, the voice would grow lower and slower till it ceased, unless one went to wind the handle. It was a glorious new way of pleasure. In time, my father amassed a vast collection of phonograph records, housed in upturned orange crates in his garrets. He never lost his first delight in them. Coming into his room in mid-morning in later years with a tray of food or some message, I would find him stretched on the bed in the swelling sound, drowsing, a black cloth over his eyes to shut out the light.

Back then, when my mother went off to see Oma and Opa, leaving my father alone, he wrote her a letter about another musical event in their lives: "I forgot to tell you that the S-S now have a guitar and there will be songs warbled and melodies whistled to the low Mexican thrumming of Paula-and-Cully's new stringed instrument. The bungalow is all out of order. I don't eat anything at home and I am cultivating the philosophy of a lodger in a Furnished Room and I am sure it will be good for you and for me when you come back. And speaking of 'coming back,' this is a very important matter and should not be neglected. Unless we have further communication, that is to say, no matter how our letters get crossed and mail service fails us, the Time is 9 A.M. next Friday, the Place is the St. Paul station, the girl is Paula."

Thirteen

The Dark Period

Part of my father's dream of changing the world came true with the socialists in power in Milwaukee. This was their chance and the country was watching. One Milwaukee weekly ran an article describing Mayor Seidel's office "by Carl Sanberg, Mayors' Private Secretary [sic]." "No where else is there the excitement of a newspaper office with the added gloom of a charity bureau combined with the life and color of a railway station. . . . Letters from the world over come to Comrade Seidel in the morning mail. There are constant inquiries as to who the Socialists are, what Socialism is, and how the Socialists expect to do this or that. . . . There are complaints from Milwaukee citizens of ashes not collected, scarlet fever not reported, high taxes, street lights not burning, holes in pavements, and dead dogs to be removed."

My father sent articles in continually to the Milwaukee *Social-Democratic Herald*. "This is the age of investigation. Is there a crying wrong, is there a brutal, filthy social condition revealed? That does not mean action. It means investigation. . . . Out with you, you investigating loafers! Out with you, you investigating pretenders! We have had enough of investigation. Let us have action. The facts are at your finger-tips. The proofs have been laid before you. Less investigation and a little more action, gentlemen. The people may not always slumber. C.S."

Then, because of his fire for the cause and his zeal for newspaper reporting, my father was withdrawn from his secretarial work and assigned to the *Social-Democratic Herald*. Also, there was a new four-page tabloid, *Political Action*, selling for a penny a copy, a quarter a year, just being launched by the socialists. It was Victor Berger's creation. "WHAT HAVE THEY DONE IN MILWAUKEE?" ran their headline, and just below, "You hear this question asked very often nowadays. And whether the present working class administration of Milwaukee has made good is an important matter. This article was prepared especially for Political Action by Carl Sandburg. Because of the increased vicious assaults of the capitalist daily papers, Sandburg was transferred from his office as secretary to Mayor Seidel and put on the job of writing the accomplishments of the administration for the Social-Democratic Herald. His straight-talk pamphlet, 'You and Your Job,' is known to thousands of Socialists. And his thorough acquaintance with the Milwaukee city hall and his experience as a Socialist organizer make this summary particularly valuable."

My father wrote to Rube Borough about the change, "Perhaps you know I was shifted from Seidel's office to the Herald at my request. The Herald has been weak, failing to present many of our strongest points. So I am a sort of administration editor, or S.D.P. publicity man, writing about a page and two columns a week—hurling the shrapnel into the Daily Liars, &c."

The last of the small booklets by my father signed "Charles Sandburg" was published at the end of 1910: *Joseffy: An Appreciation.* My father had kept track of his friend, Joseffy. Back in Appleton he'd written Mother, "Joseffy has given me some fur stuff, *rare* quality, for a collar for *you.*" She had answered, "Will you like me better when I have a collar made of this stuff you like! If so—why." And he had said, after visiting with the magician, "Joseffy is with you—he is for you strong."

The other recent pamphlet of my father's, *You and Your Job,* had been signed "Charles Sandburg" also. It was doing well. The Local Philadelphia Socialist Party had written, "Dear Comrade Sandburg:— . . . We printed 10,000 copies and consider it the plainest pamphlet printed in America. We especially like its distinctive American appeal."

By then Rube Borough had married his Laura. Borough was still with the buggy plant in Marshall, Michigan, and my father sent congratulations to the new couple, "from the two of us who are one to the two of you who are one. . . . It would be mighty good if you . . . could come over here for a few days. We have some of the choicest chicken ever fried to put before you. . . . One thing after another is crackling and sizzling in the office these days. So don't mind if I get romance and fried chicken mixed. . . . Yours always, Sandy."

Then it was 1911 and a year since my father had been made secretary to Mayor Seidel and then taken over his city editor job on the *Herald.* He told Rube Borough, "We expect to have a little red babbling heir-apparent arrive this summer, June. He (or she) will constitute our vacation, probably. So it will be up to you and Laura to visit us." On the third of June, my sister Margaret was born, my father writing about it at once and selling the article, called "My Baby Girl," to *LaFollette's Magazine* before long:

It was just a week ago she came. . . . And when I walked away from the hospital in early gray daylight with a fresh rain smell in the air, treading the blown-down and scattered catalpa blossoms under my heels, I had above all else a new sense of a sacredness of life. A grand, original something the full equal of death or first love or marriage as an experience, this I knew I had touched. . . . All that day and the next, however, I was compelled to draw on my resources of patience and humor. The remark of a startlingly large number of my friends was: "Too bad it's a girl." I learned it for the first time to be positively true that fathers and mothers generally know what they prefer as a first child and they prefer boys to girls. Could they have their choice from the God of Things as They Are, they would say: "Give us a boy." And so, while a few understood my joy, some actually took it as a half-grief, a kind of sorrow, and commiserated me: "Too bad it's a girl."

Thus at the very start of life, prejudices and dispreferences follow the footsteps of one sex as against another. . . . And I have wondered how far they are right. Tonight however, as I hold in my arms for a few moments, this new-come beginner in the game of life, I think I would as lief be this baby girl as any man alive. For this baby girl, as sure as luck and health stay by her, shall see wonder on wonder that will be denied to our eyes. . . . She shall see women go forward and cast ballots and speak and write and with passionate earnestness take part in political movements. . . . She—this little soft-breathing thing in my arms—will be alive when typhoid, tuberculosis and babies born blind have become forgotten, improbable things . . . she, my baby girl, will walk the streets of cities from which all dangers of the now commonest and deadliest diseases have been driven out.

In this week, when her name is registered among the births, woman, the common woman—the wife of the workingman—is the slave of a slave, cooking, sewing, washing, cleaning, nursing in sickness, and rendering a hundred personal services daily for a man who is himself not in power to dictate a constant job and living wage for himself. My baby girl shall see the slave achieve freedom for himself and his class, and "the slave of a slave" broken away from the harsh interests that hold him in the dark to-day. So rapid and sweeping are some of the advancements to-day, that I think it possible that the wise sweet mother who bore her, and I, her father, may look on these things forecasted. But whether we see them or not, sure it is that the world is moving forward with strides so fast and vast that all the Tribe of Intelligence agree that these and more beyond our reckoning will be. . . . Time was when it may have been right to pity the baby girl. That time has gone by. I am glad it was a girl.

He wrote a poem to my sister after a while, calling it "Margaret":

> Many birds and the beating of wings
> Make a flinging reckless hum
> In the early morning at the rocks
> Above the blue pool
> Where the gray shadows swim lazy.
>
> In your blue eyes, O reckless child,
> I saw today many little wild wishes,
> Eager as the great morning.

In July, when Margaret was six weeks old, Mother took her to the farm at Menomonee Falls. She wanted to visit with Oma and Opa and to help in the summertime canning and preserving. She wrote back, "Margaret is having a splendid time rusticating on Opa's 3½ Acres! Paula enjoys seeing a full sweep of sky & wide fields and open meadows again! Margaret routes me out of bed early enuf mornings so I can see The Gray World of mists & shadows before the Dawn breaks. Then to nurse her in the Quiet Hours with Grayness & Shadows about—is to harken back in memory to the dim beginnings of Things! A babe makes you live again! . . . We are lonesome for you . . . Love & love Paula."

My father wrote a friend, William Leiserson, "The missus has gone to her folks' farm near Menomonee Falls. 'Tis fruit season and we must get busy now or we will not have what we want when the wintry winds blow cold in January. I join her tomorrow. . . . You remember Thoreau's saying, 'It is a great art to saunter.' Beginning tomorrow night, I shall SAUNTER for three days."

The living wage stayed the problem in my parents' lives. A friend, C. L. Edson, out in Girard, Kansas, on the *Appeal to Reason—A Socialist*

Paper, said, "Dear Old Sandburg. . . . You are dead right in being dissatisfied with $25 a week and the building up of an outside market is the solution of the problem. . . . I will keep you in mind in case I see anything that would benefit you. . . . Socialism is going to develop a press that will make a good market for us and we will get a few bones before the utopian stage comes when no one will write for money. Best wishes to Mrs. Sandburg and that perfect baby. . . . Yours ever."

Victor Berger was launching another socialist paper, the Milwaukee *Leader,* in December, its slogan under the masthead: "Unawed by Influence and Unbribed by Gain." My father would be labor editor there in 1912, one article going: "NOTHING TO LOSE BUT CHAINS. . . . You newspapermen and you lawyers, you preachers and doctors, you well-fed and well-dressed brain workers who make so bold as to get up in clubs and churches and public places and discuss the labor question, understand this well. You shall never understand the labor problem and you shall never speak anything but wicked nonsense, or useless half-truth unless you go down into the working class world and understand how through the combination of low wages and high prices, there are men, women and children living with too little to eat and too little to wear and with houses and furnishings that are nothing but a terrible travesty on a race of men having strong hands. Take a week off and toil down among the tanners of Milwaukee. Or, go out to the rolling mills and help make steel for a few days. Carry your dinner in a tin lunch box. During your short noon hour eat with grimy hands holding your hard-earned bread. And find out for yourself just how little, how absolutely little, it is that the workers have to lose through any movement, however revolutionary. Find out for yourselves how true it is that the workers of the world would have nothing to lose but their chains. Then it may dawn on your brains that the labor unions and the Socialist movement rise from the very depths and out of the supreme forces of civilization. As the working class becomes conscious of how and why it is supreme, then society will effect the great change outlined in the Socialist program."

Pay stayed short. "My dear Sandburg: In spite of my returning your manuscript, you will know, I am sure, that I like your article and would be glad to publish it. . . . I am going to run at least one socialist article each month during the national campaign." So wrote Charles Zueblin of *The Twentieth Century Magazine.* Seidel had been defeated in his run for reelection as mayor by a coalition of the Milwaukee Democrats and Republicans, and was running for vice president on the Socialist ticket led by Debs. My father had propaganda articles he tried to sell, besides various others. *LaFollette's Magazine* had paid $10 for "My Baby Girl" and the same for "The Man, the Boss and the Job." For a piece "Where Is My Wandering Girl Tonight," which was about "municipal dances" sponsored by the Milwaukee socialists, he was paid $40 by the New Idea Publishing Company who featured it in their *The Woman's Magazine.* And all the time, of course, my mother typed fresh copies of articles and poems which kept going out to periodicals and journals and returning mostly with rejection slips.

Then my father had a chance for a job he liked in mid-summer of 1912. The Chicago papers—the *Daily News* and the *Tribune*—had shut down because of a strike, and the Chicago *Daily Socialist* was the only one on the stands. The socialists saw their chance, changed their name to the Chicago *Evening World* and their circulation soared. They asked my father to come on at once. He liked Chicago and came, taking a furnished room. My mother and Margaret went to stay at the farm. It was August and she was waiting to see whether they would remain in Milwaukee or go to Chicago to live. She wrote him, "Send us a copy of the World with some of your stories marked—every now and then. . . . And, Carl, I wouldn't bother with the coffee in your room—except once in a while when you have lots of time and can take pleasure in brewing your own stuff! As a regular thing—cooking your own breakfast is likely to waste more time than its worth. . . . Margaret is chasing Opa's cat around the room. She has cornered Tommie now and is pulling his ears. Tommie is wonderfully patient. . . . Margaret has picked out Opa for her special friend! She leaves Oma and myself for her dear old Opa! . . . I've been laying plans. The upshot is I believe I'll be in Chicago week after next to look over renting possibilities in the north suburbs. . . . That's if you are reasonably sure that Chicago will be *a go.*"

My father said yes. The *Evening World* was a success, and he and Chicago from the first were heart to heart. He was sending out a new poem that my mother typed up, starting:

> Hog Butcher for the World,
> Tool Maker, Stacker of Wheat,
> Player with Railroads and the Nation's
> Freight Handler;
> Stormy, husky, brawling,
> City of the Big Shoulders. . . .

My mother wrote, "Oma and I are making a start at packing. Today

I had another ad inserted in the paper & as a result sold our gas range for $5.00. . . . And meanwhile Margaret is exploring the paths in Opa's garden—plucking the silken petals of poppies (her favorites)—never giving one little thought to 'renting possibilities' in the City where daddie works."

The home Mother picked out in Chicago was at 4646 North Hermitage Avenue in the Ravenswood area. They rented the second story—roomy and with enough windows and a securely fenced backyard. She and Oma finished packing and the goods were freighted. It was late August. "I have the bill of lading in my purse. . . . I am going to the farm and will stay there till I hear from you that the goods *have* arrived. You can phone or telegraph to the farm. I will try to plan everything so it will run smoothly." It did and the new home was a success. But then the strike of the Chicago newspapers was abruptly settled. They began publishing again, their copies filling the newsstands. The circulation of the *Evening World* slowly dropped. By December, the paper had folded altogether. My father was again out of a job.

Years later my mother told me they called that time "The Dark Period," and that it was the only really hard part of their lives financially. My father walked the streets looking, and then was taken on the staff of *The Day Book,* published six days a week, a cent a copy, small in size—six inches by nine. He wrote William Leiserson, "Since the end of The World last December and checks for two weeks wages never cashed and tribulations various and unique at that time, I have been working for the Day Book. It's a Scripps paper, takes no advertising, and therefore tells the truth. Chicago, however, is unfamiliar with the truth, can not recognize it when it appears, so the paper is having a steady, quiet growth and seems to have large destinies ahead. . . . My two girls, the one I married, and the one which came a couple of years ago, are both coming fine. . . . Here's our blessings and good wishes. Your fraternally."

Looking about for a better-paying position, he wrote *LaFollette's Magazine* in January of 1913. "Dear Sandburg," they replied, "Unfortunately for us, your letter came to me just at a time when neither *LaFollette's* nor the State Journal is in a position to take on another man." Then my father landed a job at *System Magazine* that paid thirty-five dollars a week. He talked about his work and his new pseudonym in a letter to Rube Borough: "I wrote the High Cost of Government series, two signed stories on accident prevention in the July and August numbers, and in September and October numbers will have 'I' stories signed by W. C. Colson, a retail clothier who keeps country trade from going to the city. . . . You might say at first shot that this is the hell of a place for a poet but the truth is it is a good place for a poet to get his head knocked when he needs it. In fact, it is so good a place for a healthy man who wants to watch the biggest, most intense, brutal and complicated game in the world—the game by which the world gets fed and clothed—the method of control—the economics and waste—so good a place is it from this viewpoint."

It may have been during this "Dark Period" that my mother lost her second baby. I never knew for sure when it was, but in long years later she told me that if a girl had come, she'd picked her name—Madeline. Always when she spoke of the event to me though, she was firm and fierce and allied with Oma against the physician who'd attended the home birthing and, they said, let Madeline perish by protracting the delivery. Margaret had been born in Milwaukee's Misericordia Hospital, an easy delivery, and Mother had decided, on her doctor's advice, to have this baby at home. Perhaps it happened just before her summer vacation at the farm in 1913 when Margaret was two, for she wrote my father, "Dearest Carl—Write me as soon as you know whether you are coming. Margaret insisted you should 'Come home—then din-din—then bye-bye—tchu-tchu car—with papa'—yesterday evening. She took me down the road bent on *find papa* . . . I'm beginning to feel how much good the country is doing me. I notice a big change. I feel *almost* my old self again! A couple of weeks more of this and I will be quite strong! . . . Much much love. . . . Paula." One of my father's poems—and I don't know when he wrote it although it wasn't published for seven more years —would go:

NEVER BORN

The time has gone by.
The child is dead.
The child was never even born.
Why go on? Why so much as begin?
How can we turn the clock back now
And not laugh at each other
As ashes laugh at ashes?

He visited them at the farm and she wrote after he left, "Here's love to you and kisses from Margaret and Paula at the Farm! We wish you were here again today. Margaret wailed 'Come back, papa' even in her sleep last night! . . . Yesterday was a Big Day. The Joy of it is with me yet. It helps me grow strong faster."

Before coming back to Chicago, Mother and Margaret took the train up to Appleton to visit the George Foxes. She wrote, "Dear Carl—Margaret and I are in the old room that we two used to have! Margaret is enjoying the children's company immensely. . . . all the cubs are as husky as can be. . . . send me the address of my wash woman, Mrs. Krause, so I can write her from here when to come when I get back to Chicago. The address you will find on a post card which is in the green velvet box on top of the black dresser in my room." And then as autumn came on and the train returned them to the farm, "I enjoyed the days at Fox's but life was pretty strenuous for me, with all the clamoring kiddies! I'm not quite strong enough for such adventures! Saturday I'm coming home—so remember you have an engagement with me for Saturday afternoon *and* Sunday! . . . Marny has many stories to tell Daddie—all about . . . the swings & hammock, & wonderful tree-house in the boughs of an apple tree! A Big tree-house with chairs & bench & rustic seat 'way high up! You climb up a long ladder to reach it! . . . Take good care of yourself and get plenty of sleep so you will be in fine shape to *enjoy* the Homecoming Festivities! I'm going to do my part—so I'll be alive, real alive, nerves in fine shape & all! . . . Saturday & Sunday we will kick up the leaves in our backyard—daddie & Mama & Marny together! . . . Love from us all in the white farmhouse with the holly hocks!"

He wrote her one of his rambling love letters, that she could save and read over, "Now it is only a couple of days till we again maintain our establishment—huh?—a really truly home. And unless some over particular people rake up the leaves, it will be a fine yard for a homecoming celebration. It's been mystically wonderful lately, that backyard, with a half moon through the poplars to the South in a haze, and rustlings, always high or low rustlings on the ground & in the trees, a sort of grand 'Hush-hush, child.' And as the moon slanted in last night and the incessant rustlings went on softly, I thought that if we are restless and fail to love life big enough, it's because we have been away too much from the moon and the elemental rustlings. The more I think about Jack London and his John Barleycorn fear of The Noseless One and his intimations that Truth is too terrible to hunt down and face, I think he's had too much books and introspected himself too far as a genius. I like better Walt Whitman musing among 'ashes of dead soldiers' and talking as tho he knows there is a thing he calls 'love' which is a reality finer than 'death'—I haven't got room here to work it all out. Sunday we shall go hand in hand. Love now from Carl. P.S.—The Ravenswood station agent says a train leaves Milwaukee 4 p.m., you transfer at Kenosha 4.45, and get off at Ravenswood at 6.25. Unless I hear otherwise I shall look for you on that train. He said that was the only one. If I hear there are others I will meet them, to grab you & Marny."

The dark time seemed to stay with them. From *The American Magazine*, "My dear Mr. Sandburg: I am returning herewith your poems, 'Chicago,' and those 'done on a late night car.' While they have interested us very much, we have decided we are unable to use them. Thanking you very much for letting us see them. Very sincerely yours."

Then in November, from his present employers at *System Magazine*, misspelling his name, "Dear Mr. Sandberg: I want to put our relations on paper so that we both can consider them thoughtfully, as I know you wish to. You came with us, I think, in the Spring. . . . I want to be frank. Observation leads me to believe that you have not the habit of thought nor the method of approach to work which would enable you to develop fully in this organization of ours. It seems to me that your imaginative qualities and abilities lead toward the poetic rather than the selling. . . . Consequently, I feel that you ought to get into another line as soon as possible."

There was nothing for my father but to cast about again. He wrote to the Chicago *Tribune*, "From the enclosed pages, which were entirely written or supervised by myself, you can judge for yourself whether I am able to shape up business facts so as to get the editorial point of contact which is wanted. . . . As to salary, I would expect $35 a week, provided your field is the one in which I find the opportunity I want for the hard work, new ideas, and quick co-operation I can give you. . . . Yours sincerely."

The job my father did find after again walking the streets for some time and which he would not keep for long, was with *American Artisan And Hardware Record*, published on Saturdays and stating on the masthead that it was the "Representative of The Stove Tin Hardware Heating and Ventilating Interests." Sometimes my father wrote under the pseudonym "Sidney Arnold" for them in a column called "Random Notes and Sketches." The material for the column, as always, came from the voluminous pockets my mother had sewed into his coat, which stayed filled with clippings, articles, his notes, his poems and what he called "the mess of stuff that sometimes clutters my pockets."

Perhaps it was now that my mother thought of leaving my father. I know, because she told me of it once, that she reminded him that they'd had a pact from the first that if one wanted to go, the other would consent freely. She said that it had happened when Margaret was little and the only child. They had had a minor argument—he had stormed about something. She'd told him, "Remember our pact." But all he would answer was, "Do you think I'd go through all that courting again!" Over the years she told it with slight variations, but his line was always the same. She didn't remember the original disagreement. Perhaps she sometimes dwelt on old unkept promises. I have wondered if ever she was discontent with her role as keeper of the home place in that early time. Had she thought romantically that they'd do more things together—camping out in tents now and then, organizing workers for the cause while going hand in hand? Did she reproach him because he seemed to be away so much? My father had a drive for work in the evenings, rather than for taking my mother to weekly concerts, the opera, the plays and musicals which she'd gone to in Milwaukee before she married. And there was his strong, unsettling temper that she was familiar with.

My father has been described variously at this time in his life. He was thirty-five. Sherwood Anderson later said he was "somewhat heavy, a cumbersome fellow with a good deal of working-class prejudice and a gloomy Danish nature but very fine and sincere in his slow heavy way." And Ben Hecht wrote of "a stranger . . . who from his slouch and rig and the shy and smoky look of his face appeared to be a cowhand. The stranger wore a celluloid collar and had an arc of stiff hair slanting across his forehead and sticking into one eye." And Eunice Tietjens, a poet and helper to the editor of *Poetry: A Magazine of Verse,* said he was "lanky, warm and human, slow-spoken and witty, his eyes very blue behind his thick glasses."

And then, in that fall of 1913, it seems there was a momentous day in my parents' lives. My father, poems in hand, had decided to look in on the *Poetry* office at 543 Cass Street. The magazine was just a year old, and they had received his poems now and then, Mother sending them there and receiving them back. The *Poetry* office was a front room in a renovated North Side mansion. There was a gilt-framed mirror over a white marble mantel, roller-top desks, a table, chairs, and a cushioned wicker rocker which came to be called "the poet's chair." "I was not prepared," Eunice Tietjens wrote, "for the sweep and vitality of the Chicago Poems which he brought into the office the first day I met him. They quite took us all off our feet and it was with much pride that we introduced this new star in the firmament. . . . we adopted Carl at once and loved him. He used to drop over often after work, and we would go out and eat pork chops . . . and have much fine ranging conversation on the universe in general and the injustice of man in particular. He had a deep sympathetic sense of humor which always kept him from being the usual thumping radical."

The family story I was brought up with was that my mother had mailed in the Chicago Poems and that it was through her persistence that they were finally read and recognized. It seems it wasn't so. Alice Corbin Henderson, the assistant editor, had passed the poems on to the editor and publisher, Harriet Monroe, who spoke later of the "stalwart slow-stepping Swede," and said, "Alice had handed over to me a group of strange poems in very individual free verse, beginning with 'Chicago' as the 'hog-butcher of the world.' This line was a shock at first, but I took a long breath and swallowed it, and was laughed at scornfully by critics and columnists when we gave it the lead in March, 1914. Carl was a typical Swedish peasant of proletarian sympathies in those days, with a massive frame and a face cut out of stone. . . His delicate-featured very American wife told me that ours was the first acceptance of Carl's poems, although for two years she had been collecting rejection slips. . . . Carl would come in often to sit solidly in our 'poet's chair,' and talk of life and poetry with whoever might be there, weighing his words before risking utterance in his rich, low-pitched, quiet voice."

And wasn't that how light from an unexpected source ended my mother and father's "Dark Period"?

Fourteen

The Poet

By the time the March, 1914, issue of *Poetry: A Magazine of Verse* was on the newsstands, my father had left his position on *American Artisan And Hardware Record* and was back on *The Day Book,* a job that seemed to suit him, at twenty-five dollars a week. He would stay three years and more at *The Day Book* until it folded. The staff was small—five or six— and it was enthusiastic about the cause of the workingman. The quarters were in a basement at 500 South Peoria Street on the West Side. The boss was Negley D. Cochran, who posted notices to stir his staff on techniques and policy:

> Day Book Staff: It will help amazingly if everybody will get the most news into the fewest possible words. . . . The Day Book would be improved 100 per cent if most of our stories were boiled to half the space they take now. Dont try for writing. Give 'em the news—boiled down. The more news items we print in each issue the better. . . . If we can cut our stories in half, we can get twice as much news in the paper. Please, everybody try and help out on this. N. D. Cochran.

And there was my father, his free verse heading the current issue of *Poetry,* which he spotted on the newsstand in that windy March as he headed for *The Day Book* offices. For the group of nine poems that led that March issue he was paid a hundred dollars. Some of the poems had been around awhile; one, "The Road and The End," written back in his firehouse days in Galesburg, was almost unchanged, The other eight were "Chicago," just recently turned down by *The American Magazine,* and then "Jan Kubelik," "The Harbor," "The Hammer," "At A Window," "Lost," "Who Am I," and "Momus."

It was an era of revolt in the nation against all the old standards, and as a matter of course poetry and prose were in a revolution too. *The Little Review,* edited by Margaret Anderson and just launched, stated on its masthead, "A Magazine of the Arts, Making No Compromise with the Public Taste," and "the Little Review is not a chatty literary journal; it is not written to amuse, to conciliate, or to increase contemporary stupidity. It is an effort to establish some sort of intellectual communication between New York, London and Paris, and to break through the ingrained refusal of thought which one meets on every side in America. THE MAGAZINE THAT IS READ BY THOSE WHO WRITE THE OTHERS." No one was paid to work there and it is told that when they were low on funds once, Eunice Tietjens gave Miss Anderson her diamond ring and said, "Sell it and bring out an issue." Harriet Monroe wrote in *Poetry* about "the new Pegasus": "Congratulations to Miss Margaret C. Anderson, editor of *The Little Review,* upon the completion of the first year of her high-stepping charger! May it spurn the ground and sniff the air and champ the bit for many years to come, and never quite throw its rider!"

The Masses in New York announced on its masthead: "This magazine is owned and Published Co-operatively by its Editors. It has no Dividends to Pay, and nobody is trying to make Money out of it. A Revolutionary and not a Reform Magazine; a Magazine with a sense of Humor and no Respect for the Respectable; Frank; Arrogant; Impertinent; Searching for the True Causes; a Magazine Directed against Rigidity and Dogma wherever it is found; Printing what is too Naked or True for a Money-Making Press; a Magazine whose final Policy is to do as it Pleases and Conciliate Nobody, not even its Readers—A Free Magazine."

When Miss Monroe advertised *Poetry: A Magazine of Verse* in its first issues, she stated that they were "endowed for five years through the generosity of over one hundred Chicago people, for the encouragement of the art and the development of a sympathetic public."

My father's friend who ran the St. Louis *Mirror* read the March issue poems and wrote, "Dear Mr. Sandburg: . . . I wish you would modify your socialistic devotion to the extent of refusing to sacrifice yourself on the Day Book and get out into the larger writing game. You can deliver the goods, I know. Very sincerely yours, William Marion Reedy."

The poets of the day took notice too. Edgar Lee Masters wrote later in his life of the poem "Chicago": "I looked upon it as a mere piece of interesting extravagance. I felt that he did not know Chicago, except as a city of packing plants, and criminals, and dirty alleys." And Ezra

Pound, seven years younger than my father, wrote from Rapallo, Italy, to Harriet Monroe, "Glad to see Sandburg. I don't think he is very important but that's the sort of stuff we ought to print." And to my father he said, "Free verse is only part of the battle . . . I don't think you've got your 'form' yet, in the athletic sense. I think your work will be more of a temper. Also certain phrasings leave me in doubt. I am not sure whether your 'Chicago' wouldn't hit harder if it began six lines later and ended five lines sooner, for example. I am very much the grandma in these matters and numerous people dislike it. . . . For your 'harbour' and your 'road to the end' I have no carping. . . . E.P."

On the first of that March of 1914, the staff of *Poetry* invited William Butler Yeats, who was coming to the United States on a speaking tour, to let them entertain him. "We, of the editorial staff of *Poetry*, feel that you would honor us very highly if you would permit us to give you an informal dinner while you are here, to which we may invite our guarantors and contributors. . . . We hope that you will confer this recognition upon our attempt . . . to create and perpetuate beauty among us . . . Yours very sincerely." The poet accepted, from "*Stone Cottage, Coleman's Hatch, Sussex*. Dear Miss Monroe; . . . if I go to Chicago as I dare say I shall I shall certainly avail myself of your invitation, and I thank you very much . . . W.B. Yeats."

My father was asked, "The pleasure of your company is requested at an informal supper in honor of Mr. William Butler Yeats, to be given by the editors, contributors and guarantors of *Poetry*, at the Cliff Dwellers, Orchestra Hall, at half after seven on the evening of Sunday the first of March. Mr. Yeats will give an after-dinner talk on contemporary poets, and there will be brief speechs by Mr. Nicholas Vachel Lindsay and other poets and friends of the magazine. A place will be reserved for you upon receipt of $2.50."

The preparation for the "informal supper" caused a commotion among the poets and their benefactors. Yeats, along with others of the out-of-towners, would stay at Mrs. William Vaughn Moody's. She, on the death of her husband in 1912, had converted their mansion at 2970 Groveland Avenue into something of a salon, which became well known as a meeting place for the poets, among others in the arts. Harriet Moody would entertain from the tea hour until midnight. She ran a popular catering service and in the mornings was busy with it, superintending the preparation and handling of the dishes. But in the afternoons, guests were welcome. Mrs. Moody sat in a commodious black velvet swing which hung from the ceiling. At times she invited favorites or shy newcomers to sit beside her. Her dark Indian servant addressed her as "Mama" and men guests as "Papa." There, the previous year, the tall Hindu, Rabindranath Tagore, had chanted his translations of Bengali poems and songs before the fireplace. Yeats had written in *Poetry* that Tagore's translations "stirred my blood as nothing has for years. . . . his songs are sung from the west of India into Burmah wherever Bengali is spoken. He was already famous at nineteen."

My father would go to Harriet Moody's too in time, as would Nicholas Vachel Lindsay, a year younger than he. Lindsay's name as a poet was firm by the time he read my father's "Chicago Poems." He and my father, allied politically as well, always got on. Lindsay even wrote a poem called "Why I Voted the Socialist Ticket," ending:

> Come let us vote against our human nature,
> Crying to God in all the polling places
> To heal our everlasting sinfulness
> And make us sages with transfigured faces.

A few years earlier, Lindsay had walked across the country from Illinois to New Mexico and literally offered a book of poems in exchange for food and lodgings. My father's copy of *Rhymes To Be Traded For Bread*, published in June of 1912, was dedicated on October 8, 1916, "From Nicholas Vachel Lindsay to Carl Sandburg for Judicious distribution."

The Chicago *Daily News* reported on Yeats's speech the next morning. He'd said, "If America is to have great poets, they must be humble and simple. They must not stop to think whether they themselves are good or bad, but must express themselves as they are. They must give nature and themselves as they are, the evil with the good. Readers should encourage poets to lead lives of humility and simplicity." Harriet Monroe said later that Yeats had "saluted 'as a fellow-craftsman' one of the humblest, one who had exchanged rhymes for bread at farmers' doors, the obscure author of GENERAL BOOTH ENTERS INTO HEAVEN. Whereupon the young poet so honored, whose poem had 'an earnest simplicity, a strange beauty,' arose and recited for the first time THE CONGO as further proof of his dedication to the art."

Lindsay had said in a letter to Harriet Monroe, "Unless I am mistaken, you will think lots more of me after I recite the Congo—and I hope it may win Mr. Yeats a little—so I will be something more than a shadow to him. *After* that piece he will like me or damn me. . . . very much yours, Nicholas Vachel Lindsay." He chanted that evening, shutting his eyes and belting it out, whispering, hissing and obeying the "marginal instructions" which accompanied his printed chants. A refrain in the poem, with the instruction, "More deliberate. Solemnly chanted," went:

THEN I SAW THE CONGO, CREEPING THROUGH THE BLACK,
CUTTING THROUGH THE JUNGLE WITH A GOLDEN TRACK.

And "Last line whispered":

". . . Mumbo-Jumbo will hoo-doo you,
Mumbo-Jumbo will hoo-doo you,
Mumbo-Jumbo will hoo-doo you."

Yeats stayed a week in Chicago. My father, of course, attended that "famous first banquet," as Miss Monroe later called it. Edgar Lee Masters has recounted how during those days he went to "a sort of buffet supper at a club in North Michigan Avenue where Harriet Monroe, Sandburg, the *Poetry* assistant editors, and some others from New York were present. Yeats made a speech and Sandburg and I read some of our latest poems, and they were pretty audacious, as I remember it. Yeats looked amused." Masters noted also that he "laughed with Sandburg and not at him." The two had become friends right away. Masters was nine years older, a lawyer, one-time partner of Clarence Darrow.

Masters wrote later of his first meeting with my father. He had been on an injunction case involving a strike of waitresses against the hotel and restaurant keepers' association. He said, ". . . . While I was in the actual battle, at a time in the courtroom when there was a recess, a tall man came to me with a copy of the *Mirror* which contained a poem of mine, expressing admiration for it. He made himself known to me as Carl Sandburg, a reporter on the *Day Book,* an odd little daily. And he wanted some news about the injunction case I was in. He was taller than ordinary, and with a martial bearing. His voice was deep and drowsy, the smile on his large loose mouth with its fleshly lips, broad and ingratiating. He wore steel-rimmed spectacles through which his gray-yellow eyes stared or grew luminous with sudden interest. He looked much like Larson, the Swedish cobbler of Lewistown, in whose shop I used to loaf years before. It was evident enough that Sandburg was Swedish." They talked about the strike and about Masters's poem which my father had brought along, signed "Webster Ford" and published in the May twenty-ninth issue of William Marion Reedy's St. Louis *Mirror.*

My father began to stop in at Masters's law office now and then. Masters gave him a copy of *A Book of Verses*, published back in 1898: "To Carl Sandburg From a Member of the Union & with friendship, E.L. Masters, March 12th 1914." My father showed him *Incidentals*, Masters later describing it as "a little sheaf of prose poems, or aphorisms," which he read with interest but which could not "be called poetical, nor is it in any way important. . . . But there was a refreshing realism in them just the same. . . . He was off on an entirely new trail."

By now my parents and Margaret had moved from the Hermitage Avenue second-story home to a small house at 616 South 8th Avenue in Chicago's suburb of Maywood. Masters began coming out there from time to time to talk about the striking waitresses' problems and about his poetry. Mother has told me how moved my father was by *Spoon River Anthology*, then in the making. Few besides some poets, a friend or two and his own family knew that "Webster Ford" was Edgar Lee Masters. As the case of the waitresses against the hotel management dragged on into the summer, Reedy continued to publish the "Webster Ford" poems in the *Mirror*, four to ten poems at a time. Masters wrote the 214 of them over a period of ten months. He said that he spent part of the summer working out at a Spring Lake rented house and that the country was beginning to ask, "Who is Webster Ford?" He said, "Sandburg would call to see what I had done; and he was uniformly and generously full of praise, as well as wonder that I could carry on the heavy work of my law practice as it then was and write these poems in such abundance. . . . Sandburg generally had poems to show me. He carried them in his pocket, written on rough scratch paper, sometimes they were typed, sometimes they were yet in his handwriting. Some of them had beautiful imagery, or a kind of rough tenderness. Most of them were shocking, forthright with a sudden turn of rude realism. . . . Sandburg was celebrating bricklayers enjoying a chew of tobacco, wops selling bananas, Jews gathering up old iron and rags . . . and the gustatory delight of ham and eggs; and the weeds, sunflowers, cornfields, crows and sunsets and sunrises of the country about his suburban home. As I walked and went around with him I saw that there had come into being a Chicago of which I had had but faint intimidations. The town had studios where there were painters and sculptors, it had the precursors of the flappers, and here and there men and women were living together in freedom, just as they did in Paris. This year of 1914 was miraculous, not only in Chicago but over America."

As the hot weather came on, my mother headed for the farm and Oma and Opa again, hoping that with the house quiet and Margaret away with her, it might be a vacation for my father too. She reported on birthday festivities, "We are dressing an enormous rag doll for Margaret—a 'Baby Helen'—this morning. Margaret can't wait to see the last button sewed on—she is so proud & happy over 'Baby Helen's' outfit! We'll be home again rag-doll & all next Saturday or Sunday—unless you are having such a good time alone that you command us to stay on another week! . . . The birthday cake is in the oven & the three candles are ready. You should be here to see Margaret cut the cake! She will be a tremendously important little person. . . . we'll have a picnic—celebrating the little family's reunion—all day long in the woods! I'm wondering how Margaret will act when she sees her daddie again! . . . . I'm enjoying the rest & quiet at the farm—It's all doing me a lot of good. . . . . Did you remember to pay the rent? And to cut the lawn—it's your turn, you know! Oma and Opa send love—Marny sends a tight hug and many kisses—and love and love from your Paula."

My mother planned on sewing at the farmhouse too. The next day she wrote, "We fitted a nifty picnic dress yesterday—an heirloom made over! Just the thing for our Sundays in the woods! You'll like it for the color—red! And I'll like it because I can tub it & iron it—and it'll be like new again, no matter how it gets mussed a-picnicking! Today we're making over the pink silk pongee—for a more dressy summer outfit—and it's going to be fine! I'll have some things to show you when we come. . . . Your letters are wonderful, Carl. No-one ever wrote such letters as yours! I'm saving them, dear, to read over & over again! Much love, sweetheart, and I'm getting real lonesome for you. . . . —a week from today we'll be home. . . . We'll pray for moonlight for next Saturday night! . . . Let's get ready for a fine picnic on the river, Sunday! . . . Paula."

And then she said, "At last we have a letter from Ed. You'll notice it was en route 20 days, while the usual time is 10 days." Europe was up in arms—Austria had declared war on Serbia July twenty-eighth, Germany on Russia August first, Great Britain on Germany August fourth. My uncle came over from Voulangis to his Fifty-eighth Street quarters in New York for work and then looked for a home in America for his family. The Germans' speed and audacity in the invasion of Belgium and the battle of the Marne and Ypres startled the world. There was submarine war on the high seas. Uncle Ed wrote to the farm and they sent the letter on to Mother: "Dear Folks—I guess they did not suffer much in Paris—Clara & the kids—nothing more than inconvenience. Clara had her usual level head and they were ready for almost any kind of a siege—stocked in well with provisions, fuel and candles. Letters don't come very regular these days as the steamers are not running often. I'm busy and things are going a little better. . . . Love to Paus'l & Carl. Tell them I mean to write but I don't get to it. It takes no end of effort to get a letter off to Paris with each steamer. Love, Gaesjack."

At this time, in her office, Harriet Monroe was writing an editorial on "The Poetry of War" and using one of my father's poems to end it. She said, "Poets have made more wars than kings, and war will not cease until they remove its glamour from the imagination of men. . . . As Cervantes smiled Spain's chivalry away, so some poet of the new era may strip the glamour from war. . . . Now and then one hears, if not the coming Cervantes' authentic message, yet a loud word or two of grim protest against the glamour. This, from Mr. Carl Sandburg, is significant in its huge contempt:

READY TO KILL

Ten minutes now I have been looking at this.
I have gone by here before and wondered about it.
This is a bronze memorial of a famous general
Riding horseback with a flag and a sword and a revolver
    on him.
I want to smash the whole thing into a pile of junk to be
    hauled away to the scrap yard.
I put it straight to you.
After the farmer, the miner, the shop man, the factory hand,
    the fireman and the teamster,
Have all been remembered with bronze memorials,
Shaping them on the job of getting all of us
Something to eat and something to wear,
When they stack a few silhouettes
        against the sky
        Here in the park,
And show the real huskies that are doing the work of
    the world, and feeding people instead of
    butchering them,
Then maybe I will stand here
And look easy at this general of the army holding a flag
    in the air,
And riding like hell on horseback
Ready to kill anybody that gets in his way,
Ready to run the red blood and slush the bowels of men
    all over the sweet new grass of the prairie.

War will be over when such feeling as this possesses the imagination of men."

In the *International Review*, after my father's "Walsh Report" article on workingmen's rights, was another war poem, signed "C.S.":

A MILLION YOUNG WORKMEN

A million young workmen, straight and strong, lay stiff
    on the grass and roads,
And the million are now under soil and their rottening flesh
    will in the years feed roots of blood-red roses.
Yes, this million of young workmen slaughtered one another
    and never saw their red hands.
And O it would have been a great job of killing and a new
    and beautiful thing under the sun if the million knew
    why they hacked and tore each other to death.
The kings are grinning, the kaiser and the czar—they are
    alive riding in leather-seated motor cars, and
    they have their women and roses for ease, and they eat
    fresh-poached eggs for breakfast, new butter on
    toast, sitting in tall water-tight houses reading
    the news of war.
I dreamed a million ghosts of the young workmen rose in
    their shirts all soaked in crimson and yelled:
God damn the grinning kings. God damn the kaiser and
    the czar.

In the *Poetry* office in the late summer, the editors were about to award a prize. It had been announced the year before as "the Helen Haire Levinson Prize of two hundred dollars, which is to be awarded for the best poem contributed by a citizen of the United States, and published in *Poetry* during its second year—October 1913 to September, 1914. This prize is offered by Mr. Salmon O. Levinson of Chicago, in memory of his wife, who was a lover of poetry." The staff were in a quandary. Eunice Tietjens wrote of the event in later years in her book *The World At My Shoulder*, saying that she, "being then only the office girl, had no vote; but both Harriet and Alice Henderson inclined to give Carl the big prize. . . . But even they were a trifle uncertain because of the storm of protest, as well as the novelty of the loose free verse. The deciding vote . . . was cast by Hobart C. Chatfield-Taylor who was on the advisory board. He had stipulated that they do the first choosing and show him only the probabilities. I remember so clearly the day he came to vote! Alice, who was perhaps in those days the strongest of all for Sandburg, cleverly gave him Carl's poems to read first. When he had read them Chatfield-Taylor said: 'That is fine stuff. No question of it. But it is not poetry and we cannot give him the prize.' He laid the copy down and went on to the other candidates. . . . After he had read two or three more he picked up Sandburg again, only to sigh and lay the poems down. Finally, when he had quite finished, he returned once more to 'Chicago Poems.' 'They are the best of the lot,' he said, 'but are they poetry?' 'Well, what *is* poetry?' asked Alice. 'Blest if I know!' said Chatfield-Taylor. Someone suggested that we look in the dictionary, and we got down the worn copy of *The Century Dictionary* and looked it up. There we found these words:

> The art which has for its object the exciting of intellectual pleasure by means of vivid, imaginative, passionate, and inspiring language, usually though not necessarily arranged in the form of measured verse or numbers.

'So! If that is the definition I can vote for Sandburg with a clear conscience!' said Chatfield-Taylor. As he was one of the more conservative members of the organization his vote was sufficient to swing the prize for Carl. It was the only time I have ever known an academic definition to be of any practical value to a poet. Fate gave to me, who had no real right to the pleasure, the opportunity of telling Carl that he had received it. It was Harriet's practice never to tell anyone outside the office, not even the prize-winning poet, until the copies were sent out and the news given to the press. On the afternoon when the copies were being mailed she and Alice had gone home and I was just locking the office for the day, a stack of wrapped magazines under my arm, when Carl came up the steps. I knew he would know the next day and the temptation to tell him was too great to be borne. I tore a wrapper off a copy and, standing in the street, I gave it to him, open at the significant page." After walking a long way down the streets toward and past the el which Miss Tietjens took in commuting to Evanston, she says, "At last Carl stopped abruptly and looked me in the eyes. His own eyes, behind the thick lenses of his glasses, looked very big and blue and shining. 'How do you say "twice quadruple"?' he asked unexpectedly. 'I'm not sure, but I imagine you would say "octuple",' I answered, wondering on what new tack his mind was running this time. 'Then,' said Carl, 'that two hundred dollars will just octuple our bank account!' "

Plenty of rejections of my father's poems kept coming along, some laced with praise. "We don't seem to like 'em," said Floyd Dell of *The Masses;* "I wish we could have printed the one about Chick Lorimer. It's a perfect lyric—equal to the best things in English poetry. Yours ever." And he added, "Forgive our sins and let us have some more."

My father had been told at this time that out in St. Louis, Reedy was getting ready to reveal the identity of "Webster Ford." Masters spoke later of the intensity of the creative process during that long year, "Often after writing, during which I became unconscious of the passing time and would suddenly realize that it was twilight, I would experience a sensation of lightness of body, as though I were about to float to the ceiling or could drift out the window without falling. Then I would rush out of the room and catch up one of the children to get hold of reality again; or I would descend for a beer and a sandwich."

My father sent a poem on the Webster Ford–Masters hoax to Reedy, who wrote back, "I shall run your free verse to Webster Ford with great delight. I know it will also delight him. I am also going to unmask him this week, so that it will be a Webster Ford–Masters number."

The "Tribute To Webster Ford" that my father wrote was published in the November issue of the *Mirror* and Masters's work was still signed by the pseudonym. The name Edgar Lee Masters would appear in the December *Mirror* and thereafter. My father's poem went:

A man wrote two books.

One held in its covers the outside man,
     whose name was on a Knox College diploma,
     who bought his clothes at Marshall Field's,
     had his name done by a sign painter in gilt
     and never did any damage to the code of morals
     set forth by the Chicago *Tribune.*

The other book held a naked man,
     the sheer brute under the clothes
     as he will be stripped at the Last Day,
     An inside man with red heartbeats
     that go on ticking off life
     against the ribs.

Scratched into portraits here are the
     villagers, all those who walked on
     Main Street, the folks he knew down on the

Illinois prairies where his grandmother
raised eleven boys and life was a
repetition of corn and hogs.

The shadows of his soul touched the shadows
of their souls as he loved them and his
fingers knew something about the fine
dust of their blood after they are dead
and the strangeness of dreams that haunt
their graves.

When *Spoon River Anthology* would be released in 1915, the first
edition would make more money for Masters and his publishers, Macmillan, than any previous volume of American poetry. Masters wrote
his pseudonym's epitaph to end his *Anthology,* which would come out
in the January *Mirror,* a part of it going:

WEBSTER FORD

. . . 'Tis vain, O youth, to fly the call of Apollo.
Fling yourselves in the fire, die with a song of spring,
If die you must in the spring. For none shall look
On the face of Apollo and live, and choose you must
'Twixt death in the flame and death after years
of sorrow. . . .

By then Masters was ill, collapsing after the long haul, so that Harriet
Monroe came in to correct the proofs as *Spoon River Anthology* was
going into publication. "Sandburg came down one evening," Masters
wrote later, "and being forbidden by Jane [the nurse] to see me, stayed
long enough to help my wife with the evening dishes." I have been told
that my father said it never happened, but I like to think that it might
have.

Theodore Dreiser was a good friend of Edgar Lee Masters, who
had put Dreiser in *Spoon River* as "Theodore, the Poet." When Masters would write *The Great Valley* later, there would be another
poem, "Theodore Dreiser." Dreiser was seven years older than my
father. His *Sister Carrie* had been a sensation when it came out in
1900 and had been banned. *The Titan* was published in 1914. My
father had read it and admired it. On August sixth of 1915, Dreiser
wrote, "My dear Mr. Sandburg: Sometime ago I asked Mr. Masters
to get you to gather your poems together and let me see them. Last
Monday he came in, bringing them, and I have since had the plea-

sure of examining them. They are beautiful. There is a fine, hard, able paganism about them that delights me—and they are tender and wistful as only the lonely, wistful, dreaming pagan can be. Do I need to congratulate you? Let me envy you instead. I would I could do things as lovely. Mr. Dell was in here the other night as we were reading them and he said that once he had seen some earlier poems of yours, many of which were lovely and some of which should surely have been included in these. Will you be so kind as to let me see them. My idea is that if so many as a hundred and twenty-five or a hundred and fifty poems can be gotten together a publisher can be found for them. I sincerely hope so.—I mean now. A publisher will certainly be found for them eventually. If I had the others perhaps we could select a few more and complete the proposed material of the book. Incidentally Mr. Dell, hearing your poem on Billy Sunday read, wanted me to let him submit it for consideration at *The Masses*. I loaned it to him, subject to further advice from you, of course. My sincerest compliments. When I next get to Chicago I will look you up. Sincerely, Theodore Dreiser."

My father replied by return mail from the Maywood house, "My dear Mr. Dreiser: Your good letter came today. It is fine to have because I have read The Titan well and on various beer-fests Masters has told me of your aversions to throwing the bull. I am writing fast here, just an acknowledgement. I mailed to Masters at the Hotel Holley some forty or fifty additional poems, which should prove enough for any publisher by way of quantity. I add one more which is enclosed herewith after its final shaping-over. Yours faithfully."

Floyd Dell did succeed at *The Masses* and the Billy Sunday poem would be spread out there. My father wrote Dreiser again, "Such a dandy letter as you sent along to me I can't so far think out any real good answer to. For the fellowship and the sentiment of it, the enheartening element, I haven't got the reply now. When you are in Chicago maybe you and Masters and I can go out for a single sacramental glass of beer, and square things. . . . On his return here Masters said he received the 50 or so additional poems which I mailed to him in New York, and he turned them over to the John Lane & Co. man with whom he was dealing. If there's anything I can do at any time to help the publishers make a book out of what is now in their hands, I shall be glad to do so. Yours faithfully."

But then matters seemed to go askew. Dreiser set off from New York on a motor trip to Indiana, taking a month. In his absence, Masters went up to New York and gave the manuscript of poems to the Lane Company, which turned it down. Dreiser wrote to my father, "The mix-up in regard to your poems has troubled me no little. . . . As it was months since I had asked first to see the poems I did not believe there was any need or haste in placing them. Edgar Lee is one of my best friends and I sincerely believe that it was his enthusiasm for you that led him to take the matter into his own hands. When I came back from Indiana, Jones and his readers had decided against them and my voice at this late date was useless. I feel so troubled about unfulfilled obligations that I write you as I do. My compliments to you. I hope all goes well with you. And my best wishes to Edgar Lee. . . . P.S. Please send me a copy of the poem concerning the woman who is expecting a baby & digs in the garden."

My mother was with child again and looked for the birth the next June. The poem Dreiser had liked was called "June":

> Paula is digging and shaping the loam of a salvia,
> Scarlet Chinese talker of summer.
> Two petals of crabapple blossom blow fallen in Paula's hair,
> And fluff of white from a cottonwood.

Mother was wanting to go east before her new baby came, to Sharon, Connecticut, where Uncle Ed and his family were now. They had moved to America in the fall of 1914. My uncle had been busy painting and had held an exhibition in January: "PAINTINGS BY EDWARD J. STEICHEN, including 21 canvases and 7 MURAL DECORATIONS PAINTED FOR MR. AND MRS. EUGENE MEYER, JR. Motive:—In Exaltation of Flowers." My uncle had had a time getting the canvases he had done at Voulangis brought into the States and had written, "Dear Oma & Opa & Paula & Carl— Here is a message to all of you in one. Of course you realize I'm busy —so do I.—and it certainly no easy job to take up this hurricane life after Paris. The custom house seized my paintings on the dock—just to make the red tape longer—and I am only getting them out today or tomorrow and Sat. my exhibition is to be hung.—that in itself is enough to give anyone conniption fits. The nerve racking excitement and uncertainty—add to this the fact that I felt bad around my insides and for 24 hours we had an appendicitis scare but that proved wrong and Dr. Stieglitz fixed me up fine. Now I feel like a new woman." My uncle reported further, "I am living here with Mrs. Stieglitz's brother, Joe Obermeyer, in a magnificent suite of Bachelor apartments. Oh I am the real 'article.' Just think a valet to take care of me. Now Paus'l calm yourself—I don't kick him nor abuse him. We are both gentlemen 'Middleton' and I—but he is the superior one—he tips me off in the most subtle and yet firm manner as to what necktie I must put on now and then! He is one of the biggest factors in my 24 hours here—for he saves me at least 2 hours a day. He tends to everything for me.—a wonderful man 'Middleton' and I am his prophet."

My uncle had hoped to get to the farm for his birthday in March and a week of rest, but explained that it depended on how a portrait he was painting got along. He wasn't able to make it. Oma mailed him his birthday remembrances and sent a wire. He wrote her, "I got the telegram the letters and sweets from the farm—and the scarf—all made me feel good—and needless to say happy. . . . love, Gaesjack."

It took my mother and Margaret two days and a night to travel from Chicago to New York where Uncle Ed met them. They took the commuter coach out to Sharon. Margaret enjoyed the train, my mother said, "especially the diner—& the train beds. She slept fine on the train—2 naps each day—and for the night slept from 8 P.M. till 10:00 A.M. Her record broken! . . . Sunday we had a long walk Ed—Clara & I over the hills—hills all about—and brooks—I wish you were here for the walks. . . . I just asked Margaret how much love she wished to send you—she said '20 bushels, but that isn't enuf'—I suggested '100 bu.' She said 'Yes, but *that* isn't enuf—I tell you, I'll send 5 bushels!' The poetry of Numbers . . . Marny wishes for a romp with you every now & then—and wants to sing again to the thrumming of the banjo."

Then Mother said, "Yes, the garden! I have seeds from Voulangis for vines and trailing things—scarlet morning glory and verbenas and more than I can tell! This will be a wonderful spring—when we can start growing things on our own soil! Three cheers for the way you've been saving the Day Book pay!—We must surely get a wheel-barrow now! and start an asparagus bed and strawberry plants! Love and love from Marny and Paula."

It was the way of my parents and lasted their nearly sixty years together, that she was involved with the house and the land in some way —flowers, dogs, farm animals, crops—and with her children, strongly maternal. My father, in the habit of writing since he started, had made it his way of life. These two ways fitted together, their meeting over his work, the news of the world, the dinner table, the long walks on country paths. And while there was always a cot spread with some American Indian serape or rug in his attic study, there was also a large bed in a quiet room in the floor below where, when a nightmare or dream woke me as a child, I could find my way and join them. The murmur of their voices talking of whatever it was that was current in their lives is a memory of my earliest days. And I think that was how they discussed quietly the first turndown of my father's book of poems.

Fifteen

It's Hell to Be a Poet

And who was finally responsible for my father's getting a publisher for his poems? Why, the assistant editor of *Poetry: A Magazine of Verse*, Alice Corbin Henderson, who had handed the "Chicago Poems" to Harriet Monroe in the first place. They liked my father at the *Poetry* office and sat him regularly in "the poet's chair." Miss Monroe wrote, "Dear C.S. Why not drop the *Miss* for good and all? . . . I thought you were going to call me up some evening and come over. Do! Yours.—H.M."

And he responded, "My Dear Harriet Monroe: After that editorial of yours on The Fight for the Crowd, I must leave the Miss off in addressing you—for the same reasons that I don't like to call Tagore a Mister. . . . I hope to see you when the blue-misted Padraic Colum comes to town next Saddy. Yours Faithfully, Carl Sandburg."

Alice Corbin Henderson, a poet herself, was always close to my father. Not very well at the time, she would soon become seriously ill and head for the dry healing air of Santa Fe with her painter husband, Will, and their bright child, "Little Alice." Eunice Tietjens was going off to China for a long visit with her missionary sister, Louise Hammond. On her return she would take Alice Corbin Henderson's place on *Poetry*. The latter signed her editorials "A.C.H.," and so my father would address her in their early correspondence. Since my father and mother were not apart so much at this time, there are few letters between them. So it is through the exchanges between my father and A.C.H. that much of what happened here comes clear. My father was writing a piece on Ezra Pound which *Poetry* would publish, and he said, "My dear A.C.H.—I shall phone you Friday or Saturday which day I can get out. It may be the missus can come along. It's a sure go for either Saturday or Sunday, pos-i-tive-ly.

Will bring along some late wild stuff. . . . Also, I will bring along the Ezra Pound critique, what I have got done of it. . . . The Day Book is smashing ahead, making its place. Many of the Best People who know all the other Best People are getting so they don't feel they know all that's going on unless they read the Day Book. Yours faithfully, Carl Sandburg."

How did Alice Corbin Henderson find a publisher for my father's work? On a trip to New York with her husband she spoke with a friend of theirs who used to come to their parties to meet young artists and writers—Alfred Harcourt of the publishing house of Henry Holt and Company. Harcourt knew of my father and wanted to know if he had enough poems for a book. Before long my father was writing, "My dear A.C.H.—The rumors are that you not only survived New York but dented it in several places and returned to Chicago triumphant. . . . I am slaving now to get a book into shape to send to Harcourt of Henry Holt & Co. He wrote me on your suggestion. You were very thoughtful. . . . Tell Alice the Little I hope she forgives me and I will rough house to her heart's content next time I see her."

And my father reported three weeks later to her, "I have sent to Mr. Harcourt some 260 poems, each one neatly typed or pasted on a sheet by itself, all of it paged, and headed by an index, and table of contents under the title 'Chicago Poems.' I wanted much to have you go over them before they went on but he had sent me two letters about the stuff, I am behind in sleep, and work, and for peace of soul, I had to get the whole thing out of the house and off my mind. As you were the original 'discoverer' of the 'Chicago Poems,' and evocator of that title, and as it was you who told Harcourt et al these poems were worth going after, your suggestions on what should have gone into the bunch would have been worth while. You would have been a proper personage to be present at the launching ceremony to pronounce prophecies as the bottle was broken on the prow. Outside of The Missus at home I'm not even bothering anybody else with the knowledge that I'm trying to unload a book of poetry on the world. When you think we can even up the score by service to you, let us know about it."

The book would be dedicated, "To my wife and pal, Lillian Steichen Sandburg." Later Alfred Harcourt, who was three years younger than my father, said of the time that he was "glad to see that it was a fat manuscript" and that he "knew it was of first-rate importance," but he "foresaw difficulties in getting it past the inhibitions and traditions of the Holt office," and "puzzled over the problem and came to a decision about which I have had mingled feelings ever since." There was an editor upon whose advice the senior Henry Holt depended heavily—Professor W. P.

Trent of Columbia University. Harcourt slipped out the half-dozen poems that he thought Trent might feel were "pretty raw meat for the Holt imprint." Then when the approved manuscript came back, Harcourt returned the poems.

He wrote my father, "We like your Chicago Poems and want to publish them . . . we feel that there is too much in this manuscript to go into one book. Poems that are so much pictured need to be set off from each other, in good sized type and a poem to a page, unless two short ones naturally hang together, and this manuscript would make a book of about 350 pages of that character, which is, we fear, something like 150 pages too much with which to break in upon the public. Very likely most of these we would suggest omitting from this volume could find a place in the later volumes which, with the public favor, we would both want to do. You are the one to do the selecting and we are returning the manuscript for that purpose. . . . It is rare to have a manuscript in the shop which interests us as much as yours, and we think, too, it has a good chance of interesting the public. One thing more; if, as we hope, you find our proposals are satisfactory, will you let us know as soon as possible, as our spring list is on the verge of closing and, if we are to be your publishers, we should like to include your book in our regular first announcement list which has a very general circulation."

My father wrote Theodore Dreiser, "Henry Holt & Co. will bring out my poems this spring under the title 'Chicago Poems.' The one you asked me to send on to you is not to be printed. I shall mail it to you soon; can't lay my hands on it today.—Masters and others will tell you I have a bum record, a criminal record, as a letter writer. So you'll not put me in the rogues' gallery of your memory. When you're to be in Chi. I will drop all other stuff on my programs in order to hear you discourse over a glass of beer. Yours faithfully."

Floyd Dell had given my father's poem "To Billy Sunday" to the printers and it had come out in *The Masses*. My father told me once that he talked with a man who had heard Billy Sunday preach and all the man could remember of the sermon was, "You women! Cross your legs! Now the gates of hell are closed!" It was a violent poem and my father was doing his best to keep it intact: "Dear Mr. Harcourt: . . . I hope we can find a way to keep most of the Billy Sunday in. He is hyprocrisy dramatized and embodied and there is terrific tragedy of the individual and of the crowd in and about him. The question is whether I have caught the values of it intensely enough. . . . The only other American figure that might compare with Sunday is Hearst. Both dabble in treacheries of the primitive, invoke terrors of the unknown, try to throw a scare into their listeners, with Hearst the same antithesis to Tom Jefferson that Billy Sunday is to Jesus of Nazareth. Sunday is the crowd-faker pre-eminent. He is ball-player and acrobat with a sales manager gift for organizing neurotic and phsyic [sic] effects about him to gain certain results."

The poem, when published in *Chicago Poems* as "To A Contemporary Bunkshooter," would begin:

You come along . . . tearing your shirt . . . yelling about Jesus.
    Where do you get that stuff?
    What do you know about Jesus?
Jesus had a way of talking soft and outside of a few
    bankers and higher-ups among the con men of Jerusalem
    everybody liked to have this Jesus around because
    he never made any fake passes and everything he said
    went and he helped the sick and gave the people hope.

You come along squirting words at us, shaking your fist
    and calling us all dam fools so fierce the froth
    slobbers over your lips . . . always blabbing we're all
    going to hell straight off and you know all about it.

I've read Jesus' words. I know what he said. You don't
    throw any scare into me. I've got your number
    I know how much you know about Jesus. . . .

My father had cut out three "hells" and one "god-dam" from the poem as first printed in *The Masses,* and instead of "Jesus guy" used "Jesus." The Masses had titled it "To Billy Sunday" and when *The New York Call* reprinted it, the issue was impounded in New Haven by the police and its sale forbidden. In that issue the poem had started:

    You come along . . . tearing your shirt . . .
        yelling about Jesus
    I want to know . . . what the hell you know
        about Jesus . . .

Harcourt wrote, "You do not need to argue with us about the wisdom of including it, but only about the wisdom of including some phrases which do not really heighten the effect of the contrast and would alienate some readers."

My father said, "I can readily see how the Billy Sunday excoriation may be accused of lacking the religious strain that should run through all real poetry. I saw clearly your points about certain words forming what might be taken as an irreverent contrast with the name of Jesus. And I made revisions that I believe put the Sunday poem in a class of reading enjoyable and profitable to all but the most hidebound and creed-drilled religionists. If necessary or important, which it is not, I could furnish statements from Protestant ministers and Catholic priests that this poem has more of the historic Jesus or the ideal Christ in it, than does a Billy Sunday series of exhortations. . . . I am writing about Sunday at this length, Mr. Harcourt, because I want you to know what sort of foundations I see the poem resting on. When your letter came saying the Billy Sunday poem with some revisions would be used, Mrs. Sandburg commented on that first of all. Edgar Lee Masters asked first of all, 'Are they going to print Billy Sunday,' and getting 'Yes' for an answer, said, 'They are going after the soul of America.' . . . Yours faithfully."

It is said that in later years, when the poem was sent to Sunday, he commented, "Who is this Sandburg? He sounds to me like a red!" And in later years too, my father would hear from Lincoln MacVeagh of Henry Holt's, and then write to my mother, "A check for $10 came last week for right to use the Billy Sunday poem in a Macmillan anthology of 'The World's Great Religious Poetry.'"

Harcourt wanted a proper jacket for the book and my parents had suggested that my uncle design it. Uncle Ed wrote Mother, "Dear Paus'l —Hello everybody. It just seems like an age since I've been in touch with you all— . . . Has Carl his book under way? Is there anything I can do about it.—I want to if I can.—If it interests him I would like to collaborate with him in the appearance of the book—perhaps decorate it . . . If he thinks it would be worth while. . . . every natural effort should be furthered that will bring the work of modern men into closer inter-relationships. . . . Don't you think so—you and Carl? love—to all, Gaesjack."

Harcourt said that he was "glad to hear about the New York artist. Perhaps he can come in to see me. . . . No design at all would be better than a poor one or one that did not fit the book." And Harcourt wanted Masters on the jacket too. "Dear Sandburg: One of our salesmen now on the road writes in that it occurs to him that 'if it could be procured diplomatically, it would be very useful to have an appreciation of Sandburg's poetry by Masters for the jacket of "Chicago Poems".' How do you feel about this, and do you feel like passing the suggestion on to Masters? Don't do it, if you have any hesitation about it. Mr. Steichen has been in and the cover design is progressing."

214

The finished jacket was gray with a black border. Dominating it was Edgar Lee Masters' statement and signature. It ran in part:

"It is with high explosives that Carl Sandburg blasts from the mass of Chicago life these autochthonous masks and figures of modern circumstance. . . . He derives from no one, sees with his own eyes, touches with his own hands, is hearty, zestful, in love with life, full of wonder; fundamentally naive. He looks calmly on great blackness, poverty, sordidness, abject misery, hopeless agony, but with the self-possession of an artist. He loves stormy water like a Norseman, and the blue skies of Olympus like a Greek. He has a Slavic gaiety for pastoral delights and the natural reactions of healthy flesh. He is a comrade of great loneliness, has outstared Fate that thwarts, is a friend of Death as Nature's doorman at the house of Life."

In that same month Margaret Anderson splashed four of my father's poems to lead *The Little Review*. The first was the same one that Floyd Dell had praised when rejecting it—the one Masters called "Chick Lorimer," saying it was the only one of my father's which was a "character picture" and anything like his *Spoon River* epitaphs. "Gone" was its title in *The Little Review*; the other three poems were "Graves," "Choices," and "Child of the Romans." "Gone" started:

> Everybody loved Chick Lorimer in our town.
> > Far off
> > Everybody loved her.
> So we all love a wild girl keeping a hold
> > On a dream she wants.
> Nobody knows now where Chick Lorimer went.
> Nobody knows why she packed her trunk: a few old things
> And is gone. . . .

Mr. Harcourt wrote, "It looks now as if we should have 'Chicago Poems' ready on April 22nd. . . . I am very sorry to hear that Mrs. Henderson has had to go away for a rest. I hope it is for a rest and good time rather than because of real illness." But A.C.H. was very sick. "Dear C.S.—I wanted to review your book for Poetry—. . . I can't do it—at least not yet." My father replied, "Dear A.C.H.—I think I shall send you telegrams. You don't want letters with news and knowledge. You know all you need now. You've got layers of knowledge risen into stalactite

215

cliffs. . . . I'm sending a hello instead of news. Amy Lowell came and went amid the same sort of furors as last year, doing good work, with a brave air of a Cyrano de Bergerac facing life's impulchritudes. Harcourt says our book will be out April 22. I will shoot one your way immediate. . . . I am having a holy picnic with some gnarled massive ones I hacked out lately. Say, you be a turtle, one of those big slumbrous idling fellows three hundred years old, satisfied with everything, people, politics, arts, and linear distance between the earth and Canopus. Go to it. Be a turtle six months, lady. C.S."

And it was then that my father and Amy Lowell began their friendship. Miss Lowell was four years older than he. She came on the Twentieth Century Limited from New York, taking a day for the trip, and arriving in time for lunch the next day with Edgar Lee Masters and his wife among others. Masters said Miss Lowell's "descent upon Chicago was comparable to that of an Italian diva." He said that "a poem, so called, which she had then just written on the theme of herself taking a bath gave the press just what it wanted in the way of colorful sensation." The poem was a section of a long one called "Spring Day," part of the first stanza, "Bath," going:

> . . . The sunshine pours in at the bathroom window and bores
> through the water in the bath-tub in lathes and planes of
> greenish-white. It cleaves the water into flaws like a jewel, and
> cracks it to bright light.
>   Little spots of sunshine lie on the surface of the water and
> dance, dance, and their reflections wobble deliciously over the
> ceiling; a stir of my finger sets them whirring, reeling. I move a
> foot, and the planes of light in the water jar. I lie back and
> laugh, and let the green-white water, the sun-flawed beryl
> water, flow over me. The day is almost too bright to bear, the
> green water covers me from the too bright day. I will lie here
> awhile and play with the water and the sun spots . . .

Miss Lowell wrote a Boston *Transcript* reviewer about the poem, "I do not mind any serious criticism, no matter how severe; but I do object to all this nonsense about the bath-tub which has been appearing in various papers. . . . My treatment of the bath-tub was a purely pictorial matter —a question of the play of light, etc.—not at all the kind of thing they represented, and also, the bath-tub was the shortest section of a long poem. It is hard for any artist to do serious work when so many of the newspapers persist in this ridiculous attitude."

Masters called on Amy Lowell in her suite at the Congress Hotel and said "she was enthroned in state attended by a companion-secretary. She offered me a Corona cigar, and smoked two of these huge rollers of nicotine while I smoked one. We talked very pleasantly until I made some comment on a literary judgment that she had recently published; whereupon she stuck up her finger with authority and exclaimed, 'Your reasons, sir?' Not wishing to get into a debate with her I glided away from the invited dialectic. But all the while I was fascinated with her eyes. They were large and blue and luminous. I have never seen more beautiful eyes."

Amy Lowell spent a week in Chicago. She visited our house in Maywood and wrote on return home on her stationery with its neat heading that was already becoming famous: *Miss A. Lowell, Heath Street, Brookline, Mass.* "My dear Mr. Sandburg: . . . Thank you for what you say about my being a colour-bearer. Sometimes the flag jerks and the nails tear, but it has not pulled away yet, in spite of all the firing, and I think it will flutter to the end, although as a mere rag of what it was. I wish you ever came East. I enjoyed our talk so much, I want another. I have not seen your book yet, but I see it is out, and I am going to get it at once. Good luck to your work! Sincerely yours, Amy Lowell."

My father sent her his poem "Alix," part of it going:

> Dark, shining-velvet Alix,
> Night-sky Alix in a gray blanket,
> Led back and forth by a nigger.
> Velvet and night-eyed Alix
> With slim legs of steel.

And he told Miss Lowell, "Remember that color-bearers invite sharpshooters, and as you go further in ultimatums declaring your literary independence, there will be cross-fire. Many, many lucky days! Yours sincerely, Carl Sandburg."

Miss Lowell had liked my father's work in *Poetry* and the "little magazines." She even set herself up as his champion at times. Once she wrote him, "By the way, it was on your account that I had such a terrible row in Philadelphia, because I brought you up and compared you to Walt Whitman and gave you a general send off, and then a little cur dog of a man got up and slammed you and said he did not know that anybody took you seriously, and then I slammed back good and plenty, and there you were. I hope I have sold you too in the process. I tried hard enough. . . . Very sincerely yours, Amy Lowell."

Alfred Harcourt wrote my father, "Dear Sandburg: I am very much gratified that you like the book, and that Mrs. Sandburg does too. We have sent 25 copies to the Radical Book Shop by express, and we are billing to them direct, but I have had the account marked as guaranteed by you. . . . I have re-read the book about three times since I have had it in print, and it keeps growing on me. It will be one of the books of the year that we'll have real satisfaction from, and, I hope, some fame and profit, and I have good hopes of a fair share of the rewards for us both."

Copies went out about the country, to Grandma Sandburg and Oma and Uncle Ed, to Eunice Tietjens and Masters, to Miss Lowell, who said, "I am perfectly delighted with your book! I do not know when I have read anything that gives me so much pleasure." Vachel Lindsay complimented Harriet Monroe, "I think Carl Sandburg is a real feather in your cap. As soon as I can get human again, I want to write him about his wonderful Chicago Poems. Every time I reread one it seems stronger. I don't in the least approve of free verse—but I cannot help but approve of Sandburg and Masters. I am certainly glad they are alive."

Amy Lowell reviewed *Chicago Poems* for *The Poetry Review*, telling my father, "I am afraid you will not like all of it, for I have taken exception to some of your diagnoses. However, I trust that a slight difference of opinion like that will not obscure for you the very great admiration I have for your work, and the sympathetic praise I have given of it as a whole, and my delight in various individual pieces. . . . When you know me better you will know that I must be honest at all costs, in reviewing among other things, and you will forgive any individual differences for the sake of the fundamental unity of our attitude toward life."

My father didn't mind, saying, "That's a pippin of a review," and adding, "We have a new daughter, Janet, who sends you her love." Janet was born on the twenty-seventh of June, when Margaret was five. It was a time of contentment for my mother and father. He was on the upward path, his book a success. And she had another baby in her arms. There are the photographs in the album. Janet is beautiful, dark-haired. My mother has told me that she was the pleasantest of her children as a baby, not a fussy one. She is dressed in a wide-collared linen outfit. My mother, who is thirty-three now, holds her up for the photographer, smiling and serene. Her hair, which had started to turn in her twenties, is an iron gray now; loosened from the bun in back, it wisps and curls about her face. She is wearing a long dress with a white middy collar and a row of buttons down the front.

Harcourt wrote, "My love to Janet. I hope she and her mother are all right. It has been awfully hot, and I have worried about them." My father reported to A.C.H. too: "It's a girl and perfection frog legs fastened to a perfection torso. Avoirdupois: 8.5 pounds. Wavy dark hair, this notably Northern French. Mother: 100%."

And there is the poem for Janet, ending:

> On the lips of the child Janet,
> Wisps of haze on ten miles of corn,
> Young light blue calls to young light gold of morning.

Ezra Pound was writing then from Rapallo, "Dear Sandburg, A copy of Lustra is on its way to you. I hope you'll let me have Chicago Poems in return, but it isn't compulsory. I have sent the book without dedicatory inscriptions as all books have to go from the publisher direct, because of the censorship. yours ever, E.P." When my father's book reached Italy, Pound wrote back at length, "Dear Sandburg, The 'Chicago Poems' have came at last. Complimenti miei! The thing that strikes me most is that you have kept the whole book 'down to brass tacks' . . . The address to Billy Sunday (??) was refreshing. There is a great deal in the book I had not seen. In the language of the immortal Prufrock 'I grow old, I shall wear the bottoms of my trousers rolled.' Masters' panygeric [sic] on the cover seems to me florid and rhetorical and NOT criticism. I think the place where Villon 'has it on you' is in the sense of restraint, which comes from his rhyming on the precise word. I don't mean I want you to immitate Villon or to rhyme, and I dont see how you could do some of your things in any dialect save the one you have used. . . . What I am getting at, is that sometimes your dialect or your argot seems to me not the best way, not the most controlled way but simply the easiest way. . . . This surface critique may bore you. I think you are right in the main. All I mean is that there still are Catullus and Villon and that one mustn't forget it. . . . What I do believe is that if you had the patience to learn latin for the sake of Catullus,

> Glubit magnanimi Romae nepotes,

and french for the sake of Villon

> Si ils n'ayment que pour l'argent
> On ne les aime que pour l'heure,

or even for Corbiere.

> Je voudrais etre chien a une fille publique,
> Lecher un peu d'amour qui ne soit pas paye.

> [I would like to be the dog of a prostitute
> Licking a bit of love for which I should not have to pay.]

If you had the patience to listen to an old maid like myself and undergo these boredoms it would put more weight in your hammer. 'I have spoken. . . .' Yours ever, Ezra Pound."

My father had done a review on "The Work of Ezra Pound" back in the February *Poetry*. He had said, "If I were driven to name one individual who, in the English language, by means of his own examples of creative art in poetry, has done most of living men to incite new impulses in poetry, the chances are I would name Ezra Pound. . . . People write poetry because they want to. It functions in them as air in the nostrils of an athlete in a sprint. . . . It is a dark stuff of life that comes and goes. . . . Some win their public while they live. Others must mould a very small public while alive, and be content with a larger one after death. Still others need no public at all, and in the role of by-standers they get more enjoyment and knowledge of life than as performers. . . . I like the pages of Ezra Pound. He stains darkly and touches softly. The flair of great loneliness is there. . . . He is worth having."

Then, in turn, as the poets of the time reviewed each other, my father wrote to Amy Lowell, "I've been looking through Men, Women and Ghosts. . . . In my day's work I get so much of sweeping, chaotic vivid life that when I turn to art between-whiles, I demand it deliver rapidly. . . . Sometimes you press the keys and get a chord. You fail in the succeeding and contrasting chord. That is, the piece should end or should have some kind of an interlude or new key or something else. . . . All this of course, is personal and one reckless dauber to another. I know your sins by mine own. . . . Here's much luck to you!"

And he wrote of the new members of his household to his friend, Alice Corbin Henderson, out in Santa Fe, she who had found a publisher for *Chicago Poems* in the past winter, "I have had a love affair with a dog this summer: Mrs. Moody gave me an Irish setter I'll swear has as immortal a soul as any of us: He's a marvelous listener.—Janet, the new kid, has her mother's hair and face whereas the other daughter has mine; so the household is at a glorious standoff."

He wrote a poem to the setter and my sister:

Two faces I love in a corner.
One is the child Margaret.
The other is the dog Dan.
I love one for no reason at all.
I love the other the same way.
They wrench my heart and I am glad.
They wrench my heart and I wonder why.

Mrs. Henderson answered, "I've thought often of the little new-born daughter—and I wish her every joy in the world—chiefly health—Please give my congratulations to Mrs. Sandburg, whose days, I imagine, must be full! . . . And then sit down & give me a real account of yourself and your book. I want to know how it has gone. . . . Have the season's poetry parties set in yet? Do you, François Villon—& Dan Chaucer of Spoon River get together o' times?"

And he, "Our letters met, along in western Nebraska . . . Ezra Pound —yes—I am for him stronger than ever . . . if only his letters and personal relationships had the big ease and joy of life his art has I would hit it off great with him. . . . Masters I haven't seen much of. In fact I'm off the literary, even the poetry crowd, lately. The why of it is all huge and mixed with me but I guess more than anything else I like my politics straight and prefer the frank politics of the political world to the politics of the literary world. The betting chances are all that I wouldn't have had any book out this year if you hadn't got busy last year." My father called her "Rihakku," who was Li Po, China's great ancient poet, in return for her calling him "François Villon." He ended a letter, "And this—will not this do for a Saturday afternoon's gossip? Rihakku?"

Masters had turned over the proofs of his new book of poems, *The Great Valley*, to my father, who wrote to Mrs. Henderson that in "power, range of pictures, play of motives it will surpass Spoon River . . . and will bring a hell's storm of censure. . . . So I write you to know E.L.M. is virile and alive and is going to crack the tribe of criticus about the ears this coming November and December." One of Masters' poems, "The Houses," was seven pages long, and my father added, "Today Masters read me Old Houses. A haunting other-worldly thing, phantom-talking, persuasive, insidious, beautiful." The jacket of *The Great Valley* would be done in the same plain style as *Chicago Poems*—tan with a dark blue border enclosing the title and a signed statement, which would be by William Marion Reedy, publisher of Masters' "Webster Ford" verse, who said that the book was ". . . poetry permeated by thought, not mere musing or revery." The copy Masters gave my father was inscribed,

"With compliments and friendship." My father also wrote to Mrs. Henderson that Masters and he agreed on various literary matters, including voting Sara Teasdale "the best lyrist in the U.S." And he said that a syndicated magazine had asked him for a Thanksgiving poem. "It will be run with a precede that this is the way Free Verse writes about Thanksgiving. . . . Much luck. Janet—that's the Littlest One—and Dan—that's the Red Dog—send you our love. C.S."

My father was asked for a Christmas poem too. It came out in the Chicago *Evening Post* as well as the Denver *Express,* and was illustrated. Some of it went:

WHY DOES THE STORY NEVER WEAR OUT?

> . . . Back in a barn in a Bethlehem yard,
> In a haze of Galilee nights,
> A baby's first cry mixing with the crunch
> Of a mule's teeth on Bethlehem Christmas corn,
> Baby fists softer than snowflakes of Norway,
> Love-lips, the Mother of Christ calling "He is here!"
> And tall rough men, dust on their hands and shoulders,
> Tall wise men of sun-tan faces, looking on:
>
> All in a barn on a winter night,
> And a Baby there for all the hands
>   and all the hearts of the world,
> A Baby there in swaddling clothes on hay—
>   Why does the story never wear out? . . .

And then a Christmas gift came to Janet from Santa Fe, and my father responded, "Dear Alice: We send you all the New Year's wishes there are. It's impossible to tell you all the ins and outs of our wishes for you. That Indian rattle fits into Janet's hand and accentuates the papoose look I always liked about her. . . . The Missus, Marge, Janet and The Dog, all send New Years Love to you and Will and Alice, Jr. For the latter I must cook up something in exchange for that rattle which was so real a remembrance. Yours Faithfully."

The New Year came round, and spring. *Chicago Poems* had been out just a year. My father's stance as the Poet of the People was now pretty secure. A group of his poems would head the April issue of *Poetry.* There were seventeen of them and he called them "My People," leading them with a piece:

222

My people are gray,
    pigeon gray, dawn gray, storm gray.
I call them beautiful,
    and I wonder where they are going.

The last of the group went:

Cover me over
In dusk and dust and dreams.

Cover me over
And leave me alone.

Cover me over,
You tireless, great.

Hear me and cover me,
Bringers of dusk and dust and dreams.

It would be some years later when my father would write Jake Zeitlin, antiquarian bookman and friend and then attempting poetry, ". . . remember it's hell to be a poet and if it isn't you're not a poet . . . do what your heart tells you to, valuing comment on your work slightly or hardly at all." And he was writing Mrs. Henderson of his feelings about what he would call "the literary crowd." It was May and he said, "Dear Alice:— . . . I know what you mean. I'll show you. The goddam academicians haven't got me! . . . I'm through—through—with some people and things just because I feel about them the death you tell me keep away from. For months this isolation has grown. So now more than ever I prefer politicians, saloon keepers and thieves to the general run of poets and critics for company. I'm glad for your outcry. I lifted my head and howled to the night stars and the wilderness just like that. . . . Carl."

There was a direction to my father's life now. He enjoyed his family, bringing friends out for long evenings, the guitar or banjo present. While he didn't yet know just what his role in the country would be, he would manage to remain recognized as one of its poets. And, true to his feelings, he would fraternize with the people rather than other poets. That would come to be one of his recognized characteristics. I think he knew he was on his way now. Was it a "feeling of destiny" that he had?

Sixteen

A War Song

My father was still on the staff of the adless daily, *The Day Book*, in early 1917 when the Russian Revolution climaxed in the takeover by the Bolsheviks. They were the minority of the Social-Democratic Party of Russia and before long would form the Russian Communist Party. Of course, they had ties with the Wisconsin Social-Democrats, many of whom were friends and relatives. How would my mother and father stand as America became committed to war and their friends took sides?

Conrad Aiken, in a review in the Boston *Poetry Journal* in January of 1917, had stated that "Mr. Sandburg is a socialist, and consistently preaches socialist morals. Next to his deficiencies as regards form, it is perhaps Mr. Sandburg's greatest fault that he allows the poet to be out-talked by the sociologist. If Tennyson is now regarded as a tiresome moral sentimentalist, who knows whether a future generation to whom many of Mr. Sandburg's dreams may have become realities, will not so regard Mr. Sandburg? That is the danger, always, of being doctrinaire. Doctrine is interesting only when new."

Indeed, my father had told Amy Lowell, "Glancing over some old and genuinely propaganda material of mine of ten years ago, I got a sneaking suspicion that maybe you're right and maybe I have struck a propaganda rather than a human note at times." He also said elsewhere, "If I must characterize the element I am most often active with I would say I am with all rebels everywhere all the time as against all people who are satisfied. . . . I am for unrest, discontent, revolt and war to whatever extent is necessary to obtain the Russian Bolshevik program which centers on the three needs: bread, peace, land. . . . rather let the people suffer and be lean, sick and dirty through the blunders of democracy than to be fat, clean and happy under the efficient arrangements of autocrats, kaisers, kings, czars, whether feudal and dynastic or financial and industrial."

My mother shared these opinions, and when it became inevitable that the United States would enter the war, she and my father left the Socialist Party to become Independents—in truth Democrats. Not so with many of their friends. The midwest socialists were mainly pacifists and opposed to war when it was directed against their fatherlands. Victor Berger, born in Austria-Hungary, termed World War I "a capitalist orgy of blood-letting." President Woodrow Wilson's administration would suspend the second-class mailing rights of Berger's Milwaukee *Leader* before long. On the fifteenth of June, 1917, Congress would pass the Espionage Act, and Berger would be indicted on grounds of disloyalty and interference with the draft. The same would happen to Eugene Debs. The Espionage Act provided a possible twenty years in jail and $10,000 fine for offenders. Before Debs would be tried and sentenced, he would tell a crowd in Canton at the Ohio State Socialist Convention that he denounced all forms of militarism—foreign and domestic. He praised the Bolsheviks and said, "Do not worry over the charge of treason to your masters but be concerned about the treason that involves yourself. . . . We Socialists are the builders of the world that is to be. . . . we will proclaim the emancipation of the brotherhood of all mankind!" A federal grand jury would indict Debs and sentence him to ten years in the penitentiary.

But my parents, patriots, stood for the war. It was to make the world safe for democracy, and it would be the last war. In April of 1917, the United States joined the Allies and by mid-May universal conscription was announced by President Wilson. My father wrote his socialist friend Upton Sinclair, author of *The Jungle,* which Sinclair had dedicated "To the Workingmen of America," and of *King Coal,* just out in the book stalls: "My Dear Upton Sinclair: . . . I'm glad about your war stand. It was just one more war, a clash of dynasties and junkers—now it's something else—a big gamble with the odds on the red."

Uncle Ed stood for the war too. By July of 1917, he had joined up, saying he "wanted to be a photographic reporter, as Mathew Brady had been in the Civil War." He went to Washington to offer his services, with the endorsement of the Camera Clubs of America. The Signal Corps accepted him and he was commissioned a first lieutenant in the Historical Section. Later he was transferred to the Photographic Section of the Air Service. Their base of operations was outside of Paris at General Pershing's headquarters at Chaumont with the American Expeditionary Force.

My uncle left for France with the first convoy of American troops, in a seized German liner. His old friend, Auguste Rodin, had died on July 17. Uncle Ed read it in the newspaper headlines on arrival in Cherbourg. My uncle had hoped to go to Rodin's home at Val-Fleury near Meudon and show himself dramatically in his uniform "as a symbol of America coming over to help France." Uncle Ed was given leave to attend the funeral as an unofficial representative of the American Army. French fighter planes circled overhead to protect the scene—the pavilion of red brick, the columned portico and the huge rotunda, the hundreds of people assembled to see Rodin buried beside Rose, whom he had officially married a few days before her death not long before. Their joint grave would be at the foot of a great bronze statue of "The Thinker."

And where was my father at the same time? Representing *The Day Book* in Omaha, Nebraska, reporting on a labor conference for the American Federation of Labor, involving a building trade strike. From there he went on to cover another labor convention in Minneapolis. He wrote to Alice Corbin Henderson, "I have been among strikers in the coal fields, to the American Federation of Labor convention in July of 1917 in Omaha, among pacifists, Sinn Feiners and German spies, and there has been such a tumult in my head lots of times when I wanted to write you that I couldn't get to it." And to Harriet Monroe, "Big days—a great conference—Vachel couldn't find enough boom-boom words to tell the story."

And then *The Day Book* was shutting down. My father, true to his position on "literary politics," continued to drift away from the poets. He wrote his publisher, Alfred Harcourt, "Met Frost and Lindsay last week. What with letter writing, lectures and being lionized, I felt their minds were mussed up worse than the day-by-day newspaper worker." But for Amy Lowell he kept a long-standing friendship. My mother liked Miss Lowell too and said she was "no more New England than Popocatapetl." Amy Lowell had a book in manuscript to be titled *Tendencies in Modern American Poetry*. She was including six poets, grouping them in twos: Hilda Doolittle (H.D.) and John Gould Fletcher were the "Imagists," Edwin Arlington Robinson and Robert Frost were the "Evolutionists," Edgar Lee Masters and my father the "Revolutionists." It is said that after the book came out that October of 1917, Vachel Lindsay never wrote to Amy Lowell again because he was not included; nor did Masters write her again, on fire for another reason. He told Harriet Monroe that he was furious that Amy Lowell "bracketed Sandburg with me," and my father told me that he called her "Amy Barnum Lowell," saying of her first book of Poems, *A Dome of Many Colored Glass,* published four years before *Chicago Poems* came out, "Her work was not of precious or semi-precious stones—but of colored glass—American make."

My father wrote Miss Lowell, "I call your *Tendencies* the most human-and-alive book of commentary and discussion that has thus far come off a printing press in America. I would say this as readily if you had put some other guy than myself in to represent the 'multi-racial' or any link necessary to your thesis." And he said, "I admit there is some animus of violence in Chicago Poems but the aim was rather the presentation of motives and character than the furtherance of I.W.W. theories. Of course, I honestly prefer the theories of the I.W.W. to those of its opponents and some of my honest preferences may have crept into the book."

Amy Lowell wanted a photograph and my father sent her one by Uncle Ed, asking that the latter be credited and that she return it because "properly it belongs to Mrs. Sandburg and was made by her brother who is now Lieut. Steichen in France in charge of photographic war board." When the book was off the press my uncle was not listed under the picture. The strong poet wrote, "I could not credit the photographer with having done your picture because none of the pictures are credited in this volume." She added, "I cannot tell you how much I hope that you will like it all."

He did. "I'm more than glad about your book. The first and big thing about it is that it is alive and well free of the taint of the academic. Your thesis is stated and supported but not allowed to dominate and sap the human companionship quality. You make so interesting a book that I wonder how fate slipped me a ticket to be one of the six. . . . I will my volume to whichever of my daughters is most devilish." As it happens, my sister Margaret has the book—by right of possession. And my father told Miss Lowell too, "I am off the suspended Day Book, the world's greatest adless daily, and am now writing editorials on the Daily News, the world's greatest ad sheet, bar none."

My father had finished a new war poem and sent it to Harriet Monroe, who ran it in *Poetry* that October. It was called "The Four Brothers— Notes for War Songs (*November, 1917*)," and my father would read it to groups—a large one the next year at a librarians' convention on the Fourth of July, and then to friends at Miss Monroe's house. One poet there, Muna Lee, said afterwards that she'd tried to say at the time how she believed it was a great poem. "Since reading it for myself in 'Poetry,' I am more than ever sure of its greatness . . . Miss Monroe's secretary told me that fifty copies were being sent to newspapers over the country. It ought to do a great deal of good—and it will! More than anything else I have seen, it draws the line between war and this war— more than anything, it helps overcome personal grief. Thank you for it. Will you tell Mrs. Sandburg for me that I was sorry not to have an opportunity to bid her goodbye when I left Chicago? Give her my best wishes."

It was a long poem and parts went:

Make war songs out of these;
Make chants that repeat and weave.
Make rhythms up to the ragtime chatter of the machine guns;
Make slow-booming psalms up to the boom of the big guns.
Make a marching song of swinging arms and swinging legs, . . .

Cowpunchers, cornhuskers, shopmen, ready in khaki;
Ballplayers, lumberjacks, ironworkers, ready in khaki; . . .

I heard one say "I am ready to be killed."
I heard another say, "I am ready to be killed."
O sunburned clear-eyed boys!
I stand on sidewalks and you go by with drums and guns
     and bugles,
       You—and the flag!
And my heart tightens, a fist of something feels my throat
       When you go by,
You on the kaiser hunt, you and your faces saying, "I
       am ready to be killed."

They are hunting death,
Death for the one-armed mastoid kaiser.
They are after a Hohenzollern head:
There is no man-hunt of men remembered like this.

The four big brothers are out to kill.
France, Russia, Britain, America—
The four republics are sworn brothers to kill the kaiser. . . .

Look! It is four brothers in joined hands together.
     The people of bleeding France,
     The people of bleeding Russia,
     The people of Britain, the people of America—
These are the four brothers, these are the four republics. . . .

I say now, by God, only fighters to-day will save the world,

nothing but fighters will keep alive the names of those
who left red prints of bleeding feet at Valley Forge
in Christmas snow.
On the cross of Jesus, the sword of Napoleon, the skull
of Shakespeare, the pen of Tom Jefferson, the ashes
of Abraham Lincoln, or any sign of the red and
running life poured out by the mothers of the world, . . .

Good-night is the word, good-night to the kings, to the
czars,
      Good-night to the kaiser.
The breakdown and the fade-away begins.
The shadow of a great broom, ready to sweep out the trash,
is here. . . .

Out and good-night—
The ghosts of the summer palaces
And the ghosts of the winter palaces!
Out and out, good-night to the kings, the czars, the
kaisers.

Another finger will speak,
And the kaiser, the ghost who gestures a hundred million
sleeping-waking ghosts,
The kaiser will go onto God's great dustpan—
The last of the gibbering Hohenzollerns. . . .

Look! the four brothers march
And hurl their big shoulders
And swear the job shall be done. . . .

Lloyd Lewis, a close friend of my father's and a fellow newspaperman
on the Chicago *Herald*, wrote to him right away, "I read it coming down
on the train and it stands up majestically. . . . Whitman's 'Out of the
Cradle' is the only thing of this kind I'd rank with this masterpiece of
yours. I'm nutty about the thing and go about wanting to read it to
everyone but I can't read it aloud without weeping. It is a great parade
coming down Michigan Boulevard in the sun." And Sherwood Anderson
said it made his "heart jump to know we have a man like you in our old
town." Poets congratulated him, calling it splendid, and Charles Dennis,
managing editor on the *Daily News*, said he thought it "the greatest
poem the war has produced," and asked to print it, saying he wanted
"to star it," which he did. Fanny Butcher, on the Chicago *Tribune*, said

she hadn't "seen anything about the war that has touched me so deeply. My love tō Mrs. Sandburg and the big little girl and the little little girl."

The poem would close a new book my father was assembling that he would dedicate "To Janet and Margaret." He wrote Alice Corbin Henderson, "Only the last two months I began to be sure that I had a new book that would surpass and put it all over the first one." Alfred Harcourt said, "*Cornhuskers* is a mighty good title. . . . It is a better book than the first one, now, a good deal better. . . . we want to publish it, and this autumn." Harcourt told him he'd shown the book to Robert Frost. "Frost has read *Cornhuskers* and says, 'Sandburg is better and better. He was a great find for you. He's man, woman and child all rolled in one heart.' " My father had written to Louis Untermeyer, poet, critic and anthologist, about Frost, and Untermeyer had answered that he was "more than happy to know that you like Robert. He's one of the finest persons still left on this crazy planet. It may please you to know that he reciprocates your sentiments. I spent a couple of days with him last week, and he said so."

Henry Holt and Company had published Frost's *North of Boston* about a year before *Chicago Poems*. Harcourt has described Frost at this time as "a rangy man of about forty, with an extraordinarily sensitive face," saying he'd been writing poetry for twenty years and had "taught school off and on, had made shoes, edited a weekly paper for a time and had owned a farm near Derry, New Hampshire." The inner jacket of *Cornhuskers* would carry advertisements of Frost's books: *A Boy's Will, North of Boston, Mountain Interval, Selected Poems* and *New Hampshire*.

It seems that critics, newsmen, acquaintances and friends of my father have done their best to wring out anecdotes about his and Frost's relationship, losing track as a rule of the beginnings of the two poets. Frost was three years older than my father. Both were first published at a time of personal financial difficulties, made the grade with The People and always wrote for them rather than for the literati. I knew Robert Frost in his last years and had memorized his poems since a child. I met him frequently as a guest in Secretary of the Interior Stewart Udall's home in McLean, Virginia. Lee Udall would place me next to Robert, who never failed to speak courteously and affectionately of my father. My attitude toward him was one of outright tenderness. I was single at the time and considered my role there as something of a mascot. No one minded my recording notebook and pencil either. When Frost's *Complete Poems* was published, he asked my father for my address, and mailed me a copy, inscribed "with a good share of the friendship I feel for her Poet father, as of February Second Nineteen Fifty-One." When Frost gave my father *North of Boston* back in 1915, it was "from his friend, Robert Frost." In *Harper's Magazine* in 1920, would be a poem by my father called "Pot Gold (*To Robert Frost*)" that started:

> The pot of gold at the rainbow end
> is a pot of mud, gold mud,
> slippery shining mud.
>
> Pour it on your hair and you will
> have a golden hair.
> Pour it on your cat and you will
> have a golden cat.
> Pour it on your clock and you will
> have a golden clock. . . .
>
> Pour it in the shape of a holy cross,
> give it to me to wear on my shirt,
> and I will have a keepsake.
> I will touch it and say a prayer for you.

The poem was published later in *Slabs of the Sunburnt West* as "Gold Mud," edited a little. When *Good Morning, America* came along in the late 1920's, a line from a poem in it, called "New Hampshire Again," would run, "I remember a stately child telling me her father gets letters addressed 'Robert Frost, New Hampshire.'"

My father wrote of those days in *The American Songbag*, "Once when the night was wild without and the wintry winds piled snowdrifts around the traffic signals on Cottage Grove Avenue, Chicago, we sat with Robert Frost and Padraic Colum. The Gael had favored with Irish ballads of murder, robbery, passion. And Frost offered a sailorman song he learned as a boy on the wharves of San Francisco:

> As we sailed on the water blue,
> Whiskey Johnny,
> A good long pull and a strong one too,
> Whiskey for my Johnny. . . ."

My father told in that book also of how Frost "learned shanties from listening to sailors and dock-wallopers along the waterfront. He saved these tunes and verses in his heart. A favorite with him is Blow The

231

Man Down. It has the lurch of ships, tough sea legs, a capacity for taking punishment and rising defiant of oppression and tyranny:

> As I was a-walkin' down Paradise Street
> To me aye, aye—blow the man down!
> A saucy young p'liceman I chanced for to meet;
> Blow the man down to me aye, aye, blow the man down!
> Whether he's white man or black man or brown,
> Give me some time to blow the man down,
> Give me some time to blow the man down,
> Blow the man down! bullies!

After *The American Songbag* had been published, Frost would write to my father from South Shaftsbury, Vermont, "Dear Carl: I see I shall never be able to resist the flattery of being treated as if I knew anything about music and could sing chanteys. Neither will I that of being treated as if I had been an athalete [sic] and could still play tennis. Either form simply strikes me dumb with rapture and caution. You can see the need of the caution. If I said much I might give myself away; if I tried to sing at all I might lose the cheese out of my mouth the way I did when I was a crow in the time of Aesop. You may remember. You were possibly there in the capacity of the fox. When the fox finally said, 'Hence with denial vain and coy excuse,' I was just fool enough to try to favor him with a song. And the cheese, well,

> The cheese fell out of my mouth and onto the floor
> Turned over itself and rolled out of the door
> Mopety mopety mo-no.

. . . There are more things, in actual life than it would be humane or in good taste to work up into art—you old ballad monger. Always yours, Robert."

My father would fancy those two songs got from Frost, and I learned them as a matter of course as a child. As time went on and Frost and my father began appearing on platforms of colleges, universities and clubs into the 1920's, Frost began his mocking of my father, testy and ruffled. In one letter of May, 1922, to Lincoln MacVeagh, a younger member of Frost's publishing firm of Henry Holt and Company, he said, "We've been having a dose of Carl Sandburg. He's another person I find it hard to do justice to. He was possibly hours in town and he spent one of those washing his white hair and toughening his expression for his public performance. His mandolin pleased some people, his poetry a very few and his infantile talk none. His affectations have almost buried him out of sight. He is probably the most artificial and studied ruffian the world has had. Lesley says his two long poems in The New Republic and The Dial are as ridiculous as his carriage and articulation. He has developed rapidly since I saw him two years ago. I heard someone say he was the kind of writer who had everything to gain and nothing to lose by being translated into another language."

But at this time, in the fall of 1917, my father had his second book in manuscript, Frost had had his first three books of poems out and both were concerned with the next move. Amy Lowell said that Frost was ". . . all compounded as he seems to be of the granite and gentians of our Northern mountains," and that he wrote ". . . true pastorals of the hill country," and, "Mr. Frost writes almost as a man under a spell. As though he were the mouthpiece of something beyond himself, only conscious of the necessity of stating what is in him."

While Robert Frost, perhaps true to Miss Lowell's classification as "Evolutionist," remained one of the purest poets of our time, my father, true to his "Revolutionist" nature, was moving restlessly about the land. By early 1918, my mother was carrying a child again. My father had been to see his New York publishers and looked about the city. He wrote her tenderly, "Paula . . . I may leave tonight on the Lehigh and amble and lazy along hitting Chicago maybe Friday or Saturday. . . . We saw troopships loading on the river. Fifty thousand men swarming in khaki on the decks waiting for night. I sent the News a poetic telegram on it. . . . Got your letter at Holts. Fixed things fine with Harcourt; he says he is sure my stuff is going to go over big and its only a matter of plugging away till the public gets it. We may yet buy a farm out of 'Cornhuskers.' . . . With profound affection, your loving husband, Carlos."

And he wrote as jauntily to Harriet Monroe, "The Prairie" being the opening poem of the book:

> I was born on the prairie and the milk of its wheat,
> the red of its clover, the eyes of its women,
> gave me a song and a slogan. . . .

"Dear Harriet: . . . My own choice would be that you run this and The Prairie if you are asking for the two most representative things of late. Anyway please see if you can make a pick of what you wish to print— soon. The Dial, The Tribune, Stratford Journal, Midland, and others (non-capitalized) have asked for stuff and as Holts will put it out in a book in the fall, I say sell enough to pay my time-wage for typing, if you get the manuscripts back erewhiles. Carl."

Briefly my father got wooed away from the Chicago *Daily News* to go on the staff of Hearst's Chicago *Evening American* at a salary of $100 a week. But after three weeks he quit to go back to the *Daily News* at half pay, saying he "wasn't fated for a Hearst career." My father tells an early story of William Randolph Hearst, who had hired the American painter, Frederic Sackrider Remington, to cover the Spanish-American War as artist-correspondent. It was early 1898 and Remington had wired Hearst that a war didn't seem to be coming and he was not needed. Hearst had cabled back, "You furnish the pictures. I'll furnish the war."

My father wrote Alice Corbin Henderson, "Tumult. A world heavy with change. Who that can stand up wants to write anything but flash telegram letters? 'Sorrow and sorrow,' 'guardsman fed to the tigers.' . . . Sometimes I feel lucky my desk hasn't been wrecked by a shell. . . . Today it has reached its highest pitch: revolts in Hungary, reported killing of Czar Nick and son, reported overthrow of soviet government and capture of Moscow by Korniloff and German forces, Von Kuhlmann's resignation forced because of admission that war will go to a fifth winter. Wilson about ready to announce big plans backing Russia, Kerensky materializing a phantom puppet out of a dead past in London on his way to America, the western front holding like a God's miracle, Americans more and more throwing themselves into war trim ready for the supreme sacrifice—say, here where the cables come in every few minutes they all feel as sleepwalkery as you out there where the adobes doze in the endless sun." He told her also, "I read my war stuff before American Library Assn. at Saratoga July 4. Vers libre gets its foot in the door."

It was "The Four Brothers" he had read, and he sent the poem on to an editor friend, Sam T. Hughes, saying he was enclosing another reprint, making about thirty daily newspapers and several magazines that had published the poem in full. "I merely point to this record. I am never going to brag of my patriotism, like a virgin of her chastity, or a chorus girl of her shape." Hughes was editor in chief of The Newspaper Enterprise Association, with offices in San Francisco, Washington, New York, San Diego and Chicago as well as London and Paris. Its main office was at West Third Street and Lakeside Avenue in Cleveland. Of the N.E.A., H. L. Mencken would say later, ". . . the N.E.A. Service is one of my pet abominations. . . . It is journalism for street-car conductors, baseball fans, policemen and cads. . . . It glorifies the sort of reporter who prints interviews with women taken in raids on hotels," adding, "Sandburg is a man I respect."

Sam T. Hughes spoke to my father on the tenth of July, 1918, about an idea he had and followed up with a letter: "My dear Carl:—Regarding my proposition to send you as our correspondent to Eastern Europe with headquarters at Stockholm. As you know, Stockholm is next door to both Germany and Russia. The very latest and best German news gets to Stockholm faster and better than it gets to either Berne or Amsterdam. It is much more authentic from Stockholm than it is from Holland or Switzerland. Also Stockholm is only a short run from Russia. I am convinced that the Russian news is going to be just as important, if not more important than from any other part of the world. I know that you are better fitted than most newspaper men, mentally, temperamentally and otherwise, to cover this particular place and that particular section of the world. Of course I am not offering you the Stockholm thing as a temporary assignment. I want you to be a regular and fixed member of the Scripps institution. You know our ways and our ideals. We know you and we like you. We would not look on you merely from the standpoint of exploiting your brains. We are in sympathy with men of your kind. When the war ends, or when this Stockholm assignment ends so far as you are concerned, we want you in the office here."

My father responded at once, "Dear Sam Hughes: It is a go. On hearing that you can finance the stunt, I will begin packing for Stockholm."

Hughes wrote, "How soon can you break away from the *News*? . . . You will have to make application to the Federal Court in Chicago for passports. . . . Regarding your salary of $100 a week. During the first few days that you are in Stockholm I imagine that your expenses will be over the regular $25 a week. . . . But after the first week or two I am confident that you can get inside the $25. . . . We don't believe in slinging money around except when it gets big stuff. . . . We want our men to live decently, though not extravagantly."

My father asked Hughes for "a statement on why you send me to Stockholm," adding, "Tell them I have co-operated actively with the American Alliance for Labor and Democracy, which is the loyalty legion of the American Federation of Labor, and that the alliance gave wide circulation to my war poem, 'The Four Brothers.' Make me important as hell. Make it look as though there ought to be brass bands and girls in white dresses strewing flowers on my pathway to the steamboat." My father said he was going to Galesburg to get Grandma Sandburg to swear that "I was born when I was. . . . I figure on leaving the *Daily News* Wednesday of next week. . . . It seems to me I've got to hunt up some sort of live copy and stories or some good friends will be sore. My hunch is that I will find several Big Stories. . . . They want to know every mole and scar on a guy's frame. And he has to go get mugged and hand in three pictures of what kind of a pickpocket he looks like."

And so my father was leaving Maywood and heading for Cleveland and last minute talks with Hughes. He wrote home, "Dearest Paula: That was a wonderful good-by face you gave me this morning. It was luminous. . . . I was glad you and the little ones were in Maywood with trees and plenty cold running water. . . . I plan going to Washington tomorrow or Saturday . . .—As always, a lot of love—for all—for you and the Homey-glomeys—for Oma and Opa—for the guitars, the books, the manuscripts, the stove where we fried eggs, the autumn sun on the dear garden,—and most of all and all the time: you and the Homey-glomeys."

He told Mrs. Henderson, "I'm going to write Pound from Stockholm that he may hope and hope on that now I acquire a continental suavity. —There's a Big Wind blowing over Europe. Maybe I will write The Song of the Big Wind.—Sometime I shall see how it goes trying to warm myself when the Northern Lights are Playing their mystery pieces, trying to warm myself with Pictures of the adobes where you are and how the sun never fails there. Whenever you see ice think of me, please! while this stunt of Folly is on. . . . As I said before—love, regards, hope— everything. C.S."

And to Amy Lowell, "I go to Stockholm, Sweden, soon. . . . I may write a true poem of the Ocean, and one of Rocks, Pines and Fjords, and dark thoughts and lighted whimsies of the winter under the short Yule days. Though I expect to come back in a year or two and go to Brookline and tell you the ins and outs of vast actions, if my luck went the other way, I want you to know I have counted you friend and counselor. . . . I shall remember you to Gustav Froding and Selma Lagerlof and write you sometime from over there of your friends whom I am sure are there. . . . In all events, luck and regards! Yours, Carl Sandburg."

Miss Lowell answered, "Write fairly often, even if it is only a line on a postal card. Let us keep up; you do me good. Did I ever tell you how greatly I admire your 'Prairie' poem? . . . I think that it is one of the most extraordinarily beautiful poems I have ever read. I am not sure that it is not your very best thing. I can only say that I would have given much of my own work to have written it . . . I take my hat off to you."

Harcourt was delighted with the turn of events: "We look forward with unusual interest to the book which will be a permanent record of your sojourn in Sweden. We hope that the sacrifice you are making to undertake this job will be amply repaid."

My father wrote to Harriet Monroe from the Newspaper Enterprise

Association's Washington offices, "Dear Harriet: . . . Probably go in three or four weeks. 'My life has been measured out in coffee spoons.' . . . Yours, as a leaf in a wind, Carl."

At this time my father and mother began to call each other "Buddy." They would use the mutual term all their days. It was a time of war and a buddy—a diminutive of brother—was a tentmate, a fellow soldier, a companion; and then, with wartime separations, it took on romantic connotations. A song popular on a Victrola record went, "I think about you all through the day, my buddy!" My father had dedicated *Chicago Poems* "To my wife and pal." That was the same idea.

Now it seemed that red tape troubles were creeping in, connected with his passport for the trip and a draft exemption certificate. "Dearest Buddy," my father wrote home from New York, "I hope I get the exemption without going to Maywood, because a day stay, and the brief spitty smacky kisses of Janet would be a pain. When I come back to Maywood I want it to be for YEARS. . . . You will get by special delivery affidavits answering questions on which the draft board should base an exemption. A Spanish war veteran with a wife and two children, 40 years old, ought to make an easy and immediate decision for the board. Your letters are beautiful. Out of my tumults I try to get one a day to you, one of some kind, sometimes just a Hello My Buddy. Carl."

Through August and September of 1918, the messages came home to my mother. "I am there on the Art of Twiddling Thumbs and stoking up for the hunger of the Midnight Sun. . . . No passport today. . . . Thanks for the picts. The ones of you I wanted. The latest one of Janet, standing by her kiddie car, is one of the best. . . . We will all, like Pershing, Wilson, Foch, and Brother Ed, become better at Watchful Waiting. . . . as I get Paula in her dandy letters, she is in fine trim for her job which is a duty to The Republic and the world's greatest Little Family. . . . I'm saying over again everything I ever said about your being The Best. . . . I scribble idly because I like you a hell of a lot. . . . Here yet. No passports. Plenty of hope. . . . I'll wire you when I take boat. That may be any time or no time and it don't bother me to be a leaf in the wind of a world storm."

My mother was seven months pregnant when, on the twenty-third of September, Local Board Number 4 of Cook County in Maywood, Illinois, authorized my father's leaving the country and certified that the War Department had no objection to the issuing of the passport. Hughes wrote the secretary of state that the applicant was to conduct a news bureau in Stockholm and serve as a correspondent for 326 newspapers of the Newspaper Enterprise Association, that there would be "upwards of 4,500,000 subscribers" and that it would be of "utility and convenience to our correspondent and his readers in the United States" if the passport were amended to include Norway, Denmark, England and France.

My father wrote Hughes about others waiting for passports, "I'm going to be patient over delays in getting to Stockholm, the nest of spy nests." He worried about his socialist background and how he had "known Bolshevist friends," and whether that held him up. "While in New York I have kept away from the Socialist and I.W.W. bunch. . . . In Russia, the Terror is on and all who have issued from the hot breath of it have their nerves gone fliv and can only gibber a disconnected story. I'm going into chaos when I go, Sam, and I'm going to wear the same physiog and try to take it all from week to week like a game I played once with a small town ball team against a champeen big league bunch." He said he could handle the presently proposed salary. "I was brought up on herring and potatoes, and my forefathers lived on black bread the year round, with coffee and white bread only on Easter and Christmas. . . . And about my being with N.E.A. permanently, well, I know if destiny so spake I would rather go down with Petrograd cholera while working for the N.E.A. than any other newspaper organization I know of."

"Dearest Paula," he said, "You certainly got quick action on the exempt certificate. I give you a hug on that. . . . Now the way seems to be clear for a getaway next week. I wire you before I go on the ship and leave a letter to be mailed you after I sail. . . . Dinner with Harcourt today. We are getting to be quite pals. The dine was at Columbia Univ. club. Have eaten at Harvard club and Yale with other Parties. Getting to be very quite-so. All the fat I've put on, which is not a much, will be needed in Stockholm. . . . As I said once before: Love, regards, hope, everything."

He let her know he was prepared: "I am taking no scrap of printed paper except my Swedish dictionaries. Am listing all things in trunk for customs men. Bought rubbers, overshoes, wool leggins, medical kit, cold cream, orange marmalade and am a man of property. . . . Whatever you do in all these events, don't hurry, don't worry. With a Woodrow Wilson in the world things will come along—Jesus, that New York speech was a hummer—sort of the finale to 'Four Brothers'—hurray!"

And then, during the waiting as the leaving came closer, he mentioned their coming child. "Paula dearest. . . . God be good to you and John and ours, all the time, blessed girl. I still have a picture of your face the last morning at Maywood . . . lovelier face never had any woman than you in the goodby. It was a morning glory. . . . Take care of John: he

238

may see great days never known to our eyes . . . I know John will be a Holy Terror. . . . . Maybe we will sit under our own cherry tree some day with John plucking our shoe strings and I reel off the gossipy things that didn't get written . . . prayers for John. . . . The day John comes cable me, if all signs show me to be at Stockholm—cable to whatever my postal address is—whether it's John or another little sissenfrass . . . Carl."

I have wondered how my mother felt then, large with child and sure to face the birthing alone. Everyone read in the news all the time of submarines hunting ships on the open sea. I know she always stood strongly on her own feet, not depending on my father, except for total devotion and for the marvelous excitement she had about what she called his genius. Was she that way then? I hope so.

Seventeen

The Big Black Valise

On the afternoon of the third of October, 1918, the S.S. *Bergensfjord,* a ship of the Norwegian-American line, left the New York pier. My father wrote home that they "were held till Sunday afternoon the 6th near the Statue of Liberty. Saw three whales blowing today." In his pocket he had Mother's goodbye letter, ". . . here's 'So long, Buddy'—. . . . love and all my love and goodbye dear and I'm not sorry I can't be at the pier to kiss you Good-bye! Because maybe I wouldn't be as brave as I'd want to be. And I don't want your voyage marred by a picture of Paula crying on the pier! And it wouldn't be a true picture—the one of me smiling at the Maywood depot is nearer the truth—for I want you to go, dear—for your own sake and for the service I know you can do as a pro-ally Stockholm correspondent. I am happy over it all—but anxious over having to entrust your very life to the chances of a wooden boat on a big sea with its hidden threat of mines & submarines! We are all hoping & praying for our dearest one—all love & love & luck to you— and kisses from us all—Bye-bye with waving of hands from Janet—Good-bye to Carl from Paula. Send me your Stockholm address—and give Paula's love to New York for having been good to Carl!—So-long Buddy!"

He wrote an answer that would be posted when they reached Norway: "Just gave a third reading—and the first real quiet reading to your good-by letter. There were tears in it and a big gladness and a stronghearted woman—my pal—in it.—What we are having is only a breath of the world storm. We will hope that resolves and consecrations enough have been born out of the millions of separations, enough for the remaking of a world.—What with your line about Janet waving, and Margaret's dear note, and the Shewolf's kiss too, it all tugs at me tonight. I got the warm kiss of your calling me 'Buddy' at the finish. What we know is that all the chances are in favor of our sitting under our own cherry tree some day and talking about the year Carl went away and the Third Child came. (No Indian name. Maybe 'Mary Illinois' if it isn't John Edward.) And when I say God keep you and God keep you I mean it in its oldest and deepest way. Your Carl."

It was twenty-one days after he'd boarded ship that my father walked down the gangplank at Bergen, Norway, a big black valise in his hand. He got busy right away meeting newsmen and anybody he could communicate with. The N.E.A. sent out a flyer on their correspondent, "WHO SANDBURG IS," telling how he had had years of training "in the hard Chicago newspaper game," that he understood the language of the Scandinavian peoples, and was "a student of labor and social problems, the very problems that are being answered with varying success by the elements in control of various sections of Russia and the nations that have thrown off the German yoke," and that "his fame as a poet admits him to the confidence of the north European leaders of thought and governing classes, where a less known reporter might fail to make an impression."

Then my father was aboard the train to Christiania, now renamed Oslo, after picking up a Norwegian dictionary. He sent off his first cable, which the N.E.A. reported "shows that Sandburg got right on the job as soon as he landed. You may expect many other stirring news stories . . . from the one frontier where Germany has access to a large section of the outer world." An inch-high headline in a flyer of October 25 went: SAND-BURG'S THERE, and, "He Lands in Norway and Cables This Hot News Story: RUSS REDS PLOT GERMAN REVOLT, and Fifty Bolshevik Agents Daily Cross HUN Borders to Aid Popular Uprising."

Word went to my mother from Christiania, "I cabled a 165-word story last night which may be a hello to you. . . . Landlady here is a nut pro-German and curses Wilson all over the map." The story my father had wired referred to President Wilson's Liberty Loan speech of late September in which Wilson said that there could be "no peace obtained by any kind of bargain or compromise with the governments of the central empires" because they had made peace with Germany to save their own hides and that they were without honor. Wilson meant the peace pacts made with Rumania at Bucharest and with Russia at Brest-Litovsk near the Polish border. My father had gotten his story from a Norwegian newsman just back from Moscow, seat of the Bolshevik Russian government, who represented the trades union daily newspaper of Norway. The news was that "Bolshevik Russia was fomenting a Bolshevik revolution in Germany"; fifty "red" couriers were crossing the borders daily into Germany and Austria, their pouches filled with propaganda, guaranteeing that the resources of the "red" army of Russia would support the German people if they revolted against the Hohenzollerns, who ruled Prussia and Germany.

My father reported on the "Red and White Terrors," the Bolsheviks and the Anti-Bolsheviks. "Both kill people singly and *en masse*. Both expropriate property. Both break any law, ride over any tradition, throw down any and all old customs and usages that threaten their hold on power." When the Kerensky regime was ended by the Bolsheviks in the October Revolution in 1917, and the Lenin-Trotsky regime sued for a separate peace with Germany in the following March, many hoped that the White, the anti-Bolshevik Russians, would be able to gain control of the country again. It didn't work. My father said, "There are differences between the Red Terror and the White. What those differences are the historians and scribblers of future years may write out cautiously and accurately with the documents and the assessments of time before their eyes. Today in a huge rough dark way, Eastern Europe knows and understands more about these two Terrors through experience than does the rest of the world. A wide stream of information and purported information about the Red Terror has gone world wide among all nations. Only in Eastern Europe, however, has the knowledge been spread of the workings of the White Terror in the Don regime, the Volga, the Caucasus, Ukrainia, Bohemia, Poland, the Baltic Provinces, and Finland."

He wrote home, "Kristiania is proving a very friendly town. I go on to Stockholm tomorrow. Every night and morning I pray for the three of you to be snug and happy. My health never better and hopes and wishes for yours never deeper. Carl."

Then he was on a train again, crossing Norway, heading for Stockholm. From scraps of poems from that time as well as letters, there is the flavor of the people he met and the stories he heard. Stavanger was down the coast from Bergen and my father started a poem:

In Stavanger is an American consul whose heart asks to
understand the language of flowers & the sloping white shoulders
of women in decolte at faroff legation functions.

At Stavanger, however, he writes a friend at Göthenborg, there
is only herring to eat & a sea backed by stone mountains
to look at.

In Bergen is Erling Odner who testifies it nearly always rains in Bergen & the children are born with umbrellas in their hands & often a baby arrives with skin full grown between the toes & thus equipped early for the street of Bergen.

From Stockholm he said, "Dear Paula:—These are big days. Looks like I have five or six fierce months of it and then home. Correspondence goes so slow from here that I will cable more than first expected. . . . Had to pay $20 import duty on tobacco, & glad to do it & have some real American nicotine.—When I get home I will talk & talk for you— impressions. Lucky I know some Swedish for getting around & most of all for reading papers.—A thick note-book to bring home!—Love to the homey glomeys & you——all prayers for you and the littlest one." He subscribed to the Copenhagen *Politiken,* the Stockholm *Social-Demokraten* and the Christiana *Social Demokraten,* the latter daily labor papers. And he bought *Dagens Nyheter* and Stockholm's *Dagblad* on the stands.

It was a long time before his letters came to my mother, and hers to him. "It's a whole month now since the day you sailed—and a very long month it has been with no letters. . . . The kids are fine—Margaret full of stories & dreams, more and more a real companion!—and Janet lovable imperious eager for action, a little dynamo!—They are wonderful together. You should have seen them tonight marching to the 'Soldiers Parade'—Janet waving her flag and shouting 'Mar, Mar' (March, March) in time with the music! . . . I get fifty regularly each Monday from N.E.A.—so we'll be ready for them when the nurse (35.00 a week these days!) and doctor and John Edward arrive!—I'm glad I've another 4 weeks to wait, as doctors & nurses are busy day and night with this Influenza Epidemic—they simply can't take care of all cases. But the crest of the epidemic seems to have been passed. Schools reopen Monday after 3 weeks shut-down. So by the time John Edward is due—Dec. 5— there won't be the present scarcity of nurses. . . . Oma had a good letter from Ed—written Oct. 1st—from Pershing Headquarters—he was just back 3 weeks at the *very* front where he was personally directing the work of the September drives—all photography from air-planes of German positions—locating enemy batteries—enemy movements back of lines etc. You & Ed will have some big stories to tell when you both come home! Ed wrote too how glad he was of your new work—work you must be keen for. . . . It looks more every day like a collapse for Germany —her allies going and gone—her army retreating—and inner revolt brewing."

Was it a tearful time for my mother, eight months pregnant and only the chatter of children to amuse her, Margaret seven and Janet two? She wrote, "Peace seems nearer than ever.—And it won't be everlastingly long that you stay over there!"

Uncle Ed had been promoted to major by now and wrote Oma and Opa, "Just a hasty line to reassure you I'm on the job. As a matter of fact I've been so hard at it I forgot everything else. Have been at the front for over a month—helping Uncle Sam get his stranglehold on the *vital part* of the line. We have it now and it's going to do the work. It will soon be over. It's been a hard job—and lots of fine fellows have paid the big price. Uncle Foch knew what he was doing when he put the yanks in that sector. I don't think any of the other troops could have done it. Will write soon now I'm back at my desk again—so here's to joy—and peace, love, Gaesjack."

Mother told my father that the "last letter from Ed was from Strassburg! He sent photos of himself in birdman's uniform in air-plane! So he has been flying all right! He was at the front the last 8 weeks of the war." As a child in later years I became familiar with photographs in an album, taken before I was born, of my uncle at the front in the cockpit of the open "flying boxcar," wearing his bulky suit with fur-trimmed collar, tight cap and goggles, holding his ponderous camera. He has heavy gauntlets and his chin is muffled and it seemed a romantic occupation. And there are pictures of him when he visited Maywood later, jaunty in his khakis, black-haired, smooth-shaven, spurs on his tall shining boots, his figure lean and elegant, as he pushes Margaret in a swing—she in her velvet coat, a wide ribbon in her hair and high-button shoes. And he towers, with his arm about Oma in a long gray dress and fresh lace collar or a feathered cap and a home-knitted coat. I was told that Oma advised Uncle Ed, "Fly low, Gaesjack, close to the ground so you'll be safer." And I was told too, by my mother, of a romantic liaison my uncle had with a beautiful American woman there in France while he served his country and the Cause of the Allies and put his Art aside.

From Stockholm my father wrote, "Dear Buddy: Nothing to report, absolutely nothing till I get back home again and we sit in the swing in the back yard and talk. That is, Stockholm and eastern Europe are all such a blur and a chaos now that nothing in the future seems much of a certainty except that a circle of expeditions will get to the bolshevik soviets and wipe them off the map. A New York Evening Post man I came over with says the war will be over soon in every way and 'then the old universal human muddle will go on again.'—There was a thrill about seeing the soil of Sweden, setting foot on it, and hearing the speech of one's forefathers spoken by everybody and on all the street signs. And the Norway waterfalls are memory to keep. Much that is homelandish here. But . . . I look forward to when I can go home and have the everlasting youths tousling my hair and giving me spitty smacky kisses. I want to go ahead on the Homeyglomey book. I have seen enough sophistication and ignorance to last me a good while."

My father had not yet written his stories for children, the Rootabaga books, but with his present homesickness and the tales he'd heard in Bergen of children born with umbrellas in their hands and webbed toes for the rainy streets, perhaps the first stirrings came. One of his Rootabaga characters, "Hatrack the Horse," would instruct three umbrellas, "If the three wild Babylonian Baboons come sneaking through the house, then all you three umbrellas open up like it was raining, jump straight at the baboons and fasten your handles in their hands . . . never let go till I come."

The sun rose behind clouds at 8:30 in the morning and set behind more clouds at 3:30 in the afternoon. My father was given bread and potato cards and he bought a ticket to the Riksdag, the parliament of Sweden, letting him into the gallery. And then less than three weeks after my father landed at Bergen, the war was over—Armistice Day, the eleventh of November. I was not yet born and all that war means to me is family stories and photographs and the songs we would sing to the guitar, "There's a long, long trail a-winding . . . where the whipporwill is calling . . . while our hearts are yearning . . . and the white moon beams . . . and the roses will die with the summertime, and our paths may be far apart . . . my heart's right there . . . and we won't come back 'til it's over, over there."

In later years my uncle, who had been stationed then at General Pershing's headquarters at Chaumont, France, in the Haute Marne country, said, "The wholesale murdering was over, and wild celebrations began that night: cheering, yelling, screaming, booze, noise. I went into my room at the barracks and flung myself on the bed. The whole monstrous horror of the war seemed to fall down on me and smother me. . . . A state of depression remained with me for days." France had been a second country to Uncle Ed and he'd defended her position from the outset of the war. He had been hurt in another way too. My uncle, like my mother, had a green thumb and a passion for flowers. Before the war broke out in Europe in 1914, he had started his garden of delphinium at the Villa l'Oiseau Bleu, where he had divided his time between painting and photography and his interest in genetics and the hybridizing of the flowers. Then Clara had left Voulangis with the children and maids just two days before a patrol of German troops trampled over the fields and gardens.

Mother wrote my father that Oma had got a postcard from Uncle Ed saying he'd visited Bivange, where he'd been born, and that "all her folks are alive and not much the worse for the German occupation but mighty glad the Prussians are *out*! You can imagine how all Oma's and Opa's folks welcomed Ed coming with the American army—a major! It would have been wonderful enough if he had come as a drummer-boy! But. . . . Their cousin an American Major! Their Liberator!"

A fortnight later, on the twenty-fourth of the month, a Sunday, at six in the morning, I was born. My mother wrote of it to Harriet Monroe, while reporting that at last a letter had reached her from Christiania, taking more than a month to come: "So Carl's 'passage over' was safe. Mine too—'to more than India'—for we have a husky little new-born baby girl—as colorful and clamorous as you could wish. . . . Mary Steichen Sandburg. We are at home—and we wish you could come to see us. . . . Of course, I understand that we live at the far end of no-where—and it's hard to get out here. But it would be good to see you and show you our newest rose-red little one! . . . With Victory & Peace, we must all be well now. Sincerely, Lilian Steichen Sandburg."

It had taken my father's letter over a month to reach Maywood. Mother wrote him that ". . . baby Mary has settled down to good regular hours for sleeping & feeding. . . . I could not write Saturday & Sunday—a little milk fever. . . . We are wondering where you will have your Xmas. In Berlin maybe? Thierry has had a few cables the last couple of weeks from Berlin. I clipped them for you—but Janet managed to swipe them & tear them to pieces! Anyway they were *not* big news stories. . . . If we could only have you here Xmas eve! Margaret is so eager for Santa Claus—Janet & Mary Ellen take it more calmly! You should be here for the burst of joy when they first see the tree and their toys!— I pray this is the last Xmas without You, Buddy!" And in her P.S. there is a feeling of the interminable waiting for news at home: "Received the letter you wrote on the steamer Dec. 18—just 2 *months* after you landed in Kristiana! Nov. 29 I had a letter you mailed the day before you left Kristiana for Stockholm. These 2 are all the letters I've had so far."

My mother named me for Oma and perhaps my middle name came from the Presbyterian minister's yellow-haired youngest daughter who lived, I am told, across the street and was fond of children—Mary Ellen. My name would change variously in time, but when the birth was recorded six days later in the Cook County Bureau of Vital Statistics, I was Mary Ellen and my father's occupation was listed: Artist.

Meanwhile he was coming to feel Stockholm:

> I saw roses in a street garden in Karl Johansgatan . . . & the
> palace of the King was on one hand & the house of the People's
> congress on the other . . . & the leaves of many roses lay
> knocked off by the rain & the requests of autumn.
>
> I crossed the street & stood in front of the Grand hotel . . . my
> elbows just evading the elbows of spies & diplomats in spats
> speaking yes-yes & ab-so-lute-ly & per-haps to each other . . .
> & street girls by one & two passed, making eyes, making
> eyes . . . by one & two flinging up over a camouflage of smiles
> along the lighted sidewalks . . . & I crossed over & back to
> the roses, the rain & the requests of autumn.
>
> I had come three times a thousand miles in fog & salt of the
> sea & half a thousand miles on a rockland hurling ribbons
> of water, flying sheets of water, keeping always songs, day
> songs & night . . . songs no matter what happens or who
> goes by & never remembers . . . songs sliding always in
> a white scarf flurry of virgins washing their hair before a
> wedding day or young wives saving all & everything for one loved
> to the throne of God & back.
>
> I had left God & home in another country . . . & picked up
> God again on the sea & among the rocks & white waters . . . &
> I picked up God again across from the lighted sidewalks,
> among the roses, the rain & the requests of autumn . . .
> on Karl Johansgatan . . . & the palace of the King on one hand
> & the house of the People's congress on the other.

The setting for this poem is Old Stockholm, called Old Town. At the south end is the market, Karl Johanstorg, and if you walk north toward the city proper where the Grand Hotel is, on one side will be the Riksdaghuset, the Parliament House, inaugurated in 1905, and on the other the Kungliga Slottet, the Royal Palace. When I was in Stockholm in May of 1961, traveling for the United States Information Agency, I stayed at Hotell Reisen on Skeppsbron across from Old Town and would walk over to the Grand Hotel to use their stationery, drink their *kaffe* and sample their smörgåsbord. Two years before, in August, my father had come over, also for the U.S.I.A. and he also stayed at Hotell Reisen. There were flowers in my room and the man at the desk asked me, "And how are your father?"

And didn't it happen, as in his poem, that my father walked out of the Grand Hotel one afternoon and crossed the boulevard to sit on a bench in the brief sunshine, where a man whom my father has described as having "a big nice smile on his face" introduced himself as Mitchell Berg and sat beside him? My father noted this in a memo he prepared forty years later for Theodore Draper who wanted to write of the incident in *The Roots of American Communism*. In the memo my father also stated that the incident occurred in Oslo, but I am reasonably sure that it was in Stockholm, where he wrote the poem. My father also noted about Berg that "it was significant that he had waited at the hotel until I left and he had not come to my room." Berg was Russian born, of a Jewish rabbinical family, his real name Michael Grusenberg. He'd gotten into the Russian revolutionary movement through the Jewish Bund and in 1903, at nineteen years of age, joined the Bolsheviks. When he got in trouble with the government, he left for the States, shortening his last name to Berg and making his first into Mitchell. He entered Valparaiso College in Indiana, married a Russian student there, and before long the two set up a school on the north side of Chicago where they taught English to immigrants. When the Revolution came ten years later, Berg returned to his homeland to help the cause. He changed names again and became a Russian agent: Michael Borodin. One of his tasks was to get money and propaganda to pro-Bolsheviks in the States, which was why he approached my father.

Borodin had been close to the socialist movement in Chicago and surely knew of my father in those days and had no trouble striking up a conversation and offering information, using his Chicago alias. One of the stories my father cabled back that he got from Berg-Borodin was about the shelling of Jaroslav, Poland, then a part of Russia, by the Bolsheviki, the headlines going: STRONGHOLD OF CZAR IS REDUCED BY HUNS. "Red Guards Pillage and Destroy Unrestrained." The article went on, "Jaroslav was the seat of the czar's military academy and a favorite haunt of the Russian general staff. News of its destruction was brought to Stockholm by Mitchell Berg, a former Chicago school teacher. 'A large group of the former czar's officers had fostered a revolt against the soviets,' said Berg. 'About 2000 were killed, and no counter revolutionists were made prisoners. The Red Guard which attacked numbered 25,000 men. The civil population were given three days to remove from the city.' "

The plight of Finland, with Russia across her long Eastern border and below the Gulf of Finland to the South, was close to my father's heart. Finland had been a grand duchy before the revolution and the Russian czar its grand duke. The Social-Democratic Party of Finland elected the majority of the national parliament in 1916 and after the Bolshevik revolution in Russia, proclaimed the People's Republic of Finland, with its own police and military forces. However, General Carl Mannerheim, born in Finland and serving in the Russian army since the age of twenty-two, had returned to his native land in January of 1918 and led a fight against the new socialist government. His army was known as the White Guard and, as my father said, "was hemmed in on a thin strip in the far north of Finland by the new Socialist government army known as the Red Guard. In April there came to General Mannerheim's help, thousands of German soldiers. They were crack battalions taken from the western front in France. . . . This additional force . . . with machine guns and howitzers and all the paraphernalia that had played hell with Belgium and northern France, swept across Finland from north to south. . . . In July, the new White Guard government announced that 90,000 persons, men, women and children, were in prison camps . . ." and it was estimated that 10,000 were killed in mass executions.

My father reported that he had been given photographs "by a Norwegian Red Cross chief" showing prisoner executions by the "White Terror" of Finland, as the new White Guard government was now termed. He intended to bring the photographs back to the States. He wrote about secret reports published by Hjalmar Branting in the daily labor paper of Stockholm, the *Social-Demokraten*, regarding prisoner deaths by starvation in the Finnish camps. He said Branting was a strong anti-Bolshevist and "openly condemns the White Terror of Finland as far more bloody and cruel than the Red Terror of Russia." Everywhere was fear and in the States the N.E.A. offices received my father's cables. The headlines ran: KAISER'S FINNISH PALS SHOOT DOWN LABOR AND RADICAL LEADERS . . . HORRORS OF THE WHITE TERROR! PRISONERS STARVED TO DEATH BY PRO-GERMAN FINNS. All trades unions, socialist parties and farmers' leagues were abolished, ran the stories.

All the while, my father was filling his big black valise with materials: documents, photographs, postcards, clippings from Scandinavian socialist and labor papers on the Russian and German situations, Russian pamphlets, books and newspapers and magazines, the Izvestia files on the

Soviet Congress of the past June, a three-volume history of Russia by V.O. Kliuchevsky, and in time he would have three pocket notebooks containing material on numerous interviews. How can I sort out from the dispatches, letters and conflicting papers what went on in those times? I do know that Michael Borodin, alias Mitchell Berg, was packing up "a trunkful of literature" that my father intended to take back to the States with him. It wasn't possible for the deposed Finnish socialist government to communicate by cable or any way with its official representative in New York—Santeri Nuorteva, who was considered a "Bolsheviki Red" by the U.S. authorities, who had an eye on the round-faced heavy-set Finn. Nuorteva had sent a letter to President Wilson: "Sir . . . the treacherous minority representing the aristocracy in Finland, has temporarily succeeded, with the help of invading German troops, in subduing . . . the Finnish people . . . these forces are now destroying the last vestiges of liberty and democracy." It was an appeal for recognition that the legal government in Finland was the one supported by the majority of the people and deriving its sanction from a legal election. My father collected a pamphlet written by Nuorteva, listing him as "Representative of the Finnish Workers' Republic." It was titled *An Open Letter to American Liberals* and was put out by the Socialist Publication Society, sold for five cents and contained thirty-two pages. It stood strongly against "the White Guard Government of Finland, who have sold themselves body and soul to the Germans," and against outside interference in Russia, not only from the Germans who had given refuge to the royalists, but from Americans, British, French, Italians and the rest.

Nikolai Lenin, eight years older than my father, had written his pamphlet too, published in that December of 1918, which my father collected. It was put out by the same Socialist Publication Society, consisted of fifteen pages and sold for the same nickel a copy. It was titled *A Letter to American Workingmen From the Socialist Soviet Republic of Russia* and was in English translation. My father said years later that he secured it in an inside pocket of his coat and so brought it over safely to the States.

It was a time of riots and strikes and slaughter for the workingman back in America. Deportations of aliens and known communists continually took place. Billy Sunday was shouting from platforms about how the "ornery-eyed Socialists and I.W.W.'s" ought to be "stood up before a firing squad to save space on our ships." And "Big Bill" Haywood of the I.W.W. was about to skip the country, leaving on a fake passport for Russia where he would be introduced to Lenin by Michael Borodin himself. Haywood wrote home later to a friend, a radical sometime communist, Ralph Chaplin, who in 1909 had written an I.W.W. song to the tune of "John Brown's Body":

> When the Union's inspiration
> through the workers' blood shall run,
> There can be no power greater
> anywhere beneath the sun.
> Yet what force on earth is weaker
> than the feeble strength of one?
> But the Union makes us strong.
>
> Solidarity forever!
> Solidarity forever!
> Solidarity forever!
> For the Union makes us strong.

Haywood said, "I asked Comrade Lenin if the industries of the Soviet Republics are to be run and administered by the workers." Lenin's reply was that yes, that was Communism.

Lenin, in his *A Letter to American Workingmen* pamphlet, had stated that "America, like a few other nations, has become characteristic for the depth of the abyss that divides a handful of brutal millionaires who are stagnating in a mire of luxury, and millions of laboring starving men and women who are always staring want in the face." Lenin had declared just before Armistice Day in another letter, this one to the joint meeting of the Soviet Central Executive Committee, the Moscow Soviet and the trade unions, "The imperialists of the Anglo-French-American group . . . are thinking of building a Chinese wall to protect themselves from Bolshevism, like a quarantine against plague. . . . The bacillus of Bolshevism will pass through the wall and infect the workers of all countries." In the pamphlet also was a reference to an old friend of my father's. Lenin said, "I recall with pride the words of one of the best loved leaders of the American proletariat, Eugene V. Debs, who said in the *Appeal to Reason* at the end of 1915, when it was still a socialist paper, in an article entitled 'Why Should I Fight?' that he would rather be shot than vote for war credits to support the present criminal and reactionary war, that he knows only one war that is sanctified and justified from the standpoint of the proletariat: the war against the capitalist class, the war for the liberation of mankind from wage slavery. I am not surprised that this

fearless man was thrown into prison by the American bourgeoisie. . . .
The greater the bitterness and brutality they sow, the nearer is the day
of the victorious proletarian revolution." And Lenin's words had ended,
"We are invincible, for invincible is the Proletarian Revolution."

My father collected not only Lenin's words but a love letter from the
czarina, which would be published on his return, her last letter to
Nicholas Romanoff before his abdication: ". . . My dear, all you need is
to be firm and show the strength of your hand! That is just what the
Russians need. You have never failed to show them kindness and goodness of heart—let them now understand that your fist is doubled and
ready! They ask that of you themselves. Many have said lately to me,
'We need the knout.' It is strange, but such is the nature of the Slav. . . .
I wish we could find a way to live in quiet and peace. . . . I understand
only too well how 'the bellowing mob' acts when you are near. They are
afraid of you now and they must be made still more afraid of you.
Therefore, wherever you go they must tremble before you. Among the
cabinet ministers, too, you are a power and a leader. . . . Ah, my God,
how I love you! Always more and more, my love for you is deep as the
sea . . ."

And then my father was boarding the train back to Christiania, figuring
to sail home on the same liner that had brought him over two months
before. The editor of the Christiania *Social-Demokraten,* Olaf Scheflo,
offered him moving picture films that had passed Norwegian censorship
and had been shown to the public. They were half propaganda film and
half educational, and were issued by the Bolshevik government of Russia.
My father wrote to the military attaché at the American legation in
Christiania, Major Berger Osland, "I should like to take these films to
America when I go on the Bergensfjord next Saturday. . . . many of the
pictures have a news value . . . the Newspaper Enterprise Association
would utilize reproductions from these films. . . . even if the Committee
on Public Information should decide that it is against the nation's best
interest to use or publish these photographs at this time, they would be
of interest to officials in Washington."

My father wanted authorization to carry the films to the port of New
York and there to turn them over to the customs people to have custody
and disposal at their discretion. He wanted also to stipulate that if the
films were released, any profits from their showing should be "devoted to
the food supply and sanitation of the prisoners in Finland convict camps.
. . . the latest available report . . . places the number of these convicts
at upwards of 27,000." He cited the words of Wilson to Congress on the

second of December in which the President hoped that "the news of the next fews months may pass with the utmost freedom and with the least possible delay from each side of the sea to the other."

But Major Osland took a dim view of the whole matter. He asked my father what kind of an American he was, whether he was seeing the right kind of people, and hadn't he been spending about a third of his working hours with radical socialists and Bolsheviks? Osland said that it was not "strictly American conduct and was unfair to the readers of the 320 American newspapers" my father was writing for. He advised my father to "lay off from talking with 'Reds.'" My father answered Major Osland that he had been doing the same thing in Christiania that he had always done in Chicago, that he wouldn't write labor news without seeing labor men, and that he "believed it viciously unfair for the cafe correspondents to send news stories to America based only on information from royalist conspirators and Russian counter-revolutionists."

When my father was about to leave Christiania for Bergen where the S.S. *Bergensfjord* would put out to sea, the man with the "big nice smile on his face"—Michael Borodin–Mitchell Berg—approached again and asked my father, who agreed, to take along four hundred kroner of Norwegian money for Mrs. Borodin-Berg in Chicago. He also handed my father two drafts for five thousand dollars each, payable to Santeri Nuorteva in New York, saying that the ten thousand dollars was "for the purpose of getting the Finns and Scandinavians of America informed of how Finland's fate in death, sickness and hunger is worse than Belgium, Serbia, Poland or any other nation that has known tragedy the past four years." My father accepted the drafts, although he took the precaution of showing them to Minister A. Schmedeman in Christiania before leaving. He told Schmedeman that he was not certain whether it was proper for him as an American citizen to deliver the ten thousand dollars to Nuorteva, and that before he did so he would lay the matter before his boss, Sam Hughes, at the Newspaper Enterprise Association and would of course inform the New York port officials of his possession of them on arrival. As for the four hundred kroner for Mrs. Borodin, my father felt that that was a personal affair and he kept it in the same inside coat pocket as the Lenin pamphlet, planning to deliver it to her in time.

Then he was on the liner heading home. It was the fifteenth of December, 1918. Had the journey changed him? Would he ever want to return to the land from which Grandfather and Grandma Sandburg had come? He would not make it back to Sweden for over forty years. My father never seemed interested in visiting foreign and far-off places. He was committed to his own land. He felt his American roots, his patriotism, more strongly now. And looking back, there on the shipboard deck, he finished a poem he'd begun in Stockholm:

> Cast a bronze of my head and legs & put them on the
>   king's Way.
> Set the cast of me here alongside Carl XII, thus making
>   two Carls for the Swedish people & the utlanders to
>   look at between the palace and the Grand Hotel. . . .
> The summer sun will shine on both the Carls and
>   the November drizzles wrap the two. . . .
> I would remember last Sunday when I stood on a jutland of
>   fire-born red granite watching the drop of the sun
>   in the middle of the afternoon and the full moon
>   shining over Stockholm four o'clock in the afternoon.
> If the young men will read five lines of one of my poems
>   I will let the kings have all the bronze—I ask only
>   that one page of my writings be a knapsack keepsake
>   of the young men who are the bloodkin of those who
>   laughed nine hundred years ago: We are afraid of
>   nothing—only—the sky may fall on us.

Eighteen

The Liars

My father was still out at sea the day before Christmas. My mother received a letter from an Otto Johansson, a member of a delegation of Scandinavian journalists, who wrote from the LaSalle Hotel in Chicago on the twenty-fourth, "I have with me from Stockholm many greetings to you and your whole family from Mr. Carl Sandburg. I also have a little parcel for you. . . . I should be very glad if you could fetch the parcel. . . . You can perhaps phone to the hotel and tell me when you or your representative can come. I hope you will excuse my very bad english." I don't know whether or not my mother got the package, but I am sure that she would not feel safe or secure about my father until she heard that the S.S. *Bergensfjord* had docked and he was aboard.

When the liner did arrive at the New York port, it would be two days before my mother knew of it. My father was met and detained by a group of customs officials who, aside from his personal effects, took charge of the contents of the black valise as well as the bank drafts. In a memo my father set down years later he said that he was not searched personally and so the four hundred kroner as well as Lenin's *A Letter to American Workingmen* remained in his inside pocket. But his baggage was gone through and items broken, including even a jar of cold cream, he said, which he used for shaving. In this memo my father also noted that he didn't lose touch with Borodin-Berg and that when he had occasion to answer a cable from the agent in Stockholm, he would sign the name of Mitchell Berg's alderman when he'd taught school in Chicago—Eddie Kaindl.

My father was held over Christmas day and the day after, and then he went to the N.E.A. offices to send his explanation to Sam Hughes and to write Mother, "Dear Buddy, . . . May leave here for Cleveland next week and after three or four days there then Maywood. . . . Well, well, as a family now we number as many as the fingers on a human hand— what do you know about that—I'm proud of you.—I sent along some Scandahoovian knickknacks for the kids but nothing for you yet, tho I hope we can be real Christmassy before the winter is over. Your Carl." How different my father's situation was from my mother's. He was elated to be home, was filled with arrogance and assurance, and knew there was love in Maywood waiting for him. There she was, as intellectual as he and impatient for all he would have to tell, and held back by three vigorous small daughters.

My father wrote a long letter to Hughes at the Cleveland N.E.A. offices, and said that when he was "asked by Customs Inspectors Kingsland and Tracy to show them any and all papers, I handed them two drafts for $5,000 each, payable to Santeri Nuortava [sic], head of the Finnish Information Bureau in the United States, and a former member of the Finnish lantdag. I told them these drafts were given to me by persons whom I can not name, that I showed the draft to U.S. Minister Schmedeman in Christiania. . . . I told Minister Schmedeman that from such a distance I was not sure what sort of service I might be rendering and that before I delivered the drafts to Nuortava [sic] I would lay the entire matter before the editor-in-chief of the N.E.A. and that I would inform New York port officials as to the drafts." My father also said that when he took the drafts "it was with the purpose partly of raising the issue whether an American citizen is to be denied rights to communication in a human cause while an imperialist utterly hostile to American democracy, is permitted to come to the United States with unlimited funds for a propaganda of confusions, garblings and lies concerning the operations of the Red and White Terrors. The foregoing is in substance my statement to the War Work Committee which is now handling my 'case.' I am told that telephonic conversations are being held with the State Department at Washington and it is possible the department may wish to inform itself further to make certain that I am not unconsciously being made the instrument of conspiratorial interests inimical to the United States. The censorship office informs me that a squad of workers is employed on our printed and written material and a completion of the task may be expected next Monday. While I mark time in New York I shall try to send you stories from my mental notebook."

Back at his hotel, my father wrote another letter to my mother. "Dear Buddy: The Authorities loosened up to the extent of one suit case of stuff today. . . . Busier than a cranberry merchant these days. American and British Intelligence officers and an assistant district attorney spent three hours asking questions. 'Which group do you personally favor, the Liebknecht-Luxemburg Spartacans or the Ebert-Scheidemann government?' 'Well, I can't say I favor either of them!' 'Huh—well, who do you favor? Why are you so reluctant?' 'If I favor—as you put it—if I favor any one group, it is the Haase-Lebedour Independent Socialist group.' 'That is not answering our question strictly. As between the Ebert-Scheidemann group and the Liebknecht-Luxemberg group, which do you favor?' 'I would rather answer that question by saying that I regard Liebknecht and Rosa Luxemburg as honest fanatics while they lived and martyrs now that they are dead. And I have no other opinion than that Ebert and Scheidemann are crooks and will never establish a stable government in Germany.' So it goes . . . Your Carl."

And the next day, walking the windy, cold December streets of New York to the N.E.A. office at 110 West Fortieth Street, did my father think of the warm house in Maywood? He was soon typing a letter to my mother: "Paula Dearest: Still marking time here. . . . Have a tremendous story of Finland; it will be a big story even if they don't let me have my mass of corroborative details and photos. Love to Mary Illinois. God bless you and her and the whole holy homeyglomey crew. Your Carl." And he said too, "Not a line from you here. I have a notion to wire you that you must wire back whether you love me which is what I want to know not having heard it in weeks and weeks and weeks. Carl. It is possible I may have to stay here a week or two yet. Write me New York NEA office. My hope is that I go on to Cleveland in a few days and then Maywood."

Sam Hughes also wanted my father in Cleveland and wrote to Frederick Kerby, chief of the New York bureau, "If it had not been for that $10,000 that Sandburg brought back from the Finnish radical party, I would have raised all kinds of hell today with Washington by telegram over that censorship business. But I know that if I did raise such a rumpus, they would very innocently come back at me and say that Sandburg's effects were not searched because he was a correspondent of N.E.A. but because he was an agent of the Finnish Reds, the Finnish Bolsheviki. I know all right that Sandburg took the matter to the American ambassador in Norway before he sailed with the money; I know that he declared then and there that he would not deliver the money until he had consulted the American authorities in New York and that he afterwards did this; I know that he also declared that even if there was no objection whatever to his delivery of the money in this country, he would not deliver it until I had given him the word. We could say this and publish it broadcast, but we would say it and publish it on the defensive. That is,

Washington would immediately follow our first blast by charging quite truthfully that Sandburg had made himself an agent of the Finnish Bolsheviki by taking charge of the money they wished to send to their compatriots [sic] in the United States. That, of course, would put us on the defensive. However, there is probably another way to attack the thing. For this reason I'd like Sandburg to come on to Cleveland as soon as possible."

Hughes also telegraphed the secretary of the navy, Josephus Daniels, to "Please look sharp that naval intelligence office does not destroy our property consisting of five reels of films delivered by our staff correspondent Carl Sandburg to naval attache at Stockholm and sent by him to Washington. We would like you to render the decision. We have been given impression by attaché Marrix and others that film would be destroyed on arrival at Washington because it happens to have some Bolshevik pictures. As newspaper organization sending a man to ends of the earth we feel that he should get complete information and pictures, and not merely the facts on one side of a news matter. This whether we use information later or not. As you know N.E.A. supported Wilson and stood by government to last ditch during war. Why should we be placed under rigorous censorship at this late date. Why is government stopping our men at frontier and seizing our property but interfering with no other newspaper organization. Sandburg has at last been allowed to proceed from New York to Cleveland to see me and I am outraged over the reports of his treatment by U.S. government officials in New York and Europe all because he carried out my instruction to get Bolshevik information as well as anti-Bolshevik information. As a newspaperman you know that this is an absolute necessity for intelligent opposition as well as for intelligent approval. And surely you know and the government knows that we could not approve any such system. When you investigate you will realize why I am indignant. . . . S. T. Hughes."

New Year's Eve came and my father sent a night letter home. Then he wrote the next day, ". . . am hoping to have some sort of word from you to-morrow. If I don't get it I shall wire again. . . . I want to know whether you have any assurances of affection, esteem—thoughts—stuff like that—the shimmer of moonbeams—a young star winking through a cobweb—send a line to your CARL."

At the same time she wired: HAPPY NEW YEAR BUSHELS LOVE ALL WELL CHILDREN AND PAULA.

And he answered at once; "First your telegram came, then your letter today, and it's a fine start for 1919. Bushels of Love. Carl."

My mother had written, elated, "Dear Buddy-Bud— . . . Your New

Years telegram was great stuff! It made over a lonesome day into a big day of love & joy! . . . Home again! and I have no address to write you! I'm guessing you'll be in Cleveland sometime soon—and will send this there! Hurrah! Anyway! Wherever you may be now—In two weeks we'll hang out the flags! I haven't even told Margaret for I don't know whether she could keep such a glorious secret! Only Oma, Opa and I know and I've whispered it to Baby Mary Ellen! *She* won't tell but she's so happy that her daddy will see her soon! Do write and send an address. I have so much to tell you—but want to know that my letter will reach you before I write! This is just *Three Cheers for Daddy Come Home!* I can hardly wait for 2 weeks to pass! Love and Love, dearest Buddy! from your happy Paula. Bushels of Welcome Home kisses from the kids! I have wished so hard for *this*—my Wishes must have brought you home, dear!!"

My mother may have heard rumors. She became afraid my father would leave her again, her youngest barely a month old. "Last night I dreamed," she wrote, "you had gone off again to Sweden after a mere Visit home! I awoke in tears! Buddy, if you feel you have to go again— it will be much harder for us to let you go! I'm hoping and hoping that Hughes will feel your 'Mission' to Eastern Europe has been fulfilled! that it won't be worth while to send you back considering the slow transmission of news by mail! (Yesterday I received your first letter from Stockholm dated Oct. 28—so this letter was *10 weeks* on the way!) However, Buddy, I'll be game! . . . I have an idea that when you get to Cleveland you and Hughes will lay your plans for the future—so I want to get in my word ahead! I want you to know, dear, that I'm game and won't hold you back if you really feel a call to go off somewhere again. I don't want to interfere with your destiny—or your future—or any big chance for your development—or a new inspiration to write! You must be free—till the time comes when your family is sufficiently *mobile* to go with you wherever you go!—But meantime you must know *too* how we love you and need you—and so if a proposition is made to you that is. *not* very attractive—if you feel 50-50 about it—throw our love for you & need of you into the balance, and stay home! The kids are a wonderful trio now—so there will be many compensations here for what you will miss seeing over there! But I don't want to over- persuade you either way, dearest! It wouldn't be worthy of me nor of Oma's, the She-Wolf's daughter, nor of Gaesjack's sister! Oma and Gaes- jack would both say shame to me—if I kept you from any chance to make more of yourself—a chance for growth in experience—a chance for new freshening inspiration! You get me?"

Seeing the letters of that time, I can feel the total dedication my mother had toward my father, her early high resolves and ideals unmoved, insisting on being "game" and speaking of his "destiny." I can hear the noise of the small house in Maywood. Baby Mary Ellen—me—is always wanting feeding, changing and attention; Margaret is seven and a half and is always on hand and Janet is in her "terrible twos." Oma must have come to visit sometimes and to help, and surely Mother had a "girl" to assist in the washing, ironing, cleaning and cooking. She told him, as the first week of January passed and the days went by, that she was saving the Christmas tree, hoping he would be there soon. "It's hard to keep from telling Margaret that you're coming home soon—because she is very lonesome for you—and disappointed that Xmas and snow & Jack Frost—none of them brought you, as she had hoped! . . . Janet has changed *so* much! But she's just as naughty! Only more so!— We not only have to keep all drawers & book-cases locked downstairs— but we can't put books or anything on the mantel or on tops of book-cases or piano! She reaches everywhere by bringing up chairs & climbing up! I keep Mary Ellen up-stairs for safety whenever Janet is downstairs! We have your cupboard securely locked—also the 2-drawer filing case. But the big storage filing cases are not locked. I thought the drawers were too heavy for her to open. Yesterday while she was thought to be taking her nap, she managed to open one of the old storage filing case drawers and work havoc there! Luckily the stuff she got was not important! I'll nail these cases shut—one little nail will do the job—easy to pull out too, if you want to get into the old cases. But don't worry all your other stuff is safely locked!—and these old storage cases will be securely locked against our little Bolshevik Janet—and before this day is spent!! 14 below zero here! You could use your heavy overcoat—interlining and all!! Glad you have warm things!! Yesterday evening the Post had the start of your story of secret graft exposed in correspondence between Russian envoy in India & Petrograd government. I inclose clipping. It was on front page. The Post is waking up! A Bully story! Had a postcard from Ed yesterday from the City of Luxembourg—said he was feted at a dinner party given by Joseph Steichen (Opa's cousin) who is state counselor of the (Lilliput) Grand-Duchy of Luxembourg! Of course Ed was thrilled at being in his old homeland again! So you & Ed were both in the land of your fathers at the same time!! . . . Love and all there is of it—from us all—kids and your Paula."

Then briefly my father was in Maywood. He had taken the train to Cleveland and had his talk with Hughes. He was home for a week-end with my mother. She met him at the door holding me, the child he'd never seen, so that when he returned to New York to the N.E.A. office, he wrote back, "Dear Buddy: . . . Never can I forget your opening the door and looking into my face and then turning your eyes to Mary Ellen Alix, the emotional arithmetician and the wop war baby. Your Carl."

I wonder how it seemed to my father, thrown briefly into the family again. Surely he wanted to relate every adventure to my mother. There were Margaret and Janet clamoring for his attention, hanging onto his tobacco-scented figure, liking his rough face, his coarse hands, how he swung them strongly up in his arms. I surely wailed or complained as babies do from time to time. And there was my mother, soft in his arms at night. He wrote back also, "I don't know why—but it seems like the bunch of you is very close to me. The earth is my home and I am with my family. Of course, I know if I should stay any long while, more than a few weeks, it would be terribly lonesome. But when I have to be doing what I am doing, and when I have just had a glorious homey time of it with you all, it seems almost as though you're right here with me. It's something real and sure the bunch of us has found."

Where did my name Helga come from? Was there some wonderful Scandinavian woman that my father met over there? Did he feel his Swedish roots upon this voyage and claim one child of his daughters for himself to name? When I needed a passport to travel for the State Department in later years, and went back to birth records, Mary Ellen was still there. My father tried ways to change the name my mother had given me that January of 1919, trying out "Mary Illinois" and then "Mary Alix"—after the racehorse Alix, about whom he'd written the poem. Mother rejected his changes so he wrote her, pacifying, "Don't worry about 'Alix,' the name. Let it be my private name for her. I'll whisper it when Marge is around. Hugs for everybody. And your face when you opened the door with Mary in your hands, is with me often, the finest Madonna I ever saw. Carl."

He wrote about his "case" too, "Buddy: . . . Still lagging along here; may get my stuff tomorrow or next summer. I am told by district attorney there will be 'no trouble' so it seems they mean only to bother, heckle, or razz meh. Let us be very Epictetian, patient as Standard Oil and the Catholic Church. . . . Your Carl."

Then, as advised, my father made an official statement for the authorities:

I, Carl Sandburg, do hereby consent that the Military Intelligence, of the War Department, the Bureau of Investigation, of the Department of Justice, or the United States Attorney for the Southern District of New York may retain in their possession or in the possession of any one of them all of the books, pamphlets, newspaper clippings, magazines, magazine articles, manuscripts and other similar material brought by me into the United States from Christiana, Norway, on or about the 25th of December, 1918; and I do further consent that any of the agencies above-named may allow any department or agency of the United States Government to have free access to the said material and to use the information contained therein, and I do waive any and all rights that I may have to protest or object to such retention and use of the said material.

It is understood that all the said material will be returned to Mr. Sandburg, providing an investigation by the United States Attorney or any of the other above-named departments shows that the said material if published or otherwise used, would not constitute a violation of the Espionage Law or any other law of the United States.

Signed this 28th day of January, 1919.

That was the end of it. I think it was the questioning of his patriotism that had incensed my father. He had written Sam Hughes that he was "one who holds an honorable discharge from the United States Army of 1898 and whose loyalty is a matter of record from the day we went into the war, and whose allegiance to France and England was spoken the day the Great War started. Clarence Darrow and N.D. Cochran will recall that I was not neutral but pro-ally from the start." My father still had contact with Berg-Borodin, at least so he said later in his life. He also said later that he delivered the four hundred kroner to Mrs. Borodin in Chicago and that it was "in the presence of Alderman Rodriguez." He heard from Santeri Nuorteva, who wrote from a New York office in the World's Tower Building, "Diplomatic Department, Bureau of the Representative, Russian Socialist Federal Soviet Republic," that he'd not received copies of my father's correspondence with the naval attaché in Christiania. My father let him know how events stood and said afterwards that he even gave Nuorteva the Lenin propaganda pamphlet to spread through the land.

He was traveling about, and wrote to Mother from the Washington bureau of the N.E.A., ". . . not a line from you in sight. . . . Where do you think I am? Or have you quit me? Or are your hands full of trouble? Has the flu come to Our House? . . . I miss your notes when they don't come. Ain't much news. Here maybe two or three days, then

New York about two or three days, and then I hope to be through with this all-over-the map stuff.—Kiss Mary softly once for me. Carl."

She said, "Carl—Tonight I'm going to write to you twice, to Wash and to New York. . . . I name proud Janet with the rest of us! The way she touches your belongings—your chair, bed, clothes, typewriter, guitar —saying solemnly 'Papa, papa'—You'd know, if you heard & saw, that she loves her daddy all the bushels there are!! Your banjo is all fixed— new drum—new strings—polished all clean, it looks like a new banjo. Heigh-ho! Mary takes all the soft kisses you send her . . . *now* Mary signals for her bottle." She told him that my uncle was coming back to the States: "We have a hunch that Ed will be here on his birthday, March 27th (You remember the date!! And the ride!) . . . Arrange your time so you'll be here . . . if he's in the country and it's humanly possible—he'll eat his Birthday dinner at Oma's. Oma is looking over her Birthday Cake recipes accordingly! And therefore! It's going to be *al*mighty interesting—You & Ed here at once. (Ed writes he got your book—and it's great stuff especially the war pieces). . . . Your Paula." He answered, "that about Eddy listens good and I'll sure try to have March 27, anniversary of a rainstorm night, laid by for the Homey-glomeys."

My parents were making up their minds whether he'd work in Cleveland for the N.E.A. or go to Chicago, and he said he'd "met Robert Frost's eldest daughter. . . . They are going to move somewhere but don't know whether to go to New Orleans, California or Spain. So you see it ought to be easy for us to decide on whether it's Chicago or Cleveland." He wrote that he'd had "an eight mile walk last night and a ten hour sleep rivaling Alix," and from Hotel Cleveland that he was studying the layout of the city. "For a while may switch to & fro to find out how it goes for half-time here & Chi. Smoke & smoke over the whole town; location not easy." He reported, "Got a furnished room with two west windows in a smokeless end of town, the Oak Park of Cleveland, and start in to-night. Hotels lately tur-a-bul, overheated, no circulation. Unless some assignment turns up I expect to make home by end of next week and then stay two weeks. This depends on cyclones, wars, strikes, explosions, floods, crimes of violence, and acts of God. . . . Just through third rewrite of The Liars, the sequel to The Four Brothers."

Viewing my parents these many years later and studying their lives, it always helps that when they were apart and restless they wrote of love and news back and forth. Whenever they settled together for a while, comfortable, my contact with them stops. He was working on a powerful after-war poem and wrote her of it, and she instantly responded, "Let me see 'The Liars' soon—or won't the mails carry it! Anyway I must see it when you come—unless it's against 'Interstate Commerce' Act and you can't bring it into Illinois! We'll look for you end of next week—March 14 or 15—hurrah! You'll need no latch-key— the door will be open day & night!!"

He liked his room "with a west window in a frame house like home. . . . Supper tonight with Vachel Lindsay and his sister . . .—The Liars is a terrible piece and I guess it's just as well you don't get it for a while. . . . I can feel your big heart pulsing today. We are sort of all living one foot in today, one foot in tomorrow, and yesterday just a big sticky muddy bloody Dark. And as I said, I feel your heart pulsing."

And then he mailed her the poem, so her letter went back, ". . . 'Liars' —terrible yes. But great stuff!"

The poem would be in my father's third book of poems, *Smoke and Steel*, which he was starting to assemble in manuscript now, and which would include a "Passports" section on his trip away. "The Liars (March, 1919)" would go in part:

> A liar goes in fine clothes.
> A liar goes in rags.
> A liar is a liar, clothes or no clothes.
> A liar is a liar and lives on the lies he tells
>   and dies in a life of lies. . . .
>
> A liar lies to the nations.
> A liar lies to the people.
> A liar takes the blood of the people
> And drinks this blood with a laugh and a lie,
>   A laugh in his neck,
>   A lie in his mouth.
> And this liar is an old one; we know him many years.
>   He is straight as a dog's hind leg.
>   He is straight as a corkscrew.
> He is white as a black cat's foot at midnight. . . .
>
> The liars met where the doors were locked.
> They said to each other: Now for war.
> The liars fixed it and told 'em: Go.
>
> Across their tables they fixed it up,
> Behind their doors away from the mob.
> And the guns did a job that nicked off millions.
> The guns blew seven million off the map, . . .

So I hear The People tell each other:
    Look at today and tomorrow.
    Fix this clock that nicks off millions
    When The Liars say it's time.
    Take things in your own hands.
        To hell with 'em all,
    The liars who lie to nations,
    The liars who lie to The People.

My father had sent the "Passports" poems to Alfred Harcourt who wrote, "I found the sheets with your Stockholm impressions on my desk. . . . It's good stuff and will all be grist for the mill next time you want to go to market." It would not be long before Harcourt would leave Henry Holt and Company and be on his own. He had gone over to London as soon as the Armistice was signed, to "be the first American publisher on the spot," as he said later. He bought a short book by Bertrand Russell, whom Harcourt called "perhaps the most conspicuous radical of the day." A pacifist, Russell had spent four months in a British prison for opposing the war. The book was called *Roads to Freedom* and Harcourt cabled Holt that he'd bought it just as he was taking the boat. Henry Holt was shocked, canceled the contract by cable and told Harcourt that he had done so when his ship docked. Harcourt persuaded Holt to honor the contract and to publish the book under an emended title, *Proposed Roads to Freedom,* and the book subsequently did well. Harcourt recounted later that "I saw I was not going to be able to publish books dealing with the new ideas with which the world was seething, and that Henry Holt would never feel safe with me again. . . . On May 8, 1919, I resigned."

My father was suddenly out of a job at the same time. On May 16, Sam Hughes wrote to him, "Dear Carl:—I have to tell you frankly that you and NEA are not hitching well together. I hasten to say that I realize that you are a remarkable man in many ways. You are a great writer—your poems are sufficient evidence of that. You are a fine, keen thinker. But admitting all these things, you don't fit into the NEA scheme of things. Perhaps it is my fault that we do not make you fit in. If so, I can't help it. The Lord knows I'd like to be able to do so because I like you personally a whole lot and admire you greatly. But that's the situation. I know that you are not dependable on NEA for a job. I know that there are newspaper concerns with a lot more money than NEA has that will be glad to get you. Nevertheless I don't like to say the word to you that we are through. What do you say? Sincerely, S. T. Hughes."

"Dear Sam," my father replied at once, "You're right, I guess. Your letter was exactly what I wanted you to send if you looked at it that way. . . . When I go Cleveland way and stop off I'll look you up. And I hope when you're in Chicago you'll see me once in a while. I don't want to say I'm through with the NEA for good and always. When I stopped in to see you last summer on my way to Saratoga it was because I wanted a look-in on an American institution a lot more important than Harvard or the Smithsonian Institute. . . . Where I go next I can't say now because I have not been keeping touch with other openings. Two offers were made me in February, to go to work then. I suppose a week or two will clear things up. You have been more than generous and thoughtful with me and you will never hear otherwise directly or indirectly from me but that you were on the level all ways with me. Sincerely."

It seems that my father's firing had been part of a general cleaning-up at N.E.A., for on 30 December, seven months later, Hughes would write, "My dear Carl: . . . There has been quite a revolution in N.E.A. The Bolshevists are all getting out. In the summer, the old opposing faction got control of the N.E.A. trustees board. . . . The board passed a resolution—5 to 2, Canfield and Scripps voting for me—ordering that I 'retire as editor-in-chief on Oct. 1, but to remain on N.E.A. as a contributing member in an advisory capacity at full salary.' Of course I wouldn't stay under any circumstances if it were not that I bought a 10 percent interest in Autocaster last June, and it is of the utmost importance that Autocaster shall remain in this N.E.A. plant for at least six months longer. That is, until we make enough money to establish a plant of our own. My presence here, and the 'advisory' stuff is calculated to make things pleasant for Autocaster while it stays in the 'den of lions.' . . . How are you and what's doing with you? I still see your name in the magazines in connection with your poetry. Here's very best wishes."

My father's letter to Sam Hughes had been dated May 20, 1919. On that same day Alfred Harcourt had mailed him a handwritten letter from his home in Mt. Vernon, New York, "Dear Sandburg, I've resigned from Holts, leave July 1st. The news is not quite public yet but I want you to hear it first from me. . . . Mr. Holt & I get on each others nerves when I publish a liberal, not to say radical, book. . . . If I am second rate I'm a fool to have a good job, if I'm first rate I'm a fool to stay. So I bet on myself. . . . Have arranged with H.H. & C. that when an author says he'd be uncomfortable here without me, that they will sell me or the publisher he turns to, the rights, plates, stock etc. of books now in their hands. I may want such a letter from you, if you want really to write it. What do you think of me—deciding to lunge off this way?"

Harcourt was three years younger than my father. He'd been with Holt's since 1904. He called my father a "red shirt" and the two had got on and always would. Henry Holt agreed to let Harcourt take some of the authors he'd brought into the firm with him, if they wished to go. Some did. Robert Frost was one, writing, "Dear Alfred: There is only one answer possible to your question. . . . You are all the Henry Holt & Co I have known and dealt with. Where you go I naturally go. I am with you with all my heart." But Holt's then refused to release the copyrights on Frost's first books, *A Boy's Will* and *North of Boston,* and so he stayed with them. They would not sell Harcourt my father's first two books either, but my father was not as established as Frost yet, he had put his new manuscript in Harcourt's hands and he intended to stay with him. The new firm would be called Harcourt, Brace and Howe. Donald Brace had been assistant treasurer at Holt's, had known Harcourt since college, and the two had worked together at Holt's for fifteen years. Will Howe, who would stay with the house for about a year, came in to develop a textbook department. When he left, the firm would be known as Harcourt, Brace and Company for many years.

At this time, early June of 1919, my father's book that Henry Holt and Company has just published, *Cornhuskers,* was about to get some attention. The Poetry Society of America and Columbia University were getting ready to award their second annual prize of five hundred dollars, given by an unknown donor for the "best book of verse published in the United States during the last calendar year." Sara Teasdale, who had won the prize the year before, was one of the judges, and had written Harriet Monroe, "Just a word to say that I have learned that Sandburg's book has not been entered for the prize." She asked Miss Monroe to send a copy to Columbia University at once. "I shall undoubtedly vote for it," she said, "please don't mention this to anybody as the judges are supposed not to say what they are going to do." There was dissension among the judges, and Harriet Monroe said in the coming July issue of *Poetry* that "all lovers of the art may thank the kind fates that Carl Sandburg got even a 'look-in' at any prize for which William Lyon Phelps and Richard Burton formed two-thirds of the jury award. The third member was Sara Teasdale . . . who is as competent in criticism as she is in the art itself, and who has long been an ardent admirer of Carl Sandburg's work. The result emphasizes the point so often insisted on by POETRY, that all such juries of award should consist entirely of professionals—that is, of poets. . . . This rule would have relieved the committee of Mr. Phelps, whose recent book, The Advance of English Poetry in the Twentieth Century, proves him an incompetent. It is to laugh that he should have had a place on such a jury. Mr. Burton, though hardly a leader in the art, is at least a poet. POETRY may be permitted to smile in remembering the clamor of journalistic guffaws which greeted its award of the initial Levinson Prize to Carl Sandburg's first POETRY entry, Chicago Poems,—his first appearance anywhere as a poet."

Miss Teasdale had told Harriet Monroe, ". . . have fought, bled and very nearly died over the Poetry Prize, and have finally made the judges agree to split the prize." And so it was announced in the press then that the money "has just been divided between Miss Margaret Widdemer for her 'Old Road to Paradise,' and Carl Sandberg [sic] for his 'Corn Huskers' [sic]." Louis Untermeyer wrote his congratulations to my father and said he wasn't surprised and that he'd placed Cornhuskers "first among the best books of the year (I may tell you right out loud that Margaret Widdemer's Xmas-card volume didn't even finish thirteenth on my list). . . . Yourn, Louis." My father was delighted and wrote back, "About that prize I'm going to take the money and write a nice note to Sara Teasdale: I think she must have led this bombing party; tho I haven't heard airy a tale of how it come. The Widdemer party wrote a book of poetry she titled 'Factories,' which was so rough a name for a book of poetry that she ought to have been handed something on that."

Miss Widdemer, who was about two years younger than my father, had started her poem, "The Factories":

> I have shut my little sister in from life and light
> (For a rose, for a ribbon, for a wreath across my hair), . . .

and ended it:

> Round my path they cry to me, little souls unborn—
> God of Life! Creator! It was I! It was I!

Miss Teasdale wrote Harriet Monroe that she had "had a nice little note from Carl Sandburg about the prize. I do wish he could have had all of it but his getting any of it seems to have been a surprise to a lot of old fogies."

The acting editor of the N.E.A., Leon Starmont, had written my father, "I am taking your name off the pay-roll this week. But I echo most fervently your expressed desire that this shall not be a final parting of your way and our way. We like you, and I know I speak for all of us.

We shall miss you. But we can't forget you, and I want you to remember us. Perhaps our methods can't coincide. But I don't believe you're as dangerous as some people would have us imagine, and I know we are not as stodgy as some folks would have you think."

It wasn't long before my father was hired back at the Chicago *Daily News*. His first assignment was down in Atlantic City, where the American Federation of Labor was holding a two-week convention. Before he left, my father wrote to a poet he'd known for a year, Lew Sarett, whose book would be published by Holt's pretty soon—*Many, Many Moons*, with an introduction by my father. He and Sarett had talked and had an idea for a new venture. My father wrote Sarett that he was going to see the head of the J. B. Pond Lyceum Bureau "here this week and ask about hopes and horizons." My father said, "I'm started on building a show as will be a show. . . . What I am day by day more sure of is that this is a field where I will have to end up because I'm trained for it. I'm going to keep my eye out for dates for the two of us next fall and winter. . . . Figure on an afternoon or evening with Mrs. Sarett and yours out at our place such as it is. . . . Sandburg."

Ever since his Chautauqua days, the lecturing field had been one that my father liked. He had mastered it—the platform—and was at ease there now. He had a new idea. He would play the guitar and sing his folk songs and read poems and be featured as "The Poet of the City." Lew Sarett would be "The Poet of the Wilderness." They would appear as a "Joint Lecture and Recital." Sarett knew the Indians and the wilds of Canada. My father asked him once to drop into his office sometime "and tell me what a grizzly looks like," and Sarett responded, "Drop in and tell you about grizzlies? Lord, I could do it! My patrol for the last two months was in the Shoshone Valley and the Absaroka Range where the silvertip is copious, as it were,—too damned copious a couple of times when they walked off with a side of bacon and made my horses bolt. I wasted a day looking for those damn fool horses,—tracked them all over the face of the earth."

In the four-page lecture brochure put out by the J. B. Pond Lyceum Bureau to advertise the pair, were listings of their books—*Chicago Poems, Cornhuskers* and *Many, Many Moons*, and also the program:

PART I

I. CITY POEMS by Carl Sandburg
II. FLYING MOCCASINS by Lew Sarett
III. FOGS AND FIRES by Carl Sandburg
IV. CHIPPEWA MONOLOGUES by Lew Sarett

The brochure also stated, "Out of the tall timber and the white nights of this North Country comes Lew Sarett—known among the Chippewas as 'Lone Caribou'—woodsman, guide and forest ranger, author, lecturer and Associate in English at the University of Illinois. With him he brings to the literary world and the platform his Indian chants and dances, his wolf cries, his French-Canadian chanson, and remarkably refreshing poetry."

When Emanuel Carnevali reviewed their first recital in *Poetry* he said, "It was a grand show! There was something human and healthy and never before beheld, in the way the two poets treated the audience— gave the audience some credit for being human too, chattered and gossiped and talked with them, and had, themselves, as much fun as they gave to the bewildered spectators. No evening clothes, no dissertations on art: Carl Sandburg read, then brought forth a guitar of his and sang, most delicately and lovably, old ballads: *Jesse James, Frankie and Albert were Sweethearts, The Boll Weevil* and *This Morning, This Evening, So Soon;* and Lew Sarett came out with a tom-tom (or what was it?) and shrieked and bellowed, snorted, squealed and squawked, chirped and warbled—just like the many animals he had carefully listened to during his stay in the forests of the Northwest and Canada. Sandburg is a kingly reader. His reading is exactly as beautiful as his poetry and his person. He is one of the most completely, successfully alive human beings I ever saw: from his sturdy shoes to the tuft of hard gray hair over his granite eyes, to his voice and his words; from the majestic dignity of his voice to the dignity of his poems—Carl Sandburg is, in and out, thoroughly expressive of one beauty and one glory—himself. Lew Sarett recited like a versatile actor—perhaps too much so—his fine Indian songs. But he certainly was insuperable at imitating wild animals—gave us the sadness, the horror, the weirdness, the vastness, the humor of the forest as it is expressed by its worthy and heretofore misunderstood inhabitants."

Meanwhile Harcourt was busy thinking up ideas for his new house. He had set up shop with Don Brace, Will Howe and had some advisers

—Walter Lippmann, an editor of the *New Republic,* whom they would consult on economics and international relations; Joel Spingarn, a professor at Columbia, who became a partner of the firm; Louis Untermeyer, who would be poetry consultant; and William Claude Heaton, who would supervise systems of accounting and organization. Their quarters were an old Georgian house at 1 West Forty-seventh Street, where first they set up in the basement and then took over the first floor.

Harcourt wrote my father that he wanted to put out a Pamphlet Library that wasn't to be "wholly radical—anybody who honestly thinks should have his say—and it should give facts facts facts—let 'em show what they will." He said, "We mustn't let our anxiety to have a book of yours on our early list induce either of us to publish before you have just the book that most nearly means you now. You and Frost, anyway, are the long time people, and a season more or less mustn't count. I take enough comfort for the moment out of your wish to be in on my game soon. . . . Don't get into the lecture business too deeply. . . . I'm glad you like the pamphleteering idea. Ever yours."

On my father's return from the Atlantic City labor convention, he had reported on a race riot in Chicago during the last of July. Joel Spingarn had seen the series of articles, talked with my father, visited the riot zone and sent some of the clippings to Harcourt, who wrote, "Dear Sandburg: . . . I'll be glad to have the 18 news articles. We'll pray over what to do with them. I can get Spingarn or Lippmann to explain about them in a preface." And then Harcourt was writing that he wanted to make the articles into the first volume of the pamphlet library. He said that "Each bust-up in the world has been followed by an age of pamphleteering, and very often the pamphlets have the facts. I have written to a man in England, and we are watching the continent . . . so that we can build up a list of pamphlets of straight goods. We can publish these from 25 to 50 or 60 cents, so that they can be used by the people who are scared off by the present necessarily high prices of the cloth bound book." And he added, "You never answered my letter asking if you weren't pretty nearly ready for another book of poetry. We're having the most fun there ever was. I hope all goes well with you."

My father's race riot articles had told of how a Negro boy, swimming one Sunday at a bathing beach, had crossed "an imaginary segregation line." The story went on, "White boys threw rocks at him and knocked him off a raft. He was drowned. Colored people rushed to a policeman and asked for the arrest of the boys throwing stones. The policeman refused. As the dead body of the drowned boy was being handled, more rocks were thrown, on both sides. The policeman held on to his refusal to make arrests. Fighting then began that spread to all the borders of the Black Belt. The score at the end of three days was recorded as twenty negroes dead, fourteen white men dead, and a number of negro houses burned. The riots furnished an excuse for every element of Gangland to go to it and test their prowess by the most ancient ordeals of the jungle."

It was a time of trial for the Black Man in America. Whippings, tarrings, brandings and destruction of the property of Blacks and their White sympathizers swept the South. The Ku Klux Klan was active. Lynchings took place, twenty-eight by July of that year, one report from Blakely, Georgia, going, "When Private William Little, a Negro soldier returning from the war, arrived at the railroad station here a few weeks ago, he was met by a band of whites who ordered him to remove his uniform and walk home in his underwear. Bystanders persuaded the men to release him. Little continued to wear the uniform as he had no other clothes. . . . Anonymous notes reached him warning him to quit wearing it. Yesterday Private Little was found dead, his body badly beaten, on the outskirts of town. He was wearing his uniform." And another in Vicksburg, Mississippi: "Lloyd Clay, Negro laborer, was roasted to death here last night. He had been accused of entering a white woman's room. . . . A mob of between 800 and 1,000 men and women removed the prisoner from the jail. He was taken to the corner of Clay and Farmer Streets, covered with oil, set afire and hoisted to an elm tree. Bullets were fired into the body."

My father had written a poem on the subject, that was in the manuscript he was working on. It was called "Man, The Manhunter":

> I saw Man, the man-hunter,
> Hunting with a torch in one hand
> And a kerosene can in the other,
> Hunting with guns, ropes, shackles.
>
> I listened
> And the high cry rang,
> The high cry of Man, the man-hunter:
> We'll get you yet, you sbxyzch!
>
> I listened later.
> The high cry rang:
> Kill him! Kill him! the sbxyzch!

In the morning the sun saw
Two butts of something, a smoking rump,
And a warning in charred wood:
                              Well, we got him.
                              the   sbxyzch.

He wrote to Louis Untermeyer, who had objected to some explicit
terms in the poem in its first form, "Dear Louis:—You're right about the
S.O.B. Let it read 'crying, "Kill him, kill him, the . . .",' deleting 'the
Judean equivalent' and 'Son of a Bitch.' I would never have put this in
but that its come over me clear the last two or three years that in a
group killing of a man, in a mobbing, the event reaches a point where
all rationale is gone; such a term as 'anarchist' or 'traitor' or 'Boche' or
'Englander Schwein' disappears and they babble hysterically only one or
two epithets, in our language usually a tenor of 'Son of a Bitch' with a
bass of 'Cocksucker.' Since some of the finest blood of the human family
goes this way poets and painters have a right to try to employ it or at
least not kid themselves about what actually happened at Golgotha.
Since I've tackled with men who were in the trenches and since I've
seen race riots I am suspicious that the sponge of vinegar on the spear
is a faked legend and what probably happened, if the historicity of Jesus
is ever established, is that they cut off his genital organ and stuck it in
his mouth.—The Black Belt is arming. Big strikes coming.—Carl."

When *The Chicago Race Riots* was published, Walter Lippmann,
one of Harcourt's advisers, did the "Introductory Note." My father seems
not to have been wholly pleased with it, writing flatly in the early copy
of the book that I have, "With regrets over the uninformed Lippmann
introduction." Perhaps he objected to Lippmann's emphasis on "race
parallelism." Perhaps the two didn't get on, and argued later on the same
subject. Lippmann and my father had known each other over the years.
When Lippmann had been secretary to the socialist mayor of Schenec-
tady, George R. Lunn, my father was secretary to Mayor Seidel. In
1916, when Lippmann had covered the Republican Convention and
written of it in the *New Republic*, my father had complimented him,
"Dear Lippmann:—Your Chi. convention story had the teeth and passion
of democracy in it. When you write of actual contacts—when you do
real reporting—I get you. I get more hope from your cry of despair
about that convention than any of the masses of reasoning and cool,
clever assemblage of facts in much of your work. By this sign of your
cry of despair, I know you are now strong for battling, even futile

battling. I have wondered about you. I feel safer. As a member of the Amalgamated Secretaries to Socialist Mayors, I am free to write you this way." Lippmann had replied, "I am afraid it is a good deal easier to do the reporting than it is to keep cool and reason. Don't you think it is not quite fair to do the easy thing all the time? Some day I hope to see you. If you come to New York be sure to let me know. Yours."

In *The Chicago Race Riots,* my father not only reported what happened in that hot July of 1919, but he went back into the origins of the flare-up and said that there were factors that made its character different from other riots. The Black Belt population of 50,000 had more than doubled during the war and stood at at least 125,000, while housing stayed the same. Then, the returning black doughboys wanted to remain in the North, rather than go back to the oppression of the South. It seemed also that the mixed Chicago races and nationalities—Poles, Negroes, Lithuanians, Italians, Irishmen, Germans, Slovaks, Russians, Mexicans, Yankees, Englishmen, Scotsmen, now were for the first time organized union labor. My father went into the migration of the blacks to the north, the subsequent dynamiting of their homes when they merged into white areas and the heavy influx that Chicago got from the South after every lynching there. He discussed "Trades for Colored Women" in one chapter, "Unions and the Color Line" and "About Lynchings" in others. And there was a piece too on "Colored Gamblers," describing the craps and poker enterprises that various blacks ran—"Billy" Lewis, "Louie Joe," "Mexican Frank," "Wiley" Coleman, and how they would stand on the street and "pick out faces from the human stream flowing by." They'd saunter out, he wrote, and ask someone, "Try your wrist to-day? Try your wrist?" Sometimes in one of the "clubs" as many as a hundred men would come in and out of the passageway when the "going" was good. The pamphlet ended with interviews in which leaders stated that "The negro is the equal of the white man in brains," and that the race question was national and federal and that no city or state could solve it alone.

The pamphlet sold well. One song-hunting friend of my father's didn't like it. He was John Lomax in Austin, Texas, from whom my father had gotten ballads and folk songs that he used in his recitals with Lew Sarett and sang at home and to friends. Lomax wrote a long letter: "I refer especially to your digs at the South where you seem to go out of your way to stimulate and encourage the prejudice growing out of our Civil War." Lomax said that my father spoke "of a series of lynchings in Texas, as though the practice was as prevalent as railroad accidents or fires or what-not." And, "Perhaps I can tell you something about the psychology of the negro that you do not know. A negro educated or uneducated when approached by a white man will tell the white man what he thinks the white man wants to hear rather than what the negro himself actually believes. A witty old negro friend of mine puts it this way 'the white man talks with the front of his head, the nigger talks with the back of his head.' In other words the negro doesn't tell his whole mind but always keeps something in reserve. Remarkable, distinctive, but true." Lomax had ended, "I hope you are doing well and happy. I read your poems and enjoy them. I will ask Macmillan to send you personally a copy of my new book, 'Songs of the Cattle Trail and Cow Camp.'"

My father answered that he had "not met any man with a keener sleuthing instinct than yourself for these wonderful, vivid singing qualities in the negro soul. I know you would understand, if we had the time to go over all the evidence, that there is a prejudice which if it could achieve its desire would segregate, repress, and again make a chattel of the negro if that status could again be restored. Both north and south this prejudice was loosened with the end of the war and was given added impetus by the very physical hysteria of war. I believe that this prejudice, as sheer prejudice, runs deeper and wider down south than up north and that this is the basic reason why the southern business interests have completely failed in their endeavors to induce movements of negro population from northern points back south again. There is no place in the south that I have heard of where the negro has the freedom of ballot and the political equality and economic opportunity accorded him in Chicago and other northern cities. I did go out of my way, probably, in my writing, to throw a flashlight on discrepancies in the 'democracy' of the ruling class of the south just as I also went out of my way to show the terrible shortcomings of the Chicago stockyards overlords, whose work and wages policy across the last twenty years must be counted as a factor in the production of hoodlums, white hoodlums. Whatever reflections I may have cast on the south, however, were merely incidental and cursory as compared with the direct indictment of the intelligence of my own home town for its lack of plan in housing, its economic discrimination, its collusion of police and gamblers by which negro crap joints exploit the negro workmen by wholesale. I want to thank you for writing that letter just as you wrote it. It has just the thing about it that used to make me go out of my way to look you up and learn new things worth knowing, when you were here. Faithfully yours."

Then, as *The Chicago Race Riots* was being published that fall, a nice change suddenly happened in the life of my family, as they decided to sell the small crowded house in Maywood and move. I was nine months old and have no memory of the excitement of the change, but there is my father's letter of the twenty-sixth of September to Alice Corbin Henderson in Santa Fe. "Dear Alice: . . . Just suddenly picked up all our chattels and flitted away from Maywood, where we owned a place, and moved into debt at Elmhurst with wonderful pines and poplars and a chance for the daughters to sit in with values of silence if they so choose. Why should I be the first poet of misery to be keeping out of debt? Wishing you always all the luck there is."

Changes took place in Uncle Ed's life too. The World War had been over for ten months, making its impact with all of the scars as well as the freedoms that went with it for the men and women who served. I have listened always to Mother's stories about my uncle. Here was a letter from my father to him, "Dear Ed: What can we say, more than that we are all tied up closer to you and with you than ever before, and as fate deals the cards sometimes there is reason to say, 'This is the worst of all possible worlds.'" Whatever it was that happened— divorce impending, headlines and sketches or photographs in the roto- gravure section of the papers, courts, doors slammed, fingers pointed, an alienation of affection suit, scandal, tears, the difficulty of picking up art for its sake after weeks of war work with the Photographic Sec- tion of the Air Service overseas—my uncle wrote to my parents of the crisis. And my father answered, "Come along sometime, if only to see Janet. She's got your own elusive way and she is a hunter of beauty and will be hungry all her life. She is your kin all over.—Paula keeps more beautiful forty ways than ever before and is worth your knowing more.—If luck can come from wishing, daytime and night-time wishing, you will have it from us out here." Perhaps Uncle Ed considered moving to the Midwest then. My father told him to "remember what you said about Chicago having no art at all and so being possibly a place worth trying out as a place to live in. . . . Great times moving from Maywood to Elmhurst. Paula is having the time of her young life. Be ready to look over some live branches of nieces of yourn when you come this way. You're in our thoughts and speech often."

I think my uncle came to visit us then at the new house. It may have been at this time in his life that he started his custom of arriving always at Christmas. Soon Oma and Opa would move to Elmhurst—into a house a couple of blocks down York Street from us. It seems that Uncle Ed marked that Holiday Time of my childhood. My sisters and I thought him the most comical man we had ever known. Once Mother set up a huge cardboard cutout of Santa Claus and my father sang "The Ship That Never Returned" and Uncle Ed fell upon Santa Claus, sobbing and clutching. I remember rolling on the floor with laughter. His enthusiastic presence moved through my life. He tiptoed secretively with us and did the same with my own children years later, planning tricks and misdeeds. He crouched on the floor, growling and barking and yet lovable, so we could pat his head. He make-believe ate a walnut as if it was a chewy caramel and we were giddy with delight. With my son in league, he took our doors off their hinges and returned them. He brought Janet twin boy and girl cloth dolls from Paris, called Jack and Jill. The doll he gave me was tall and beautiful with blonde hair and a garden hat that matched her lavender dress and shoes. I named her Mary Jane and she survived all my young days. My parents, as well as my sisters and I, thought Uncle Ed was wonderfully funny, and yet my father said once that when Janet and Margaret were shown a certain tragic photograph of Abraham Lincoln and asked who it was, they answered, "Uncle Ed."

He had left the army with the rank of colonel and the Legion of Honor ribbon. He called us—his three nieces—"humdingers." He made photographs of my parents together under the spruce tree in our new backyard, naming one print "Mr. and Mrs." He wrote of it, "I have the photo of you & Carl up in front of me—I want to tell you both—in case you don't know—that it's a humdinger, that picture, in fact about the humdingerest I ever made. Of course I will admit the material was humdinger too. And how are all the little humdingers? In the main there is a hell of a lot of tall scrapping going on in Europe to celebrate 'Peace'—and the Bolchis are coming on the double trot. A lot of people who do not exactly like the Bolchi idea are at least ready to say, 'Well they can't give us worse.' I think I'm getting neurasthenic. It is time some one started a nice war again so as to occcupy my mind. Am taking art too seriously, which is indecent."

My father had decided to dedicate the new book of poems, *Smoke and Steel*, to my uncle, who had now abandoned the continental spellings of "Edouard" and "Eduard." He said, "Say I'm just tickled bald headed to have Carl dedicate his book to me. I never imagined such a thing could happen. How many copies do I have to buy—!! Please be sure they spell my name *right*. Every time I pull off something first class like that they call me Stickmen or Strecher or something—EDWARD J. STEICHEN please. I tell you what I did the other night. I took Chicago Poems to bed with me and read them *all* to myself *out loud.*—When I got through—it was daylight and the birds were commencing to notice it too. I never did that with a book since I stopped getting 'Nick Carter' once a week. . . . Be as good to yourselves as you can, Brother Ed."

The dedication of *Smoke and Steel* went, "To Col. Edward J. Steichen —painter of nocturnes and faces, camera engraver of glints and moments, listener to blue evening winds and new yellow roses, dreamer and finder, rider of great mornings in gardens, valleys, battles."

When my father sent the manuscript for *Smoke and Steel* to Harcourt Brace and Howe's cramped office, where as Harcourt said, they "made the rooms into offices as far as was possible with Georgian mantels, fireplaces, and closets meant for clothes and dishes rather than business records," Harcourt wrote my father, "Spingarn and I and Louis when he dropped in later in the afternoon have spent most of the day gloating over your manuscript. We have decided it is best to let it go just as it is. . . . I think we will both make a nice little dent with that book. We are very proud of it already and are going to be more proud." Ellen Eayrs, who ran the office, dashed off a handwritten letter, "Dear Mr. Sandburg:—This office has been on a complete bat today:—no one has done a lick of work. Mr. Harcourt came upstairs at ten this morning with the ms. I could not get a word out of him until 11:30 when he began to read from the ms. to Mr. Spingarn. Then Mr. Spingarn took part of it and read it back to him and me. They went out to lunch and when Mr. Spingarn got back at 2:30 he started on it. At 3:30 Mr. Untermeyer came in then and he and Mr. Spingarn started reading it—and now here comes Mr. Harcourt again and all four of us have begun all over again. Really—see what you have done."

One critic, an Arthur Wilson, was furious about the book when it was released. "Either Carl Sandburg is dead or he is very sick. Some of us, who annunciated this great poet when his epiphanal accents crashed out in Chicago, now look up from the useless pages of Smoke and Steel with a gasp of astonished grief. . . . Surely one who has wept and raved over the true Sandburg may be permitted to repudiate the false. . . . For the poet is not dead. He is merely whoring after alien gods." Louis Untermeyer read that piece and asked my father, "Who in hell *is* this pup, anyway?" But there were other well-known critics, one William Allen White, editor and owner of the Emporia *Gazette* in Kansas, writing, "My dear Mr. Sandburg: I have just finished reading your "Smoke and Steel"; You have done a real thing. Of all of today's modern poets, it seems to me that you have put more of America in your verses than any other. The others are academic, theoretical, remote, but your verses stink and sting and blister and bruise and burn, and I love them. I am sending your book on to my boy who is in Harvard. I wish every student in America could read these verses. They are as good as a trip across America, vastly better than a trip in a pullman or in a motor car, for they are American. . . . Sincerely yours." And Sara Teasdale wrote a note from New York: "Dear Carl Sandburg: I like to think it was yourself who sent me 'Smoke and Steel.' You know how much I have loved your work all these years—how it seems to me more real in its tenderness and sympathy than any other poetry being written in our language to-day. I'm not going to say a formal 'Thank you.' My new book 'Flame and Shadow' will reach you in a few days."

My father had copies of *Smoke and Steel* sent from Harcourt's to his family, one going to Grandma Sandburg, about seventy now. Sure in the Swedish tongue and never really familiar in the English, she wrote to Mother with whom her ties were strong, "Lilian dear, The book of poems has come with its spicy words and deep thought it will take more than a life time to learn what it all means and is impossible for plain simple working people to understand even Mary and her surrounding look upon it as too hard." Grandma Sandburg talked about her own way of life, mentioning Uncle Allie, Aunt Mary's husband, "Allee came over this afternoon for Martha myself,—Children Mary and the new baby for a long ride in the country Mary said she hade company one evening last week Edith Dopp the hardware merchants Daughter and Brynolf Brynelson saying Carl Sandburgs Books are now taken up for study at Lombard College. the modern poets and their work is discussed sifted out with ethusiasm and interest while some of them are more vild about it Registratiars days Martha is at the schoolhous serving as clerk and we have the Children hope all is well with you all with love from mother."

There were poems in *Smoke and Steel* for our Irish Setter, Dan; for my sisters; and for the first time two for me, two years old now and safely renamed—not Mary Ellen or Mary Alix or Mary Illinois—one ending:

There are dreams in your eyes, Helga.
Tall reaches of wind sweep the clear blue.
The winter is young yet, so young.
Only a little cupful of winter has touched your lips.
Drink on . . . milk with your lips . . . dreams with your eyes.

And the other, called "Helga," went in part:

The wishes on this child's mouth
Came like snow on marsh cranberries;
The tamarack kept something for her;
The wind is ready to help her shoes.
The north has loved her; she will be
A grandmother feeding geese on frosty
Mornings; she will understand
Early snow on the cranberries
Better and better then.

And, as always, a love poem called "Paula":

Nothing else in this song—only your face.
Nothing else here—only your drinking, night-gray eyes.

The pier runs into the lake straight as a rifle barrel.
I stand on the pier and sing how I know you mornings.
It is not your eyes, your face, I remember.
It is not your dancing, race-horse feet.
It is something else I remember you for on the pier mornings.

Your hands are sweeter than nut-brown bread when you touch me.
Your shoulder brushes my arm—a south-west wind crosses the pier.
I forget your hands and your shoulder and I say again:

Nothing else in this song—only your face.
Nothing else here—only your drinking, night-gray eyes.

Nineteen

The Homeyglomies

It is only when people are apart that events and emotions are recorded. That is, unless someone about is addicted to keeping a journal
or is a reporter or an editor or a collector. A long-time friend of my
father's, the Lincoln collector, Oliver R. Barrett, used to empty the
wastebasket when my father left after a visit, because he fancied the
handwritten abbreviated reminders my father had thrown away. Alfred
Kreymborg, a friend of my father's and Uncle Ed's, wrote an account
once for the magazine *Troubadour* back in the early 1920's, that gave a
feeling of my family's days then. Kreymborg wrote of walking about the
Loop in Chicago with my father and how they stopped into a shop
where my father bought a child's ball for a nickel and how the two went
over to Lincoln Park and "threw high flys at each other, tore around in
pursuit of them and succeeded in missing most of them." Kreymborg said,
"Had not Carl instructed his wife—'that Steichen girl', as he called her—
to lay an extra plate for dinner, the pair would have played right on
into the twilight." When they reached our house, Kreymborg says that
"two flying figures came sliding down the banister from the floor above.
Spink and Skabootch, as their father hailed them, had to be caught, em-
braced and set on the ground for a run to the top of the stairs and
another slide down to the floor—a rondo the girls repeated until Carl
could catch them no longer."

I am dependent again during this time on Alice Corbin Henderson,
to whom my father wrote easily and who saved his letters for a sense of
his life when no pain, no tragedy, death, illness, or small trouble, seemed
to be in it. It was May of 1920. "Dear Alice: . . . The kids at home are

a tantalization of loveliness. And the Missus takes life all the time with finer zests. We walked eight miles in fierce winter weather last Sunday. The kids are a loan, only a loan, out of nowhere, back to nowhere, babbling, wild-flying—they die every day like flowers shedding petals—and come on again. Well, I'm writing you my Peer Gynt heart today." He told her, "Today I feel I won't put out another book of poetry in forty years. Anyhow before another of poetry I'm going to do a Kid book."

Years later Harcourt said, "Through May Massee, then editor of the American Library Association Booklist, I learned that Carl had been telling some stories to his three daughters, Margaret, Janet, and Helga. . . . May was a friend of Carl's, and had been helping him get them into readable shape. When I read them, I was sure they were going to become classics for children." Harcourt wrote my father, ". . . we are more than interested in the idea of your doing a children's book. Do keep on with that material."

Perhaps it was a reaction to the war, or then again because they had five young girls between them to listen, but at this time it seems that Uncle Ed as well as my father wanted to do a book for children. Cousin Mary was nearly sixteen, Cousin Kate near twelve, Margaret was almost nine, Janet about four and I almost two. My uncle had been experimenting at Villa l'Oiseau Bleu with forms and had become intrigued with the triangle, starting with a special rectangle in the proportion of root 5, which was said to have been the basis of the Parthenon and Greek vases. He divided this rectangle "into three triangles, each of which was . . . in extreme and mean ratio, or the Golden Mean. . . . In experimenting with the three triangles I had cut out, I was fascinated with the curious shapes that could be formed, and I started using these shapes as the subject matter for a children's story I wanted to do. I called the images evoked by assembling the three triangles The Oochens. Oochens lived in a special kid kind of imaginary republic, of which an Oochen named Khor was the President. Some of the other characters were Thinkrates, the Philosopher; Mushton-Slushley, the Lyric Poet; and the Pink Faced Politician, who always wept because the world was going to the dogs. . . . As I worked on the Golden Measure or Golden Section, I discovered that everything growing outdoors had become exceptionally alive to me. In the small tempera paintings I made of the Oochens, I experienced a sense of freedom I had never experienced before in painting. I believe it came from the knowledge that I was doing something based on nature's laws. The inexorable discipline gave me a new kind of freedom." Uncle Ed wrote my parents, "I have given up hopes that grown ups can understand the thing we call 'art'—in its real creative sense so—it's 'Begin with the kids' for me I guess. These pictures are all of a certain kind of oochens or thingmabobs that never were on land or sea. And yet they are as alive as alive can be.—each one is made out of *three triangles*. I miss a big guess if you kids don't enjoy them. I don't really know if it is a thing for kids in the real sense of things.— I doubt if kids *really enjoy* or understand anything but what they *create themselves*. The things we do as grown up kids is possibly for grown up kids. . . . Love to all, Brudder."

Amy Lowell wrote my father that someone had told her he was writing "a book of fairy stories," and that "I think they will be good." And in September of 1920, he was reporting to Santa Fe on being made the *Daily News* movie critic, "Dear Alice: . . . I am the cinema expert, the critic of the silent celluloid"; and, "Steichen is painting flowers near Paris and says if he keeps on some day he may do something worth looking at"; and then, "One satisfaction—the book of kid stories, tales of impossible villages, out next year, will be a hummer. Fifteen done and passed. These are my refuge from the imbecility of a frightened world. . . . I was out in high winds along the Du Page river yesterday . . . blown red haws in yellow green river water among great grey roots of trees . . . and three hawks flapping hoarsely out of a big treetop."

Harcourt was happy. "Good for 'Liver and Onions'. There'll be a book a year from now." Harcourt had read the story which would open the book in the making, in which Gimme the Ax says to his children on the railway train—his son, Please Gimme, and his daughter, Ax Me No Questions, "The next we come to is the Rootabaga Country where the big city is the Village of Liver-and-Onions."

The book would be called *Rootabaga Stories* and be published in 1922, dedicated to my sisters: To Spink and Skabootch. At two years of age then, I had no fairy-tale name from my father yet, perhaps because the hoped-for boy, John Edward, had not arrived, and perhaps because I was something of a poker face, as my father would claim from time to time, and a baby with no patience for having stories read to me. When I was older, I would get my name: Swipes. It would stick for as long as my father lived. In time, too, my father would formally inscribe a book for me: To Helga. It would be his next and fourth book of poems and be put out by Harcourt's in the same year as *Rootabaga Stories*. It would be called *Slabs of the Sunburnt West* and would remain an ununderstandable mystery to me until well into adolescence. The closing poem would be the title one, all about Alice Corbin Henderson's Santa Fe country that he came to know on lecture trips out that way:

Into the night, into the blanket of night,
Into the night rain gods, the night luck gods,
Overland goes the overland passenger train.

Stand up, sandstone slabs of red,
Tell the overland passengers who burnt you. . . .

A bluejay blue
and a gray mouse gray
ran up the canyon walls . . .

Margaret was the bright child of the family, or at least the center of my mother's attentions as her first, and demanding of my father's. Marie Montessori had devised the "Montessori Didactic Apparatus" in 1907 and Margaret was used in their advertising brochure. Her picture, at the age of four, holding a basket of young rabbits, was featured along with a reproduction of her clear handwriting, "margaret oma daddy." Margaret was an eager reader and retold what she read to Janet and me whenever we were quiet enough for her to do so. Janet, nearer my age, was my inseparable companion. She had clear olive skin, the handsome Steichen features and a pleasant disposition that stayed with her always.

In the Rootabaga story called "How to Tell Corn Fairies If You See 'Em," my father wrote,

Spink, who is a little girl living in the same house with the man writing this story, and Skabootch, who is another little girl in the same house—both Spink and Skabootch are asking the question, "How can we tell corn fairies if we see 'em? If we meet a corn fairy how will we know it?" And this is the explanation the man gave to Spink who is older than Skabootch, and to Skabootch who is younger than Spink:—All corn fairies wear overalls. They work hard, the corn fairies, and they are proud. The reason they are proud is because they work so hard. And the reason they work so hard is because they have overalls. But understand this. The overalls are corn gold cloth, woven from leaves of ripe corn mixed with ripe October corn silk. In the first week of the harvest moon coming up red and changing to yellow and silver the corn fairies sit by thousands between the corn rows weaving and stitching the clothes they have to wear next winter, next spring, next summer. They sit cross-legged when they sew. And it is a law among them each one must point the big toe at the moon while sewing the harvest moon clothes. . . . If it is a cool night and looks like frost, then the laughter of the corn fairies is something worth seeing. . . . And whenever the corn fairies laugh then the laugh comes out of the mouth like a thin gold frost.

My father was traveling now on lengthy lecture tours—Charleston, New Orleans, Salt Lake City, San Diego, Los Angeles, Albuquerque, Austin. He wrote home of the "long desert stretches" and, "How are all my shiny faces? . . . Sleepy Carl." By now he was set in his way of going off for long periods of time—gathering folk songs and giving recitals in which he used them along with his poems. My mother wrote, "Margaret is fine—and Helga and Janet are radiant & wise & know it all and tell each other & us very importantly that 'daddy tummy home a-night.' You can imagine all the inflections of voice & wise waggings of heads that go with it!—They miss you all right. Write us a line now and then—because it will be such a long trip this time—we must hear from you." She mentioned Oma and the trouble in the family with Uncle Ed's divorce under way: "Oma writes wearily about the case, but is glad she is near Ed anyway. I am writing Ed to save his visit till you return from Texas. I filed your income tax return today. I mention this so you'll know I attended to it. Good luck! And did you like the Grand Canyon? And Los Angeles? Write! We want to know. Four million bushels of love from the four of us—Paula & kiddos."

My mother hired carpenters while my father was gone and added a porch in back and raised the roof over the laundry area and made more room above for my father so there would be more space for the wooden file cabinets, the book shelves, the upended orange crates he used for supplies, to hold the Victrola records, and to set his typewriter on. She had windows put in and reported that, "at last we can talk to the spruce face to face! You will like it all."

Then he was home and writing back to Santa Fe about how the manuscript for *Rootabaga Stories* progressed: "Dear Alice: . . . Work goes forward on the kid stories, 36 of them now. When I get 100 I'll pick out a book." And he said, "Amid the tide of events I suppose the most exciting in its portents for me of late was an affair between a beetle and a spider in our house about midnight. I brushed the beetle off my arm. Next I saw him he was against a wall sort of hunching himself up and down like a slow bucking bronco. Ten minutes later his feet were off the floor and by quarter inches he was making a slow ascent. I looked under the window sill and saw a spider letting down webs and hoisting them up. Sometimes he ran down a web and inspected the beetle. Later he went down and took off a few legs and front tentacles of the beetle.

After an hour the spider had hauled up into a nest under the window sill this beetle five times his own size and weight. The next morning the husk of the beetle, all insides gone, hung in a nest of thin silk webs under the window sill. And a fat spider ran out, dropped to the floor, and scurried. . . . Made a cleanout of junk in my home workshop. Tossed away many old muckrakers' documents. The very language and lingo of the muckrakers is gone. Justice is a dying word. Power is the new password—power. Another dying word is Liberty. The fight is for control. Let us have power, control—and justice and liberty will automatically be put where 'Us', whoever we are, want 'em."

My father worked hard always, becoming more secure as time went by in his "destiny." I think he always knew he would produce great work but was not sure that he would ever make more than a modest living. He said at this time that he'd "been home four days sleeping nearly all the time." What of my uncle? Financially he'd been a true success and his art was well known in America and on the continent. Since the war's end and then the divorce proceedings, he'd returned to his Voulangis studio. There he had been working on his Oochens, but also with a camera, using as he said "the principles of volume and form." He set himself to studying plane and solid geometry and learned to use a slide rule, saying that he was "particularly interested in a method of representing volume, scale, and a sense of weight." He began to photograph a white cup and saucer and didn't stop until he had a thousand prints. He took lengthy time exposures of apples and pears. He photographed wheelbarrows, flowerpots, grasshoppers, snails, butterflies, sunflowers, begonias, roses, spider webs, raindrops.

Later Uncle Ed wrote that he'd "worn myself to a frazzle on the problems connected with the spiral and the extreme and mean ratio," and decided to take a vacation and got on a train for Venice, planning to spend "a week or ten days flat on my back in a gondola." There, drifting on the Grand Canal, he came upon Isadora Duncan in a gondola with her pianist, Walter Rummel, and some of her pupils—girls adopted by her as children—among them the talented Thérèse Duncan. They asked him to come along with them to Greece where they were going the next day. Isadora told Uncle Ed that he might find a movie camera there and make a film of her dancing on the Acropolis. My uncle had never been as far as Greece. He was easily persuaded and in the morning the party boarded a steamer for Piraeus. In Athens, at the Parthenon, however, Isadora seemed to be overwhelmed by the setting. She said that she felt like an intruder and refused to let the movie be made. She preferred to be a legend, she told my uncle. But she would let him do some stills, she said, and so Uncle Ed borrowed a Kodak from the headwaiter at their hotel. Isadora still was hesitant: "Edward, I can't. I can't do it. I can't do it here." It worked in time, though, and Uncle Ed made studies there of Isadora Duncan as well as Thérèse Duncan who was, my uncle said, "a living reincarnation of a Greek nymph."

Those photographs were the only ones of Isadora ever made at the Parthenon. Nowadays nobody can go up on the Parthenon. Guards blow whistles and forbid tourists to do so, a trial for me at least, used to climbing up and posing in some portal, thinking of Uncle Ed and the legend of Isadora and himself. My uncle has told the story of how, on that same trip, one day the group were making their way back to the Parthenon and came to the place where Pericles spoke to the multitude. Uncle Ed got up on the platform and declaimed my father's Billy Sunday poem to the pianist and the dancers, who were not quite sure it was poetry.

Uncle Ed brought framed prints to Elmhurst when he next visited the States, of Isadora in loose Grecian robes, her arms limp, leaning against an enormous column, or standing with arms lifted or outstretched under the Parthenon's portals. He inscribed one photograph of Isadora's pupils, "For my three nieces—to look upon, to ponder, and to remember. With love from their Uncle Ed." My mother hung the pictures about our house.

It was mid-November of 1921 and we had been in the 331 South York Street house a little more than two years. There was a swing in the tall spruce and my mother's flowers ringed the house, climbed the arbor over the front porch and were laid out in masses in a garden in back with paths to walk. We had always had dogs since Dan and my father wrote to Mrs. William Vaughn Moody, "Dear Harriet: We have lost our dog. If you get hold of a setter, sheep dog, collie, German police dog, mastiff, Danish bloodhound, or any dog spotted or unspotted that growls at strangers and is good to children—bring him along." And he said, "I am trying to get some final revised copies of some of those kid stories done next week and hope to send some on to you. . . . I hope your reading eyes will be in good form because there will be almost fifteen or twenty of these babies of literary destiny sent to you. Your black-hearted renegade, Carl."

When my father gave his recitals or lectures, he didn't just read his poems and sing songs to the guitar any more. There were three parts to his programs now—poems, songs and the Rootabaga stories. He wrote a sponsor, "The kid stories are now in such shape that I can bring 'em along and read three or four in a program." He said too, "I have a new guitar bought from a man who had it eighteen years. . . . Anyhow I'll offer you two great ballads: Stackerlee, and Jay Gould's Daughter—both classics—each a child on the doorstep of the neglectful parents, Mr. and Mrs. American Culture."

Then it happened that trouble entered the lives of both my father and Harcourt. It seems often that suddenly, when ambition and health and youth are all one feels, pain strikes into one's life. Harcourt wrote to my father, "The stories are great stuff. Sometimes I like one best and sometimes another. . . . Mrs. Harcourt has been ill and is still in the hospital." In his letter ten days later Harcourt asked, "What is the matter with your oldest girl? These spells of illness when the only thing to do is to keep your mind on the day you are in take it out of one. Mrs. Harcourt is just back from the hospital. . . . Don't worry about the contract, I'm not. Yours, Alfred." Harcourt's trouble stayed with him for two years. In August of 1923 his wife, Susan Hareus Harcourt, would die. After a few months, Harcourt would marry Ellen Eayrs, who'd been in the Harcourt firm since its beginning.

It was in that mid-November of 1921 that Margaret had the first intimations of the nocturnal epilepsy that was to take a number of years before coming under control. In those days—not much over fifty years ago—a sort of stigma was associated with the disease, so that I was into my teens before my mother gave me a name for the ailment. All I knew was that Margaret had fallen asleep in class at school—at least so it was described to me later—and at ten years of age was taken out of the public school system and did not return. By the first of December Mother and Margaret were in Battle Creek at the sanitarium. My father wrote, "Dear Margaret: This is only a little letter from your daddy to say he thinks about you hours and hours and he knows there was never a princess or a fairy worth so much love. We are starting on a long journey and a hard fight—you and mother and daddy—and we are going to go on slowly, quietly, hand in hand, the three of us, never giving up. And so we are going to win. Slowly, quietly, never giving up, we are going to win. Daddy."

He wrote my mother, "Dearest Buddy: Every day and some days every hour the thoughts go to you and the little battling one. . . . Helga & Janet blooming miracles of good will, mirth, health." And he wrote my sister again, "You asked me often when the stories would be ready and printed in a book for you. I am able now to vouchsafe the information and knowledge to you that this event will probably be realized in September of the year 1922, which is the year beginning on the first of next January. The title of the book will be 'Rootabaga Stories.' It was understood that I should let you know as soon and at the earliest possible moment I should know."

In that time, it was thought that diet might help control seizures. If a special ketogenic diet, one with high fat and low carbohydrate content could induce a state of acidosis in which the blood and body fluids became so acid that the activity of the nervous system was depressed, the tendency to convulsions might be reduced. My father wrote Margaret, "Stick to it with that strong will of yours—set your teeth——listen to your mother—and you will win the battle you are fighting. Your mother tells me you are a wonderful sleeper, that you are making a grand fight, and everything looks like a gay and merry Christmas. The fat, fat gobbler of a turkey is ready, and though you won't eat any of it probably, you will enjoy your sisters eating, and you will enjoy drawing a picture of it. I showed your letter, the one signed 'Yours forever,' to several people and they said you are a very much alive girl. Harcourt, our publisher, liked the pictures you made at the end of it. Yours forever too, Daddy."

My father's old friend Joseffy had been invited to come to our house with "Balsamo, the Living Skull" answering questions from its dark box and clicking its human teeth in its ghastly fashion. In dream and reality I have remained terrified of the skull as well as its ventriloquist master since I first saw them. My father promised Margaret, who was not afraid and understood illusion, that "a great magician who performs strange, fantastic marvels with mysterious paraphernalia has promised us he will be at our house on Christmas Day, when you are expected to be home."

But she didn't come and instead answered in her clear round hand that she was "glad the old gobbler is ready. . . . I am eating now, Saturday. That is drinking orange juice. But as for the turkey and other sweets you are going to have on Christmas, I don't care about them at all, for I am going to have egg on toast for Christmas and chicken broth for dinner. I don't know what for supper. Besides when there are so many surprises for Christmas, who cares for eats. In about four or five days I will have rusks. . . . I'm making some scrapbooks for the children and mama bought some toys here too. We are going to hang up our stockings on Christmas, too. Perhaps you have been told that already, but I didn't know so I thought I'd tell you. Ever Yours Truly, The Spink. P. S. Give my love to those at home, and read my letter and show the pictures also. . . . I'm glad the magician will be there."

When my mother wrote Uncle Ed about the problem and her hope, he responded at once, "Dear Paus'l—Hurray & Hurrah—It looks as if you had it nailed at last. Now it is simply a matter of your patience and

HEROIC COURAGE on the part of Margaret. I'm awful proud of her and when I get rich again will buy her a marvelous Hero present. In the meantime I will turn over my cross of the Legion d'Honneur to her. Love to all, Gaesjack."

My father said to a friend in the last of December, "The going is all better now but it was a Christmas of grief." May Massee wrote, "Now of course Carl needs money. . . . I do know a bit about books, children's and others, and I am sure that Carl's are literally great stories, among the best that have come from America and the equal of any, anywhere. . . . And they are so ab-so-lute-ly American. They couldn't be translated even into British. . . . I am enthusiastic because I have lived with them since the first of August but we did not send them even to Harcourt's until the middle of November. I have copied many of them, read them innumerable times and they are better to me today than they were in the beginning. Why that old Potato Face Blind Man is as wise as Socrates and a deal more companionable. Carl has never worked so hard on anything; he's been doing them for several years but has only just got them to the point where he's willing to let go. We are all going to burst with pride to think that we had anything to do with presenting them to the public."

As January came around, my father was saying, "It has been a winter of work, with two books for Harcourt this year, and our girl, Margaret, with a month of hard luck that she's pulled through finely." And my father was seeing an old friend again, who came visiting at our house and had had his share of trouble—Eugene Debs, who was ill. Just before Christmas Day, President Warren Harding had commuted Debs's prison sentence, though not restoring his citizenship rights. Debs went home to Terre Haute, Indiana, and before long was sent to Elmhurst and the Lindlahr Sanitarium, two blocks from our house. My father wrote him, "Dear Gene, You will always be close to us. . . . My signature goes for the whole bunch under our roof. As you went away out the front door one of them said, 'He's a big rough flower.' With you it isn't really a good-by because you are still here."

As my father's lecture schedule took him about the nation, he heard from Amy Lowell, "I have just discovered that you are to give a reading at the Women's City Club on February 4th, and I want you to come and stay with us while you are here. We could put you up quite easily, and it would be a great pleasure to see you and show you the town, so don't under any circumstances say no, and don't have a prior engagement. I have an idea that I never thanked you for inscribing my books so splendidly. If I have been a little remiss in not mentioning this before, you must put it down to all the thousand operations that they have insisted upon my having; I have had two since I saw you and am no better from either of them, but I have now refused to act as a surgeon's model any more and think I shall improve under the policy of being let alone. . . . I was coming out to your town this Autumn, but the doctors put their feet down and squashed the project, and now I doubt if I see Chicago this Winter, which will make your coming here all the pleasanter. Of course I shall see you anyway, but not half so nicely as though you were in the house, so I am anxious to know that you will come and make this your headquarters while you are here." Amy Lowell's close friend and companion was Mrs. Harold Russell, who'd been an actress in her early years. Stories went about of how when she and Miss Lowell went abroad in 1914, along with them went Miss Lowell's maid, her maroon automobile, and one of her two chauffeurs with his maroon livery. Miss Lowell finished her letter to my father, "Please remember Mrs. Russell and me most kindly to Mrs. Sandburg and give the kiddies our love. Sincerely yours, Amy Lowell."

My father accepted her invitation, "Well, I know there will be good talk at your house." She said, "Our letters passed each other. I was delighted to get yours telling me that you will come to me while you are in Boston. You must let me know what train you will arrive by and I will send the motor in to get you, as I live quite a little way out of town. . . . I hope the children are all well." Then on the small elegant stationery headed: *Sevenels, Brookline,* my father reported to my mother, "Buddy! This is it—where we live the higher life—and tell all about it when we get home. Mrs. Russell gives me a good line from a letter of yours, 'I married a slow man.' Luck to you, dear battler, Carl. Sunday night."

It was February, three months since my sister's trouble began to show itself. My mother wrote, "Dearest, these are busy days. Margaret is on an exclusive milk diet—milk—milk—nothing but milk—4 oz. every half hour during day—32 feedings in 24 hrs, including 2 during night. Rest in bed all the time—no reading—no occupations of any sort—absolute rest. Believe me it means little rest for the rest of us to keep her resting!!!! Today the new girl comes—she looks like a good one—we shall see! I should have mentioned that the windows are open in Margaret's room day & night—so the cure is milk—fresh air—and rest—the milk is 2% milk (half the cream removed from whole milk) and given in such small portions that the stomach is not over-loaded at any time. The total intake per day is 4 quarts—so this is a generous diet enough to correct any condition of under-nourishment from the fast and the relapse at

Xmas. This is an old-time Russian cure—worth a trial . . . if it does not effect a cure, it will help put Margaret in condition for another fast."

My father would be home briefly and off again, sending notes from hotels. "It was hard leaving & I have memories of lovely faces & voices." And she, "This is what Margaret said today: 'You don't know how often I think about daddy. Every time I hear the front door open, I think what a beautiful surprise it would be, if it was daddy coming in'—She has mentioned writing you—but is really very weak from being in bed all this time on a low diet. She is getting more to eat now, and her diet is more generous every day—so she will be up and around again very soon." And she told him some news she'd gotten on the phone, that ten of the Rootabaga stories had been sold to the *Delineator* for $1250, and "I have the fun of springing the news on you first! I think it's a mighty big piece of news—hurrah! We'll dance an Indian dance in celebration when you get back—Helga, Janet, Marge, Carl & Paula—but you will have to teach us the Indian dance out of your New Mexico Santa Fe experiences. . . . We are all looking for you—it's been a long absence. I'm glad there are no other long trips this spring. All the love there is from us all."

On the fifth of May, 1922, Harcourt wrote, "Dear Carl: We are just publishing 'Slabs of the Sunburnt West.' I like its looks, and it, and hope you will, too. We are sending you ten author's copies separately. Enclosed is a check for $300, the advance agreed on. You must know we are proud to publish it. The more the folks here see of 'Rootabaga,' the more it grows on us all. . . . Yours, Alfred."

A copy of *Slabs of the Sunburnt West* went to Grandma Sandburg, who wrote of her delight. "Dearest Sweetest and most beloved of all! Y thank you a thousand times for the beutifull book the pretty covers as well as inside arengement. Oh how we all feel the fullness of gratitude to you and gladness that your patient work have ended in a so large and so pretty book. Y wish Y could give something or do something in return. Y have sense New Years made yokes for corset covers for all of us and Lina too. Y thoutht of Lilian to have some of the insertion crocheted on the novelty brede it is pretty for pillowcases would like to make a pair for your pillows they are a good large sice are they? Wish Y could run over with a dozen of eggs now and then we have so much of them. This is just my feeling. Y only stand bewildered and would praise God for having moulded his clay into a so beutifull piece of ornamet in his kingdom. With much love from all of us as ever yours, Mother."

292

My dreams and memories of childhood are of an unhampered free time. Perhaps it is because it was that way—my mother occupied with my sister, and Janet and myself unguided. When Mother and Margaret went to Battle Creek again, my father reported on Uncle Ed's visit, of the dog, Pooch, and how everything went, "Janet and Helga coming fine; Ed took some particular looks at their legs and said their legs are more than perfect; that should be final.—Oma shook hugging Ed, in the house, then rallied and from the porch waved a grand gay good-by.— Pooch learns; we can get him so he won't give long vocal performances; but he will never learn to stop his passionate enjoyment of scaring people by rushing them with his terrible eyes and teeth; he must have seen himself sometime in a magnifying mirror so that he imagines he is six or seven dogs in one.—Kitty Whispers seems to have many thoughts about the creche and the layette.—It is rich luxury to walk around the house and goddam any ghosts I please and nobody hears, nobody is bothered, the echoes are musical.—The reports could be endless. The book grows. You and your Marny, and mine, are missed all over the map. Carl."

Margaret wrote, "Dear Daddy, I'm so glad that you wrote to mamma and me. It was certainly funny to hear how Helga threw a spoon of sand into your coffee and the next day how the kitty got her foot into the butter. But it wasn't funny to hear how Helga threw a stick into Janet's eye so she had to be bandaged all the time. Poor little Janet! I don't think Helga meant to do any real harm, though, do you? But won't you write a long letter all to me please, if you're not busy?. . . Mamma gives me a dollar a week for fasting though I can't see why she should. It's for my own good. . . . Give love and kisses to Scabooch and Pooch and all the rest. With a bushel of kisses from your loving Spink."

"Out of the window," my father said, "I can see the wild ruddy face of Helga with its wonderful curves. She is at the sand box. For hours those kids have been talking and laughing out there. I am only living in the present with them, which is what I am going to do with Margaret. The worst is to come and if it doesn't come what we get is so much velvet." He started a poem:

> Helga in a sand box dabbles.
> Dabble your fingers in the sand.
> Let the wet sand snuggle in your knuckles.
> Let the dry sand go wiggly and ticklish through your
>   finger tips.

So far all you know for an answer to a question, is,
      "no."
Oh, your slow sure way of saying "no," to everything.
Do you want fresh wheat bread soaked in fresh Jersey
      cow milk? No. And then you drink it.
Do you want to go to bed? No. And then you fall asleep
      in the sand box and your limp beautiful ankles
      look like something the wind blew off an elm.

Then Harcourt was asking for a second Rootabaga book to follow the *Rootabaga Stories* coming out in September. My father wrote, "Buddy: . . . Harcourt says it is important to have the second Rootabaga book ready for illustrators this winter, if we want early copies next year so salesmen can have them to show to the booksellers in the summer."

"Dear Daddy," wrote Margaret, "Yesterday I began on my fast. In the morning I was awfully hungry but toward evening I wasn't so hungry. Mamma wanted to go on a fast with me but I wouldn't let her."

From home, his letters went to them regularly. "The main regret of the day is that you couldn't be here to see Janet and Helga. They never were better. Their laughs ripple. Janet has color, is growing. And Oma was gay today. I am going to get tickets to 'Lightnin'' for Oma and Lina at a matinee some afternoon next week when I will stay home with the shiners. Margaret's letter to Lina today made us all feel she has big and deep vitality. That a girl fasting six days could write so keenly of so many things and in such a handwriting, was testimony. I am deep in the final rewrite and shaping up of the second Rootabaga book. . . . Kitty Whispers is gracious and friendly and I am betting on the kittens having one or two we want to keep. Mona languishes; she was washed in sand today, Helga scrubbing her with a pear she called soap; Alice B gets shinier. While Rhoda tops 'em all; the chances which were one in five that we would raise her I now put at one in three. Such is news from your old empire and domain of days. There is love from all, includin' Carl."

"Dear Spink: We are all thinking here that you are a very much alive girl, and very strong, to be able to write such letters as you do, after more than a week of fasting. Your handwriting stands up as though your fingers and fists are good for many long, steady, hard fights and struggles. But then you are now one of the champion, long-distance, unconquerable and invincible fasters of the United States—you are a veteran—and since Uncle Ed pinned the Legion of Honor cross of France on you, I don't

294

know what further honor and acknowledgement can be made. Everything here at home is elegant, hunky dory, up to snuff, 100 per cent and first class. Only when you and mother get back, it will be more so—see? . . . Here is love to you and your mother—from—Daddy."

"Dearest," Mother said as the long year neared its end, "Here we are the morning of the 8th day of the fast—and Margaret is holding her own fine. It is 8 a.m. and she is reading the Blue Fairy Book (from the Public Library here)—reading fast and with utter concentration as always. Her brain seems unaware of the fast—for mentally she is as active as she ever was. Her body wants rest though. She is in bed all day except for an hour or so sitting up in a chair. . . . Take good care of yourself, Buddy. You ought to get a rest this month as you have no lecture dates except the Lincoln Centre one—have you? and next month you will have a bunch of them probably. So you must manage to get a lot of exercise this month and get in good physical trim against the trials ahead! Margaret sends a bushel of kissess—and here is all the love there is from Paula. And you'll have to smack-kiss Helga & Janet for me. *Gee*—it will be great to be back home again! And that good day will probably be the day before Xmas." And, "We are starting on our twelfth day today —and all's well. . . . she hasn't had much pep the last few days. However Dr. C. says she is eliminating toxins much more freely than last time and expects good results. . . . Be sure to bring the mss for the second Rutabaga book. I will have time here to go over it thoroly—without a million interruptions. So be sure to remember to bring the Mss along."

As they were leaving Battle Creek, she said, "I feel I know the whole technique of fasting—as far as Margaret is concerned—and if we try any more fasts I think it will be at home. First we must see what results we get from this fast. . . . I am well satisfied that Margaret never needed a fast as badly as this particular time. Margaret looks fine—and is so very eager to get away from Battle Creek—to get home . . . she thinks and talks constantly about home—the two sisters—and daddy! You can tell Lina & Oma that we will be home Tuesday. . . . So long dearest and 'See You Soon!' "

In my album photograph taken before that year, my sister sits on the branch of the spruce in the backyard, swinging her feet. Her hair is held back with a ribbon and falls to her waist. She's pretty and round-faced. In the photo afterwards, though indeed in my childhood memory I never knew she'd been fasting, she stands with bobbed hair, gentle face and hands, emaciated. She never would go back to public school, though she would attend a convent school awhile and go off to summer camps.

As a consequence, unrepressed, Margaret would read avidly and continually in the literature of the house and libraries, very well self-educated.

Death is a different sort of trouble. Alfred Harcourt would lose his wife. When George and Hopie Fox's son, Randall, had died in an accident back in 1919, my father had written them, "A world that could produce a Randall can't be a crazy world. . . . With Janet and Margaret, I am ready for anything all the time. Every day I come home and find them alive I take as a day snatched from Death. I think too about how they die every week. The little fluff of a Janet we had a year ago is dead. The Margaret that was learning to talk three years ago is dead and replaced with an endless chatterer. Every beautiful thing I know is ephemeral, a thing of a moment. Life is a series of things that vanish. I had two brothers go with diptheria and we had a double funeral on a bitter winter day when I was a boy. I buried a child that had not lived long enough to be named. . . . A day of life is a day snatched from death. And the only fool is the one who can prove that death is a blank nothing or something less than life."

Back then too, my Aunt Mary, at close to forty-five, had lost her baby, my mother saying, "I feel very sorry for Mary—a child would have meant so much to her—and she would have been a very real mother. Of course, the big thing is she came thru alive." Aunt Mary, a strong woman, and her husband, Allie Johnson, had adopted a son, Eric, after their loss. Then, after only five years of marriage, in the fall of 1922, Allie was hurt in a motorcycle accident and wasn't expected to live. In February of 1923, my mother was writing to my father, "Take best care of yourself. Everything fine at home. Margaret is in fine shape again. Good-natured & everything. We are trying a more bland diet. . . . We've had a couple of fine days, spring in the air. Lilac buds are swelling and Helga & Janet parade the sidewalk on their kiddy cars. . . . I had a telegram from Mary last Monday that Allie died. The funeral was last Wednesday. Of course I could not go and leave Margaret—for things were pretty uncertain at the time. In fact on Wednesday (the day of the funeral) Margaret was ill. . . . I wrote Mary that you were away on a lecture trip West and that I could not leave the children to attend the funeral. I sent five dollars for flowers from us (or for a more practical purpose as she wished) and an additional $15.00 for herself. I suggested that she come up here now for a vacation with Eric—change of scene would do her good and it would mean a real rest for her. Or she could leave Eric with Grandma Johnson where he has been since last fall when Allie had the accident. I felt we could afford to send Mary that much now when she has much extra expense—and if either of us had made the trip to Galesburg for the funeral it would have cost that much too. Mary writes that she is thankful that she has Eric now to live for. . . . I can imagine how hard it was for Mary & Allie's mother to see Allie go. But Eric has helped them all thru it—Allie's mother just worships him—and he will round out her life as well as Mary's. It's the little tykes who keep things going. . . . The children have been outdoors a good part of the day—and it has been a restful Sunday. Just now Margaret is at Oma's house playing dominoes wtih her."

Cousin Eric did come to visit with Aunt Mary—a handsome child, dark-haired, wearing rompers and black button shoes, maybe two years younger than I. Grandma Sandburg came to visit too from Galesburg in a long print dress, her white hair back in a bun, writing on return, "Dear sweet Marney How childish it sounds and homy seems so I can hear Janet yet call Marney but I was so glad to have your little newsy letter and glad to hear thath Oma is well and happy togather with you yes we have much to be happy and greatfull for in this especially in this awfull days with so many awfull happenings both in nature and people among themselves do and cause so much bitter feeling yays Margaret dearie it is good learning to knit to work with our hands usefull things as well as with our brain. I know you can write beautifull stories which requier much more knowledges and strenght to our mind than does the handwork I love to read your stories wish we were not so far apart but thath we could run over and see each other oftener you allmost live in tow places good to have preveledges. . . . with much regard and love to Oma as well as all the rest of your people ever yours Grandma."

Soon the second book of Rootabaga tales would be published, *Rootabaga Pigeons,* inscribed: To Three Illinois Pigeons. The stories were going into the French language too, Leon Bazalgette translating them; they would be titled *Au Pays de Rootabaga.* Now the first glimmerings of a Lincoln book were coming along. My father's old *Day Book* boss, Negley Cochran, wrote, "Glad to hear from you always. Especially that you have been reading Lincoln. Good thing we have him to read about. He always appealed to me more than Washington or any of the rest of them. . . . Go on with Lincoln. He's about all we have left thats worth a shrine in this country. When I think of Warren Gamaliel Harding as president of the U.S. I shudder and get goose-pimply with apprehension for the future of the race. If animals could only talk I'd like to attend a barnyard convention called to discuss what they know about humans who think they are enjoying liberty and dont know what it means. All the same, I dont lose my optimism. I keep on thinking there's a good time coming. The world still gives me a good laugh."

And a few weeks later, Harcourt was asking, "How's the 'Lincoln' getting along? I hope all this traveling doesn't hinder it too much, and that it just gives the material a chance to settle into order. Plan a firm outline for it. All this month my mind has been turning to you and that job. It will be a great book. Tho not written for boys it will be open to them. Yrs, Alfred."

Later Harcourt wrote that when he and my father had discussed a book of perhaps 400 pages, my father had said, ". . . it might run a little longer." Harcourt said that during their talk, my father "had agreed to try his hand at what we described as a 'boy's life of Lincoln.'" It was at this time that Harcourt Brace and Company moved their quarters. "We had grown out of our adolescence," Harcourt related later. "We had such an affection for 1 West 47th Street that we played with the idea of remodeling an old house somewhere in Washington Square." Instead, "we signed a twenty-year lease for a floor in a building going up at 383 Madison Avenue. The picturesque time was over."

My father's busy wires are there in the files and my mother's responses. He said: CROSSING THE DESERT TONIGHT ARRIVING SWEETWATER TEXAS ON SANTA FE TRAIN SUNDAY EVENING ARRIVING DALLAS MONDAY MORNING EIGHT OCLOCK (STOP) HARD PROGRAM BUT COMING FINE (STOP) WISHING LOVE AND LUCK TO YOU AND THE BUNCH (STOP) WIRE ME CARE WESTERN UNION DALLAS TEXAS IF ANY NEWS MONDAY (STOP) EXPECT HOME THURSDAY CARL.

"When your wire came this morning," she wrote, "your dear thoughts for us made us all very happy. I called the good news to Helga. She was playing house on top of the big wood-pile. Helga was much impressed with your special message to her and declared she would let you play with Shep on top of the wood-pile when you get home. I don't know which she thinks she owns & controls, Shep or the house on top of the wood-pile. Margaret is coming along fine. Went on a six mile hike with the Girl Scouts Friday morning and to dancing class in the afternoon. . . . The steam-plant will be installed before your return, so you escape the noise and general upset state of the household. Also the kittens have opened their eyes—and Kitty Whispers looks well again & happy. Bushels of love from all. We are looking forward to the first days of May & your return, sweetheart."

"Just left Santa Fe," he answered, "new songs & new friends—now I can give a good long reading to your letter & think over every newsy love line. In weather you've had it all over me—snow & wind at Santa

Fe like an Illinois March day. . . . it was a friendly place tho not home. . . . The Hendersons were fine; their girl is a radiant simple genius; I hand it to her over all except our own. About 10 days now, taking the last leg of the trip. Chinese things from Frisco & Indian stuff from Santa Fe will come along to you—pay the express—a singing blanket—rain gods, animals for the kids—have kept well all along, every show a go. Love to you, dearest, Carl."

My father said too, "I am being slowly killed by date lines." But he seemed to thrive on his way of living. He told Harcourt, "Sometimes I think the Lincoln book will be a sort of History and Old Testament of the United States, a joke almanac, prayer collect, and compendium of essential facts."

Harcourt said, "It's a sweet & noble book." And, "Ellen arrived yesterday afternoon and I've just finished the piece of the Lincoln book she brought. We've had not more than one or two books in this shop as good as this piece, and if it keeps up it will be the brightest feather in our cap—a regular plume! You're just the boy to do this—to understand Abe and make him real in real times when life went on so differently. The sense of reality in the setting is wonderful. . . . Say, we've been right so far to keep this job fairly dark. Let's both continue, then when it's practically done I want to send a handsome announcement—all at once to Everybody—of it as an event. And it is. . . . I'd like to publish next fall. Do you see yourself having it done by May? . . . Bless you—go on— don't get sick or anything."

"The wife and friends are saying the job will kill me if I don't slow down," my father told Harcourt, "BUT it's exactly the kind of a job that with me has to be a spurt job; if I had one of those retentive efficiency memories that took a never-let-go grip on names, dates, places, actions, I could slow down—One thing I'm sure of; the biggest part of American history has all to be rewritten; and it will be done."

Abraham Lincoln: The Prairie Years would be published on Lincoln's birthday in 1926. Before printing the trade edition, Harcourt's would go all the way and put out a two-volume boxed deluxe first edition on "imported Dutch charcoal rag paper," numbered and signed. The book would total nearly a thousand pages. The trade edition would combine the two volumes in one. Grandfather Sandburg was gone, but the book was dedicated: TO AUGUST AND CLARA SANDBURG, Workers on the Illinois Prairie. Grandma Sandburg would die in that December, not knowing that the Lincoln biography would swell to six volumes in time, as *The War Years* came along, and earn a Pulitzer Prize for history fourteen years later.

Then in 1925, before the book was released, a magazine bought the serial rights to it and called it when published "The Unfathomed Lincoln." My father sent a wire home from Commerce, Texas, as soon as he heard: HARCOURT WIRES BOOK SERIAL RIGHTS SOLD TO PICTORIAL REVIEW FOR TWENTY THOUSAND FIX THE FLIVVER AND BUY A WILD EASTER HAT.

My mother answered by Western Union at once: YOUR WIRE WITH BIG NEWS CAME SUNDAY OVERJOYED LETTER FROM HARCOURT TODAY CONFIRMS FIGURE OF TELEGRAM PURCHASER OF SERIAL RIGHTS WISHES FIGURE KEPT SECRET BECAUSE UNPRECEDENTED FOR NUMBER WORDS USED YOU MUST TAKE LONG VACATION FROM ALL WORK THIS SUMMER ALL JUBILATING HERE IN GAY EASTER BONNETS EVERY OPPORTUNITY ASSURED MARGARET NOW HIGH HOPES AND BUSHELS OF LOVE   PAULA.

Twenty

What Is a Memory?

What is a memory? A sound down in the lake of the mind? A sensation dragged up from dark waters? A feeling of strong gentle hands? A dream of a tall looming figure who picks me up and walks me upside down on all the ceilings, upstairs and down, of the house? The same hands lift me behind the handlebars of a bicycle, hearing the whirr of the wheels, the air spinning in my flung hair, the rustle of cornfields passed on country roads, the honk of frogs at the quarry, the voice behind calling me one of his homeyglomies.

Can the past be pulled up from a photograph of a bald smiling baby in a large oval dishpan on the lawn, a strange young yellow-haired girl seated beside with laced calf-high shoes and frilled blouse? There is an old wood standing swing in the background that creaks, and trellised grapevines, sweet-smelling in the fall, and a shambling small barn with pigeon holes in the loft, and a vacant lot where the sun burns in the summer days and fireflies twinkle in the dusks. Who is the child who looks nothing like me in red and blue coveralls or a smock, sewn and embroidered or cross-stitched by my mother, and always with a hand on a puppy or a dog called Prince or Pooch or Bimbo or Shep, who lies across my lap, or varied cats or kittens or rabbits in my arms or in baskets or a box or somewhere about?

Who is it on the tricycle or wheeling the wicker doll carriage with the cat or the rag doll asleep? What is clear, for it returns in dreams or half-dreams sometimes, is the scent of the flowers in my mother's gardens, the overshadowing tall iris bed at the end of the flagstoned path, the half-seen figures of pedestrians going by the hedge and the fence that are between me and the old St. Charles Road bordering that side of our lot.

Whose old dusty letter scrap is this, saved, unfamiliar, incredible to memory:

> dear daddy
> thank you for the
> cards I love you
> dear daddy yes I do
> like you very
> much oh I do like
> you frum Helga
> to daddy
> dear daddy
> good-bye Helga Sandburg

There is the heat of the sun and I am going back and forth with the doll carriage, singing; and somewhere, observing, is my mother, who does not sing at all herself, but hums and has little sense of tune, thinking I may be on key, and reporting to my father, "You should hear Helga this minute singing off the old nursery rhymes softly to her little old rag boy-dolly. She has the *resonant* voice—a quality of voice that reminds me of yours, buddy—I think she's going to be the singer of the three—at any rate Helga has a rare voice—with those lingering resonances."

Mother stands me with back to the piano and strikes the notes. "What is that one?" "C." "Yes! And that one?" "E!" And so piano teachers will come and go and the metronome tick through my early years, some of those about hoping that I'll come to like the keys. I endure the "Recitals" arranged periodically along with "Dance Programs," Mother and Margaret in the audience, not my busy father. It will not be until I reach my teens that I will openly rebel and the music lessons cease.

But not the singing. That catches and holds. I write to Oma, "These are some of the songs that we sing, The ship that never reterned, Sweet Tilly Tailor, Mamie reilly, She is the daugter of officer porter, Mister doolly-ooly-oolly-oolly-oo. Sweet Tilly Tailor, she loved a sailor, on board a whaler that sailed down the bay, her heart was aking, 'twas almost breaking, for that ship was taking her sweetheart away. 'Clap, clap, clap,' that is the song of tilly tailor. Lovingly Helga."

And the letters tell of noise, "Dearest . . . Helga & Janet gloriously well and noisy as the 4th of July. . . . Helga & Janet happy dare-devil gypsy babes as always. . . . We miss you & your voice—and we don't like it at all that the guitars are silent and the hasp on your door always fastened!"

We are never spanked or struck. There is only one law and it is in effect when my father is home. "Quiet! Daddy's sleeping. Hush! Daddy's working." "Hush," we tell each other, "Shhhh."

Oma I know well. And Opa too, distant and kindly. They are nearby. Grandma Sandburg is far away. She writes to my mother sometimes, "Dearest Lillian . . . Times flyes it seems one day after another. . . . we certainly all of us were delighted to se Carl the Sunday evening his raidiant face shining I thought traveling around having a good time as it seems but as I read the poem O wondrous gifted pain teach thou The God of love let him learn how knowlege how great, not only books but know thyselves hope you are all well my love goes with to all ever Yours Clara Sandburg." There she is in the photographs—in the yard I know and on the trellised porch and seated on the bench and standing before the flower bed with her arm about me. My matching bloomers come to my knees, my socks slip down, one leg is across the other, the toe on the ground. Or I hold the cat who is playing with the long light brown curls my mother has brushed round her finger that morning. Grandma Sandburg is patient-faced, her smile a little tense. My dolls are there, those well remembered—Betsy in my arms with velvet coat and round cap and Nell at my feet. The grass and the air and the feeling of the time are all caught in the snapshots my mother has pasted in a book to help me hold onto the memory.

Upstairs in the house there is a playroom where there are blackboards and a low table, paper to draw on and a box of crayons. The old house creaks and at night I listen to the sound, knowing it is Santa Claus or God going about their business and I am not afraid. There is a letter to Sinclair Lewis from his wife, Gracie, that holds the atmosphere, ". . . at Carl Sandburg's house, out at Elmhurst, with Gene Debs. . . . Elmhurst. A dusty flat suburb, stoopid as a Main St. town. But a few good shady streets of big maples— . . . Carl's house—small, littered, not uncomfortable, wonderful photographs by Mrs. Sandburg's brother, Steichen—e.g. Isadora Duncan posing between the columns of the Parthenon. Terrible food—stews and greens. Three noisy but nice and unimaginative daughters . . . we sit about the table on the screened porch till eleven." "Red" Lewis had planned to write a novel based on Debs's life, but never got around to it. Debs calls our place, "that delightfully hospitable home on the edge of the jungle and near the flower garden." He and Sinclair Lewis and my father are close. Debs says, "Lewis and Sandburg are fit companions, genial, fun-loving, wholehearted and generous, as well as princes of the pen and masters of the literary art."

Who is that in Debs's lap in the garden, six years old with long curls, the socks still falling down, in a red and white checked frock and bloomers, sewn for me on the treadle machine where my mother makes her own dresses and aprons, our rompers and nightgowns, and even elaborate costumes—a clown, a brownie, a witch? Debs is holding a rose I have given him. He pushes me in the swing. He lets me pat his bald head. And later he will write down a beatitude for my father, inscribing it "with boundless love and admiration":

> Blessed are they who
> expect nothing, for they shall
> not be disappointed.
> > Eugene V. Debs
> > Elmhurst, September 4th 1924

And a poem too, that he'd composed while serving time. It seems that Debs, like my father, had a "sense of destiny." It was called "Prison Ode":

> Beyond these walls
> Sweet freedom calls;
> In accents clear and brave she speaks,
> And lo! my spirit scales the peaks.
>
> Beyond these bars
> I see the stars;
> God's glittering heralds beckon me;
> My soul is winged: behold, I'm free!
>
> > Eugene V. Debs
>
> To Carl, with love and loyalty
> > Gene
>
> Elmhurst, Sept. 4—1924

After Debs goes away, he writes my mother who has taken snapshots, "Each of the prints you send is an excellent reproduction of the life which had its being in your garden and in the jungles surrounding it when it was my good fortune to be your guest and to be decorated with beautiful roses pressed upon me by the loving hands of your little household gods. . . . Carl shows his usual discriminating taste in expressing preference for the very happy little picture of Helda [sic] and myself on the bench. That particular picture is a gem. It could not possibly be better, and it flatters me enormously. Helda's eager, searching and amusing expression and pose is a subject for the best of the movies, and I am sure that Carl never saw anything of its kind to excel it. It is so utterly and so beautifully characteristic of the sweet, innocent child full to overflowing with the spirit and animation of childhood. It requires only a glance to see that she and I are lovers and that we are in delighted and blissful communion with each other. How my emotions are quickened and thrill within me as I recall this happy scene and look once more, as I often shall in the future, into the sweet face, the quizzical eyes of that lovely child!"

There are visitors throughout the year. Uncle Ed goes tramping with my father out into the countryside where the cornfields are, sometimes a railway track cutting through one. The two buy beer, or popcorn if beer isn't to be had. My mother makes pancakes for us all when they return, or corn fritters topped with syrup, or doughnuts, hot and just fried. There is a bowl of apples and a dish of walnuts to crack. Arm in arm, my father and uncle sing "Where Is My Wandering Boy Tonight?" and "A Boy's Best Friend Is His Mother." And then Uncle Ed roars out a poem and I am told later that I burst into tears:

> It was the schooner Hesperus
> That sailed the wintry sea,
> And the skipper had taken his little daughter
> To bear him company . . .

There is trouble in the poem and the inevitable happens and:

> The salt sea was frozen on her breast,
> The salt tears in her eyes.
> And he saw her hair, like the brown sea-weed,
> On the billows fall and rise.
> Such was the wreck of the Hesperus,

In the midnight and the snow!
Christ save us all from a death like this
On the reef of Norman's Woe!

At Christmas, Uncle Ed brings his new wife. It is twenty years since
he married Clara Smith. Dana Desboro Glover is beautiful, fashionable,
auburn-haired, creamy-skinned and freckled, humorous. She is an actress
and a photographer too. Uncle Ed met her at the New York School of
Photography. My father knows Dana. He's told us how when he and
Uncle Ed stayed overnight in the New York apartment where Dana
and her sister and mother lived, in the mornings the two men would
come into the hallway and chant at the top of their lungs: "WE WANT
BREAKFAST! WE WANT BREAKFAST!" My father got a song from Dana's
mother that he has taught us. He put it in *The American Songbag*, where
he speaks of Mrs. Glover and one of his visits to their apartment: "In
the first Oklahoma land rush in the late 'Eighties, was a woman who
rode a wild horse and staked out a claim worth having. In the years
that came she raised corn, broom corn, alfalfa, soy beans—and three
daughters who had freckle faces, hair of a dark gold corn silk, and sweet
dispositions. Time passed. The family moved. New York was their
home, the address was on Eighty-eighth Street, and the number in the
phone book. They were now far from Oklahoma. Yet there came one
cold rainy night to their fireside, their steam radiator, a young man who
had raised corn, broom corn, alfalfa, and soy beans in Kansas, the next
state to Oklahoma and standing on the same big prairie. They sang on
that cold rainy night, those people around the steam radiator. And one of
the songs was Rosie Nell. 'It was a comfort to us in those days of the first
Oklahoma land rush,' said the woman who rode a wild horse to stake
out a claim." The lilting song started:

How oft I dream of childhood days,
Of tricks we used to play
Upon each other when at school
To pass the time away,
They often wished me with them,
But they always wished in vain,
I'd rather be with Rosie Nell,
A-swinging in the lane!

Uncle Ed recounts again how in Voulangis he burned his paintings.
He'd been doing oils and pastels of flowers, and one morning at break-

fast his sabot-shod Breton gardener, François, came in to show him a painting he had just completed. My uncle stared at it—it was a copy of one of his—then he shouted, "It's better than mine!" And he told François to follow and they marched to the studio and hauled out every painting there and piled them up and made a bonfire. Uncle Ed says he sang a song while he watched his works burning that he'd sung with General Billy Mitchell in the war:

Where will we all be one hundred years from now?
Where will we all be one hundred years from now?
Pushing up the daisies, pushing up the daisies,
That's where we'll all be one hundred years from now!

When my uncle got to New York, he shredded what paintings he could lay his hands on there and told the janitor to come and take the junk away.

At this time Uncle Ed is working in New York. He is about to give up Villa l'Oiseau Bleu in France and settle full-time in the States. He makes fashion photographs for *Vanity Fair* and *Vogue* now. And he is doing pictures to advertise everything from cigarette lighters to mattresses to hand lotion to shoes. For one photograph he might get a thousand dollars. At one point he's said to be the highest-paid photographer in the world. Poets, dramatists, actors and actresses, prize fighters, musicians, composers, millionaires, come to his studio in the Beaux Arts Building in New York.

Amy Lowell arrives at our house one September, and my father writes her, "We are glad you came and that among our few traditions we have added one for the south porch that you supped with us there." She replied, "My dear Sandburg: You and Mrs. Sandburg gave me a very pleasant two evenings while I was in Chicago. I only wish we lived nearer together. I enclose a little poem which perhaps expresses my feelings better than I could do in prose. I hope you will like it. . . . Remember me to Mrs. Sandburg and my friends, Margaret, Janet, and Helmar [sic]." Part of her poem goes:

I think I am cousin-german to Endymion,
Certainly I have loved the moon a long time. . . .

To-night I saw an evening moon
Dodging between tree-branches
Through a singing silence of crickets,
And a man was singing songs to a black-backed guitar. . . .

The moon stops a moment in a hole between leaves
And tells me a new story,
A story of a man who lives in a house with a pear-tree
    before the door. . . .
There is a woman in the house, and children,
And, out beyond, the corn-fields are sleeping and the
    trees are whispering to the fire-flies.
So I have seen the man's country, and heard his songs
    before there are words to them.
And the moon said to me: "This now I give you," and went
    on, stepping through the leaves,
And the man went on singing, picking out his accompaniment
    softly on the black-backed guitar.

And then there is the poet Ernest Walsh, writing from the Etruscan Apennines in Italy, "My visit to Elmhurst, my night in your home was too sharp a pleasure for me to recover immediately. . . . The face of your wife, one of the most beautiful faces I have ever seen, and of Margery [sic], Janet and Helga come back to me here in Italy like good news in bad weather, like promises of good luck tomorrow. I see all of you standing in a row in the garden looking up at a new crescent moon. And I hear you saying:

        'Well, Old Wish-Bone!
        What luck tomorrow?'

and it's all rich with the flavour of the salt and bone and brain of a country I love better, perhaps, than most men love women. To me, Carl Sandburg is my United States. . . . Yours in the name of Margery, Janet and Helga and with my love to your wife."

My father, when at home, goes when it is cold or raining up the steep back stairway to his upper-story workroom, where the windows overlook the high spruce, the garden, the vacant field beyond, the small barn, the roof of the added-on kitchen. The house was once a farmhouse and there are additions here and there and the rooms are many and little. My father has thumbtacked press clippings all about, and Chinese print decorations on tissue-thin paper painted pink, green, orange and gold, and there are sepia halftone pictures and newspaper cutouts from the rotogravure section. His Santa Fe Indian rugs are on the floor and a Mexican poncho, and a Navajo blanket covers his narrow iron army cot.

When it is warm and sunny and my father is home from his lecturing trips, he writes outdoors behind the barn. The corner lot is ours now. A little while back, when *Rootabaga Stories* was published, my father had written Harcourt, "Dear Alfred: . . . now to a matter of a kind that I won't bother you about maybe again in a lifetime. We are buying a lot next door south of us in Elmhurst. If we don't get it somebody else will and we will have a house we may not care to look at slammed close to us. The price is $2,300, of which $1,300 must be cash down, the rest time payments. We have paid $200 earnest and borrowed $500 and need $600. If you can find this $600 it will go into good land. It has two marvelous sugar maples in front. At the rear it has the biggest incomparable lilac bush in northern Illinois. It is the only place I ever found glow worms. I spaded it all and raised sweet corn year before last. Our cats have their kittens there in special sunny lying-in corners. So you see we know what we're getting. And all we need is $600 spot cash greenbacks of the national government. The man who owns the lot has notions; now he'll sell and now he won't; and this week is the first time he has been in a selling mood and would talk prices.—If you don't have the $600 available would you wire me collect? And I know you'll understand that only a very special situation would let me bother you like this."

Harcourt sent the money as an advance on *Rootabaga Stories* and now my father is carrying out the orange crate, on the sides of which Mother has screwed little handles for easy lifting. He has set a typewriter on it, and there are pencil stubs in an empty cigar box and a handful of papers. He stays there in the waist-tall weeds and brush where a cow was pastured not long since, and where the sun glitters continually. I am making my way to him, carrying a glass of milk. Seeing my approach, he spits brown juice to a side and there is a bulge in his cheek where his tongue has pushed the tobacco. He is sun-brown and fragrant, his sleeves rolled up, his collar turned under. He takes the glass and sets it in the grass where he forgets it. I am wandering away, back to the yard and the creaking swing.

I've no idea what he is writing, but the Rootabaga people I know. Under our front porch a blue fox lives who has always been there. He comes into the kitchen through the window at times to drink cream from a saucer left for him. He has to measure himself all the time to be sure that he can get back out. He is there now, panting lightly, his blue coat shining, his teeth white. I know about the White Horse Girl and the Blue Wind Boy who go away and find the sea where the white horses come from and the blue winds begin. I know the Green Rat with the Rheumatism and the girls Sweeter Than the Bees Humming and

Wednesday Evening in the Twilight and the Gloaming. I know the Potato Face Blind Man and Blixie Bimber and Henry Hagglyhoagly who plays the guitar with his mittens on and Snoo Foo, the Snow Man, and Shush Shush, the Big Buff Banty Hen who lays an egg in the Postmaster's hat. Over the years our kittens will be named Blixie Bimber and Snoo Foo.

When my father goes away, he wires Mother at times: KISS THE KIDS FOR ME AT BREAKFAST OCEANS OF LOVE TO YOU. And writes, "Dearest Paula —All going okeh.——Talked with Ed and Harcourt over the phone today— blessings on you—sleep much—and sing your little humming songs every day. Carl." He sends her an envelope with dried flowers, "Violets from the Chattahoochee River." And she says, "We miss you every day and more than ever on this Special Day—when Helga blew out the candles on her birthday cake and counted Six of them. Helga did not like it at all that you were not here to help blow out the candles. Frank Lloyd Wright dropped in for a few minutes today on his way home from Chicago. He wanted to know whether we would come out to his place for Thanksgiving. I told him you would probably not be home till after Thanksgiving. Wright liked Ed's pictures tremendously and suggested that we all come out to his place between Xmas & New Years and bring Ed along. Ask the Gaesjack what he thinks of the plan! I think Ed would like Wright—He *looks* mighty interesting anyway. Margaret is fine again . . . and everything looks good. Love and bushels of love to you & Gaesjack from the children and Paula."

Wright is a Rootabaga fan. "Dear Carl—I read your fairy-tales nearly every night—before I go to bed—they fill a long felt want—Poetry. I'll soon know them all by heart . . . lucky Spink and Skabootch—to have a daddy—'fire-born' who understands blue. . . . I'll be waiting for you, at this Station in the Rutabaga Country, to bring Spink and Skabootch to play with their uncle—Frank."

We never get there. We never travel anywhere as a family of five. But my mother takes my sisters and me up over the Wisconsin border where the lake country begins and where the love of water and sand becomes a part of us. One of Mother's letters to my father from Williams Bay goes, "I hope you will somehow manage to get some rest after the book gets into page proofs. We are sorry that you can't join us. . . . the children are not so noisy here. You would be surprised how quietly they can play here—it must be the water that has effected this 'sea-change' in their natures. Anyway, whatever it is that has brought it about, we have a surpassing Peace here these days. . . . So long, sweetheart, and now at last, you too must take a real vacation—and before the fall lecturing begins. . . . Paula & children."

Our car is a narrow-tired two-door Model A three-pedal Ford, my mother a skillful, somewhat fast driver. She wears white—her brimmed hat, her middy blouse, her skirt that comes nearly to her ankles, her stockings and shoes. Margaret sits beside her in the front seat, and Anna, our maid and helper at the time, in back with Janet and me. We have made the two-hundred-mile jaunt up to Lake Geneva or Williams Bay in a day, stopping on the way for ice-cream cones, rainbowed, gigantic in memory, slapped on in one color after another with a paddle —lime, strawberry, banana, chocolate. Half an hour later, I retrieved my bathing cap from the floor to be carsick in it. "Thank goodness, she's got the seat by the window," Janet had yelled as I'd hung my head out in the rushing air.

We got our flivver straight from the Ford Dearborn plant—my father drove it home from there and it cost five hundred dollars that way. He has no skill with machines. Mother has tried teaching him but he always goes off the road, distracted by some sight, and when backing out of the driveway he rammed into the wire fence that separates our yard and our neighbor's. My father has been in an accident already, his face cut and shoulder bruised, so that a lecture date at Wellesley has to be cancelled and it was reported in the newspapers. Ole Rölvaag saw the account and mailed my father "The Blessing of Automobiles" in Latin, and sent a translation too:

O God, our Lord, vouchsafe to hear our prayers, and bless this car with Thy right hand; bid Thy holy Angels stand by it, to save and protect from every danger all those who travel in it; and, just as, through thy levite Philip, Thou didst grant faith and grace to the Ethiopian who was sitting in his chariot and reading Thy sacred words, show likewise to Thy servants the way of salvation, that, helped by Thy grace and ever striving to do good works, they may, after all the vicissitudes of their life and journey here below, rejoice forever. Through Christ our Lord. Amen.

My father thanked Rölvaag and said, "If you come across a Typewriter Blessing or Fountain Pen Blessing, please let me know. As ever, Sandburg."

We rent a small summer cottage in Williams Bay for two weeks or so, spending our days in sandied striped wool bathing suits that come almost to the knees, smelling of mothballs and darned where moths have attacked them during their wintering in some drawer. The cottage is of wood and unscreened and sparely furnished. In the kitchen is a musty-smelling ice safe. There is a card that we set up in our window every other day: ICE. The van stops and the man brings us a block held in his tongs. Mother chips off pieces with a pick and gives each of us one. We go out onto the porch and down the sandy path that leads to the water. A lifeguard watches the bathers from his high platform behind the piers and the little boats. The men swimmers wear long wool suits like ours, and often rubber caps. We have tire tubes to buoy us up, dog-paddling along. Only Margaret knows the recognized "breast stroke," not Janet or me.

My mother seldom goes into the water with us. She was not used to water as a child, but she likes the sunlit scene and feels her responsibility for our health: "I wish I had weighed the children before we left— for I know they have all gained in weight! Such appetites! . . . special kisses from each & all."

And then hasn't time dawdled by in its summertime way? We are back in the Model A, treasures of skipping stones in our pockets, along with prizes that came in the bags of jawbreakers we have bought—a tin clown or a pottery doll. What are plastics or television or moon travel? The radio is a fact and Opa has a set in his living room—a tall affair, and he is skilled at keeping the stations from drifting. At home, my mother and Oma are speaking the Luxembourg tongue over my head. Out in the yard the spruce towers and Janet sits on a low branch in a photograph my mother makes with a Brownie. There, looking nothing like me, is a small figure in knee socks and summer dress, on a far-up limb, swinging sandaled feet so that while mother comes placidly to click the shutter, Oma will not stir from the doorway, "Ach, du lieber!"

A trapeze hangs from a tree limb on the other side of the house, and there are iron rings—large ones to sit in and small ones to hold and swing on, and there is an old tire tube and a swing with a wood seat that fits in that I can remove, and so sit on the rope, which I prefer. It is September and summer is almost gone. The blue fox under the porch has white stripes around his neck like a collar and white stripes up the legs like stockings. He is taking the stripes off and putting them back on. "It is early in the morinng and I am getting ready to go to our Blue Fox school," he says. "I am in the first grade of the Blue Foxes. And in the first grade we all wear stripes."

There is the class picture in my album. The teacher is standing to one side. She smiles serenely. Each child laces his fingers and folds his hands on the desk before him. Most of the boys wear knickers and long socks and bow ties or knotted ones. The farm boy wears a tie too above his overall bib. A couple of the girls wear glasses—round lenses and wire frames. Not the small child with light brown long hair, brushed into curls around Mother's finger as always that morning. She has her hands folded on the desk and has been seated in the front row because, near-sighted, she cannot make out the alphabet on the board if she sits farther back and no one in her family has noted that she squints to see in the distance. Has she ever made out the stars yet? Or the moon except as a distant vague ball? Will the child in the photograph outgrow the dress she wears, comprehend the uses of the twenty-six letters the teacher has chalked up there that she can barely make out? Who is she?

The Search Is Over

Now my journey into the past is over. There I found memories. In the recalled warmth of my parents' bed after a nightmare. In the scent of the chocolate cake Martha baked in the long flat pan, the fudge icing half an inch thick on top. In the remembered voice of my father as we sat on the porch with chairs side by side and he gazed into the woods. "Listen. What are the trees telling each other?" Not only memories, but dreams lie in the past, so that over and again, I am in the houses I lived in, the yards I played or fought in, the lakes I rushed into. But memories and dreams can alter over years so that bitter becomes sweet or sweet bitter. That was the reason for turning to letters, papers, albums, the recorded fact of the time.

What did I find in my search into the past? Devotion, the fire of genius burning, pain, steadiness, love. When I took a friend once to visit my parents' home, he told me later, "I have never been in a house before with an undivided feeling of harmony." That was because, like a great wheel, everything spun around my father—his wants—quiet, food, sleep, companionship. When he died, the wheel stood still and it was never the same in the world again.

My father died at eighty-nine years. The night before, he had looked into my mother's face, suddenly seeing her, and said, "Paula!" At Uncle Ed's ninetieth birthday party, at the Plaza Hotel, seated in a chair beside my mother, my uncle stamped his cane and said, "I shouldn't be sitting here. Carl should. There are some men who should live forever—Carl was one." My uncle died two days short of his ninety-fourth birthday. What did I find in looking back at him but romance, sensitivity, sweetness, gaiety?

And what of my mother, born on May Day in 1883? "I don't know why I don't die," she said at ninety-two, "I've done everything I wanted."

At ninety-three, two and a half months before her ninety-fourth birthday, having lifted her frail hand two days earlier and pushed the nurse away, she died. In her I found firmness and beauty. When she had been very old, every so often a new great-grandchild had been placed in her arms —Sascha Michael, Tristan August and Helga Sky. It is ninety-nine years since my father's birth. Let the journey into the future begin.

January 1977

Page 68

In Reckless Ecstasy, published in 1904, has thirty-nine pages. It measures about 5½ x 7½ inches. The beige-colored rag paper folded sheets are bound together with a brown cover, and a crimson cord is tied through the three punched holes. There is a list of contents, a prefatory poem, "And a Man's a Fool," the Foreword by Philip Green Wright, the Dedication to Grandma Sandburg, and an introduction by my father to the book. The first poems are free verse: "The Ideal," "The Sphinx," "Complacency: Austerity," "Vengeance: Pity," "Experience," "The Plow Ox: The Spanish Bull," "Charles XII, of Sweden," "To Whom My Hand Goes Out." Then comes a section of prose pieces: "Wayside Words with Comrades," "Pastels," "Millville." After this are eight poems done in rhymed form: "Pulse-beats and Pen-strokes," "An Old Tragedy," "The Dead-Sea Apple," "Revelation," "The Quick and the Dead," "A Homely Winter Idyl," "Survey," "Quatrains." The last two included are prose again: "The One Man in all the World" and "Invocation."

The Dial of the Heart was produced in the same way as *In Reckless Ecstasy* and is approximately the same size. There are fifty-five pages. The rag paper folded sheets are white and bound into a dark blue cover with a red cord. It was first published in Boston in 1894, and reissued in 1904 by Wright's Asgard (Norse home of the gods and slain heroes) Press, with my father's two-and-one-half-page introduction. There are thirty-five poems, many about love, for Wright had been married five years when the book was first published, to his cousin Elizabeth Quincy Sewall. The dedication goes:

> **To her**
>
> who for many years has watched with
> anxious brow and sympathetic under-
> standing the hours and minutes told
> off by the moving shadow,

To my dear Wife
I dedicate these verses,
                The Dial of the Heart.

Page 77

The Dreamer was also put out by the Asgard Press. It was approximately
4 x 7¼ inches. My father's foreword runs about a page and a half. Wright's
dedication was:

> To Dreamers who see the solid earth
>   A fiction of the years,
> Who hear in Chicago's wheat pit
>   The music of the spheres;
> And when men say, "Tis final,
>   This dogma, custom, style
> Is like the rock"—gaze over them
>   To the phantom hills, and smile.

Page 98

The small book *Incidentals* by Charles Sandburg measures 3¼ x 5⅞ inches. The
cover is of light brown, heavily textured paper with a 1¼ inch fold to the inside
so that there is room for a quote which appears at both front and back. The title
is dark red and set in old German type over Alton Packard's black-hooded figure
whose toe is pushing a large single dice. There are thirty-two pages, light tan,
the last four being advertisements for "THE SANDBURG LECTURES," as well as for
The Plaint of a Rose, Philip Green Wright's *The Dreamer* and for the Asgard
Press. The book was printed by the Asgard Press in early November of 1907.

The book *Joseffy* by Charles Sandburg would measure about 3⅜ x 5⅞ inches.
The makeup was the same—a brown cover with tan pages inside, bound with a
thin red cord and using dark red for the cover title. There are twelve pages,
the next to the last carrying advertisements for Wright's and my father's books
published by the Asgard Press, stating in part, "Besides this fine appreciation
of his friend by Mr. Sandburg there are two other things by the same author
which the Asgard Press has put out—INCIDENTALS and THE PLAINT OF A ROSE.
The former is a vest-pocket collection of essaylets, thoughts, observations, and
reflections by a young man who has seen and felt much. It may be had for twenty
cents. The latter is a prose-poem; only a few hundred words but each one
selected as for a mosaic, it has the poignant, unforgettable quality of the prose-
poems of Tourgueneff. It is, as it were, the spirit of the author's philosophy
exhaled from the petals of a rose." *The Plaint of a Rose* was priced at fifty cents,
Incidentals at twenty cents.

Page 99

The booklet *The Plaint of a Rose* by Charles Sandburg is a 4½ x 7¼ inches. The heavyweight cover of my copy, for there were variations, is cream colored, with the title in brown bold type, and the design of roses by Mrs. Elizabeth Wright in bright red. The inside pages are of a lighter cream color, and there are ten. The booklet, advertised as of "Strathmore Deckle Edge Paper," is bound in heavy red cord. There are no advertisements in back or front and the copy is undated, although said to have been published in January of 1908. It cost fifty cents then.

Page 161

You and Your Job, by Charles Sandburg, is a twenty-eight-page booklet measuring approximately 3¼ x 5 inches in one of its printings. It was priced at five cents a copy, with a special rate of sixty copies for a dollar. Some of the issues, according to Reuben W. Borough, were "red covered."

Page 195

Poetry: A Magazine of Verse, measures about 5½ x 7¾ inches. The cover is gray with black and red printing and a cut of Pegasus is there. The contents are listed on the cover along with the date and the price, fifteen cents a copy or a $1.50 a year. In order to read *Poetry,* it was necessary to cut many pages as one went along.

Page 273

The Chicago Race Riots, published by Harcourt, Brace and Howe in 1919, measures about 5¼ x 7¾ inches and the paper covers are tan with bold black printing. There are seventy-one pages and sixteen chapters. The "Introductory Note" by Lippmann runs two pages and is signed from "Whitestone, Long Island, August 26, 1919."

The author and the publisher wish to thank the following for permission to quote from the sources listed:

Edward Björncrantz for the letters of Carl Björncrantz; Grace Hegger Casanova for her letter to Sinclair Lewis; Margaret Conklin, Literary Executor of the Estate of Sara Teasdale, for the letters of Sara Teasdale; Marguerite Debs Cooper, Literary Heir, for the letters, speeches, and biography of Eugene V. Debs; Doubleday & Company, Inc., for *A Life in Photography* by Edward Steichen; Alfred C. Edwards, Executor and Trustee of The Estate of Robert Lee Frost, for the writings of Robert Lee Frost published here for the first time; Edwin S. and Marguerite F. Fetcher, Literary Heirs, for the letters of Harriet Monroe; Stuart Fitton, Literary Heir, for the letter of May Massee; Maurice C. Greenbaum and Frank M. Parker, Trustees of the Sandburg Family Trust, for the unpublished writings of Carl Sandburg and for the letters of Clara Mathilda Sandburg; the Estate of Alfred Harcourt for *Some Experiences* by Alfred Harcourt and for a personal letter written by Alfred Harcourt; Harcourt Brace Jovanovich, Inc., for *The Letters of Carl Sandburg* edited by Herbert Mitgang, © 1968 by Lilian Steichen Sandburg, Trustee, for the letters of Alfred Harcourt and Ellen Eayrs, and for the poems by Carl Sandburg published by Harcourt Brace Jovanovich, Inc. and the excerpts from *The American Songbag* by Carl Sandburg, copyright 1916, 1918 by Holt, Rinehart and Winston, Inc., copyright 1920, 1922, 1927 by Harcourt Brace Jovanovich, Inc., copyright 1944, 1946, 1948, 1950, 1955 by Carl Sandburg; Marshall Head and Janet Hart, Literary Heirs, for *The World at My Shoulder* by Eunice Tietjens; Holt, Rinehart and Winston, Publishers, for *Across Spoon River* by Edgar Lee Masters, copyright 1936 by Edgar Lee Masters, copyright © 1964 by Ellen Coyne Masters, for *Selected Letters of Robert Frost* edited by Lawrance Thompson, copyright © 1964 by Lawrance Thompson and Holt, Rinehart and Winston, and for the letters of Alfred Harcourt published here for the first time; Houghton Mifflin Company for "Spring Day" and "To Carl Sandburg" by Amy Lowell, from *The Complete Works of Amy Lowell*, copyright 1955 by Houghton Mifflin Company; Kathryn Lewis, Literary Heir, for the letter of Lloyd Lewis; Nicholas C. Lindsay, Literary Heir, for the letter of Nicholas Vachel Lindsay; Ellen C. Masters, Literary Heir, for *Spoon River Anthology* by Edgar Lee Masters; Conrad W. Oberdorfer and G. d'Andelot Berlin, Trustees under the will of Amy Lowell, for the letters of Amy Lowell; Mrs. Edgar L. Rossin, Literary Heir, for the letter of Alice Corbin Henderson; Alan Lomax for the letter of John Lomax; *The Milwaukee Journal* for the feature stories of Carl Sandburg; New Directions Publishing Corporation, permissions agent for the Trustees of the Ezra Pound Literary Property Trust, for the letters of Ezra Pound; Newspaper Enterprise Association, Inc., for the letters of Sam T. Hughes and Leon Starmont; Margaret Sandburg for her letters; Joanna T. Steichen, Literary Heir, for the letters of Edward Steichen and Mary Kemp Steichen; Louis Untermeyer for his letters; Dr. Neda M. Westlake, Curator of The Dreiser Collection at the University of Pennsylvania, for the letters of Theodore Dreiser; Mrs. William L. White for the letter of William Allen White; The Frank Lloyd Wright Memorial Foundation for the letter of Frank Lloyd Wright to Carl Sandburg, first copyright by Frank Lloyd Wright 1943, renewed by Olgivanna Lloyd Wright 1977; Louise Wright for the letters of Philip Green Wright.